Comet!

The World's First
Jet Airliner

Graham M Simons

Pen & Sword
AVIATION

First published in Great Britain in 2013
and reprinted in this format in 2017 and 2018
Pen & Sword AVIATION
An imprint of Pen & Sword Books Ltd
Yorkshire – Philadelphia

Copyright © Graham M. Simons, 2013, 2017, 2018
ISBN: 978 1 52672 677 3

Typeset in 10/11 Century Schoolbook by GMS Enterprises
Printed and bound in India by Replika Press Pvt. Ltd.

Pen & Sword Books Limited incorporates the imprints of Atlas, Archaeology, Aviation, Discovery,
Family History, Fiction, History, Maritime, Military, Military Classics, Politics, Select, Transport,
True Crime, Air World, Frontline Publishing, Leo Cooper, Remember When, Seaforth Publishing,
The Praetorian Press, Wharncliffe Local History, Wharncliffe Transport, Wharncliffe True Crime
and White Owl.

For a complete list of Pen & Sword titles please contact
PEN & SWORD BOOKS LIMITED
47 Church Street, Barnsley, South Yorkshire, S70 2AS, England
E-mail: enquiries@pen-and-sword.co.uk • Website: www.pen-and-sword.co.uk
Or
PEN AND SWORD BOOKS
1950 Lawrence Rd, Havertown, PA 19083, USA
E-mail: Uspen-and-sword@casematepublishers.com
Website: www.penandswordbooks.com

Contents

ACKNOWLEDGEMENTS

A book of this nature would not have been possible without the help of many people and organisations.

For many years Darryl Cott, the Staff Photographer at BAe Hatfield and Stuart Howe of the De Havilland Aircraft Museum at Salisbury Hall were the very greatest of help and assistance - the former making freely available to me the tremendous archive from the 'DH Days' that were then in his care. Darryl also arranged the copyright waiver that allows for so many BAe Hatfield images to be used!

It goes without saying that my deepest possible thanks go to the late Group Captain John Cunningham CBE, DSO and Two Bars, DFC and Bar, test pilot on so many Comet flights and an all-round gentleman!

My thanks also go to the staff of Dan-Air Services, Dan Air Engineering and the Dan-Air Staff Association, many of whom freely provided information, advice and photographs.

Thanks are also offered to John Hunt of Ian Allen Travel, Mr F E F Newman, CBE, MC, Michael Newman, Captain Keith Moody, Captain Yvonne Sintes, Captain Bryn Wayt, Captain Roger Cooper, Captain Arthur Larkman, John Stride, David Lee, John Hamlin, Vince Hemmings, Brian Cocks, Michelle Millar, Martin Bowman, Mike Ramsden, Mick Oakey, Ian Frimston, Warrant Officer Paddy Porter BEM. Finally, thanks also go to Laura Hirst and Charles Hewitt of Pen & Sword!

I am indebted to many people and organisations for providing photographs for this story, but in some cases it has not been possible to identify the original photographer and so credits are given in the appropriate places to the immediate supplier. If any of the pictures have not been correctly credited, please accept my apologies.

INTRODUCTION

Comet! Let it be fully and completely understood from the outset - the British De Havilland DH.106 Comet was the worlds first jet airliner, it was not the Avro Canada C-102 Jetliner, it was not anything Russian, French or Italian - and it was certainly not the Boeing 707 or it's numerous predecessors!

Not only was the Comet the first to take to the air, it was the first to enter full passenger service, and the first jet to carry passengers across the Atlantic.

In 1952, the United Kingdom was entering a new Elizabethan Age and the world was on the cusp of great changes. One highlight of that year was the introduction of the Comet into the world's passenger air services, reducing the journey times of smooth, high altitude, vibrationless flight by nearly a half. Flying in the Comet was, as De Havilland's publicity material reported *'...to arrive without the feeling of having travelled'*.

Nearly fifty years later, this remarkable aeroplane was commemorated by a new postage stamp. The UK Post Office chose the Comet to represent one of Britain's greatest achievements during that millennium. Also, whenever a driver is advised of the proximity of an airport, airfield or even low-flying aircraft, the design they see on the relevant roadsign is the outline of a Comet 1!

No praise is high enough for the team whose combined experience, knowledge, intuition, foresight, and, above all, courage, produced the world's first commercial jet airliner - only four years after the British aircraft industry had emerged from a crippling Second World War, and had abandoned several promising airliner projects in 1939.

Often forgotten today is the mood of the aeronautical world at the time. Sceptics were almost unanimous in asserting that jet propulsion may have been suitable for military aircraft, but excessive and expensive fuel consumption would rule out commercial applications. De Havilland's faith in their own project proved them wrong. Much credit must go to the launch customer, British Overseas Airways Corporation, the British state-owned airline who matched De Havilland's faith with equally enthusiastic support. De Havilland and BOAC together introduced jet travel to a world that was sceptical in some quarters.

Sadly, the devastating crashes of 1954 set the project back by four years, and provided fuel to the doom-mongers. The crashes also allowed rival manufacturers to benefit from De Havilland's enterprise. The company had leaped boldly into the unknown realms of seven-mile-high-altitude flying, meeting operational phenomena which were completely unknown at the time.

Indeed, there are echoes from this past at the time of writing with the Boeing 787 Dreamliner battery fires. Boeing came to dominate the jet airliner industry with their flagship 707 in large part because of the De Havilland Comet accidents. The Comet embraced new technologies before they were fully understood. Now, in 2013, similar things are happening again. Although the makers of lithium ion batteries work within some of the most stringent quality control standards in industry today and they make cells by the million, there are still failures up in the region of hundreds or thousands every year.

Part of Boeing's battery fix is to not just to try to eliminate battery fires but also contain any that might break out. This means, in part, thermally insulating every lithium cobalt oxide cell within the battery's stainless steel container that in itself is designed to contain any fire. However, reports indicate that this could also cause a problem. It is known that as the cells are used, they heat up, and have to be able to dissapate this heat, but if they get above about 90 degrees Celsius or so, and the heat is contained, then the battery may begin to self-heat and undergo a thermal runaway. Boeing have put forward a statement that in the unlikely event of this happening, then the fire would be contained - however, it is my opinion from this, it could mean that anyone flying on a Dreamliner would be playing Russian Roulette that the aircraft they are travelling on will not suffer a cell failure - or on board fire.

In composing this story, I have tried to remember that we all write with the benefit and the handicap of hindsight. Hindsight can sometimes see the past clearly - with 20/20 vision. But the path of what happened is so brightly lit that it places everything else more deeply into shadow. Commenting on Pearl Harbor, Roberta Wohlstetter - one of America's most important historians of military intelligence - found it *'...much easier after the event to sort the relevant from the irrelevant signals. After the event, of course, a signal is always crystal clear; we can now see what disaster it was signalling since the disaster has occurred. But before the event it is obscure and pregnant with conflicting meanings."*

The same is true of the Comet accidents; as time passes, more documents and evidence became available, and the bare facts of what happened became still clearer. Yet the picture of how those things happened becomes harder to re-imagine, as that past world, with its preoccupations and uncertainty, recedes and the remaining memories of it become coloured by what happened and what was written about it later. With that caution in mind, I had to ask whether the insights that seem so apparent now would really have been meaningful at the time, given the limits of what people then could reasonably have known or done. To that end I tried to rely on primary source documents, reporting on what was available at the time.

Counteracting that tragic episode were the Comet's numerous achievements that have been invariably overlooked by so many aviation historians, particularly those from across the pond: yes, there was high fuel consumption but this was more than compensated for by cheap price at the bowsers; the maintenance requirements were dramatically reduced because of the smooth running of the jet engines, a fact that considerably lengthened airframe lives. Yes, it was smaller than it possibly could have been, but the market at the time clearly indicated that there was a tremendous market for an aircraft of that size. When the Comet was introduced there was nothing to suggest that a 'bigger and faster' battle was just over the horizon. The Comet demonstrated an efficient swept wing, a reliable jet engine, multiple wheel undercarriage, high-level pressurization, full power controls, and many other related engineering advances. These advances, coupled with the freely available findings of the court of enquiry into the accidents meant that entire aviation world was , or at least should have been, the grateful beneficiary of DH enterprise.

Two years later, Aeroflot's Tupolev Tu-104 began service in the Soviet Union, and two years later still, Pan American put the Boeing 707 into service, just three weeks after the rejuvenated Comet 4. In the jet airliner race, the Comet had been the pacesetter, faltering early, but recovering bravely, to cross the line in advance of all others as the winner in a trans-Atlantic photo-finish.

The Comet went on to achieve many things, including opening up the world to air travel to a whole new generation when it was put to great use by UK airline Dan-Air Services.

Even after Dan-Air retired the last one from commercial service in 1980, the story was far from over, for with the Comet derivative Nimrod the RAF operated the aircraft well into the 21st Century until the MRA.4 spluttered to a halt in a political and financial quagmire!

The de Havilland DH.l06 Comet occupies a unique place in aeronautical history that can never be emulated. Without ignoring the development problems - or the terrible penalty of being first, I look in detail at the work that went on with the accident inquiry - this book tries to do justice to the memory of a tremendous technical achievement. Above all, I would like to think that not only does it put on record, but also pays tribute to the design, manufacturing and test teams, whose sleek, beautiful aircraft can be described as the result of collective genius.

Graham M Simons
Peterborough
September 2013

Chapter One

GENESIS BY COMMITTEE

On 23 December 1942 - in that grand old British tradition - a committee was formed under the chairmanship of aviation pioneer John Theodore Cuthbert Moore-Brabazon, 1st Baron Brabazon of Tara, GBE, MC, PC. to investigate the future needs of the British Empire's civilian airliner market. The study was an attempt at defining in broad overview; the impact of projected advances in aviation technology and to forecast the global needs of the post war British Empire (in South Asia, Africa, the Near and Far East) and Commonwealth (Australia, Canada, New Zealand) in the area of air transport, for passengers, mail, and cargo.

The study both recognized and accepted that the British Empire and Commonwealth as both a political and economic entity would have a vital need for aviation systems (principally aircraft) to facilitate its continued existence and self reliance in the post-war world. For military and commercial reasons, the empire simply could not continue to exist if did not understand the needs, and develop the industrial infrastructure to provide, the aviation systems and sub-systems necessary to supply and maintain a global air transport service.

Moore-Brabazon was born in London to Lieutenant-Colonel John Arthur Henry Moore-Brabazon (1828–1908) and his wife, Emma Sophia (d. 1937). He was educated at Harrow School before reading engineering at Trinity College, Cambridge, but did not graduate. He spent his university holidays working for Charles Rolls as an unpaid mechanic, and became an apprentice at Darracq in Paris after leaving Cambridge. In 1907 he won the Circuit des Ardennes in a Minerva.

With the outbreak of War, Moore-Brabazon return to flying, joining the Royal Flying Corps. He served on the Western Front, where he played a key role in the development of aerial photography and reconnaissance. In March 1915 he was promoted to captain and appointed as an equipment officer. On 1 April 1918, when the Royal Flying Corps merged with the Royal Naval Air Service to form the Royal Air Force, Moore-Brabazon was appointed as a staff officer (first class) and made a temporary lieutenant-colonel. Moore-Brabazon finished the war with the rank of Lieutenant-Colonel, had been awarded the Military Cross, and had become a commander of the Légion d'Honneur.

Moore-Brabazon later became a Conservative Member of Parliament for Chatham (1918-1929) and Wallasey (1931-1942) and served as a junior minister during the 1920s. In Winston Churchill's wartime government, he was appointed Minister of Transport in October 1940 and joined the Privy Council, becoming Minister of Aircraft Production in May 1941, succeeding Lord Beaverbrook. As the Minister of Transport he proposed the use of Airgraphs to reduce the weight and bulk of mails travelling between troops fighting in the Middle East and their families in the UK.

He was forced to resign in 1942 for expressing the hope that Germany and the Soviet Union, then fighting the Battle of Stalingrad, would destroy each other. Since the Soviet Union was fighting on the same side as the UK, the hope that it would be destroyed, although common in the Conservative Party, was regarded as being unacceptable to the war effort. Moore-Brabazon was elevated to the House of Lords as Baron Brabazon of Tara, of Sandwich in the County of Kent, in April 1942.

During 1942, the Prime Minister, Winston Churchill, sought his advice regarding the setting up of an advisory committee to formulate plans for post-war civil aviation in Britain. Initially known as the Civil Aviation Committee on

John Theodore Cuthbert Moore-Brabazon, (8 February 1884 – 17 May 1964) 1st Baron Brabazon of Tara, GBE, MC, PC.
(author's collection)

Post-War Transport, the first meeting was held on 23 December 1942; its members from the Air Ministry and Ministry of Aircraft Production were. under the chairmanship of The Rt Hon. The Lord Brabazon, Sir Henry Self (Ministry of Aircraft Production), Sir Francis Shelmerdine, William P Hildred and J.H. Riddoch from the Air Ministry, Norbert E. Rowe and Kelvin T. Spencer (Ministry of Aircraft Production)

The Committee's official terms of reference were:

1a   To prepare outline specifications of the several aircraft types that would be needed for post-war air transport.

1b   To suggest which firms should be invited, as soon as urgent war work permitted, to prepare tender designs.

2   To consider, in consultation with the aircraft firms concerned, which existing military aircraft could usefully be converted to air transport purposes for use whilst new civil types were being produced, and to plan for such conversions.

3   To prepare a plan for the immediate utilisation, in the interests of post-war air transport, of spare design and production capacity whilst the aircraft industry made its transition from war to peace.

They studied a number of designs and technical considerations, meeting several times over the next two years to further clarify the needs of different market segments.

Following the Committee's tenth meeting on 9 February 1943 a series of outline recommendations were made to the Secretary of State for Air and the Minister of Aircraft Production:

A.   The adaptation of four existing types:
1.   Avro York
2.   A civil version of the Vickers Warwick.
3.   Development of the Sunderland III - the Short Hythe.
4.   Development of the Sunderland III - the Short Sandringham.

B.   The design of five new types:
1   A large, long-range landplane for the North Atlantic route
2.   A DC-3 replacement for European services
3.   A four-engine medium-range landplane for the Empire routes
4.   A jet propelled mailplane for the North Atlantic
5.   A twin-engined fourteen-passenger feeder liner

C.   Work on these five new types of aircraft should commence as soon as circumstances permitted. Their specifications were to be drafted jointly by potential users and aircraft manufacturers whose selection would be agreed between the Air Ministry and the Ministry of Aircraft Production (MAP). However, top priority was to be given to Type I - the large, long-range landplane.

The Committee considered production numbers, as it was realised that the aircraft industry would obviously reduce considerably in size on return to peace. They included what would later turn out to be some very optimistic proposals, quoting over 1300 Yorks to be built over a three-year period! Other types were to be produced in hundreds. There was no mention as to who would operate such large numbers or how they were to be paid for.

After studying the recommendations, the Cabinet authorised the setting up of a second Brabazon Committee to undertake more detailed work; '...*to consider the types recommended in relation to traffic needs and to prepare a list of requirements for each*

The Avro 685 York used Lancaster wings, tailplanes and Rolls Royce Merlin engines. *(author's collection)*

type to provide a basis for design and development.'

This committee's first meeting was held on 25 May 1943 with the following membership: Alan C Campbell-Orde, assistant to Chairman BOAC; Capt. Geoffrey de Havilland, De Havilland Aircraft Co Ltd; Sir William P. Hildred, Director-General Civil Aviation; Group Capt. William Helmore, Technical Advisor, Ministry of Aircraft Production; Maj. J. Ronald McCrindle, Deputy Director-General BOAC; Maj. Ronald H. Thornton, Air Registration Board; Air Commodore Alfred R. Wardle, Air Ministry and John H. Riddoch, Director of Home Civil Aviation, Ministry of Civil Aviation.

These members provided a wider range of people which, in theory, meant a greater grasp of the practical problems of matching the proposed types to traffic and economic needs, considering both airframes and powerplants. They also studied such ancillary matters as pressurisation, navigation aids and runway lengths. Their government contact was Sir Stafford Cripps, the new Minister of Aircraft Production.

Winston Churchill took a personal interest in that he had already experienced first hand the hardship of long-distance travel in existing wartime aircraft flying in both the unpressurised B-24 Liberator and the Avro York. He was concerned that a comfortable, pressurised long-range airliner should be available.

In May 1943 MAP indicated to Bristol Aeroplane Co. that they would be ordering four prototypes of the definitive Type I requirement. This had not gone out to tender, as the MAP did not want design work and time duplicated between different constructors. Limited information concerning the Brabazon Type I had been made public back in March. By June it was agreed that preliminary design work on the other designs could begin '...*with no detriment to the war effort'*. The MAP asked Airspeed, aided by de Havilland, to proceed with the Type II, Avro with the Type III and de Havilland with the Type V.

The committee noted that the British aircraft industry remained fully committed to military production and could not devote much time to these new airliner requirements. However, it was felt that more notice should be taken of their recommendations, otherwise any delays might render the new airliners obsolete before entering service.

Following the Brabazon Committee's first report in August 1943, Winston Churchill appointed Lord Beaverbrook to form the Committee on Air Transport which was tasked with co-ordinating post-war civil air transport policies. Its first task was to oversee the production of the new aircraft. Peter Masefield was appointed as his secretary. Beaverbrook worked closely with the Brabazon Committee, where it was confirmed that the first requirement – and certainly the most difficult task - was for the five thousand mile range Type I transatlantic airliner. A conference in October 1943 saw representatives of Empire countries and airlines approve a derivative of the Avro Lincoln bomber, thus leading to the Tudor. Specifications for all the Brabazon designs were issued to the British aircraft industry, their initial responses being submitted to the Committee by 1944.

The Brabazon Committee's second report in November 1943 saw the Type III and Type V both split into two. The original Empire airliner now becoming the IIIA, with a new medium-to-long-range Empire airliner becoming the IIIB. The original Type V now became VA with a Type VB added as an eight-seat feeder-liner.

Following this Report, the Director General of Civil Aviation confirmed in January 1944 that the Government had decided that '...*work on design of a limited number of aircraft for civil use should proceed in so far as this can be done without interfering with war production. Certain work should be done on adaptation of existing types for use as transport aircraft during interim period before new types are ready'*.

The aircraft so designated became known as 'interim' designs eventually being developed as:

(i)   A pressurised transport based on the Lincoln for non-stop North Atlantic service. This became the Tudor I. Despite its size, the

Decidedly one of the 'interim' designs was Avro 691 Lancastrian G-AGLF. The aircraft - configured as a 15-seater - entered service with BOAC on 1 December 1944, passing to Skyways Ltd and named *'Sky Diplomat'* on 8 April 1946 and crashed at landing ground H3 in the Syrian Desert on 11 March 1947. *(author's collection)*

Another interim design was the Handley Page Halton, converted from the Halifax bomber. Here is G-AHDU *'Falkirk'* of BOAC, that was fitted out by Short & Harland Ltd of Belfast with an under-fuselage freight pannier. The aircraft was able to carry ten passengers in rudimentary comfort in the fuselage.

Tudor would only be required to carry twelve passengers plus mail.

(ii)   The Avro York was planned to be used on the major Empire trunk routes.

(iii)   A civil Handley Page Halifax III - designated Hermes - to be used on shorter Empire routes.

(iv)   A civil Sunderland (Sandringham)

Mentioned in the announcement – albeit briefly - were two of the main proposals - the Brabazon I fifty-passenger airliner from the Bristol Aeroplane Company and a De Havilland feeder airliner that was eventually to appear as the Dove. Also mentioned was the large Short Shetland II flying boat that would operate Empire routes as well as summer services across the North Atlantic.

More developments

In March 1944 the Secretary of State for Air disclosed the development of an updated list of 'Brabazon' airliners, which included two new requirements:

(i)   A large transatlantic airliner.

(ii)   A North Atlantic 100,000 lb airliner, refuelling at Gander.

(iii)   Four engines, medium range, trunk routes

(iv)   Twin engines, medium range and European routes

(v)   A high speed transport, with jet engines

(vi)   A fourteen-seat feederliner for route and internal UK services.

(vii)   A eight-seat, twin engined machine for feeder routes & air taxi work.

Having already given development of the transatlantic airliner to Bristol, the Committee selected other British aircraft manufacturers for the remaining 'Brabazon' aircraft: Airspeed; Avro; De Havilland; Miles and Vickers-Armstrongs. Miles had never produced airliners, although they had progressive ideas.

In the spring of 1944 Lord Beaverbrook was visited by his American counterpart. They discussed future aircraft and airline services, with the British offered US airliners at the end of the war. Beaverbrook felt there was no need to accept as the Brabazon aircraft would be available. Following the hectic events of D-Day in Europe. Beaverbrook and other officials visited the US in July 1944 to see first hand some of the US aircraft manufacturers, flying by Liberator transport direct from Northolt to Washington. They were following in the footsteps of some of the British aircraft designers – for instance, Avro's Roy Chadwick had visited the USA in 1943, visiting amongst others, Lockheed, Northrop and Boeing.

The Beaverbrook group were able to see that, as well as large numbers of fighters and bombers, there were many transport aircraft rolling off the production lines. Whilst in the US, it was agreed to hold a Conference in Montreal with fifty-two nations invited to consider post-war transport requirements and this led to the formation of International Civil Aviation Organisation (ICAO). Post-war this organised, amongst other matters, airline routes and tare structures. On his return home, Beaverbrook advised Churchill and the Cabinet of the progress seen in the US, with the need for Great Britain to do

The Roy Chadwick-designed Avro 688 Tudor I seen without markings on rollout at Woodford. *(Peter Clegg Collection)*

During the war early versions of the Lockheed L-1049 Constellation were put to military use. Immediately peace broke out they were used by both Howard Hughes' Trans World Airlines and Juan Trippe's Pan American Airways. Such was the level of competition on the trans-Atlantic routes, that BOAC was forced to operate a small number in order to remain competitive.

something quickly: 'converted bombers will not do, new and efficient aircraft are needed as soon as possible'. Beaverbrook now felt that it might be necessary to accept the earlier offer of US airliners, as the interim Brabazon airliners might not be up to the job.

Somewhat pointedly it was made clear that Liberator transports, with BOAC crews, were regularly crossing the Atlantic with twelve passengers and Trans-Canada Lancastrians were carrying ten plus mail. So what improvements were offered by the proposed twelve-seater Tudor I? Luckily, Lord Beaverbrook did not have to answer these questions as he stood down in November 1944 on the appointment of a new post of Minister of Aviation.

As the second Brabazon Committee started to move towards its conclusions, it was aided by the Air Ministry which created the Ministry of Civil Aviation (MCA) in November 1944. This was able to concentrate its efforts on the airlines and their aircraft. The Committee held a total of sixty-two meetings, the final one in November 1945 when it produced its fifth report. During its meetings the Committee had been dealing with BOAC, which was considered to be the main customer for the new aircraft. It was not until August 1946 that the two additional state airline corporations – British European Airways (BEA) and British South American Airways (BSAA) — came into being and so became 'new ' customers for the aircraft.

In 1946 Lord Brabazon joined the Air Registration Board, becoming its chairman in 1947. Beaverbrook's secretary, Peter Masefield, went on to become chief executive of BEA in October 1949.

The report identified four, later changed to five main types that would be required after the war.

The Type I was a very large transatlantic airliner serving the high-volume routes like London-New York, seating its passengers in luxury. This was the Bristol Brabazon I, created under Air Ministry

Specification 2/44. It built on submissions Bristols had made during the war for a '100 ton bomber'. The Type IA was the unfinished Brabazon II that was slightly redesigned and would have been powered by turbine-propellers - more commonly called 'turbo-props'. Air Ministry Specification 2/46 was created for it.

The Type II process was somewhat more complex. Several companies submitted designs to the original specification, but Vickers suggested a move to turbo-prop power. There was some scepticism on the part of the committee, and in the end they decided to split the specification in two, allowing the turboprop design to go ahead while at the same time

The BOAC board expressed a strong perference to buy American aviation products - although the balance of payments at the time severely restricted them.

BOAC expressed a wish to get a number of Douglas DC-4s but were thwarted...

...instead they obtained a number of Canadair C-4s, which were Canadian built versions of the pressurised Douglas DC-4 and powered by Rolls-Royce Merlin 624 engines. In BOAC service they were known as Argonauts, with G-ALHX *'Astraea'* seen here in flight.

ordering a 'backup' piston design as well. This led to a split into the IIA and IIB types, the Airspeed Ambassador (Specification 25/43) filling the IIA requirement, and the Vickers VC.2 Viceroy (Specification 8/46) and the Armstrong Whitworth AW.55 Apollo filling IIB (Specification 16/46).

The Type III called for a larger medium-range aircraft for various multi-hop routes serving the British Empire. This was planned as the Avro 693. Originally a turbine-propeller design, it was finalised as a turbojet fitted with four Rolls-Royce Avons, but was cancelled in 1947. Another Type III machine (Specification C2/47) that eventually became a limited success for Bristol was the Britannia.

The Type IV was the most advanced of them all, a jet-powered 100-seat design. It was added at the personal urging of one of the committee members, Geoffrey de Havilland, whose company was involved in development of Britain's first jet fighters. The Type IV could, if the whole concept of a jet airliner could be made to work, be able to replace the Type III outright, and many of the duties of the other planes in shorter routes. Type IV was a jet propelled trans-Atlantic mail plane cruising at over 400 mph, capable of carrying a ton of pay load and having a pressure cabin for the crew and passengers.

The Type V was later introduced to fill the original feeder-liner specifications after the Type II

had evolved into larger designs. The VA was a feeder-liner transport in the shape of the Miles Marathon under Specification 18/44 and the VB was the De Havilland Dove light transport under Specification 26/43.

In January 1946 a Government White Paper was published under the title 'British Air Service'. It recorded that twenty-seven Lancastrians – converted Lancaster bombers – had been delivered, with twelve on order intended for BOAC and BSAA. Twelve Halifax C.VIIIs were to be acquired for BOACs 'Tiger' route to India and also to West Africa. Twenty-four Shorts Sunderland IIIs were in service, with a further twelve to be converted by the autumn of 1946. At the time, BOAC was still operating thirteen pre-war C-Class flying boats and the one remaining G-Class. BOAC had twenty-five Yorks, with twelve on order, for its 'Springbok' services to South Africa and 'Tiger' services to India. Twenty Avro Tudor Is were due for delivery in October 1946, although they might not be available for North Atlantic services until 1947. Seventy-nine Tudor IIs would be delivered between May 1946 and May 1947. 108 Vikings were on order for European services, with the order expected to be completed during 1946. A number of Solents were on order for BOAC, along with other flying boats.

The White Paper also covered the Brabazon

BOAC also operated a number of Boeing 377 Stratocruisers such as G-AKGH *'Caledonia'* as seen here on trans-Atlantic services. *(BOAC)*

Types saying: '...*it is still necessary to draw a veil of secrecy over these aircraft which should come into service from 1948. Some of them are revolutionary in design'*. In July 1947 the Ministry of Civil Aviation confirmed that it was not intending to publish the Brabazon Committee recommendations as they were confidential and would not be in the national advantage!

In the immediate post-war years the British aviation industry still supported the Avro Tudor and Handley Page Hermes, despite the obvious advantage of the Lockheed Constellation. One reason was to support the home manufacturers but probably more importantly, Britain did not possess the requisite dollars with which to purchase the American aircraft.

Genesis

De Havillands had always built unorthodox aeroplanes, right from the day when young Geoffrey, later Sir Geoffrey de Havilland, taught himself to fly in a stick-and-string machine he had constructed with the help of his wife between 1909 and 1911. In the First World War there came a series of startling new designs from Geoffrey de Havilland's drawing-board, among them the DH.4, rated easily the best day-bomber used by either side. Modified to carry two passengers, this somewhat austere conveyance

operated the first post-war scheduled air services on international routes. And from that point onwards, British civil aviation and De Havilland's grew up together, through a succession of famous designs that each bore the stamp of fearless originality, from the rotund DH.34s that flew with BOAC's earliest ancestors, the Daimler and Instone Airways, to the stately three-engined DH.66 Hercules with which Imperial Airways pioneered the Eastern trunk routes.

Then in 1934 a sleek, twin-engined racer flashed half-way round the world to win a resounding victory in the international air race from England to Australia. It was the DH.88 and was called the Comet. From its clean lines evolved the magic aerodynamic formula that gave us the Albatross of 1938 - and from that came what was surely one of the most beautiful aircraft ever built - the Mosquito.

By all accounts Hatfield's first jet airliner drawing was dated 1941. In May that year the Aerodynamics Department made their first study of jet propulsion applied to civil purposes, using a modified DH.95 Flamingo with two Halford H.ls as Frank Halford's Whittle-inspired jet engine was designated, or De Havilland Goblins as they later became known.

Earlier that same year Hatfield had been studying a twin-jet Mosquito, talking about it with Dr Moult of De Havilland Engines and Dr Griffiths of Rolls-Royce.

The early successes achieved by Frank Whittle formed the basis of De

One 'home grown' piston-powered airliner BOAC operated was the Handley Page Hermes.*(BOAC)*

Havilland research and development, but the company's special interest in the problems of aircraft efficiency as a whole led the design team to strike out on an independent line in selecting the layout of the Goblin.

The first Goblin ran on the test bed on 13 April 1942. Flight trials began on 5 March 1943, with a Gloster Meteor in which two Goblins were mounted. Vampire fighter flight-trials began on 20 September 1943. This aircraft exceeded 500 mph in the Spring of 1944 and was the first aircraft in Britain or America to do so by a handsome margin and over a deep altitude range.

Captain Sir Geoffrey de Havilland, OM, CBE, AFC, RDI, FRAeS, (*b.* 27 July 1882 – *d.* 21 May 1965)

Goblin engines were air-freighted to America and powered the Lockheed XP.80A Shooting Star prototype; it exceeded 500 mph shortly afterwards.

As we have already seen, in the same year, an august body of experts known as the Brabazon Committee issued a series of far-reaching proposals. A committee is one of those much maligned and typically British institutions that only occasionally serve a very useful purpose; luckily, this one did!

With an eye on all the huge strides manufacturers in the USA had been making with transport aircraft such as the Lockheed Constellation and the Douglas DC-4 and DC-6, its members tried to forecast what sort of machines Britain might need when the war was over. Among their various proposals - to which, incidentally, both the Viscount and the Britannia owe their origin - was one for a high-speed mail carrier, powered by jet engines, and capable of flying the Atlantic with six passengers and half a ton of mail.

The de Havilland Goblin centrifugal jet engine developed some 3,000 lbs. static thrust. It was the first of the De Havilland range of gas turbines, and was the first jet engine to pass the British official type-approval tests.

Bishop, along with Hatfield Head of Aerodynamics Richard Clarkson and his assistant David Newman began feasibility studies and design work in April 1941, at a time when no other established aero engine manufacturer had yet entered the gas-turbine field. The aircraft and engine divisions of

the De Havilland Enterprise embarked upon the venture together, for it was realised that the much higher speeds of flight made possible by jet propulsion would bring aircraft and engine problems into closer association than ever before.

The later De Havilland Ghost was very similar in concept, but developed 5,000 lbs. static thrust. During the period January to June 1943, a short range civil design based on four Goblins was being considered. Later that year, a more detailed twenty passenger project was proposed having a Vampire layout with three Goblins in the rear of the nacelle. The design range was approximately 700 miles. From November 1943 to April 1944 the design again changed to a canard layout with three DH Ghosts in the tail.

Development and experience with the de Havilland Vampire suggested that long range flights might be possible and BOAC, who appreciated the benefits to passenger travel of vibrationless flight over long ranges, saw the possibilities of range development with increasing runway lengths and therefore heavier fuel loads.

After one of Geoffrey de Havilland Jnr's demonstration flights in a Vampire, Charles C. Walker was supposedly heard to say to Alan Campbell-Orde of BOAC: *'You know, you could have all that in a transport aircraft...'* meaning a cruising speed of 530 mph, at the time the cruising speed of the fastest transport aircraft then in service was less than half that.

Ronald Eric Bishop, CBE, FRAeS, Design Director, De Havilland Aircraft Co. Ltd (1903 - 11 June 1989)

The jet-propelled airliner project – designated DH. 106 in October 1944, was proposed to the Brabazon Committee as a scaled-up DH.100 Vampire De Havilland Halford H.2 engines, later named Ghost. Bishop is supposed to have called it a '...stupid aeroplane' with a London — New York payload of 18 passengers and 1,800 lb of mail.

However, this project was becoming so specialised that an alternative proposal was made for a more conventional airliner. Studies were made with various fuselage designs in March 1945, seating twenty-four to thirty-six passengers.

In October 1945 - after Bishop and Clarkson visited Germany to see their swept wing research - a tailless design was proposed having a 40° sweep wing, weighing 75,000 lbs. and powered by four DH Ghosts. This idea was dropped in March 1946 as it was considered basically uneconomical, due to the limited effectiveness of the flight controls in this layout. However, much experience on this design was later obtained with the tailless DH.108, three of which were built. Although its efficiency was amply demonstrated, the controllability factor proved to be marginal at very high speed and, in addition, it was found that the landing weight for a given landing speed would be uneconomical. Data provided from the DH.108 showed the sweepback to be uneconomical due to the lower maximum lift coefficient and higher structural weight. It was therefore decided that, with the knowledge then available, the tail-less layout was not suitable for a passenger aircraft.

By May 1946, a more conventional design with 40° wing sweep was proposed showing an Atlantic payload of 5,000 lbs.

To De Havilland's, who had been largely responsible for persuading the Brabazon Committee— rather against the judgement of the majority of its members—to include a jet airliner in its recommendations, this looked like a somewhat specialized and extravagant requirement. However, they decided to see what they could do about meeting it and a project team set to work under the leadership of Ronald Bishop, the brilliant Chief Designer who had joined de Havilland in 1921 as an apprentice of eighteen and was now a director of the company.

Bishop realized that it was going to take far longer than they could afford to get the bugs out of the tailless layout. The United Kingdon was in desperate need of an aircraft with which to win back the share of international air traffic lost to carriers using US designed and manufactured aircraft. The first post-war hope, the Avro Tudor, was turning out to be an expensive, unmitigated disaster, and her present motley fleet of adapted military aircraft was proving quite incapable of taking business away from its competitors, with the inevitable result that BOAC was losing money fast. Even the new Handley Page Hermes, when it was ready for service, would be barely a match for the fast, economical Constellations and DC-6s, and as an interim measure the Government sanctioned the expenditure of precious dollars on a few American aircraft with which BOAC could defend its prestige routes.

Bishop realised that if the sweepback was eliminated payload could be almost doubled. As a compromise, a more orthodox 20° sweepback wing aircraft was settled upon, incidentally saving about a ton weight of wing structure – it also greatly improved take-off and landing lift.

The words 'straight wing' appeared in an Aerodynamics Department report dated July 1946.The next month Bishop drew the final layout. The tail now had elevators, and the cabin was 120 inches wide compared with the original 100 inches.

So the final Comet shape was established. The final configuration, agreed upon in the closing months of 1946, represented a logical step forward rather than a too-hasty step into the unknown. BOAC and BSAA said they would order fourteen if performance and weights could be guaranteed - and they were. By November 1946, a complete weight and performance statement was available with performance guarantees, all of which were met by the time the Comet entered service in 1952.

Different perspectives

Wilfred Nixon, the Managing Director of the De Havilland Aircraft Company Ltd, gives a different perspective to the background.

"It was our experience with a jet fighter, having our own jet engine, and in

The De Havilland team - left to right: Frank T Hearle, Wilfred E Nixon, Sir Geoffrey de Havilland, Charles C Walker, Francis E N St Barbe, Alan W Butler. *(DH Hatfield).*

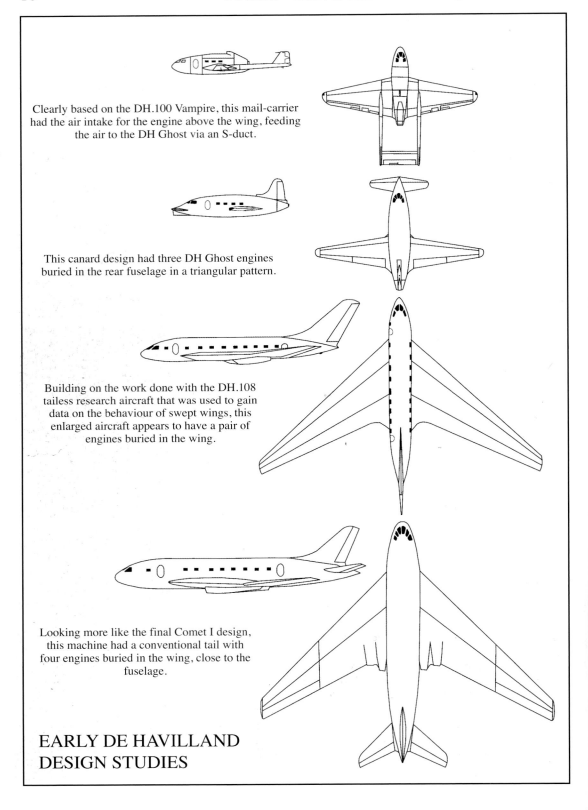

Clearly based on the DH.100 Vampire, this mail-carrier had the air intake for the engine above the wing, feeding the air to the DH Ghost via an S-duct.

This canard design had three DH Ghost engines buried in the rear fuselage in a triangular pattern.

Building on the work done with the DH.108 tailless research aircraft that was used to gain data on the behaviour of swept wings, this enlarged aircraft appears to have a pair of engines buried in the wing.

Looking more like the final Comet I design, this machine had a conventional tail with four engines buried in the wing, close to the fuselage.

EARLY DE HAVILLAND DESIGN STUDIES

particular the inherent simplicity and robustness of our type of jet engine, and the high degree of reliability which we quickly attained with it, which gave us confidence that a larger aircraft with four such engines, in fact a passenger liner, could be evolved as a sound proposition. On the economic side, whilst the fuel bill must be considerably heavier than the fuel bill for a comparable piston-engined liner the jet liner would fly so much faster that it would be able to accomplish a great deal more transportation in the year, and this would bring down the cost per passenger-mile to be keenly competitive with that of the piston-engined type. And, of course, the accomplishment of much more work in the year— about half as much again, would mean increased turnover and earning capacity. Thus the advantages of a much faster and much smoother journey appeared obtainable at a competitive cost. Moreover, the simplicity of the jet engine appealed enormously, for the extraction of more and more power out of the piston engine has made it so complex that airline operators are finding its maintenance a most serious problem.

The propeller-driving turbine had attractions, particularly for exceptionally long range, but for ordinary mainline operation the fast jet aeroplane was more attractive; the pure jet engine had reached a more advanced development than the shaft-driving turbine, and it was much simpler. It was an unusual case where a large step forward was easier to take than a smaller one.

Because we were ahead of the Americans in turbine development we saw in the jet airliner an opportunity to re-establish British leadership on the airways of the world, which had been denied us from the middle thirties when British airline operations had not been encouraged to anything like the degree enjoyed by American airlines. The leeway had been increased by the war period in which, by agreement, America concentrated on heavy bombers and transport aircraft while British effort was devoted to fighters and other combat types.

The Comet airliner with our Ghost jet engines, as we conceived it in 1946, represented the greatest step forward in design which we felt justified in taking, assuming that we should go straight into production from the drawing board. Had we built and tested a prototype first the aircraft would have been out of date before it could be delivered to the airlines, and we should miss the market altogether; to build a prototype airliner is, in our opinion, wrong in principle.

The financing of the Comet project was a matter of great importance to its success. Doubtless we

De Havilland Men!

Charles C Walker CBE, AMICE, Hon FRAeS. Director and Chief Engineer. (b. 25 Aug 1877).

Richard M Clarkson OBE, BSc, ACGI, FRAeS. Assistant Chief Engineer, Aircraft. (b. 14 July 1904).

Major Frank B Halford CBE, FRAeS, MSAE. Chairman and Technical Director, Engines. (b. 7 March 1894).

Wilfred E Nixon Managing Director. (b. 1892).

Eric S Moult PhD, BSc,(Eng) MIMechE, FRAeS Chief Engineer, Engines. (b. 15 June 1903).

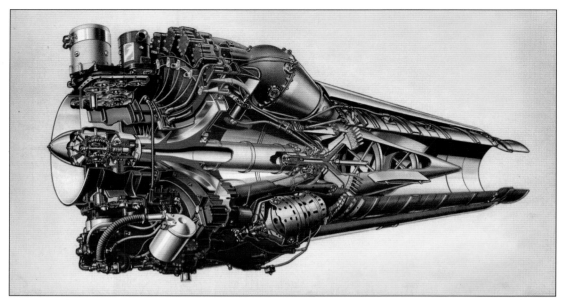

An August 1947 release of the De Havilland cutaway artwork for the 5,000 lb static thrust De Havilland Ghost engine that embodied the principal of single impeller for maximum installed efficiency. *(DH Hatfield)*.

could have obtained Government finance, but it would mean loss of control in some degree and we know that a good airliner can evolve only from the direct partnership of the two naturally responsible entities, the builder and the user, this partner- ship taking the form of a straight contract with guarantees of technical performance, delivery date and price. With that system there can be no misunderstanding of liabilities, no passing of blame. Knowing where they stand, both builder and user can go forward with enthusiasm and with a joint interest in making a success of the project.

With these principles very firmly in mind we put forward a proposal to British Overseas Airways and to the Ministries concerned.   We explained that we could not proceed without an order for a reasonable number of Comets - not sufficient by any means to break even because that would call for some dozens of aircraft - but a sufficient quantity to make the prospect of selling the remainder a worthwhile commercial risk. BOAC, interested in the possibilities of at last offering the most up-to-date airline service in the world, were confident enough to give us the order we needed, an order for 14 aircraft, with the price and delivery date fixed and the performance guaranteed by us. The Ministry of Supply ordered two more aircraft at the same time and at the same commercial price, these to be at Government disposal for development and experimental work.

On the basis of these orders we were able to go ahead with the design, and three years later we had

the first aircraft flying. We have surpassed the guaranteed performance figures and hope to better the delivery dates. Now we face the difficult task of securing world-wide business from the established airlines, bearing in mind that for 15 years or so they have been using American equipment and forming happy and satisfactory associations with our American competitors. The Americans will, of course, do all they can to save their market and we know that we must press forward with the development of the Comet to still better capabilities. As I said before, it represented the greatest technical advance that we felt justified in making at a single step ; in its initial form it can carry an economical payload on all but the very long Empire stages at a speed approaching 500 miles an hour, compared with the present-day speed of something under 300 miles an hour.

Ronald Bishop: 'The Comet has resulted from a joint effort by builder and operator. At the end of the war we were faced with the problem of catching up the American lead in transport aircraft. We felt that to embark upon the design of an aeroplane similar to the Lockheed Constellation or the Douglas DC-6, or even a little in advance of those designs, would be fruitless, since our aircraft would inevitably be five years late. We felt also that the American airliners would be able to take advantage of engine developments up to the stage of the propeller turbine, and that we would always be trailing along behind them and striving to catch up.

Chapter Two

DEVELOPMENT OF THE CONCEPT

The Comet design specification represents a substantial advance in airliner performance without calling for radical changes in operational procedure. The Comet is an aircraft of moderate wing loading - far less in fact than some of the latest propeller driven airliners of its time. Thus in all ordinary handling respects the Comet is orthodox'.

So said the opening paragraph of De Havilland's General Statement for the Comet 1. As dramatic as it reads now, even then it was a case of typical British understatement. De Havilland's were taking highly advanced, rapidly evolving engine technology and merging that with an airframe that was designed around advanced lessons learned in World War Two. Ronald Bishop, De Havilland's Chief Designer provided a greater insight: *'We had considerable experience of the Goblin jet engine in Vampire fighters since September, 1943, and we had the larger engine, the Ghost, entering the test-bed stage.*

We felt that it should be possible to produce a useful civil aeroplane based upon the Ghost engine. At that time, 1945 and 1946, the axial form of gas turbine showed great promise of achieving better fuel consumption, but we considered that the axial was not sufficiently developed for adoption in a civil project. Nobody had yet succeeded in de-icing an axial engine, neither had the problem of tapping the blower for pressure cabin air and de-icing air been tackled by anyone. Looking back, six or seven years later, it appears that the decision to fit a centrifugal engine in the first version of the Comet was a wise one. Had we adopted an axial engine from the first we should not yet have got the Comet into commercial operation.

The specification for a civil jet aeroplane on which we first focused our thoughts was for flying the Atlantic with 1,000 lb of mail and six passengers. We were told that there would be a use for a high-speed

The starting point for the Comet was the De Havilland Goblin jet engine. The design featured ensured the shortest, simplest, engine obtainable within a given cowled diameter. A compact engine with a minimum divergence of gas flow was clearly necessary when handling a hundred tons of air per hour, compressing, heating and expanding it, and ejecting it at a nozzle velocity of over a thousand miles an hour.

Above: The first Ghost engine - a military type - with fourteen combustion chambers, compared with the ten-chamber Comet I engine on the right. On the latter are visible the manifolds for cabin pressurising and aircraft de-icing. *(DH Hatfield)*

transatlantic mail carrier of this capacity. We envisaged it as a sort of enlarged Vampire with three Goblin engines grouped in the rear fuselage, and with twin booms carrying the empennage. Our own inclinations, however, were towards an airliner in the true sense, and we felt that it should be designed around four Ghosts. This would not give us in its original form a transatlantic passenger vehicle, but we thought that it would be a valuable aeroplane for the Empire routes and a step in the right direction. At first we saw it as a vehicle of moderate size, with a fuselage of about the size of that of the D.C.3, with its diameter of 8 ft. 6 in. and accommodation for 24 passengers, but the more we studied the problem the more confident we became that a full-size airliner for about 40 passengers was justifiable.

Concurrently with these considerations, one of the main technical decisions which occupied us was whether or not to employ a wing of marked sweep-back, and to eliminate the tailplane and elevator. The same problem was engaging us in connection with fighter development, and we decided to study it in a practical way by building a tailless swept-wing adaptation of the Vampire. This was the DH.108 and we had it flying by May, 1946. The work which we did with it during the next two or three years has proved invaluable to our fighter projects and to the Comet. And by September, 1946, we were decided that a tailless airliner, based on our knowledge at that time, would be less practical and economical than a more conventional design.   The tailless formula would take more time to resolve than we could allow ourselves. We had recognised from the first the importance of being able to go into production straight off the drawing-board. And this meant that we had to reach sufficiently far ahead in design to take good advantage of the new form of power unit, but not so far as to involve ourselves in highly

experimental features. In every way the design must represent a logical step forward. We were keen to retain a moderate wing-loading. Thus we came by stages to the Comet design as we know it to-day. In 1946 we saw this as a valuable aeroplane for the Empire routes and as a design having sufficient 'stretch' in it to take advantage of the more powerful and more economical axial engines, when, as we expected, they would be developed to civil standards.

The decision to go into production without waiting for a prototype was made possible by the foresight and initiative of BOAC in ordering a production batch. They were willing to place orders, provided that we would give contractual guarantees under penalty, relating to performance and delivery date, and agree the price in advance. This decision, which was a very courageous one at that time, has, I think, been justified.

Of course, the orders which we were able to obtain on this basis, amounting to 14 aircraft for the airlines and two development aircraft for the British Government, all at a fixed price based upon the costs which were current in 1946, did not amount to a break-even quantity, but we had not expected that. What we secured was a starting order for 16 Comets and we considered that offered us a justifiable commercial risk in proceeding with the project.

Serious design work was started in September, 1946, and the first aeroplane, built by our experimental department, made its maiden flight on July 27, 1949. The second machine, which was built by our production department, took the air a year later to the day. British Overseas Airways started their proving flights in April, 1951, and their passenger service 13 months later on May 2, 1952. The period of two and three-quarter years from the start of design to the first flight, and a further two and three-quarter to the commencement of passenger

Two turning and two burning! The De Havilland Ghost turbojet engines took to the air for the first time when the outer Rolls Royce Merlins on Avro Lancastrian VM903 were replaced. The first airborne testing of the Ghosts occurred in July 1947 as the Lancastrian is seen taking to the air from Hatfield. *(DH Hatfield)*

Once airborne the Lancaster flew on the outboard Ghosts alone. The tests were made by John Cunningham and Chris Beaumont, with a second Ghost Lancastrian VM729 added to speed the testing up. *(DH Hatfield)*

service, was less than we had expected. Certainly, had we waited for a prototype to fly before starting production, we should have added at least two years to the overall time of getting into service.

Design and Experiment

Detail design work had barely begun when, early in the New Year, there came the stimulating news that no less than sixteen of the new aircraft - costing, at that time, about £450,000 apiece - had been ordered on the strength of the preliminary plans. This did not amount to a 'break-even' quantity, but it was sufficient to reduce considerably the tremendous commercial risks in starting to build.

Two machines were for the Ministry of Supply - the rest were a bold move by BOAC and British South American Airways, both of whom had been pushing the project right from the outset, to ensure that full production could start straight away, without having to wait perhaps two years or more for the results of tests on the prototype.

Whilst this served to emphasize the urgency of the whole programme, it also called for considerable courage on the part of De Havilland's, who had not only to guarantee exact delivery dates and performance figures before they had even begun building, but had to fix the price while design work was still in progress.

It also meant that they had to risk a mass of last-minute modifications to all the production aircraft on the assembly lines, if any serious faults should show up on the prototype. With such a revolutionary design, this was quite possible, for even the most conventional aircraft have their share of teething troubles. De Havilland's resolved to use every possible means of avoiding this costly contingency, and even as the first jigging and tooling began, they put in hand an urgent programme of research aimed

at eliminating as many faults as possible at the laboratory stage, and also to discover ways and means of lightening the construction. This was particularly vital, because, of the total weight of the aircraft, exactly half consisted of fuel and only one eighth was payload. One pound of extra structure meant one pound less payload, and every pound of payload was worth £50 a year to BOAC.

Ronald Bishop again: ' *Tare weight may be mentioned as the first of the design problems. Since the payload would be little more than 10 per cent of the all-up weight at take-off, great efforts were made to keep the structure weight and equipment weight down to the minimum. We went for the smallest fuselage diameter which would accommodate two passengers on each side of the aisle with reasonable comfort. A great deal of investigation and testing was done to achieve the most efficient wing structure. We had been employing Redux cement extensively; it was used in the Dove light transport first built in 1945, and we had been working on the process for three or four years before that. We decided to use it in the Comet wing and fuselage, including double-curvature applications, and a method of construction was evolved for the wing, making use of extruded top-hat sections Reduxed to the skin, which enabled us to employ high allowable compressive stresses in the skin and stringer combination. This construction appeared to be very suitable for a wing having integral fuel tanks, due to the lack of rivets.*

Since the jet aircraft is very sensitive to drag we made every effort to reduce this to a minimum. The Comet has a relatively thin wing, the thickness-chord ratio being 11 per cent. All aerials are buried within the contour of the aircraft and the windscreen also forms part of the fuselage profile. There was a certain amount of doubt about the view from such a windscreen and we decided on a practical test at an early stage in the design. This we accomplished by making a special nose and mounting it on the front of a Horsa glider which we then towed behind a Halifax. The view for the pilot, both in clear air and in rain, proved to be quite adequate, and it has in fact never been criticised.

The Horsa, which happened conveniently to be the same diameter as the new Comet, with a Halifax bomber acting as tug, toured the skies of Britain looking for some suitably severe rainstorms. At the controls of the hybrid glider was Group Captain John Cunningham, OBE, DSO and two bars, DFC and bar, who had now become Chief Test Pilot. It took several weeks of searching before he was satisfied that he could see out clearly under any conditions. Several

years later a French jet airliner, the Caravelle, was to adopt an identical nose section, the first few actually being purchased from de Havilland's - an interesting tribute to the original design.

Among the first steps was the building of two very important models. One was a super-accurate scale pattern of the complete aircraft, which could be suspended in the wind tunnel and exposed to a hurricane blast of air, while technicians studied its behaviour 'in flight'. The other was a full-size facsimile, or 'mock-up', of the fuselage and inner wing section, built mostly of plywood and used for planning the layout, colour scheme, furnishing and lighting of the passenger and crew accommodation, the details of the engine installation with its cavernous air intakes and huge jet pipes, and the intricate geometry of the wires, ducts and hydraulic lines that snaked throughout the interior of the machine.

It might be thought that all this sort of thing

Below: this strange looking vehicle built from a three-ton truck chassis. A pair of transverse I-beams at the front held a pair of Mosquito main undercarriage units as outriggers and a Comet nosewheel leg with tanks of scrap metal on either side to simulate the loads on the nosewheels. The gentleman in the trilby is Sir Geoffrey himself.

Left: Charles T Wilkins, Assistant Chief Designer applies himself to navigational as well as technical problems with the device. *(DH Hatfield)*

could just as easily be done on the drawing-board, but as so often happens, there is a world of difference between paper and practice, and things that look fine on paper have a disconcerting habit of getting in the way of something else when they come to be fitted, or of being completely inaccessible to the unfortunate mechanic who has to work them. Similarly, there is only one way of making sure that the positioning of the various instruments and controls will be convenient for the pilot, and that is to let him spend some time sitting in the mock-up trying them for himself.

Ronald Bishop continues: *The problem of carrying fare-paying passengers at a height of 40,000 feet in comfort was one which caused us considerable worry. The temperature of the outside air at this altitude is frequently as low as minus 70 degrees Centigrade, so that the cabin heating and insulation became extremely important. One great advantage of the jet engine is that hot air under pressure can be readily tapped from the main engine compressor, thus doing away with the complication and weight of separate cabin blowers and combustion heaters such as are used at the present time on piston-engined transports. In fact, the temperature control on the Comet is effected by cooling the incoming air.*

We were faced with cabin differential pressures nearly double those in use on existing transports, and the consequences of a

pressure- cabin failure would be so serious that the fuselage must be designed rather like a submarine, so that it would never fail. A great deal of testing was done on large specimens of the fuselage with this object in view. In the early stages, after a failure using air pressure, we found that the only safe way of testing these large fuselage specimens was to submerge them in water and to employ water pressure instead of air pressure. Apart from the danger of the air-pressure method, a failure brought about such a disruption that it was not easy to determine where it originated ; in a water- pressure test the failure was localised. We built the first water tank for this purpose in this country and we have found this method of testing to be entirely satisfactory.

We adopted a policy of testing every part of the pressure cabin to destruction, never relying entirely upon calculations, and we employed factors on the pressure part of the fuselage considerably higher than those demanded by the Airworthiness Requirements. Requiring a cabin differential pressure of eight and a quarter pounds per square inch, we

The windscreen rain clearance capabilities of the new design were tested 'in the real world' by putting a mock-up nose on the front of a Airspeed Horsa glider and flown from Hatfield during the bitter winter of 1946.
(DH Hatfield)

designed to a safety factor of 2.5 , i.e., twenty and a half pounds per square inch, subjected test pieces to a factor of 2 (sixteen and a half pounds per square inch.) and we test all fuselages to a factor of 1.33 (eleven pounds per square inch). We treated the windows as a special case and tested them to a safety factor of 10 (eighty-two pounds per square inch).

The pressure cabin came in for more than its fair share of torture, or so it seemed to some people at the time. But jet engines have an extravagant thirst for fuel at low altitudes, and the entire economic success of the Comet was going to depend on its ability to operate at very great heights. In one of their earliest destructive tests on a specimen of the fuselage, they had pumped it up with air pressure until it burst, and the resulting explosion had been so shattering it had virtually destroyed all the evidence they were seeking.

They solved this particular problem by building a large tank, submerging each fuselage specimen in water and then bursting it quite gently with water pressure. This enabled them to see where every break occurred.

The cabin windows were treated as a separate case, and a set of test windows were pressurised every day for three years under simulated airline conditions which even included cleaning them with scratch remover in case this should affect their strength. Bishop goes on:

The supply of air for pressurising the fuselage is completely duplicated - in fact, any one engine will maintain the pressure-cabin supply. From the first we insisted upon inward- opening doors and hatches throughout. Considerable care was necessary to ensure that materials would not get brittle after several hours in temperatures down to minus 70°C. To explore this problem and to test equipment which must function in very low temperatures and air pressures we built a decompression chamber, capable of taking the full diameter of the Comet fuselage, in which we could simulate air conditions at altitudes up to 70,000 feet and with temperatures down to minus 70°C. We soon found that the standard materials used for such things as bag tanks, flexible hoses, etc., were useless, and a great deal of development work was undertaken before we were able to obtain materials which would remain reasonably flexible after soaking for five or six hours in air at such temperatures.

We decided to use power-operated flying controls, and although perhaps it could be argued

Tucked away in a screened-off area the Comet mock-up took shape out of timber, plywood and brown paper.
(DH Hatfield)

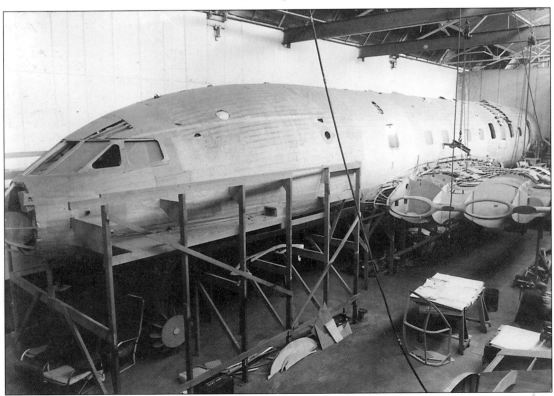

A test section of the Comet fuselage in the water tank at Hatfield. As the company said *'The use of water inside and outside the test specimen, instead of air, removes any danger of an explosive burst and localises the damage if a rupture does occur'.* (DH Hatfield)

that we might have made a success of aerodynamically balanced controls on an aircraft of this size, the advantages of power controls are so great that they seemed to us to be worth the effort. The uncertainties of aerodynamic balance appeared great, especially for an aeroplane with the speed range of the Comet, which operates at high altitude and cruises at a relatively high Mach number. It is significant that we were able to do 200 hours of flying with the Comet prototype in the first five months of trials, and I am convinced that had we had normal aerodynamically balanced controls we should have spent most of this time getting the controls right.

The great advantage of a power control system is that it can be got right on the ground on a test rig.

Powered controls have the additional advantage that they allow controls of larger chord to be used, and larger angular travel. Very considerable precautions have to be taken on a power-controlled aircraft. The hydraulic rams and valves are completely duplicated. The primary power control system serves no function other than the operation of the ailerons, elevator and rudder. The undercarriage and flaps are operated by secondary systems. There are three separate hydraulic- power-supply systems on the aircraft, available for flying controls.

John Cunningham and his fellow-pilots also played an important part in the early development of the power-operated control system. This was a system of powerful hydraulic rams which moved the control surfaces up and down for him at the touch of a finger - so effortlessly, in fact, that the cockpit control column and rudder bar had then to be restrained by springs in order to give the pilot an artificial sense of the 'feel' of the aircraft and prevent him from inadvertently overstressing it. The precise degree of response and 'feel' was something that could only be worked out in practice, and a complete set of powered controls was accordingly tried out in the air, first on a Hornet fighter and afterwards on the Swallow.

The next step was to prove the mechanical

Another test rig was the huge gantry that checked the strength of a Comet wing. The tests called for many thousands of reversals of load and besides providing an effective check of the structure strength they also served to establish the leak-proof quality of the integral wing fuel tanks, which were filled with kerosene during the tests. *(DH Hatfield)*

reliability of the system beyond all doubt. To be on the safe side, every vital part was triplicated throughout the system so that even if two failed, another could take over, and this reduced the risk to negligible proportions. Nevertheless, a full-size set of control equipment was put to work on a ground rig at the Hatfield works and only after it had run continuously, day in and day out, for over three years, were the engineers satisfied that nothing was likely to go wrong with it in the normal working life of the aircraft.

This was typical of the exhaustive ground tests undergone by practically every other part of the Comet - as it was now known. Because of the need to keep all structural weight to the barest minimum, a radically new method of construction had been adopted, using a thin skin of aluminium alloy - about the thickness of a postcard - attached to the skeleton framework of the aircraft not by the usual rivets, but with a special metal cement known as Redux.

Redux has become known as the generic name of a family of phenyl–formaldehyde/polyvinyl–formal adhesives developed by Aero Research Limited at Duxford, UK, in the 1940s and subsequently produced by Ciba-Geigy. The brand name is now used for a range of epoxy adhesives manufactured by Hexcel. The name is a contraction of REsearch at DUXford.

It was devised at Aero Research by Dr. Norman de Bruyne and George Newell in 1941 for use in the aircraft industry - at that time specifically De Havilland. The adhesive is used for the bonding of metal-to-metal and metal-to-wood structures, and the adhesive system comprises a liquid adhesive and a powder hardener.

Above: A Comet I cabin window under pressure test - the steelwork was there to prevent the pieces from flying if the window burst. There is a popular misconception that these windows were 'square', with sharp corners, but as can be seen, they were rectangular with rounded corners. wrinkles on the fuselage skin disappeared.*(DH Hatfield)*

Right: Comet cabin under full pressure is twisted to check its strength. The torsion wrinkles in the skin are clearly visible. The photograph shows the fuselage under a torsional load many times more severe than would ever occur in flight. On this occasion the cabin was not pressurised. When cabin air-pressure was applied at a later stage in the test the stress wrinkles on the fuselage skin disappeared.*(DH Hatfield)*

Another test section of the Comet fuselage 'on the rack undergoing torture' at Hatfield. This picture appears to show the centre-section with parts of a wing structure installed, but one that does not have the apertures for the engines. *(DH Hatfield)*

In this and a hundred lesser ways, pounds were pared off here, ounces off there, but always the strength of the finished component was kept up to standard, proved in a seemingly endless series of gruelling tests in which wings, with their integral fuel tanks filled, and a fuselage under full pressurization, were strained and twisted by powerful hydraulic jacks, the loads being steadily increased until the structure finally failed.

Bishop explains about the fire and fuelling problems that had to be overcome: *'Since we had engines buried in the wing, we realised from the start of the design that very great attention must be paid to fire precautions. The hot parts of the engines are separated from the main structure by steel fireproof bulkheads, and the whole of the tailpipe is enclosed in a steel tube with cooling air passing down the annulus. Perhaps the greatest need in regard to fire risk with a jet engine is a reliable means of detecting the fire quickly should it occur, since once the pilot knows that there is a fire it can be put out instantly by cutting off the supply of fuel to the engine. I am convinced that one of the biggest steps forward in safety from fire in the air is made by the use of*

paraffin instead of petrol. I hope that there will never be any talk of using in civil aircraft fuels other than paraffin, such as the new American J.P.4 jet fuel which is, in effect, a low-grade petrol.

Since the advantage of the speed of the jet aircraft can so easily be lost by long stops on the ground, it was essential to develop a good, reliable means of pressure refuelling. The Comet carries 7,000 Imperial gallons of paraffin, and it can be refuelled in 20 minutes. The pressure-refuelling system has been used from the first flight of the prototype in 1949 and has proved entirely satisfactory.

Because of the relatively thin wing and the large amount of fuel to be carried in the aircraft—which, incidentally, could not be carried in the fuselage—we decided to go for integral tanks for the major part of the fuel. By using Redux to cement stringers to the skin and by the use of bolts for assembly, we were able to avoid rivets in the integral-tank area. This system appears to have worked out well, and the integral tanks have given no trouble at all in service.

During the designing of the aeroplane we were concerned about noise in the cabin. After a flight in the Nene Viking we decided to shift two rows of passengers from the back of the cabin to the front to get them away from the area of jet-pipe noise.

Early in the period of test flying we were worried by the whine of the impeller in the front part of the cabin. After a lot of sound- proofing experiments it was eventually found that this high-pitch noise was transmitted through the structure from the engine, and it was cured by mounting the engine on rubber. Although the Comet may not be a lot quieter than conventional civil aircraft it does appear that it has a less unpleasant sound, and a much more important thing is that there is an almost complete absence of vibration, which results in the passengers arriving at their destination feeling less fatigued than they would be after a flight of the same time in a piston-engined

aircraft. This, coupled with the fact that the flight itself takes much less time in the Comet, is without doubt going to add considerably to the passenger appeal of the Comet'.

Meanwhile it had been established that the Ghost engines were not affected by the intense cold. They had even proved capable of swallowing considerable quantities of ice, including, on several occasions, large chunks weighing several pounds each—with no more than a hesitant cough. This was due mainly to the rugged simplicity of their centrifugal type of compressor, and was one of the main reasons for De Havilland's decision to use this engine for the first Comets, instead of waiting for the more efficient axial turbojets which were coming along; these were more

The air conditioning and cabin pressurisation system took air from the engine impellors and then ducted it around the cabin. Due to the altitude the DH106 was to fly at, the system operated at much greater pressures.
(DH Hatfield)

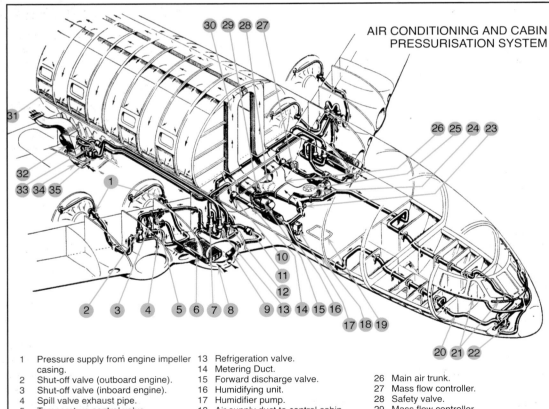

AIR CONDITIONING AND CABIN PRESSURISATION SYSTEM

1	Pressure supply from engine impeller casing.	13	Refrigeration valve.
2	Shut-off valve (outboard engine).	14	Metering Duct.
3	Shut-off valve (inboard engine).	15	Forward discharge valve.
4	Spill valve exhaust pipe.	16	Humidifying unit.
5	Temperature control valve.	17	Humidifier pump.
6	Primary heat exchanger.	18	Air supply duct to control cabin.
7	Mass flow valve.	19	Access door.
8	Cooling duct for heat exchanger	20	Warm air duct to pilot's feet and windscreen.
9	Ram-air inlet, auxilliary ventilation.	21	Pilot's warm air valve.
10	Non-return valve	22	Warm air distributor for windscreen.
11	Non-return valve, auxilliary ventilation.	23	Ground conditioning adaptor.
12	Non-return valve, refrigeration.	24	Recirculating fan motor
		25	Recirculating fan.

26	Main air trunk.
27	Mass flow controller.
28	Safety valve.
29	Mass flow controller.
30	Main air supply to cabin at bulkhead 18.
31	Air supply through louvres in cabin upholstery.
32	Secondary heat exchanger.
33	Non-return valve from cold air unit.
34	Retractable cooling duct.
35	Cold air unit.

This picture is something of a mystery. Some sources have claimed that it shows the modified Mk 1 Vampire that John Cunningham used to break the altitude record on 28 March 1948 - and now in a partially dismantled form - to test the effects of 'jet noise' on this forward fuselage section. However, it seems puzzling as to why the Comet section is canted nose-upwards at that strange angle and why the Vampire is 'reversed'. *(DH Hatfield)*

compact, weighed less and used less fuel, but at that time were much less reliable than the centrifugal type and were very sensitive to icing conditions. This decision can be reckoned to have saved the best part of two years in getting the Comet into airline service.

Running experience with the Ghost began in September 1945, and two were airborne for the first time on July 24, 1947, in the outer engine nacelles of a Lancastrian 'flying test-bed', its normal piston engines being retained in the inboard positions for use primarily on take-off, and as a 'get-you-home' policy in case of trouble with the jets—an infrequent event, as it turned out. It was afterwards joined by two similar aircraft, and during the next few years they put in many hundreds of hours of valuable flying, in which a number of teething troubles on the engines were overcome.

Their service ceiling, however, was limited to about 25,000 ft, and in order to carry out tests at upwards of 40,000 ft, a Ghost was also installed in a special Vampire with extended wing tips. It was in this that John Cunningham established, on March 23, 1948, a new World Height Record of 59,492 ft. Over the next few months, a useful amount of experience was steadily built up on the Ghost-Vampire (later to become the Venom fighter), which showed that the new engine had no unexpected vices at high altitude.

During this period, John Cunningham also spent time with BOAC, making several trips to America and Australia as a supernumerary crew member and generally getting to know some of the practical aspects of airline operation, in preparation for development flying.

The Design Concept
By April 1949 De Havillands were able to publically announce how the Comet was intended to be used - for express services along the trunk routes of the British Commonwealth. It would also be suitable for inter-continental services generally, for it was seen as an airliner for world operation. Its high speed compared with then present-day aircraft, besides being an advantage to communications, would materially aid its economy by rendering it possible to fly more miles and carry more ton-miles of payload in the year. The company stated that high speed was not to be secured at the sacrifice of slow-flying ability; in point of fact, the wing loading was less than that of some conventional propeller-driven airliners of the time, and the stalling speed was correspondingly modest. Thus, although the D.H. 106 would cruise at high speed above the weather it could descend through cloud steeply at slow forward speed and would be perfectly capable of flying a standard circuit, approach and make a landing in the manner of any other aircraft. It would not require

The prototype Comet 1 comes together in the Hatfield Experimental Shop. Prominent in this view are the square windows installed in this version. *(DH Hatfield)*

exceptional runways and could operate from normal main airports along the trunk routes.

Contemporary thinking of the day suggested that mainly due to fuel consumption, the aircraft would require prompt handling by the terminal flight control organisations; indeed, the development of the technique for landing aircraft in bad weather was rendered doubly urgent by the advent of jet-propelled airliners, which could not economically be delayed long periods before landing. This aspect of the D.H. 106 was carefully studied by the authorities and by BOAC, all of whom were fully aware of the need to quickly evolve a safe and dependable system.

The comfort of passengers when flying at great heights demanded unprecedented attention to the problem of air-conditioning. The aircraft was to fly at about 40,000 feet in order to achieve optimum economy. The cabin, including the control room - as De Havillands were then calling the flight deck - also the luggage, freight and mail storage all had to be pressurised to a differential of 8.25 lb. per square inch, which was nearly double the pressure employed in airliners then in service. This provided a 'cabin altitude' of 8,000 ft when at

40,000. The conditioning equipment included cooling as well as heating apparatus, along with humidifiers to replace the moisture that was absent at such heights. The design was for ventilation air in the aircraft to be changed every three minutes.

The Comet Series 1 was best suited to stage lengths of up to about 1,750 miles, and down to as low as 600 miles. These figures had full regard to the fuel reserves and all other operational features of the aircraft. Nevertheless, the Ghost engine - being a first-generation turbine - suffered from low thrust that was coupled with high fuel consumption and it was fully expected that this would evolve over time. Indeed, even before the Comet 1 entered airline service, plans were already in hand for the Comet 2, powered by Rolls-Royce Avon axial compressor turbines, as they were then known. This version, with a greater all-up-weight, would be capable of working the longer and more severe stages of the world's airline network.

The use of rockets

De Havillands had always kept a watching brief on all developments likely to attain a significant place in the science of aeronautics. In view of wartime advances in the design of rocket power units. Major Frank Halford appointed A V Cleaver as Special Projects Engineer whose job was to evaluate the various known forms of aircraft rocket and their applications and the development of units for manufacture by the de Havilland Engine Company.

For some time the small team concerned itself only with the most general study of the possibilities of rocket propulsion for aircraft. These arose from the two outstanding characteristics of the system, namely, its ability to deliver extremely high thrusts from very small units of light weight, and the independence of that thrust upon atmospheric conditions.

As against these advantages, the very high fuel consumption of the rocket was a serious drawback, which inevitably limited its possible use to applications of short duration. Two such applications had been extensively exploited by the Germans in the war, the first in performance boosting of fighters and the second in the assisted take-off (ATO) of heavy aircraft.

Of these two cases, the latter had an accentuated importance in connection with the operation of jet aircraft from high-altitude tropical airfields, where the basic engine thrust could be down by as much as 25%. Clearly, in a case where other forms of thrust-boosting - such as water injection or re-heat - could provide the extra thrust required, it would be undesirable to go to the added complication of rocketry. There was an argument for ATO rockets in some instances as De Havillands saw no limit to the extra thrust that

could be provided by rocket units of suitable design and size. Their high fuel consumption was relatively unimportant in this application, since the whole fuel load was consumed very soon after the aircraft was airborne.

The de Havilland survey of possible rocket fuels indicated that great technical advantages might be expected from the use of hydrogen peroxide at concentrations, by weight, of 80% or more. This fluid was first produced in quantity by the Germans during the war and its use in various rocket and naval devices was very successfully pioneered by the firm of Walterwerke, at Kiel. It was being made in the UK by Laporte Chemicals at Luton.

De Havillands considered that there had been a many exaggerated stories about the dangers of handling high-strength hydrogen peroxide, but wartime German experience, and post-war experience in this country demonstrated that it could be handled just as freely as petrol, provided that comparable care was observed. The necessary precautions included the use of containers of suitable material and the observance of a high standard of cleanliness.

In 1949 the only disadvantage of hydrogen peroxide was its high cost, then about £190 per ton. In rocket motors, hydrogen peroxide could be used in two ways. It could be used primarily as a source of oxygen, with which some other fuel could be burned, creating what was known as 'hot' rocket, with a combustion chamber temperature of 2,000°C. It could also be used as a fuel in its own right, in which case the amount of energy liberated

Avro Lancastrian VM703 gets airborne under the power of three types of engine: a pair of Rolls Royce Merlins driving the inboard propellers, a pair of DH Ghosts jet engines in the outboard nacelles, and a pair of ATO rocket motors under the fuselage. There is some doubt and controversy regarding this picture: some sources state that they are a pair of DH Sprite rocket motors - others state that given that this picture was taken in 1947, they could not be Sprites, but were in fact a pair of captured German Walter 109-500 rockets. Whatever the case, the two new propulsion systems were under consideration and test for use in the Comet. *(DH Hatfield)*

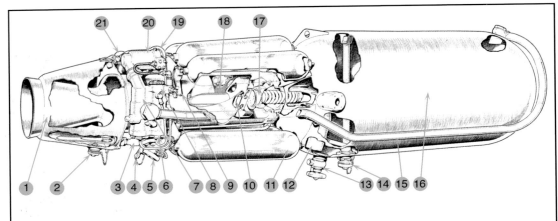

hydrogen peroxide.

1   Catalyst tank.
2   Catalyst filling point.
3   Catalyst feed to injector.
4   Air filling point.
5   Air pressure guage.
6   Air distributor valve for catalyst
7   Air distributor valve for

8   Starting valve.
9   Air bleed to catalyst tank.
10 Catalyst injector.
11 Compressed air bottles (1 of 9)
12 Hydrogen peroxide collector
    pipe.

13 Hydrogen peroxide dump valve.
14 Hydrogen peroxide filling point.
15 Air feed to peroxide tank.
16 Hydrogen peroxide tank.
17 Hydrogen peroxide injector.
18 Reaction chamber.
19 Air feed to catalyst tank.
20 Check thrust valve.
21 Air reducing valve.

Above: cutaway of the Sprite rocket motor. A pair of these were planned to be fitted between the Ghosts in each wing of the DH106.
Below: The refuelling trailer for rapid and foolproof servicing of Sprite rocket motors installed in the Comet 1.
(both DH Hatfield)

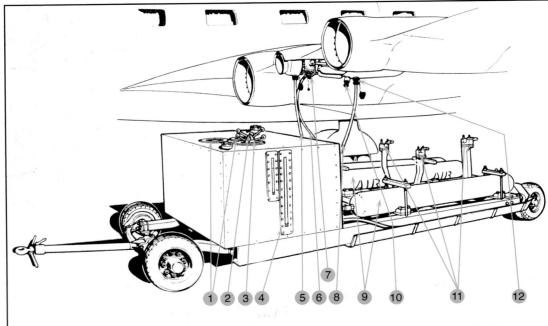

1   Air pressure guage.
2   Air control valve.
3   Feed selector control.
4   Contents guages for propellant
    storage tank.

5   Catalyst (calcium
    permanganate) filling line.
6   Air filling line.
7   Air pressure guage.
8   Hydrogen peroxide filling line.

9   Air storage bottles (3,600 lb per
    sq in.
10 Drain cock.
11 Rocket motor transport cradle.
12 Sprite rocket motor.

per unit mass was much lower – the so-called 'cold' rocket motor with a combustion chamber temperature of 500°C.

The first de Havilland rocket - the Sprite ATO unit - was of the 'cold' variety. The advantages of this low-energy system were its great simplicity and safety.

It was considered desirable to provide special equipment to permit charging of Sprite units with compressed air, hydrogen peroxide and permanganate, of such design that the possibility of incomplete filling, over-filling or spillage could be eliminated. De Havillands designed a special trailer that incorporated all possible safety features, so as to ensure quick and tidy refuelling procedure. Large air cylinders on the trailer were used to charge the Sprite air bottles, by equalising pressures, and then some of the remaining air was used to pressurise peroxide and permanganate tanks (of the correct capacity) in the trailer. This displaced the fluids up from the trailer into the appropriate tanks in the Sprite through hoses and self- sealing couplings of different size for each

fluid. All the filling operations were controlled by selector valves mounted behind the trailer control panel.

As the Sprite had been designed to give a total impulse for take-off assistance of 55,000 lb./sec, which gave a rating for a maximum thrust of 5,000 lb. and a total period of operation of about twelve seconds the design team seriously considered using it in the Comet. A pair of Sprite rocket motors were the equivalent of two extra Ghost jet engines for take-off.

Alternatively, plans were already in hand for the later Series 2 Comet with Rolls-Royce Avon engines - a long range aircraft capable of carrying its capacity payload on stages of up to 2,500 miles,and, having the advantages of a greater thrust and a lower specific consumption.

Moreover, the later entry of the Series 2 Comet into service would be facilitated by the widespread commercial experience which the Series 1 would have obtained, as well as by the developments which should have taken place meanwhile in air traffic control proceedures and technical abilities.

De Havilland's original caption:
'The team principally responsible for the development of the Sprite : (left to right) Mr. W. H. Neat, Technical Assistant; Mr. A.V. Cleaver, Special Projects Engineer, in charge of the de Havilland Engine Company's rocket development; Mr. R. A. Grimston, Technical Assistant, and Mr. E. B, Dove, Designer-Draughtsman. Other members of the team not appearing in this picture include Mr. P. I. Brittain, Chief Chemist at the Stag Lane Laboratories, Tester J, J, Bennetts and fitter B. Carrington'. (DH Hatfield)

The Sprite rocket motor undergoing firing trials in a special test bed at Hatfield. The photograph shows the engine about half-way through an early test run; the steam is tinged with the brown of manganese dioxide.
(DH Hatfield)

Aviation artist Terence Tenison Cuneo CVO, OBE, RGI, FGRA did this 1949 rendition of the Comet as it would look like during a night turn-around. *(DH Hatfield)*

Chapter Three

PRODUCTION

The question of producing the Comet presented the usual problems which were already well-known to all production engineers. They may be defined under the following headings: —

1 Tooling of the production batch in such a manner that it would assist and expedite the completion of the prototype aircraft.
2 The production of a small batch of aircraft at a reasonable cost. This involved:
   (a) A survey of essential tooling and the production of such tools at a cost justified by the contract price.
   (b) The production of tools within a period of time limited by the planning.
3 The production of the tools within the time factor and to a standard which would ensure the high quality demanded by an aircraft in the category of the Comet.
4 The first aircraft of the production batch to be made to a programme which allowed only a small gap between the flying of the prototype and the flying of the first production aircraft.
5 The development within the planned period of new processes and techniques not yet fully established.

To achieve the foregoing it was necessary to initiate planning which needed the full co-operation of Design, Experimental, Test Laboratory, and Production Departments under the auspices of Harry Povey AFRAeS, Production Director of De Havillands and his team.

The original plan was to fly the first production aircraft six months after the prototype had flown and, although this was not achieved, the first of the production batch of aircraft did fly exactly twelve months to the day after the prototype, and this performance was not considered a complete failure.

To see the achievement against the planned programme, the fact must be taken into account that the flying control system on the first production aircraft underwent extensive changes in design which, together with many other alterations, accounted for a delay of a few months. During this period, most of the tooling was also nearing completion.

An essential part of the planning was to establish a strong liaison between the Design team and the Production Department. Great importance was attached by the De Havilland Company to this design and production liaison and without it the achievement would certainly not have been possible. Povey and his Chief Production Engineer attended all design progress conferences, and this enabled the production team to obtain a forward knowledge of the design requirements. It also enabled decisions to be taken at these meetings as to how best the production team could assist the Experimental Department in the early tooling of difficult parts. Such decisions were vitally important at the early stage of the design, and a complete understanding had to be reached between Design, Experimental and Production Departments. It meant that the designers could

In the days before CAD-CAM and perception in a virtual world, the best way of planning was to build physical models - which was just what De Havilland's did with the Comet, as with this fuselage break-down model.*(DH Hatfield)*

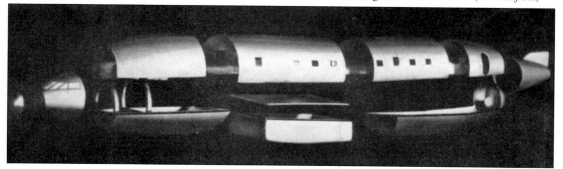

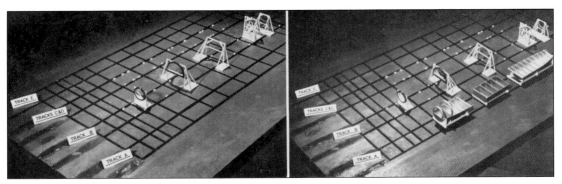

This sequence of pictures show in model form the fuselage construction lines at Hatfield. They show how each mobile trolley was moved along its track. On to track A the lower front and rear keels are manhandled from their assembly jigs on to their trolleys. The only fixed jigs necessary for track assembly are shown on track B where the location of skins, pressure domes, canopies, etc., was controlled. The small white dots in tracks represent the surface plates and vee-blocks whose correct positioning accurately controls the construction of the component. Each trolley was then moved on to track C and D for the joining of the now completed main fuselage components. On the final track all the outstanding operations are completed and a preliminary leak test of 2 pounds per square inch was made. The fuselage was then moved outside the hangar for its final pressure test of 11 pounds per square inch. The final picture, lower right was a composite view of the assembly process - all the fuselage sub-assemblies are mounted on mobile jigs which could readily be moved from one track to another.*(DH Hatfield)*

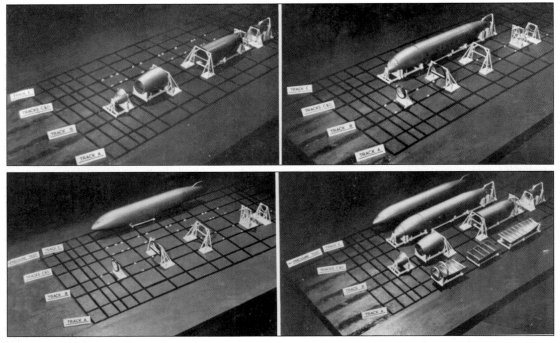

take a reasonable risk and Production could anticipate the many modifications that might be needed as a result of the early decisions.

Some results of this liaison and the assistance given by Production to enable the Experimental Department to expedite the flying of the prototype involved such things as the spar booms which were fully tooled for spar milling from the beginning. This required a very early decision and risk by Design. Another item was the door jamb and door frames, all of which necessitated the development of drop hammer technique and the production of heavy tools. The nose portion to the fuselage also necessitated the production of three-stage drop hammer tools.

There was also a large amount of glass cloth

mouldings - a technique used for the first time by DH on the Comet - which were developed by the Production Department, and to enable this to be done before finalised designs were available, 'typical' designs were used to make test samples and to develop the technique.

In order to allow the Production Department to develop their techniques and tooling, a typical design of wing and a 24 ft. section of the fuselage was planned to be built for physical testing and design of equipment needed for the final design. The production of these skins necessitated the design and manufacture of suitable presses. These were designed in-house by the Company's Engineering Department and made by the Tool Section. One 35-ft. long press was used for the wing skin, and two 25-ft. long presses for the manufacture of double-curvature skins on the fuselage.

As soon as the technique of producing wing skins and fuselage skins had been developed to a reasonable standard the Production Department

proceeded to produce a complete wing and a 24-ft. long portion of the fuselage for physical test.

By this time, the production of tools and development had gone entirely to plan, and was working out extremely satisfactorily.

All of this - the early development of spar milling, glass cloth moulding, Reduxing of fuselage and wing skins, Hufford tools for the manufacture of fuselage rings, drop hammer tools for large components, and a complete wing-building jig, together with a substantial wing drilling jig gave the Production Department an excellent start on the first batch of aircraft.

The Redux process was for bonding metal to metal by heat and pressure in order to replace riveting or spot welding on the wing skin and fuselage had already been partially developed and had been initially used on the Hornet to bond aluminium in tension to the wooden spar. It had also been used to great effect on the Dove feeder-liner.

Its use in the Comet therefore was not an innovation, though the extent of it was. The Comet

A model of the final assembly line at Hatfield. It can be seen that there are two lines of Comet fuselages, both of which are served by a single line of wings. Each fuselage runs along its track on the same trolley that it retained after the boxing-up process in the fuselage shop. *(DH Hatfield)*

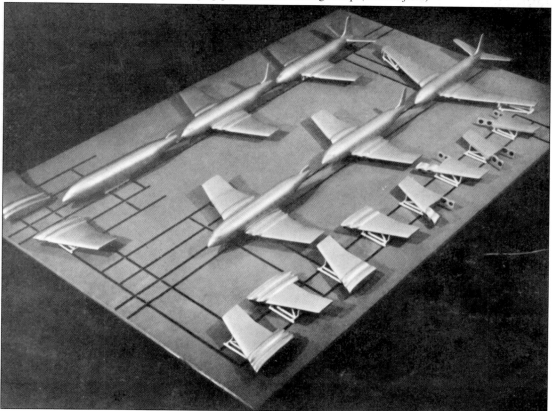

required so much fuel - quoted as 40% of maximum weight - that the wing itself had to become an integral fuel tank; that was another Comet first, but is of course standard in every jet transport of today. The tanks in the centre section under the passengers had to be bags - for safety in case of crash landing - but every other available volume of the wing outboard of the engines and undercarriage had to be used to uplift fuel.

Because rivets meant holes, and holes meant leaks, Bishop decided to make use of extensive

How stringer Reduxing tools were cast - the master pressure bar was in position close to the plaster model in preparation for a capping to be cast. *(DH Hatfield)*

The early stages in the construction and the finished plaster model of the forward part of the fuselage. From this model no less than 64 pairs of tools were produced for Reduxing the stringers to the fuselage skin. The plaster model could be rotated to bring each successive stringer station into position against the adjustable table used for casting stringer Reduxing tools. *(DH Hatfield)*

Redux bonding. Redux also saved the weight of rivets, and allowed the use of thinner plate, and was used extensively for the pressure fuselage. So the combination of bonding and riveting - flush rivets for a high-speed aircraft - was adopted.

The Redux process consists of applying heat and pressure by suitable tools to the parts to be bonded together. The problem was to produce these tools accurately and at a reasonable cost.

The mating surface of the top and bottom tools had to be a one hundred per cent perfect fit, as it was essential that every part of the surface for which adhesion was required had equal pressure. This tool was a composite unit and comprised top and bottom pressure bars with loose cappings fitted to each. The main pressure bars were made from hollow duralumin extrusions, which enabled steam to be supplied through the bore of the extrusion for heating and curing the Redux.

In order to economise, only one pressure bar was used, which was made as a master by forming to the average curvature of the fuselage nose, as determined by the plaster model.

The method of producing these tools accurately and cheaply was achieved by the use of the plaster model - the capping was the only variant in this unit and the variation of curvature was made by casting low fusible metal on to the face of the plaster model and into the dovetail grooves in the capping. Each capping, when complete, made a separate tool.

To produce these variations in the cast face of the capping the hollow extrusion and capping, formed as a unit, supported on an adjustable table placed adjacent to the plaster model. The nearest part of the unit was kept half an inch away from the plaster model, and was adjusted so that the ends of each extrusion were an equal amount away from the model at the two extremities.

Having determined the best position for this tool in relation to the plaster model, the lower extremity of the gap formed between the plaster and the tool was filled with fire clay on a plywood

support. By this means a cavity had been formed between the plaster and extrusion. This cavity was then filled by casting with a low fusible metal which keyed itself into the dovetails which were part of the capping extrusion. When cooled and set, the unit was then taken away from the plaster model and an accurate cast face representing the stringer flange had been obtained on the capping.

The tool was completed by the production of pressure bars which had to make a perfect contact with the face of the tool which was produced by casting on the plaster model.

The pressure bars are made by supporting the

The window frames were Reduxed to the fuselage skin during the assembly process on the static jig. Two castings were used, one located in the jig at the window positions, and the other, a mating jig, formed a steam box for applying the necessary temperature for Reduxing. *(DH Hatfield)*

tool on a table, re-heating, and casting the mating face of the pressure bar right on to the previously formed face on the capping strip, using a parting compound of graphite.

By this means the Company was able to produce a separate stringer Redux tool on each capping, '...*the faces of which were dead accurate to the plaster model, and which needed only a small amount of fettling to make them perfect*'. All of the Redux tools for double-curvature parts were produced at a relatively low cost by this method. The components were made in the simplified fuselage building jigs. The keynote for the design of these jigs was low cost and simplicity, easy access for the operator for all work and the ease of movement for large components leading to the elimination of manhandling.

A simple track was devised and once the sub-assemblies which formed the breakdown of the completed fuselage were received on the track and track jigs, they passed from operation to operation and eventually become a complete fuselage without any further manhandling. To feed the track a number of components had to be made in static jigs and these were the only components which were manhandled on to the track trolleys at

the head of the line.

The components manufactured in the static jigs consisted of the fuselage nose, canopy, forward section of fuselage, centre section and its pressure floor, fuselage sides, front keel, rear keel, rear fuselage sides, rear cone, and pressure dome.

The method of attaching window frames to the fuselage skin was perhaps novel, as these window frames, which were deep-drawn drop hammer pressings, were Reduxed to the fuselage skins in situ while the skin was being assembled in the fuselage side jig which consisted of two castings; one was located accurately in the side jig and determined the position of the window frames, while the mating casting was a hollow casting which formed a steam box and was drawn into position by two standard four-inch Mosquito hydraulic flap jacks, which applied the necessary pressure for Reduxing. The steam which supplied the heat was obtained from a pipe which was located over the top of the jig. Fluid pressure to the jacks was supplied by an obsolete Mosquito hand pump. The operation for fixing a window complete was approximately 25 minutes.

After the Redux operation had been completed, the outer tool was withdrawn, but the inner one

The static jigs used for the assembly of some of the larger fuselage components. This battery of jigs was designed to combine simplicity with ease of access. From these jigs the assembled components were man-handled to the mobile jigs on the assembly tracks. *(DH Hatfield)*

Left: Checking the alignment of fuselage to centre section before attaching the latter to the fuselage body. The tubular straight-edge was calibrated to be dead square with the centre-line of the centre section before it was attached to the fuselage. With the centre section in position plumb bobs were dropped from each side of the straight-edge to indicate its relative alignment to the fuselage centre-line by the position of the plumb bob heads in relation to index plates located on the floor.

Below: A murky day at Hatfield, and another fuselage was wheeled out for full-pressure testing.
(both DH Hatfield)

was left in position to locate a router template which enabled a simple hand routering operation to be performed which removed surplus metal from the window orifice and, when completed, gave the exact shape and position required.

The fuselage side panels consisted of four skins, 30 inches wide and 22 feet long, on to which all stringers were Reduxed. The panels were then formed into one large skin by riveted lapped joints on the three internal edges of the four panels.

One of the Company's great aims was to keep the external part of the fuselage free from jig structure so that the operators had ready access to their work, which added considerably to efficiency and was conducive to good workmanship.

In order to transfer the jig trolleys from one track to another a simple substitution for turntables was arranged in the form of a nine-inch square steel plate placed at intervals in the rails. This enabled the trolley wheels to be turned through 90 degrees and wheeled from track to track on the rails which join one track to the other.

At each station there was only one fixed piece of jig structure that controlled the location of skins, pressure domes, canopies and so on which were to be mated to the component contained on the jig trolley. This fixed structure and the jig trolley, when located on the Vee blocks, accurately controlled the location of the parts in relation to each other, so that they could be built on to the component which was located on the jig trolley.

With the centre section in position, and ready for attachment to the fuselage, plumb bobs were dropped from each side of the straight edge to indicate its relative alignment to the fuselage centre line by the position of the plumb bob heads in relation to index plates which were located in the floor. It was possible to adjust the centre section by shims under the centre fittings until a correct alignment has been obtained. The alignment of the centre section in relation to the centre line of the fuselage was extremely

A view of the jig used for the accurate drilling of the 252 tight-limit holes of the fuselage centre section and the stub wings. In this picture the centre section can be seen in position on the jig, and an operator was using one of the two special radial drills on the wing-root fittings. This method ensured complete interchangeability between fuselage, centre section and stub wings. *(DH Hatfield)*

Plaster models which were used for the making of tools for the wing skins and engine cowlings. *(DH Hatfield)*

important, since this determined the squareness of the wing to the centre line of the aircraft. Exceptionally good results were achieved with this method and taking diagonals on the 110-feet span of wing to the rear cone of the fuselage, the difference of only four-tenths of an inch were measured between either diagonal.

When the centre section was attached, all other jig trolleys were removed, leaving the fuselage standing on the centre section trolley only. The fuselage was then moved on to the final track, track 'E', where all outstanding operations were completed, and a preliminary leak test of 2 pounds per square inch was made. When this operation was completed and found satisfactory, the fuselage was wheeled out of the shop, still on the track, to a position on the aerodrome where the 11 pounds per square inch pressure test was applied. It was not possible to do this test in the shop because should a failure occur while approaching the 11 pounds per square inch pressure, the bursting of the fuselage would be catastrophic.

Construction of the wing

The wing building track was constructed on similar lines to the fuselage track. The stub wing building jigs were static, but when the component was withdrawn from these jigs, subsequent operations were made on the track and all components were transported to the various stations on mobile jig trolleys.

The complete track circuit provided stations for the operation of drilling the stub wing attachments to the fuselage, for the fuel tests, attachment of engine cowling, engine cowling doors, air intakes, jet pipe cowlings, the attachment of leading-edge, and the installation of ailerons and flaps.

The stub wing building jigs were rather unorthodox and were designed with three principal features in view : —

(1) To give all operators easy access to their work.

(2) All operations in the jig to be of such a working height that personal fatigue was eliminated.

(3) To obtain an accurate aerofoil when

Above: The stub wing and extension lined up in the centre-section drilling jig. This jig was designed to ensure complete interchangeability and the absolute accuracy of the wing unit in regards the dihedral, incidence and sweepback. The steel rails on the floor were for moving the jigs around the factory.

Left: As soon as the stub wings came off their jigs they were given a fluid test. Because of the confined working space in the wing, and because of the fumes given off by the Bostik protection fluid, special precautions had to be taken. The clothing and equipment provided the operator with a fresh air supply and a means of communication with an assistant outside. *(DH Hatfield)*

attaching wing skins.

The spar building jig was an orthodox building jig, but emphasised the liaison between the Production and Experimental Departments insofar that the original jig was produced by the Experimental Department and taken over by Production to be modified in such a way that would ensure production times and interchangeability

The stub wing called for very special attention and as this portion of the wing was an integral fuel tank, great accuracy was necessary in the manufacture of mating components.

As an example, the method of producing the rather complicated shaped wheel-well wall which traversed across the wing in several directions. The profile of the landing angle, owing to its path across the wing, required the production of a winding bevel and at the same time the depth of this member between top and bottom skins had to be accurately controlled and a perfect wing contour produced.

The first operation on this component was to Redux the angles to the web. These angles were controlled as accurately as possible, but the final accuracy was produced when the assembly was placed in the jig and machined by a rotary hand miller which was traversed across the surface of

Above: The stub-wing building jigs were built over pits to allow easy access from above and below. On completion of the bottom surface of the wing the component was turned over to be transferred to a similar jig for completion of the upper surface plating.

Left: This jig for the assembly of the inboard section of the flaps was built by the Experimental Department and was taken over by the Production Department who made only such modifications as would ensure good production times and interchangeability.

Below: A view of the Comet assembly lines at Hatfield. In the foreground are the starboard wing jigs.
(all DH Hatfield)

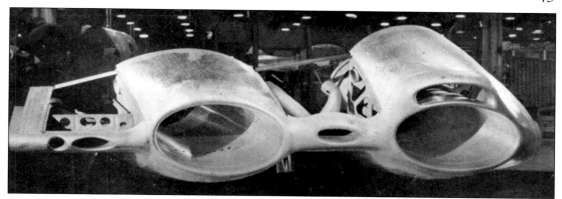

Above: The starboard-side engine air-intakes in the course of assembly. This process was one of the more complicated sub-assemblies, but a reasonable production time-cycle was achieved by the use of production jig.

Right: A stub-wing further down the production line, with its leading edge fitted.

Below: A stub wing is wheeled on its trolley into position by a fuselage for attachment.
(all DH Hatfield)

The large concrete tool used for stretching the longitudinal portion of an engine cowling was cast direct off a plaster model. Here an engine cowling is being stretched on the Sheridan stretcher press.

The interior of one of the hulls is fitted out.
(both DH Hatfield)

the angles, removing approximately 1/32nd inch of metal. The rails controlled the depth of cut, also the correct contour and winding bevel.

After machining one face, the component was reversed and the machined face from the first operation was located against a limit stop which determined the correct depth of the component, while the second operation of machining the opposite angle was done.

This was a quick and accurate method and the units had to be kept within the tolerance of approximately 0.01 inch. The final thickness of the angle was made by a router fitted with control rollers which located on the surface of the previously machined angle and by traversing the component through this router the correct thickness and inner bevel was produced.

The operation in the first jig was the location of spars, ribs, wheel-well walls and bottom skins. On completion of this the wing was transferred from No. 1 jig to No. 2 jig, and turned over through 180 degrees. The top skin was attached in a similar manner in No. 2 jig.

To enable this, the bottom skin which was previously fitted was removed to give access for the operators to complete their work inside the wing, which included fastening off the top skin to the ribs and spars. The stub wing was then removed from the jig, placed in position on the drilling jig, and while the spars were being drilled and reamed for attachment to the fuselage centre section, the bottom skin was also being attached.

By eliminating the operation of attaching the bottom skin while in No. 2 jig, and doing this concurrently with the drilling operation, the time cycle was equalised in Nos. 1 and 2 jigs.

Before beginning drilling operations, the fuselage centre section was set up correctly in the drilling jig and the stub wings were wheeled into position, and the spar booms accurately located between the high-tensile steel fish-plates which formed the attachment of wing spar to the centre section. The sweepback of the wing, the incidence, and dihedral angles were accurately set and checked by Inspection prior to drilling.

When the setting was satisfactory, the drilling and reaming for the tight-limit bolt holes through the fish-plates and spar boom were completed in this jig. When this drilling was completed, the stub wings were withdrawn from the jig and before proceeding with any subsequent assembly they were taken on the track to a position outside the shop where a fluid test was given. Each stub wing was filled with 2,000 gallons of paraffin and any weeps which might occur were remedied.

Although the actual sealing of the tank was made by an internal rubber seal, it was also given a thin coating of Bostik solution as an internal protection. Because of the confined working space in the wing and the fact that fumes were given off by the Bostik solution, special precautions had to be taken to avoid the toxic effect of these fumes on operators. Special clothing was provided for

Taken in March 1949, this photograph demonstrates the considerable progress that was made in preparing for quantity production of the Comet. A number of airframes were well on the road to completion before the prototype took to the skies for the first time. *(DH Hatfield)*

them, which enabled them to be given a fresh-air supply during the time they were inside the wing. This suit was also provided with inter-communication telephones, and the operator was kept in constant touch with external personnel.

Following the fluid test, the wing was wheeled into several station positions on the track where the various elements were assembled. One of the problems was to produce quickly and cheaply the tooling required for the engine cowlings, which were of a rather complicated shape, and for the access doors under the engine compartments. A plaster model was used tor the manufacture of the tools and the accuracy of this was obtained by using lofted printer plates. The printer plates were made into a three-dimensional structure which was filled with plaster to give the accurate three-dimensional model.

On completion of this three-dimensional model all concrete stretcher press tools were cast direct on to the smooth and accurate surface of the model. The time for pulling this complete cowl skin, which was 20 feet long and four feet wide, was ten minutes. The weight of the tool was approximately three tons.

The surface of the tool was finished by smoothing with a portable abrasive disc, filling in the small porosity caused by air bubbles, after which it was given a priming coat and a final finishing coat of Phenoglaze. This produced a tough and smooth surface and it had been found by experience that this type of tool with this finish was excellent for stretcher press work.The time for production of a tool of this size and weight was approximately seven days.

An interesting problem was the accurate and economic production of the large quantity of Hufford stretcher press tools required for the manufacture of the cross members in the engine cowling. It was decided to try, for the first time, the development of concrete tools for this job, which proved most successful.

The regular method of manufacturing these concrete stretcher press tools was to cast direct on to the same master model which was used for making the longitudinal skin. All the cross member tools were cast transversely on this model at

Above: The engine cowling doors in position on the aircraft. They give good accessibility to the whole of the underside of each engine.

Left: A set of cowling doors, direct from the jigs, await assembly on the aircraft. *(DH Hatfield)*

Production of the leading edge presented one of the more difficult problems because of the extreme accuracy of contour that had to be achieved. This was solved by the manufacture of stretcher press tools in Remak metal, spar-milled to the tolerance and set up on the Erco stretcher press. *(DH Hatfield)*

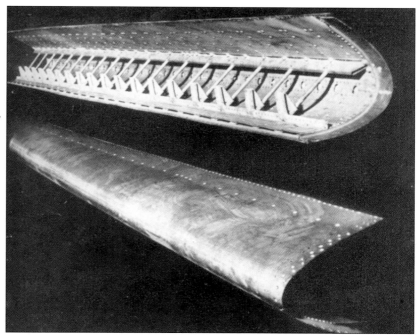

whatever position they were located. This ensured the accuracy of fit: in fact, every cross member which was made from these tools had, to use the proverbial saying, '...fitted like a glove'.

Production of the leading-edge presented one of the difficult problems, particularly as the contour had to be produced to a tolerance of 0.01 inch.

The production of any leading-edge in 12 SWG (Standard Wire Gauge) DTD. 710 - a particular aircraft material specification - with a minimum curvature of 1.5 inch on the tip within these tolerances presented a production problem.

This was solved by the manufacture of stretcher press tools in Remak metal. These were spar milled to the tolerance and by a special set-up on the Erco stretcher press leading edges were successfully and economically produced to the accuracy required.

The extension wing consisted of two skins with Reduxed stringers made in an orthodox jig. Interchangeability between the stub wing and the extension wing joint was achieved in a simple manner. This consisted of jig drilling the extension wing while in the main drilling jig and using these holes for locating a simple router jig which

The rear jet pipe fairing being fitted to the wing stub. Of interest is that this particular wing stub has the fitment for the Sprite rocket motor between the two Ghost engine spaces. *(DH Hatfield)*

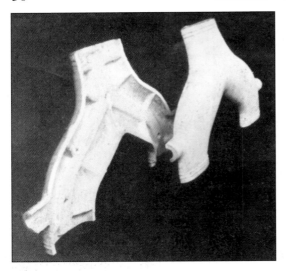

The two sacrificial plaster cores that were used to make a fibreglass component - in this case the junction of the port and starboard ducts of the cabin air-conditioning system. The picture above shows the two split cores - the lower picture the finished component. *(both DH Hatfield)*

produced the interchangeable mating edges of stub wing and extension.

The stub wing arrived at a station where it was wheeled into a position adjacent to the fuselage, and attached to the fuselage by the fish-plate joints of the centre section.

The complete track operations include engine installation, coupling of flying controls, operation of flying controls under power, final inspection, and clearance of snags for flight.

De Havilland made good use of the then-new technique of glass-cloth mouldings including a number of components of difficult shapes. The glass cloth was tailored, and then impregnated with Nuron resin, after which it was built up in

laminations on a plaster core to the correct thickness.

The laminations were held in position on the plaster core by a rubber bag which was exhausted by a vacuum pump, and the whole unit was baked in a muffle at 120 C. After curing, the internal plaster core was finally broken away and the component was complete. Other methods of moulding were also used, and in many instances metal moulds which could be collapsed and withdrawn from the Finished detail and finally reconstructed, thereby avoiding the loss which occured with the plaster core, which was entirely destroyed.

All in all, this shows just how revolutionary the Comet was but also that the manufacture made use of existing, proven techniques.

Above: Some of the fibreglass components used in the Comet. Besides its light weight and dielectric qualities fibreglass cloth was reasonably impervious to moisture absorption. This form of construction enables the most complicated shapes to be manufactured.

Below: a collapsible, permanent metal mould used on the more simple components made of glass cloth. *(both DH Hatfield)*

Hull number 06002 was the second prototype, eventually surfacing as G-5-2 and later G-ALZK. It is seem here in the shops at Hatfield having its Ghosts fitted.

Below: An overall view of the assembly shops at Hatfield photographed in March 1950.
(both DH Hatfield)

Above: number of fuselages on the track. In the background is one Comet receiving attention while outside is another in basic BOAC markings. Below: on the left is hull number 06002 G-5-2 and later G-ALZK. On the right is hull number 06003 G-ALYP for BOAC. *(both DH Hatfield)*

Chapter Four

FIRST FLIGHT!

'The de Havilland Aircraft and Engine Companies feel that the time has come when some preliminary information about their projected jet airliner, the Comet, DH 106, may be released, despite the fact that the aircraft is not likely to be in operation before 1952 and is not yet approaching the flying stage'.

So wrote an unidentified writer - but almost certainly DH's publicist Martin Sharp - in *The De Havilland Gazette* magazine No. 50 of April 1949. This was the first 'public' statement about what had been going on . The writer went on to provide more information:

'The co-operation of the British press in minimising public references to the aircraft during the past year or so has been greatly appreciated by all concerned with its development. There are two reasons why this reticence is necessary. In the first place, because this project presents an opportunity for Britain to catch up the leeway lost in the war years it was, and still is, important that no design details should be released until the aircraft is well advanced; this attitude is accepted in a spirit of friendly rivalry by the American manufacturers, with whom De Havilland have excellent relationships. In the second place, because of the complexity of modern airliners their design and development take a number of years, and if a new aircraft be given publicity in the early stages it is inevitable that, as the time goes on, there must develop a general impression that the type is materialising with considerable difficulty.

If there is no unforeseeable hitch the DH 106 may be expected to fly this year, but from their long experience the Company dislike making forecasts on this subject, and the advanced character of the new design makes even an approximate estimate impracticable.

Sixteen DH 106 aircraft are being built, the first two against contracts for the Ministry of Supply and the remaining 14 for British Overseas Airways Corporation and the late British South American Airways. Production of this quantity has been laid down directly from the design stage, a

'At eight o'clock on the misty morning of Saturday April 2nd 1949, the Comet was pushed out of its hangar for the first time, so that engine runs could be made...' So said the caption that went with this colour picture that appeared in the *DH Gazette* of August 1949. At the time only the port pair of Ghosts had been fitted. The long wooden building in the background is the pilots hut which later housed the library and tech reps offices. *(DH Hatfield)*

policy which will represent a substantial saving of time on the project as a whole.

The DH 106 is intended for express services along the trunk routes of the British Commonwealth. It will also be suitable for inter-continental services generally, for it is essentially an airliner for world operation. Its high speed compared with present-day aircraft besides being an advantage to communications, will materially aid its economy by rendering it possible to fly more miles and carry more ton-miles of payload in the year. But high speed has not been secured at the sacrifice of slow-flying ability; in point of fact, the wing loading will be moderate, less than that of some conventional propeller-driven airliners of the present time, and the stalling speed will be correspondingly modest. Thus, although the DH 106 will cruise at high speed above the weather it

Right: Major Frank B Halford, Chairman and Director of the De Havilland Engine Company - At the time of the Comet's first flight his Ghost jet engine was the most powerful transport engine in the world. *(DH Hatfield)*

This view - not used in any of the publicity material - shows that not only were the pair of starboard Ghosts not fitted, the wingtip on that same side was also not installed as was the tailcone. *(DH Hatfield)*

will be able to descend through cloud steeply at slow forward speed and will circuit, approach and land in the manner of to-day's aircraft. It will not require exceptional runways but will be suitable for operation from normal main airports along the trunk routes. It will, however, require prompt handling by the terminal flight control organisations ; indeed, the development of the technique for landing aircraft in bad weather is

Viewed from above the Comet I displayed strikingly the advances in drag reduction which were embodied in the design, particularly in the neat root installations of the Ghost engines, almost completely buried within a relatively thin wing; De Havillands did all they could to make every effort to reduce drag. *(DH Hatfield)*

rendered doubly urgent by the advent of jet-propelled airliners, which cannot economically be delayed long periods before landing. This aspect of the D.H. 106 is being carefully studied by the authorities and by B.O.A.C., all of whom are fully alive to the need for quickly evolving a safe and dependable system.

Collaboration between the builders and the prospective users of the aircraft, always emphasised in de Havilland experience, has been particularly thorough in the case of the D.H. 106. The great background of practical knowledge gathered by British Overseas Airways in the course of many years has been drawn upon, and the other principal operators of the British Commonwealth also have been brought into consultation with good effect. Relations with the Ministry of Supply, Ministry of Civil Aviation, Royal Aircraft Establishment, Air Registration

Board, etc., have been clear and satisfactory in every way.

The comfort of passengers when flying at great heights has demanded unprecedented attention to the problem of air-conditioning. The aircraft must fly at about 40,000 feet in order to achieve optimum economy. The cabin, including the control room, also the luggage, freight and mail storage, will be pressurised to a differential of 8.25 lb. per square inch, which is nearly double the pressure employed in airliners at present in service. The conditioning equipment includes cooling as well as heating apparatus, also humidifiers to replace the moisture that is absent at such heights. The ventilation air will be changed every three minutes. Air-conditioning is typical of the new services which must require a long time to develop to a degree of all-round satisfaction, and it is one of the unpredictables in regard to the

Above: Out for the first time as a complete aircraft, the Comet is manoeuvred slowly and delicately on the special standing prepared for engine runs.

Left: A company signwriter applies the soon-to-be-famous name.

Below left: De Havilland's urbane public relations manager, Martin Sharp.

Below: Unfortunately in the manner of the times, names were usually recorded with just initials - here are some of the senior technical staff of the Aircraft Company, the men mainly responsible for the Comet. Left to right : Messrs. R. H. T. Harper, F. T. Watts, W. A. Tamblin, R. Hutchinson, A. G. Peters, C. T. Wilkinson, D. R. Newman, R. E. Bishop, S. C. Caliendi, J. E. Walker, R. M. Clarkson, J. M. Wimpenny. H. A. Miles, M. Herrod-Hempsall and A. W. Torry. *(all DH Hatfield)*

The men behind the Ghost. The Engine Company's technical leaders, who turned to jet propulsion - first of the aero-engine manufacturers to do so - in 1941 and achieved the first jet engines to secure military and civil type-approval. Left to right: Messrs. I. Spittle, W. Ker Wilson, K. W. Clarke, A. R. Gay, J. L. P. Brodie, W. H. Arscott, F. B. Halford, E. S. Moult, W. T. Winter, R. Miller and G. Bristow. *(DH Hatfield)*

date of the first flight and the period of trials. Two sections of the fuselage have satisfactorily passed pressure tests in the de Havilland high-altitude chamber at Hatfield, a full description of which was published in the Gazette some time ago, and have been subjected also to underwater tests in a large tank on the airfield, this procedure being adopted to obviate the dangers associated with the possibility of a fuselage bursting. There have been large numbers of individual tests on doors, windows, windscreen, etc. All of this work has been conducted in severe conditions, more stringent than those demanded by the regulations.

The D.H. 106 will carry an operational flight crew of four, and up to 36 passengers. The passengers are to be accommodated in fully-reclining chairs with adequate leg-room, along the lines of the American 'sleeperette,' which it is expected will give all the rest that is necessary for the relatively short times which will be spent aloft, even on main-line stages. There will be two toilet compartments, a large luggage-room and a modern galley. The aircraft may be expected to show a distinct advance in the matter of freedom from vibration by reason of the employment of jet turbines for propulsion.

The new airliner will be a low-wing monoplane and the wing will have a moderate sweep-back. The

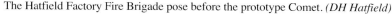

The Hatfield Factory Fire Brigade pose before the prototype Comet. *(DH Hatfield)*

The scene on the Hatfield tarmac during the two days of engine runs and taxying trials.*(DH Hatfield)*

undercarriage is to retract outward, and the nosewheel will be steerable. Because of the large quantity of paraffin fuel to be carried an underwing pressure-refuelling system will be incorporated which will give a high rate of flow for quick servicing. A fuel-jettisoning arrangement will be provided. The main controls will be power-operated and an electronic automatic pilot will be fitted. De-icing will be of the thermal type.

Simplicity is a characteristic of the D.H. 106 which will make a notable appeal as the aircraft takes shape. The absence of propellers eliminates also their control gear and permits an attractively short undercarriage leg. The power units are extremely simple, not only in themselves but in every particular of their auxiliaries and the services which they operate, there being no carburetters, magnetos or engine-cooling arrangements, and consequently no controls for these items in the cockpit.

Apart from the speed and simplicity of the jet-propelled airliner, it represents one of the greatest advances in the matter of reducing the hazards of fire that have been seen so far in the history of aviation. Experience with jet-propelled fighter aircraft during the past few years has amply

demonstrated that paraffin is a much safer fuel than petrol and this fact will come to be generally appreciated when jet airliners are in service on the routes. Taken in conjunction with the reduced opportunity for weather change due to the high cruising speed, also the relatively low wing loading of the D.H. 106, and consequently the moderate stalling speed and 'normal' landing characteristics, we see a step in the direction of increased all-round safety.

The de Havilland Ghost engines, of which there will be four, will each give a static thrust of

Rex King, Experimental Superintendent, responsible for building the first Comet, cheerfully receives the 1090 form, which was the flight clearance. Behind are Mr. A.Brackstone-Brown and Mr. F. T. Reynolds, who shared the duties of flight engineer in the early trials. *(DH Hatfield)*

G-5-1 sits in the sunshine waiting for the final preparations for flight to be made. *(DH Hatfield)*

5,000 pounds, and on this basis the cruising speed is expected to be something approaching 500 m.p.h. The development of the Ghost engine, for civil and for military purposes, has been most vigorously pressed forward during the past two years under the contractual supervision of the Directorate of Engine Research and Development of the Ministry of Supply. Thousands of hours of development running on test beds as well as in flight conditions in Lancastrian and Vampire aircraft have been accumulated during the past years, including considerable experience at speeds and altitudes appropriate to the D.H. 106. In June, 1948, the Ghost was accorded type approval as a passenger-liner power unit by the Air Registration Board. It embodies all the lessons learned in seven years of running experience with the smaller Goblin engine - now famed for its durability and reliability - and is confidently regarded as a satisfactory power unit for airline duty despite the departure which jet propulsion represents. The practical advantages of the single-entry centrifugal-compressor engine from the points of view of de-icing and fire prevention are proving substantial. In regard to performance and consumption and in all respects the development of the Ghost is proceeding satisfactorily.

Everyone knew that 'something was happening at

Above: The very first hop at 9.50am on 27 July. Three more hops were made that day before the first proper flight. Note the square cabin windows and single mainwheel undercarriage.
Below left: De Havilland's always captioned the picture on the left as '6.17pm on July 27. The first take off'. Given that the undercarriage is retracted, it is more likely John Cunningham's flyby at the end of the flight. What is not in doubt is the other picture '6.48pm. The first landing'. *(all DH Hatfield)*

Carrying the Class B marks of G-5-1 and the De Havilland emblem on the vertical fin, , the first Comet is seen airborne. *(DH Hatfield)*

Hatfield', but following the dignified promotion standards set by Martin Sharp, De Havilland's did not say much. The first Comet emerged from its assembly shed on 25 July 1949. Engine runs and 90 minutes spent in taxying and hops occupied the next two days.

The journalists gathered at Hatfield for Sharp's briefing - climbing over the fence would probably be a more accurate description - were aware that John Cunningham had been making short hops along the runway, but there was no mention that the Comet might make its maiden flight. A highly experienced PR man, Sharp knew that, if he said it would happen, there might be technical problems and he was not going to run the risk of delays. So, after the briefing and a certain amount of socialising, the Press Corps headed back towards London.

It was a fine afternoon on Wednesday 27 July, and at about 1630hr on the chief inspector said to John Cunningham: *'All's well. She's all yours'*. John gathered his crew and told them that he had decided to fly, and they went aboard to make preparations.

Meanwhile, word was being passed around the factory works and corridors of the D.H. complex that their Comet was going to get airborne for the first time. All eyes were on the Comet as it began to taxy out from the hangar area, with Cunningham at the controls and John Wilson in the right-hand seat. Cunningham had taken Wilson with him rather than the more experienced Peter Bugge. He felt that if anything disastrous were to happen on that flight, Bugge was better equipped to take over the programme.

That first flight lasted 31 minutes. On board was John Cunningham, John. W. Wilson, First Officer; Mr. F. T. Reynolds, Flight Engineer ; Mr. H. Waters. Flight Engineer, Electrics; and Tony J. Fairbrother, Flight Test Observer. In the course of it John Cunningham climbed to 10,000 feet, tried out the general handling qualities of the aircraft over a range of low and medium speeds, and flew along the runway at 100 feet in salute to several hundred members of the De Havilland technical and experimental departments. Cunningham filed the following Flight Test Report: '

Hop with full flap, and first flight.
Crew: J. Cunningham, pilot; J.W. Wilson, second pilot; F.T. Reynolds, flight engineer; A.J. Fairbrother, aero flight test observer; H. Waters, electrician.

This cheerful group symbolises the unnamed hundreds of workers from the experimental shops. Left to right : Messrs. W. Lewis, A. Lloyd, R. Pledger, H. Wells, J. W. Roake, K. Ward, H, Harris, F. Ready and S. Bolton. *(DH Hatfield)*

Right: Former De Havilland apprentice Ronald Bishop, Director and Chief Designer of the De Havilland Aircraft Company, the executive mainly responsible for the Comet airliner. *(DH Hatfield)*

As the Comet rolls to a stop outside the hangar after the first flight a crowd of enthusiastic workers assemble to applaud the flight crew. *(DH Hatfield)*

A short hop was made with full flap.

The nosewheel was held off the ground until the speed had dropped to 50kt; I had the impression that I could have put the tail bumper on the runway.

Immediately after this hop I taxied back to the grass at the east end of the runway and prepared for take-off.

The aircraft came off the ground in about 500yd, and on reaching about 50ft high I selected u/c up. As the speed was increasing rather quickly I throttled down to about 9,500-9,700 r.p.m. and 135kt. About this moment the windscreen-wiper blade on the starboard side started to rotate: a position was found where it could be parked out of sight for the remainder of the flight.

Above: John Cunningham and John Wilson seen leaving the Comet after the first flight

Left: The flight crew, with John Cunningham holding some documentation, are seen receiving a heartfelt ovation - led by John King, the Superintendant of the Experimental Shop - from those who had been working on the aircraft for two years and who could now see that the Comet which they had created was a basically sound aircraft.
(both DH Hatfield)

An original print of the first Comet in flight - a print that has been signed by test pilot John Cunningham. *(DH Hatfield)*

The ailerons appeared rather light, but very effective. The flap was taken off in two stages, and very little trim change was noted.

A climb was made towards a clear patch of sky at 9,750 r.p.m. and 240kt. Jet pipe temperatures of all engines showed 580°C and rear bearing 100°C. Engine oil temperatures were 63°C.

During the climb at 200kt I found all controls very powerful and highly geared; the spring centring of all controls produced a pronounced jerk throughout the machine on releasing the control after slight displacement.

On reaching 10,000ft I lowered 20° of flap and reduced speed to 100kt and lowered full flap. There was very little change of trim noticeable. Marked strain lines on the outboard side of the inner flap near the scissor mechanism were noted from the rear of the cabin by Fairbrother.

Wheels were next selected down, when it was noticed that no lights were showing, although the mechanical indicators showed 'Locked Down'. While Waters (electrician) was checking the circuit breakers I reduced speed to 80kt, where there was still plenty of control and no buffet.

On replacing the circuit breakers I noticed there was no green light for the port main wheel, although the mechanical indicator showed 'Down'.

Wheels and flaps were selected up and a descent made to 3,500ft with the inboard engines throttled back. At 2,500ft, cruising at 8,700 r.p.m. on all four engines, I was indicating 240kt.

A gradual descent was made back to the airfield, during which it was extremely hard to lose speed. After a low flypast at 150-160kt down the runway, a wide circuit was made, and the final approach to land was completed at 100kt.

Two of the senior aircraft designers: John E Walker, the Chief Engine Installation Designer with W A Tamblin, who was responsible for the design of the DH.106 wing. *(DH Hatfield)*

The landing and touchdown were perfectly straightforward, and very little braking was required owing to a fairly strong wind.

Two points that need attention before long are: replacement of the two curved windscreens in the nose by screens that have much better optical properties; also it is possible that the adjustment of the rudder pedals is insufficient.
DISTRIBUTION: Mr Bishop, Mr Clarkson, Mr Wilkins. Aero Flight Test, File.

Clearly the Press had egg on their faces when they returned their offices only to hear that the Comet had flown. The air correspondent for The Times vowed that he would never write the name De Havilland again - and as far as I can tell, he never did! The company was accused of being arrogant and uncooperative in the extreme, but the irritation of being left out of the big show gradually evaporated, as most journalists realised that Comet coverage would become a continuing story, and they had to be part of it.

The following morning Sir Geoffrey de Havilland rang John Cunningham to congratulate him, saying that John had given him the best birthday present he had ever had. John had had no idea that their birthdays coincided. Sir Geoffrey wrote: *"Some people have asked how it came about that the first flight was made on this day, and I have always had to say that I do not know. I asked John whether it was 'fixed' that way or was mere coincidence. John said that, strange as it may seem, it was pure coincidence'.*

In the next eighteen working days, the Comet was airborne for 32.5 hours. It flew at operational speeds and altitudes and was put through all general handling trials on a medium loading. Handling was thoroughly satisfactory in every respect both in the air and on the ground. The excellent serviceability of the airframe and of the Ghost engines, which had enabled the Comet to make four and five flights daily with little attention beyond refuelling, had been notable. The aircraft was then prepared for performance measurement and the whole programme of development trials.

Left: It was not long before airline representatives beat the path to the door of De Havillands. Hudson Fysh [centre] the founder and President of QANTAS, with his Assistant General Manager, Mr, C O Turner inspected the Comet at Hatfield. Here the two Australians are seen with Mr. P. G. Lucas (left) as their guide at Hatfield.

Below: G-5-1 photographed from a Dove over Hertfordshire in the course of a test flight. The freedom from maintenance snags, large and small, which marked the first weeks of the Comets flying programme impressed De Havilland engineers with the possibility that indirect economies resulting from the simplicity of jet propulsion would reduce operating costs below the level indicated by straight calculation.
(DH Hatfield)

Chapter Five

ROUTE DEVELOPMENT AND TRAINING

Given how the Comet was a quantum leap above every other airliner that flew, it was not surprising that wherever it went, new records were set.

A number of milestones in flight testing were achieved in a remarkably quick period - on 8 August a Mach number above 0.8 was attained in a shallow dive and on 10 November a height of 43,000ft was reached. During the same flight the 375 miles from Edinburgh to Brighton was covered in 42 minutes, averaging about 530 mph, and during a 5 hr 35 min flight at 35,000 - 40,000 ft on 14 November the 590 miles from the Shetland Isles to Hatfield were clocked in 60 minutes. A noteworthy feature of the early trials was the high degree of serviceability attained and the aircraft averaged well over one hour's flying a day during its first 110 days. The ease of engine changing and other servicing, the quick turn-round between flights, and even the simplicity of the cockpit check - which had brought favourable comment from London Airport control tower - was noticeable.

On 25 October 1949 John Cunningham took G-ALVG from London to Castel Benito in Libya and back in under twelve hours. This was the Comet's first flight to an overseas airport. The trip was one of a series of flights to measure the economy of the aircraft and to ascertain the optimum cruising conditions. For the tests to achieve their purpose of providing reliable operational data the conditions of the flight were strictly controlled with pre-set figures for cruising altitude and engine speed and no attempt was made to achieve spectacular times at the sacrifice of accurate data. Up to the end of October these flights were made on a medium loading corresponding to full tanks and partial payload. Gradually the loading was increased and in mid-November it was near to operational weight. In other respects the flights were fairly representative of commercial conditions except in the matter of the pressurising of the fuselage. Up to the Castel Benito flight only about two pounds per square inch of pressure differential had been used - higher pressures would be soon employed.

As a preliminary to the flight to Africa John

G-ALVG was prepared at London Airport in the early hours of 25 October 1949 for its day trip to Libya. *(DH Hatfield)*

Cunningham flew the Comet to London Airport on 22 and 23 October to carry out a series of night landings and Ground Controlled Approaches in mixed weather in order to familiarise himself with the airport and the control procedure. Towards the end of this series of landings the Comet was operating in very poor visibility.

On 24 October the Comet left Hatfield at about 21.30 and touched down at London Airport some ten minutes later. Cunningham and his crew retired to bed leaving the aircraft in the hands of the ground crew for refuelling and a final check.

At 0400 weather reports were examined, navigational and radio briefings checked, and after a hasty cup of coffee and to the accompaniment of flash-bulbs Cunningham and his crew of Peter Bugge, second officer. E. Brackstone Brown, flight engineer, and G. Blackett, navigator and radar-operator, climbed aboard.

Taking off at 06.33 BST in darkness and light rain the Comet climbed on course to its required height of 35,000 ft. Eyebrows were raised at London Airport when 27 minutes after take-off Cunningham sent a routine message reporting passing through tenuous cloud at 31,000 ft. At 09.56 BST the Comet touched down at Castel Benito, Tripoli, having accomplished the flight in 3 hours 23 minutes, representing a block-to-block speed including the climb and landing circuit of 440 mph. After a late breakfast, during

which the Comet was refuelled with Shell Aviation Turbine Fuel, Cunningham left the ground again at 12.04 on the return flight. During the homeward trip an accurate 500-mile stretch, in which light head- and tail-winds alternated, was covered in 61 minutes. As on the outward journey the altitude was 35,000 ft., the cruising speed being allowed to increase as the weight of the fuel lessened. Over northern Europe cloud and strong crosswinds were encountered, but over the Mediterranean the winds were light and the sky almost clear. At London Airport the weather improved during the morning and there was sunshine with occasional showers when Cunningham circled and landed at 15.19. The return flight had been made in 3 hours 15 minutes at an average block speed of 458 mph.

The Ministry of Civil Aviation, who were naturally most interested in studying traffic control problems for jet aircraft, gave the fullest assistance in handling the Comet at London Airport. At Castel Benito the airfield was in the hands of International Aeradio Ltd., and all the facilities at that place worked with smooth efficiency. Underwing pressure refuelling was used at both London Airport and at Castel Benito with fuel and mobile equipment provided by the Shell Company. BOAC, who as potential operators of the Comet were watching the progress of the tests with the keenest interest, gave their full co-operation particularly in matters of

Immediately the Comet came to a halt on the apron at London Airport on return from Tripoli it was examined by Customs, Health and Immigration officials before the crew were allowed to leave. Meanwhile a crowd of airport and airline officials gathered round to study the Comet at close quarters. *(DH Hatfield)*

meteorological and route information, engineering facilities and communications.

More record-breaking flights happened - taking off from Hatfield on 16 March at 09 hours 15 minutes 42 seconds, the Comet crossed the line at Ciampino Airport, Rome, 2 hours 2 minutes 52 seconds later, achieving a speed of 447.246 miles per hour, having been officially timed by observers of the Royal Aero Club and the Aero Club of Italy. At the speed the equivalent time from city centre to city centre was 1 hour 59 minutes 37 seconds, a figure submitted for recognition as a record. The return journey from Ciampino to Hatfield was accomplished in 2 hours 4 minutes 14 seconds, at a speed of 442.326 mph. This represented a equivalent city-to-city time of 2 hours and 57 seconds.

A few days later, on Tuesday, March 21, with a party of air correspondents, the Comet flew from Hatfield to Copenhagen for lunch, returning to Hatfield in time for tea. Two new records were established for the flight between the city centres of the two capitals. On the outward flight the time was 1 hour 18 minutes 36.5 seconds and on the return 1 hour 24 minutes 53 seconds. The measured distance was between Kastrup Airport and London Airport, and the Comet was timed as it flew past the respective control towers. The speed achieved was 453.98 mph on the outward flight and 420.436 mph on the return.

From 24 April to 11 May 1950 the Comet was in Africa for tropical trials. About forty hours were spent in the air and a great deal of valuable information was accumulated regarding 'hot and high' performance.

A strong passenger list representing many of the

The warm greetings at Ciampino Airport, Rome. The Comet carried eleven passengers, including Sir Archibald Russell, GCB, MBE. Permanent Secretary of the Ministry of Supply, and his two colleagues at the Ministry, Air Marshal Sir Alec Coryton, KBE, CB, MVO, DFC. Controller of Supplies (Air), and Mr. Musgrave, Under Secretary (Air), the official entrant for the record, also the editors of *'The Aeroplane,'*, *'Flight'* and *'Aeronautics'*, and several De Havilland executives were carried.
DH Hatfield)

The Esso refueller at Ciampino airport at the completion of the refuelling of the Comet, during which about 1,400 gallons of aviation kerosene were pumped aboard in ten minutes. By now the BOAC 'Speedbird' emblem had been painted large on both sides of the aircraft's nose.
(DH Hatfield)

technical departments of the De Havilland Aircraft and engine Companies accompanied the Comet, and the concentrated programme of performance measurement called for hard and continuous work from all. Excellent serviceability made it possible to complete the job in 17 days. Apart from a delay in Khartoum while a small undercarriage part was flown out by BOAC, the airframe behaved faultlessly. As for the Ghost engines, man-hours of engine maintenance - other than daily inspections - amounted to less than three and oil consumption worked out at between 1,000 and 1,500 miles per gallon for all four engines.

Incidental to the main purpose of the trials, new speed records were established. Outward bound on 24 April the Comet flew the 2,182 miles to Farouk Airport, Cairo, in just under 5 hours 9 minutes, at 426.63 mph. The Cairo-Nairobi flight of 2,195 miles was made next day in 5 hours 15 minutes, at about 420 mph. During the tests from Nairobi's exacting high-altitude airport, 90 miles south of the Equator and 5,370 feet above sea level, the day temperature was equivalent to the International Commission for Air Navigation (ICAN) standard plus 19° C/34°F, which was equal to 34°C/93° F, at sea level. Afterwards the Comet flew to Khartoum for tests in higher temperatures, and on 11 May flew from Cairo to Hatfield in 5 hours 39 minutes. The London-Cairo and Cairo-London flights were, subject to adjustment to the true city-to-city distances and to homologation by the FAI, inter-capital records.

The BOAC Flight Development Unit

There were concerns about operational aspects, understandably so, since the design represented a substantial advance in airliner performance without calling for radical changes in operational procedure. The Comet was an aircraft of moderate wing loading - far less in fact than some of the latest propeller driven airliners of its time. Thus in all ordinary handling respects the Comet was orthodox.

Considering handling in the broader sense, the whole problem of operating the Comet demonstrated itself to be – as it was designed - a practical proposition from the outset. Traffic control in all its many aspects was acknowledged to be in need of development, even for propeller-driven airliners; as such development materialised so the economic and practical superiority of the jet aircraft would show up to better and better advantage.

De Havillands had designed the Comet Series 1 to best suit stage lengths of up to about 1,750 miles, and down to as low as 600 miles. These figures had full regard to the fuel reserves and all other operational features of the aircraft, which had been well demonstrated, in over fifteen hundred hours of test flying accomplished in the two and a half years since July 27, 1949. Useful experience had been gained, not only as a result of the manufacturer's trials, but also by the Comet Unit of BOAC which in the course of a six month period of proving trials during 1951 flew over 92,000 miles on the Empire air routes with the second Comet prototype, G-ALZK.

Sir Basil Smallpeice (with the 'e' before the 'i') had a number of jobs within BOAC, including that

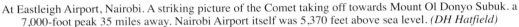

At Eastleigh Airport, Nairobi. A striking picture of the Comet taking off towards Mount Ol Donyo Subuk. a 7,000-foot peak 35 miles away. Nairobi Airport itself was 5,370 feet above sea level. *(DH Hatfield)*

Right: Topping-up at Nairobi. A local crew of the Shell Company at Eastleigh Airport replenish the oil tanks of the Ghost engines after the flight from Cairo. Between them the four engines took only one gallon; at Cairo the tanks were still full and no replenishment was possible. *(DH Hatfield)*

Below: The Comet comes to rest on the apron of Farouk Airport, Cairo, at seven minutes past two, local time (1207 (GMT), by the control tower clock, having flown from Hatfield in just under 5 hours 9 minutes. *(DH Hatfield)*

Back at Hatfield the crew and passengers disembark under the supervision of HM Customs and Immigration officials. The outstanding feature of the tests was the reliability of the Comets Ghost engines, which apart from the routine daily checks required only three man-hours of maintenance work during the 17 days and 160 engine-hours involved in the Africa flight. The engine spares packaged for the flight were returned to Hatfield unopened. *(DH Hatfield)*

The second Comet, G-ALZK, taxies up to its new home in the BOAC maintenance area at London Airport on 2 April 1951. The loan was to enable the Corporation to gain experience in aspects of operating jet aircraft prior to the delivery of Comet to the Corporation later in the year. *(DH Hatfield)*

of Managing Director. He recalls the establishment of their own dedicated Flight Development Unit for the Comet: *'Meanwhile great progress on the de Havilland Comet had been made in our Flight Development Unit led by Captain 'Rowley' Alderson. Captains Majendie and Rodley were the two pilots selected to work with him to develop the operating procedures and techniques for getting the best out of these first generation pure-jet aircraft. This was an entirely new and untried field, and they had no one else's experience to draw on. Never before had there* been *a passenger airliner which would fly at speeds of over 450 mph and at altitudes of up to 40,000 feet. Moreover, the nature of jet engines was such that aircraft consumed fuel at a higher rate, causing real problems if for some unforeseen reason it had to go into the normal holding stack at a much lower altitude while waiting to come in to land. This — and much else besides — required the mastering of new operating techniques. The best methods of using jet aircraft on civil air routes had to be tested and proved, and proved again. It was all done with the quiet competence and thoroughness which I had come to expect and was so typical of BOAC's flight operations management.*

The Comet 1 was due to go into passenger service on the route to South Africa at the beginning of May 1952. The planned schedule of training flights was well on time, and in April we took the press down to Rome for lunch and

Above: The BOAC crew which took over the Comet at London Airport. Captain E. E. Rodley, the second from the left, and Captain A M Majendie on his right. The remaining crew members (left to right) are Navigating Officer C. Evans, Radio Officer R. W, Chandler and Engineering Officer W. I. Bennett.

Right: Among those who flew in the Comet on its delivery flight from Hatfield to London Airport were (left to right) Captain M. R. Alderson, Manager of the BOAC Comet Unit, Air Commodore H. A. Fenton, Operations Manager, BOAC, Sir William Cushion, Supplies Manager, BOAC, Mr. K. Granville, Sales Director BOAC, and Mr. A. C. Campbell-Orde, Deputy Operations Director, BOAC. *(both DH Hatfield)*

back the same day. That may not sound much of an achievement these days. But in 1952 it took the most advanced piston-engined aeroplane some four-and-a-half to five hours, depending on the wind, to cover the 900 miles between London and Rome. But in the Comet, with a following wind, we reached Ciampino Airport near Rome in under two-and-a-half-hours. Distances between places, as measured in time, were on the point of being halved.

Plans were already in hand for the Series 2 Comet with Rolls-Royce Avon engines which would come into operation later. This was a long range aircraft capable of carrying its capacity payload on stages of up to 2,500 miles, and, having the advantages of a greater thrust and a lower specific consumption, its operational aspects would be less critical than those of the Series 1. Moreover, the entry of the Series 2 Comet into service would be facilitated by the widespread commercial experience which the Series I would have obtained, as well as by developments which should have by then taken place in air traffic control.

Whilst from the start of the flight tests De Havillands naturally concentrated on evaluating the performance and handling characteristics of the Comet, it was realised, even in the early design stage, that the high speed of the Comet and the basic characteristics of the jet engine would call for a close study to determine the best operating procedure to enable the aircraft to function smoothly on the established airways, and at the same time to take full advantage of the speed, comfort and economy which it could offer. It was always evident that the many novel characteristics of the Comet would call for a special study of the already acute problems of air traffic control, and, whilst this was primarily a matter for the airline operators and controlling authorities.

Comet G-ALZK landed at London Airport on 2 April prior to being handed over on loan to BOAC. This aircraft was the second of the two Comets ordered by the Ministry of Supply for development purposes. A comprehensive programme of flying had been drawn up in collaboration with the Ministry

of Civil Aviation and the Ministry of Supply.

After preliminary flight trials in the United Kingdom which were largely concerned with a series of performance measurements for the purpose of producing a BOAC Cruising Control Manual, experimental flights were being made between the U.K., Cairo and subsequently Calcutta, with extensions to other routes as experience was gained No passengers were carried on these flights, but up to 28 May, the Comet flew 147 hours.

'LZK differed in several respects from the machines being built for BOAC. The interior layout was not standard and was not fully soundproofed or furnished.

Aspect of operations

Perhaps the most controversial factor in the operation of a jet airliner concerned the inter-relation of stage length, bad-weather landings at congested airports and fuel reserves for stand-off or diversion. This is common-place operating procedure today, but at the time was revolutionary in terms of passenger travel. The jet engine offers its best operating economy at high altitudes and in the case of the Comet the most economical cruising altitude was 30,000 to 40,000 feet. Below the optimum altitude the fuel consumption increased as the aircraft descended - a condition which made it undesirable for a jet aircraft to be held for long periods at low levels whilst waiting to land, and which meant that a decision to divert to an alternative airport should, if possible, be made before the aircraft had descended to a low level. If a diversion was to be made from ground level it always paid to climb as much as possible. In this event the diversion distance was reduced and the overall endurance was greatly affected.

In the case of the Comet these limitations applied only when the aircraft was called upon to operate on maximum stage lengths with the possibility of traffic

The second Comet, G-ALZK takes off from Hatfield during route development with BOAC.
(DH Hatfield)

Every now and then a picture appears that just screams to be reproduced as large as possible - this striking picture - taken in the circuit over London Airport, is of the second Comet, G-ALZK, in BOAC livery. *(DH Hatfield)*

congestion in bad weather at the destination. Furthermore, although the Comet, because of its high speed, was economical on a mileage basis, holding time at any altitude was relatively expensive on fuel and consequently its fuel reserve represents a greater fraction of the total fuel load than was the case with the piston-engined aeroplane. This gives rise to a compensating advantage in that, having provided the necessary reserve of fuel, contingencies, such as an unexpected increase in wind strength have a relatively small percentage effect on the stand-off reserves.

The Comet Series 1 was expected to prove outstandingly economical on stage lengths of up to 1,750 miles on such distances, which represent a fair average of the world's trunk stages, the aircraft would be able to operate with adequate reserves comparable, in terms of time, with those of existing piston-engined aircraft. To what degree the stage length could be extended would depend on the conditions appertaining to the particular route, and could only be decided finally in the light of practical operating experience.

In effect the question of reserves for a jet airliner- as indeed was the ease with any type of aircraft - resolves itself to a matter of adjusting the length of

the longest stage over which the aircraft will carry a paying load, having due regard to the degree of congestion and the weather to be expected at the destination. On routes where these factors were marginal it may well be that the practical stage length would have to be reduced, or the payload adjusted, but the great majority of the air routes of the world were not overcrowded and would not be for years to come.

In considering the problem of airport traffic control, in relation to the jet airliner it was generally agreed that the systems then in use at the busiest airports was in urgent need of revision, not solely because of the new problems set by the jet airliner but for the more economic operation of all types of aircraft. Much of the delay which was occurring in bad weather was caused by aircraft which were inadequately equipped with modern radio landing aids sharing airports with modern liners and it was logical to expect that improvement should be sought by eliminating the older types, of aircraft rather than by penalising the capabilities of the more modern equipment.

While it was reasonable to expect a progressive improvement in traffic-handling methods, experience already obtained by the BOAC Comet Unit had

The absence of propellers made engine ground running safe and easy. The air-intakes of the Ghost engines were sufficiently high above the ground to avoid the risk of anyone being sucked in, but, as the picture shows, the engines themselves are readily accessible from ground level. Here someone does the famous handkerchief being sucked upwards demonstration. *(DH Hatfield)*

shown that the aircraft had a sufficient operational flexibility to allow it to fit into the existing traffic pattern. The ideal approach was a steady let down from operating altitude to circuit level covering a distance of perhaps as much as 200 miles. In conditions of heavy traffic it was preferable for the Comet to be brought in high and have its approach steepened as other aircraft were cleared from below; with airbrakes and a flexible pressurisation system this presented no difficulty, and rates of descent of up to 3,000 feet per minute were quite practicable. Experience shown that the most economical holding technique even at height was to throttle two engines and keep the other two at relatively high RPMs and that in fact whilst there was some gain in holding at altitude, the effect was not very pronounced. If instead of holding level, the aircraft was stacked and descended progressively to lower and lower levels some benefit was gained by the reduction in fuel consumption during descent, and it was found that the mean consumption for say a descent from 10,000 feet to 4,000 feet based on a landing rate of 5 minutes and a 1,000 feet separation was roughly equivalent to level holding at about 18,000 feet.

Under cruising conditions the engines of the Comet 1 used a relatively high percentage of the available power output - this brought into question the performance of the aircraft on three engines. In the case of the Comet Series 1 the effect of shutting down one engine was not so serious as might be expected, particularly after the point of no return when the fuel load was greatly reduced. Even from 40,000 feet the rate of descent to the optimum three-engine cruising altitude was very slow. To state a particular case, on the stage length of 1,750 miles, the shutting down of an engine at the half-way distance followed by a gradual descent to the most economical

The doorway of the erecting shop in which the first Comet was serviced had insufficient head-room to clear the fin. To overcome this the tail was pulled down to a trolley running on inverted rails let into the floor. This procedure required careful handling but became a routine matter, and offered no problem. Airlines were also concerned about this, but what eventually evolved were cut-outs for the vertical fin in the hangar front. *(DH Hatfield)*

Changing the engines of the Comet was simple and straightforward. During the early flight trials a team of twelve men removed the four engines from the airframe, gave them a routine inspection and replaced them ready for flying, within sixteen hours.

The engines were placed on trollies in front of the aircraft (left) then pushed back into position (below)

The detail picture below shows the hatch in the top cowling which opens to admit a slinging tackle by means of which the engine could be lowered directly onto a supporting trolley. *(all DH Hatfield)*

three-engine cruising height, which would occupy the best part of an hour, would reduce by less than 15 minutes the normal stand-off time at 1,000 feet.

This takes no account of the fact that it was normal practice to give landing priority to aircraft approaching with one engine out. The approach and landing of the Comet on three engines presented no problem. Because of the relatively high fuel consumption per hour, the landing weight of the Comet was low compared with its take-off weight and in this condition with flaps and undercarriage up the Comet's rate of climb on three engines exceeded 1,100 feet per minute; thus in the event of a baulked landing the Comet operating on three engines had an ample margin of safety and one which was considerably better than most comparable piston-engined airliners. Furthermore, because of the close grouping of the engines, there was a negligible amount of asymmetrical thrust. The improvement of the wing contour obtained by retracting the wheel doors after the wheels were locked down was an aerodynamic refinement of some importance in the case of a baulked landing.

Meteorological services demanded by a jet aircraft did not differ greatly from those of the more orthodox types. The most important requirements for flight planning were accurate forecasts of conditions relating to surface wind and temperatures for take-off and the en route high-level wind conditions. En route air temperatures were of secondary importance, as were the mean wind and temperature data for the climb and descent, but all these were of help in the making of an accurate flight plan.

The advent of the jet threw into prominence two aspects of forecasting which would require special development to meet future needs. Firstly, the prompt notification of weather deterioration at the point of destination and the corresponding alternative airfields assumed increased importance to enable a diversion, if it became necessary, to be made before the descent was commenced, with the consequent saving in fuel consumption. Secondly, a development of upper wind observation on the trunk routes of the world was an urgent necessity to enable accurate forecasts for heights between 30,000 and 50,000 feet. Until such time as the present deficiencies were made good, the accurate reporting of upper air conditions by the crews of jet aircraft assumed a special importance.

Much had been written about clear air turbulence and in this connection it was interesting to note that during the route trials conducted by BOAC the Comet was fitted with an accelerometer in order that accurate records could be kept. However, during the whole programme of some 470 hours flying no clear air turbulence worth recording was encountered.

Although scarcely heard of before the advent of the Comet, so-called 'jet streams' had been a subject of study for some years. Meteorologists claimed that these currents of air - which vary greatly in width but seldom exceed 5,000 feet in vertical depth - were usually associated with a sloping tropopause and could be fairly accurately forecast up to 24 hours ahead, thus enabling the captain of a jet aircraft to adjust his flight plan to minimise or avoid the effect of an unfavourable jet stream or to make advantage of a favourable one.

Contrary to theoretical predictions, the effect of temperature on cruising economy was found to be much less than generally supposed. For instance, on a 1,500-mile stage length an increase of 15°C. in temperature reduces the range by only 30 nautical miles. This means that if the full stage length had been flown under the +15°C conditions the reserves over destination would have been reduced by 5%.

The jet airliner would have benefitted considerably from increased accuracy in the science of meteorology but this was a reciprocal process because the knowledge gained by actual experience of sub-stratosphere flying would go far to increase the data available to the meteorologist.

The Comet employed thermal de-icing for wings and tail surfaces, and the hot air required was tapped directly from the compressors of the four engines. This system exacted a penalty in increased fuel consumption during the de-icing process, but it had the outstanding advantage of simplicity compared

It was not long before the high and famous visited Hatfield - Marshal of the RAF, Lord Trenchard, father of the Royal Air Force and, since he retired from the appointment of Chief of the Air Staff in 1929, a wise counsellor on aviation affairs in the House of Lords, visited Hatfield with Lady Trenchard on 1 March 1950. They are seen here after a flight in the Comet with Sir Geoffrey de Havilland and Major Frank Halford. Lady Trenchard became the first lady to fly in the Comet, and did so at a height of eight miles.
(DH Hatfield)

with alternative systems using petrol-fired combustion heaters, and the fact that each engine represented an independent source of supply ensures that an adequate supply of warming air was available in any eventuality. The Comet cruised well above the normal icing levels, and experience with the prototype Comet, which was flown continually throughout an English winter without aerofoil de-icing, had shown that its ability to climb and descend rapidly greatly reduced the icing problem and consequently the time during which the de-icing system was in operation, as compared with the normal aircraft. Thermal de-icing was used also for the engine air-intakes and here again experiments showed that ice accretion was very slight and that it could easily be dispersed. Even when ice formed, the Ghost engine, like the Goblin, with its robust single-sided centrifugal impeller, had shown itself capable of consuming large pieces of ice without damage.

Some critics of the jet aircraft were at pains to point out that the absence of propellers deprived the jet of a valuable auxiliary braking medium, and it was suggested that tail parachutes might be required to supplement the aircraft wheel-brakes in the absence of any form of reversed thrust. Indeed, some form of auxiliary braking proved necessary on aircraft with high wing loadings and fast landing speeds, but it was proved quite unnecessary with the Comet. With a maximum permissible landing weight of 80,000 lb. the wing loading of the Comet was under 40 pounds per square inch and the touchdown speed consequently very moderate. The aircraft was heavily flapped and on the ground it could be held tail-down in a position of maximum drag until the speed was reduced to about 60 mph. The wheel-brake operating system was duplicated throughout and each of the four wheels of the bogie undercarriage was equipped with two independent disc-type brakes in conjunction with which there was a device under development for relieving the braking force directly the wheel started to lock and skid. Extensive experience with the Comet prototype shown that it was necessary to use the brakes only lightly on the 2,000-yard runway at Hatfield even in conditions of no wind.

Experience with the Comet at Hatfield and other airports in Europe and Africa had served to dispel certain misgivings regarding the ground handling of large jet aircraft. The Comet could taxi slow or fast and could manoeuvre on the ground in the same manner as propeller-driven aircraft, and it could, if desired, be taxied on two engines. The normal taxying speed was about 30 miles per hour and the thrust required for starting from rest was not excessive. The amount of fuel used to taxi to the take-off point could be allowed for and need not be included in the take-off weight. The use of tractors for towing, which was suggested as an alternative to taxying the aircraft under its own power, did not seem necessary; the process would be slow and inconvenient and would in itself tend to create a traffic problem on busy airports.

Starting the Comet's engines on the apron had in practice caused no inconvenience and it was found possible to park it close to the airport building without intolerable noise or commotion and it was found that 150 feet clearance was sufficient for following aircraft.

The concrete apron and the runway at Hatfield had shown no sign of deterioration from the effects of jet blast. Similarly, tarmacadam runways, which are apt to suffer considerable damage by some of the smaller jet fighters, were not affected by the Comet, due to the horizontal thrust line and the large ground clearance of the jet pipes. Spillage of Kerosene had caused some break-down of the bitumen filling material in the joints between the concrete slabs, but this was no problem because petrol had the same effect.

The air-intakes on the Comet were over seven feet from the ground and it was possible to walk below them in perfect safety (holding your hat) whilst the engines were running. The height of the intakes from the ground coupled with the robustness of the centrifugal impeller made the use of intake guards unnecessary for ground running, although wire-mesh screens were normally used while the aircraft was in the hangar to prevent tools, cats or other objects being left in the intakes.

The use of kerosene materially reduced the fire hazard, thus greatly simplifying the precautions necessary when working on the aircraft. For instance, insurance companies raised no objection to the Comet being refuelled overnight and parked indoors with 6,000 gallons on board.

Within five years of its conception the Comet was almost ready to take its place on the air routes of the world. Combining as it did high speed and conventional flying characteristics, it offered a high degree of economy on the world's trunk routes not to be equalled by the best of to-day's aircraft and with this remarkable advance in speed, comfort, convenience and a capacity for work per pound of capital investment.

Like all basically good aeroplanes, the Comet offered scope for steady development in range, speed and power and De Havilland believed as they did five years earlier that it could meet the requirements of the major airlines for the next 15 years at least. The Comet thus provided a stimulating challenge to traffic control authorities throughout the world to match this progress in their own sphere of activity so that the manifold benefits offered by the Comet's speed, economy and safety could be realised in full measure.

Pressure refuelling

One of the most striking lessons to emerge from the BOAC route proving trials was the need for rapidity in all matters affecting the ground services of the aircraft. Refuelling was perhaps the most important single factor governing the time of turn-round - and as the Comet had a tank capacity over double that of contemporary piston-engined aircraft the problem assumed unusual proportions.

The early Comet Series 1 fuel supply was contained in five tanks: a centre-section tank under the fuselage with a capacity of 2,020 Imperial gallons, two inboard wing tanks each holding 785 Imperial gallons, and two outboard wing tanks each holding 1,220 Imperial gallons. The later Series 1 and the Series 2 machines were to have the fuel capacity increased to 7,000 Imperial gallons.

The system of underwing pressure refuelling adopted in the Comet design was capable of uplifting fuel at the rate of 400 gallons per minute and the Comet could therefore receive its full complement of fuel within 20 minutes, including the time taken to couple up. For emergency use each tank was provided with a filler cap reached from the top of the wings for overwing refuelling.

The pressure refuelling system for the five Comet tanks incorporated two underwing refuelling points. The port refuelling point was connected to the centre-section tank and the port inner and outer wing tanks

Above: The refuelling panel in the port wheel-well of the Comet, containing the control switches and contents gauges for the centre-section tank and the port inner and outer tanks. A similar panel in the starboard wheel-well controlled the inner and outer starboard tanks.

Left: The 3,000-gallon Dorset Refueller, shortly to be put into operation by the Shell Company, undergoes service trials with the Comet at Hatfield. The Dorset proved itself capable of delivering fuel through a single hose at a rate of over 200 gallons per minute. *(DH Hatfield)*

The contents of each tank could be measured by means of a 'drip-stick'. The amount by which the hollow drip-stick had to be withdrawn before fuel flowed from the open end gave a direct reading of the fuel level.

The two under-wing refuelling points were easily reached from ground level. The action of screwing home the Lockheed Avery coupling opened the self-sealing valves situated in the aircraft tank and in the hose.
(both DH Hatfield)

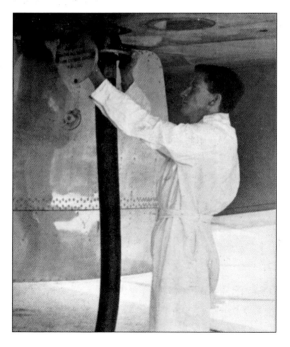

whilst the starboard point supplied the inner and outer tanks on that side. Each refuelling point consisted of a standard SBAC (Society of British Aerospace Companies) Lockheed Avery screw-type coupling, situated just outboard of each wheel well. These couplings were less than six feet from the ground, which was a convenient working height. From the couplings large-diameter pipes branched to the respective tanks, in which were situated electrically operated refuelling valves.

Each tank was equipped with float-operated cut-out switches that automatically closed the refuelling valves when the fuel in the tank reached predetermined level. To safeguard against accidental overfilling under pressure all tanks were fitted with blow-off relief valves.

Two refuelling control panels were situated in the wheel wells and contained three-position switches for each tank, a dial-reading fuel contents gauge and a red warning light for each tank. A refuelling-master switch was fitted in the belly of the aircraft, accessible through a door.

To meet the needs of the BOAC Comet services an entirely new type of refueller, known as the Dorset, was introduced at the main refuelling stations on the routes from London to Johannesburg and Singapore. Built by Thompson Brothers (Bilston), Ltd., to the design of the Shell Company, the Dorset Refueller consisted of a Leyland Hippo chassis carrying a welded steel tank sub-divided into five compartments having a total capacity of 3,000 Imperial gallons.

In the construction of the Dorset special steps were taken to ensure cleanliness of the fuel delivered. The main tank, divided into sub-compartments to conform to the Road Transport Regulations, was lined internally with aluminium. All pipework and components liable to corrosion were internally and externally hot tinned. To reduce contamination by condensation water the tank breathers were led through a vapour gallery fitted with vacuum and pressure valves, and easily accessible water and sediment drains were disposed throughout the tank and piping system. Before delivery to the aircraft the fuel was passed through a filter capable of intercepting particles down to a diameter of 10 microns.

Training

For many years De Havilland policy was that satisfactory maintenance in service ranked equally in importance with sound design and quality of manufacture. Long experience showed that by rigidly adhering to this precept the reputation of the company and its products could be upheld. Thus it was that over the years the De Havilland enterprise had step by step built up its world-wide organisation of DH service engineers supplemented at home by the Servicing School at Hatfield specialising in technical instruction for customers' engineers and pilots. It had long been the custom for every purchaser of De Havilland products to be invited before taking delivery to send suitable personnel to the School for one or more of the many courses covering airframe, engines, propellers, ground handling, etc.

With the advent of the Comet, the indoctrination of engineers in the many aspects of servicing and maintenance took on a new significance, and it was apparent from the start that this, the world's first jet transport and de Havillands' first venture into the larger airliner field, would need more elaborate treatment than had hitherto been necessary for the smaller and more conventional types of aircraft. After much preliminary study of the requirements of the Comet Servicing School and the preparation of a training syllabus the first practical steps towards the setting up of the demonstration hall were taken in March 1950. From the start the closest liaison was maintained with BOAC to ensure that the experience of the operator should be merged with that of the Servicing School to obtain the most satisfactory and practical realisation of the project.

During the succeeding months the design and equipment of the Comet School went ahead with all possible speed. The selection of a suitable site was no easy task. The project called for a building large enough to house a self-contained unit and to permit the full development of the scheme. Such buildings were hard to find within the confines of a plant already growing to cope with large-scale Comet production. Final choice fell upon a hangar which was first used for the erection of the prototype Mosquito in 1940. It was ideal in size and was well suited to its purpose in every way.

The power required to operate the many demonstration rigs was considerable and in consequence the School had its own power house, in which were located a BTH inverter, current rectifiers, dual hydraulic pumps and other associated equipment. A fan room supplied fresh air to the school building through a heat exchanger and a system of distribution trunks and adequate workshops was provided for the maintenance and repair of all the equipment in the school. Outside the main building but adjacent to it was an engine cell in which was mounted a jet engine. The running of this engine could be controlled from inside the school.

The demonstration equipment within the school building was split up into convenient units but each in itself simulated as closely as possible the actual aircraft installation. The aircraft fuel system, located on the east wall, was mounted on a steel structure

The Comet demonstration hall taken from the platform of the hydraulic control rig. The Comet air conditioning and pressurisation demonstration panel, the sectioned Ghost engine, and a flexible bag tank are prominent in the background. *(DH Hatfield)*

Left: The cockpit of the Comet fuselage mock-up from which a jet engine could be operated to demonstrate the starting and ground running procedure. The instruments on the left-hand side of the centre panel were genuine, and record engine performance. The other instruments were dummies.

Below: The remotely controlled gas-turbine engine situated in a test cell adjacent to the Comet demonstration hall. *(both DH Hatfield)*

approximately six feet above the floor to represent the height of the Comet wing above the ground. Three tanks representing the centre-section, inboard and outboard wing tanks of the Comet were mounted in their appropriate positions on the structure. Each tank was fabricated of light alloy and employed a similar sealing system to that used on the aircraft. The top of each tank contained a heavy-gauge Perspex observation panel and the interior of each was lit by fluorescent lighting below the fluid level. Situated beneath the tank platform and accessible from ground level were a Comet refuelling control panel (situated in the wheel well on the actual aircraft) and a standard underwing refuelling valve. As in the case of the actual aircraft, large-diameter pipe lines connected the refuelling valve to the fuel tanks via the standard electrically operated refuelling valves and float-operated cut-off valves. Each tank was fitted with a Waymouth contents fuel gauge installation working on the electric-capacity principle.

Underneath the tank structure was a delivery hose with a standard underwing refuelling connection which mated with the corresponding aircraft valve connected to the tank system. For demonstration purposes fluid was fed through the refuelling hose by an electric pump at the rate of about 200 gallons per minute from an adjacent 1,000-gallon reservoir.

The fluid used for demonstration purposes was a high flash-point distillate of hydrocarbon oil initially developed for the manufacture of printing ink. This liquid possessed many desirable features. Not only was it virtually non-inflammable, but its dielectric value was sufficiently close to that of paraffin to place

it within the calibration range of the fuel gauge installation. In addition, it was non-corrosive and was sufficiently clear even when turbulent to allow the submerged components in the tanks to he clearly seen.

The largest rig in the School was that which was used to demonstrate the functioning of the power-operated flying controls and the alighting gear. This rig consists of a central staging, upon which was mounted a reproduction of the Comet cockpit comprising the flying controls, the central pedestal with associated controls and indicators, an instrument panel and the crew chairs.

Flanking the central platform to left and right respectively were the power-operated flying control system and the alighting gear layout. The former was virtually a compressed edition of half the aircraft system, the aileron elevator and flap units, complete with sections of their individual control surfaces, being banked from front to rear to allow ease of inspection from all angles. The rig was coupled to an auto-pilot and gyro-compass installation. The alighting gear installation, mounted in a substantial girder structure, consisted of a complete main undercarriage leg and wheel assembly and a nose-wheel leg, the former with

its appropriate fairing doors.

This rig was a most valuable adjunct to the School because, apart from its ability to operate both the controls and the undercarriage from the simulated cockpit, typical faults could be artificially introduced and the trainees subsequently afforded the opportunity for their analysis and rectification.

As with the fuel system rig, necessity had forced the acceptance of less space than would be available in the aircraft for pipeline, conduit and cable runs, but every effort was made to retain as close a representation of component location as possible, this being particularly so in respect of the hydraulic equipment beneath the floor of the galley, which in the Comet was accessible during flight.

The Comet pressurisation and air conditioning system was well illustrated by an ingenious bubble diagram loaned by Normalair Limited. This consisted of a transparent panel showing a plan view of the aircraft cabin and a system of glass tubing representing the flow of air. The glass tubes contained a coloured liquid through which were forced bubbles of air. The panel was illuminated from behind and gave a very clear picture of flow of cabin air from the engine compressors through the inter-coolers, mass-flow controls and other equipment to the cabin. Surrounding the centre piece and upon a back panel was a selection of typical air-conditioning components, so mounted as to illustrate their inter-relation with each other.

Other demonstration units consisted of a fully sectioned Ghost engine, a complete Ghost rotating assembly, a specimen of a Comet centre-section bag

Above: The central control pedestal with transparent side panels and interior illumination used to demonstrate the control trimming gear, the flap-operating mechanism and the undercarriage retraction controls. On this rig the instruments on the facia board were represented by photographic prints.

Right: The Comet flying control system was reproduced on this demonstration rig : it was operated from the Captain's station on the right of the picture. The only difference between the layout of the rig and that of the actual aircraft was that the disposition of the control surfaces had been modified and the length of the control runs reduced. *(both DH Hatfield)*

The undercarriage demonstration rig lay to the right of the control station. The complete mechanism of the nose-wheel and main-wheel retracting gear was shown, including the wheel-well doors.

Below: The hydraulics bay, situated under the galley floor in the Comet, and easily accessible during flight, was faithfully reproduced in the School, and formed a working part of the control operation and undercarriage retraction demonstration rig. *(both DH Hatfield)*

tank, and a panel illustrating the fire-extinguisher circuits in the aircraft. Occupying a large section of one wall of the school building was a panel measuring 24 feet by 8 feet on which was mounted a representation of the Comet electrical system. Power for this panel was supplied by a BTH three-phase 8-5 kVA aircraft-type alternator. Built into the rig were a representation set of selenium rectifiers, carbon-pile regulators and D.C. motors driving inverter sets for the 115-volt alternating current supply, together with a main fuse and circuit-breaker panel.

Perhaps the most impressive piece of equipment was the full-scale cockpit, consisting of a wooden mock-up of the forward 25 feet of the Comet fuselage. This portion of the fuselage contained the complete flight deck, the stewards' galley, the forward freight hold and the eight-seater compartment, each

area being equipped and furnished.

Although to outward appearances the interior of the mock-up was complete, many of the components which were not required to work were simulated. Thus, for instance, the blind-flying panel and the engine instruments, except for one genuine set, were photographic reproductions covered with Perspex, whilst the radio equipment comprised wooden mock-ups of the various units with photographic prints attached to their visible surfaces. Other components which had no active part to play were faithfully represented so that the flight deck was accurately reproduced, proving invaluable for the familiarisation of aircrews who could thus readily become accustomed to the precise location and the function of controls and systems used on the ground or in the air.

In the rear of the flight deck was mounted an instructor's control panel from which a range of visible and audible warnings could be set before the student crew, their cancellation being, of course, dependent upon the employment of the correct emergency procedure.

One most important factor in respect of this training aid was that from the flight deck it was possible, by remote control, to start and run the jet engine which, as already mentioned, was installed in an adjoining test cell. Engine performance was recorded upon the normal range of instruments on the flight deck and was duplicated upon a set of larger external dials mounted on the school wall for the benefit of the remainder of the class.

Chapter Six

THE COMET 1

In a typical arrangement, the Comet 1 offered accommodation in two cabins for 44 passengers. An eight-seat compartment was located forward of the front-spar structural bulkhead. This compartment was equipped with facing pairs of fixed chairs and tables. The main cabin aft of the bulkhead would seat 36 passengers in nine rows of four at 39 inch pitch. An alternative arrangement for a lower passenger density could be provided to accommodate seven rows of four seats at 45 inch pitch, giving a total seating capacity of 36.

In the forward compartment two windows were fitted. In the main cabin one window was fitted adjacent to each pair of chairs when installed at 45 inch pitch. The two windows in the forward cabin, also two in the main cabin, were emergency exits in conformity with ARB requirements.

In both versions, the central gangway was 17.5 inches wide between arm rests with 77.5 inches of headroom.

Seating in the forward compartment was in non-adjustable double chairs with folding arm rests. In both versions the adjustable single chairs in the main cabin were of the BOAC 'Overseas' type, two feet wide over arm rests. They incorporated ashtrays, life-belt stowages, pockets for detachable tables, and a

The proposed passenger accommodation for the 44-seat Comet 1. (*DH Hatfield*)

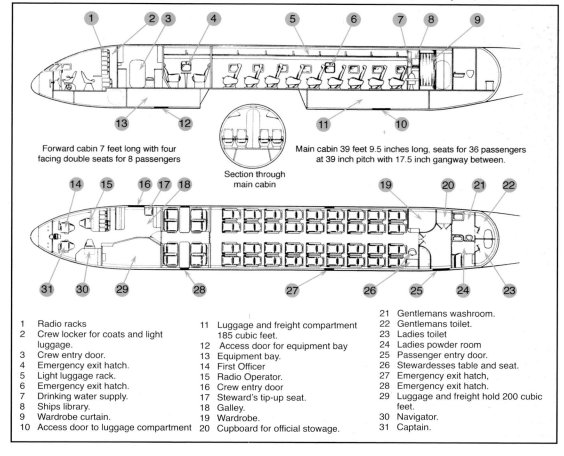

Forward cabin 7 feet long with four facing double seats for 8 passengers

Section through main cabin

Main cabin 39 feet 9.5 inches long, seats for 36 passengers at 39 inch pitch with 17.5 inch gangway between.

1 Radio racks
2 Crew locker for coats and light luggage.
3 Crew entry door.
4 Emergency exit hatch.
5 Light luggage rack.
6 Emergency exit hatch.
7 Drinking water supply.
8 Ships library.
9 Wardrobe curtain.
10 Access door to luggage compartment
11 Luggage and freight compartment 185 cubic feet.
12 Access door for equipment bay
13 Equipment bay.
14 First Officer
15 Radio Operator.
16 Crew entry door
17 Steward's tip-up seat.
18 Galley.
19 Wardrobe.
20 Cupboard for official stowage.
21 Gentlemans washroom.
22 Gentlemans toilet.
23 Ladies toilet
24 Ladies powder room
25 Passenger entry door.
26 Stewardesses table and seat.
27 Emergency exit hatch,
28 Emergency exit hatch.
29 Luggage and freight hold 200 cubic feet.
30 Navigator.
31 Captain.

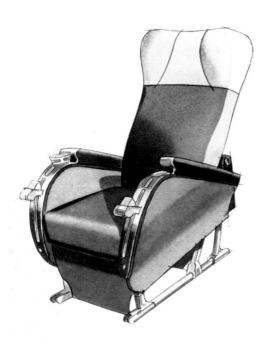

'A polite swish . . . and no vibration.

A flight in a Comet Jetliner is a memorable, oddly soothing sensation.

It takes but a minute to start the four jet engines, buried in the depth of the wings, before this low-wing monoplane taxis to the runway.

No protracted warm-up is necessary.

Easily, without apparent effort or the fury of flaying propellers, the Comet slides smartly into the air. Climbing 35-40,000 feet, she levels off on a rock-steady flight above the highest clouds in a dazzling, almost indigo sky.

The Comet is remarkably quiet and free from vibration. Little outside noise is perceptible. Lack of vibration, and the absence of any sign of an engine, propeller or other moving part, completes the illusion of being fixed rather than moving in space.

There is no sensation of distance dropping behind at eight miles a minute.

You are, in effect, sitting in a pleasant room above a painted scene..

THE COMET 1

'Speaking of comfort . . .

No smallest detail of passenger comfort has been left to chance in the Comet Jetliner

In addition to main ceiling lights above the central gangway, there is an individual reading light and steward's call button for each passenger. Gangway lights at floor level are provided in the main cabin.

Overhead hatracks are provided in each cabin, and a wardrobe for passengers' coats is located in the vestibule by the main entry door. Ample storage space for light luggage is provided adjacent to the wardrobe'.

So were the words in a 1952 brochure *'BOAC Introduces The Comet jetliner',* an elegant landscape document, profusely illustrated with colour pictures.

With echoes from the great days of the steamships, the Comet carried what was known as 'The Ships Library' for the entertainment of the travelling public. Adjacent to the Library was a filtered water drinking dispenser. *(DH Hatfield)*

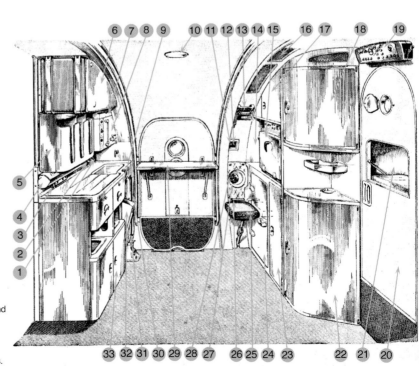

GALLEY AREA COMET 1

1. Fresh water tap
2. Fresh water tank filler.
3. Hot cup switch box.
4. Cup rack.
5. Crockery crate.
6. Fresh water tank.
7. Urn filler tap.
8. 2 gallon urn.
9. Cutlery stowage drawers.
10. Roof lamp
11. Stand-by light switch
12. Ice formation spotlamp switch.
13. Telephone and switchboard.
14. Hot cup stowage.
15. Oven.
16. Ventilation grilles
17. Pantry cupboard
18. Glass stowage cupboard.
18. Galley panel.
20. Door to passenger cabin.
21. Serving hatch.
22. Bar cupboard.
23. Dry provisions cupboard
24. Refrigerator.
25. Steward's folding seat.
26. Safety belt stowage
27. Ice detection window.
28. Ice formation spotlamp.
29. Folding table.
30. Hydraulic emergency hand pump.
31. Oxygen charging access panel.
32. Waste bin.
33. Food stowage cupboards.

Immediately forward of the eight-seater compartment was the galley along with a serving hatch into the passenger cabins. The colour artwork is the original design interior for the galley from a BOAC brochure. *(DH Hatfield)*

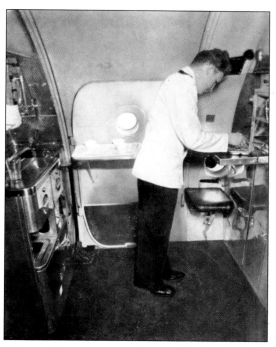

fully-reclining movement. Stowage for the tables was provided in the chair backs.

Hat racks were fitted in each cabin with a minimum head clearance of five feet above the floor. A wardrobe for passengers' coats was provided in the entrance vestibule in both versions. In the 36-seater version stowage for passengers' light luggage up to 120 cubic feet was provided adjacent to the wardrobe.

In addition to the main lights in the ceiling above the gangway, individual reading lights were provided under passengers' control, together with steward's call buttons. Gangway lights at floor level were provided in the main cabin.

Smoking was permitted during flight throughout the passenger and crew's quarters.

The main passengers' entrance door was located on the port side of the fuselage at the aft end of the cabin. The door was 4' 8" high and 2' 6" wide and provided access to the light freight and luggage stowage. The forward entry door located on the starboard side of the fuselage was 4' 8" x 2' 6" wide. This crew entry door provided access to the forward freight hold and galley. All doors and hatches in the pressurised section of the fuselage opened inwards.

Separate toilet compartments for ladies and gentlemen were located at the rear end of the pressurised section of the fuselage, In addition there was a gentlemen's washroom fitted with a wash basin supplied with hot water from an immersion heater,

Left: The Main Cabin of the Comet 1, looking towards the rear.

Below: The rear of the Main Cabin, showing the drinking water supply, the Ship's Library and the passenger entry vestibule.
(both DH Hatfield)

electric razor power sockets and a mirror. A separate ladies' room was equipped with a dressing table and seat, wash basin supplied with hot water from an immersion heater, mirror, and waste bin.

The galley, occupying a floor area of 32.5 sq.ft. and of 185 cu.ft. in volume, was located forward of the eight-seat cabin on the starboard side between transverse bulkheads fore and aft of the crew entry door.

On the forward bulkhead was a cupboard fitted with racks for food trays, drawers for cutlery, a waste bin and waste water tanks, and a working table top incorporating a sink. Above this was located a ten-gallon drinking water tank feeding a two-gallon two-kilowatt urn, and crockery racks.

On the rear bulkhead was a cold box of three cubic feet capacity, a dry-provisions cupboard and a removable box under a working top, which was used for dispensing drinks. An AEG oven was also fitted on this bulkhead. Above these were located a storage cupboard and a removable glass container. A further storage cupboard for cleaning materials was housed above the freight hold.

This was in the days before meal serving carts, each passenger receiving their meals 'by hand' by a stewardess who had the meal passed to her via a hatch in the cabin door.

Seats were provided for two stewards. One tip-up seat was located forward in the galley; the second seat was at the rear end of the main cabin in the 36-seater, and in the vestibule in the 44-seater.

A total of 585 cu.ft. in two compartments was available for mail, freight and luggage in the 44-seater. Access during flight was provided for both

these compartments. Stowage for ship's papers, diplomatic mail, etc, was provided in the forward freight hold. The forward hold, located on the port side of the fuselage immediately forward of the passenger cabin, had a capacity of 200 cu.ft. Direct access for loading was through the front entry door.

The centre hold, located under the floor aft of the centre section, had a capacity of 185 cu.ft. Loading was through an external door 31 inches long by 26 inches wide, in the centre of the compartment on the underside of the fuselage.

In the 36-seater only a rear hold of 120 cubic feet capacity for light freight was located above the floor in the vestibule, with access via the passenger entry door.

The floors of the cabin, the rear belly freight hold and the rear light freight hold of the 36-seater version were designed for an average loading of 37.5 lb./sq.ft. although within these overall limits local loading up to 70 pounds per square inch, was permissible.

Crew Positions

The control cabin was conditioned and pressurised to the same degree of comfort as the main passenger cabins, and there was a warm air-pipe at the feet of each pilot. Oxygen was available to the crew in the event of an emergency and intercommunication equipment was provided.

Stowage for the crew's hats, coats, brief cases, etc, was provided in a small wardrobe between the flight deck and the galley.

Careful consideration had been given to the grouping of the cockpit controls and instruments. A complete mock-up of the cockpit was constructed, and the opinions of experienced pilots sought on every detail before the final arrangement was adopted.

The arrangement of the crew station was to some extent flexible. Whilst it was easily possible for the second-pilot to handle the engineer's panel situated on the starboard side, a separate flight engineer could, if desired, be accommodated in a fifth seat just behind the pilots' stations. Alternatively, in the case of airlines which had already gone over to the exclusive use of radio-telephony, a flight engineer could occupy the radio operator's seat which was adjacent to the engineer's panel.

The Captain and the First Officer were situated in the positions usual for a first and second pilot in the forward port and starboard sides of the control cabin. Their seats were adjustable for tilt and height, and they were able to slide fore and aft for a distance of 16". They were also able to swivel through 60° outboard and 30° inboard. Each pilot had a direct-vision panel which could be opened during take-off or on the approach.

The pilots were provided with full dual control and a flight instrument panel each. Provision was made for the mounting of a Sperry Zero Reader on each flight panel. The engine instrument panel and

The cockpit of a Comet 1 - visible is the stowed curtain used to separate the two pilots from the navigator and radio operator in order to preserve their night vision when flying during the hours of darkness. *(DH Hatfield)*

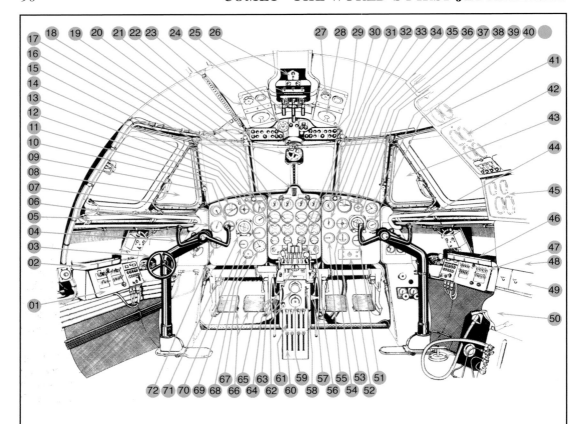

COMET 1 COCKPIT KEY

01 Captain's switch panel for interphone.
02 Captain's shelf.
03 Captain's ground steering wheel.
04 Captain's control column.
05 Hot air spray pipe for demisting.
06 Altimeter.
07 Airspeed indicator.
08 Direct vision panel.
09 Windscreen wiper control.
10 Zero reader.
11 Gyro horizon.
12 ILS indicator and warning lamp
13 Gyro Compass
14 Machmeter.
15 Hydraulic system warning lights.
16 Oil pressures and temperatures.
17 Jet pipe temperatures.
18 RPM indicators.
19 Undercarriage mechanical indicator
20 Magnetic compass and mirror
21 Fire warning light panel
22 ADF Receiver controller.
23 VHF Panel.
24 Undercarriage warning lights.
25 Power control boosters changeover levers.
26 Switch for secondary power booster pumps.
27 VHF Panel box.
28 ADF Receiver controller.
29 Fire warning light panel.
30 Throttles.
31 Flap selector lever
32 Airspeed indicator.
33 Hydraulic system warning lights.
34 Altimeter.
35 Gyro horizon.
36 Electrical supply warning lights.
37 ILS indicator and warning lamp
38 Gyro compass.
39 Clock.
40 ADF Indicator
41 Electrical supply control panel.
42 Fuel supply and control panel
43 Direct vision panel
44 Hot air spray pipe for demisting.
45 Cabin air condition indicators and temperature controller
46 First Officer's shelf.
47 First Officer's switch panel for interphone.
48 Cabin pressure controller.
49 Safety valve, refrigerator and mass flow controls.
50 Undercarriage emergency lever.
51 Cabin differential pressure guage.
52 Gyro-compass control panel.
53 Turn-and-Slip indicator.
54 Zero reader
55 Outside air temperature guage
56 Rear bearing temperature guages.
57 First Officer's Elevator trim wheel.
58 Flap indicator and emergency lever.
59 Aileron trim wheel.
60 Low pressure fuel cocks.
61 High pressure fuel cocks.
62 Undercarriage selector lever
63 Rudder trim wheel.
64 Automatic pilot control box.
65 Captain's Elevator trim wheel
66 Captain's rudder pedals.
67 Clock.
68 Zero reader control panel.
69 Accelerometer.
70 Rate-of-climb indicator.
71 Gyro compass
72 Turn-and-Slip indicator.

control pedestal were common to both. Adequate lighting and placarding of all instruments and controls was provided for all conditions of flight,

On the captain's control column was mounted a small steering wheel for use during taxying. The wheel brakes were operated by the depression of the rudder toe-pedals, and by a parking brake on the control pedestal.

Duplicated 70-channel V.H.F. selector boxes were provided for the pilots in the roof of the cockpit. A panel containing all the aircraft and engine emergency warning lights was prominently positioned just above the windscreen, and the emergency flying control boosters change-over levers were centrally positioned in the cockpit roof, readily accessible to either pilot. Both electrical and mechanical undercarriage lock position indicators were provided. Each type of indicator was entirely independent so that, should one fail, there could be no doubt whether or not the undercarriage had correctly locked.

The controls for the automatic pilot were on the control pedestal between the two pilots. This autopilot was the well-proven Smiths SEP1, standard equipment on most British airliners.

In addition to a gyro-compass on each flight panel, a magnetic compass viewed through a mirror was placed just above the windscreen for the use of either pilot. A small shelf for personal articles was provided for each pilot.

The controls and instruments for the ancillary aircraft systems and services were grouped together, on a panel on the starboard side of the flight deck.

Once the pressurisation and air conditioning controls were pre-set before flight, the cabin pressure, its 'rate of climb', its temperature, and the mass flow of conditioned air through it were taken care of automatically. On this panel also were grouped the controls and instrumentation for the de-icing system, and the electrical and fuel supply systems.

The navigator was seated on the port side of the flight deck behind the captain, and although he normally faced outboard his seat was able to swivel through 360° and to slide inboard towards the centre of the flight deck. This officer controlled No. 2 Marconi AD 7092A ADF equipment, (which could also be controller by the pilots) and the CL2 gyro compass. In the roof of the cockpit above this station was a mounting for the Hughes periscopic sextant. A stowage for loose equipment was provided at this station.

The Radio Operator's station was located aft of the first officer's station on the starboard side of the flight deck. The radio operator was normally seated

facing aft, though his seat was able to swivel through 360°. This officer controlled the Marconi AD. 107 HF transmission equipment, the AD.94 MF/HF reception equipment and No.1 AD.7092A ADF equipment. The pilots were also able to control this latter set. All this equipment and the ILS was mounted in standard SBAC racking at this station.

Aircraft Systems

The Hydraulic System - four separate power-supply systems were fitted as follows:

1   A main system with two engine-driven pumps supplied undercarriage, flaps, nose undercarriage, steering, air brakes,wheel brakes and secondary flying controls.
2   A booster system with two engine-driven pumps supplied the main flying-control boosters only.
3   A standby system with one pump driven by electric motor supplied the reserve wheel-brakes and emergency operation of undercarriage and flaps. Twin hand-pumps, also part of this system, were fitted to provide a second emergency method of lowering undercarriage only.
4   A booster emergency system with one pump driven by electric motor supplied the secondary flying-control boosters only. This was a completely independent system, complete with header tank.

Failure of any engine did not effect the main or the booster systems and change-over from primary to secondary boosters would be by manual control from the cockpit. Two special accumulators were arranged to feed the boosters through separate pressure lines during the period of change-over. A separate accumulator charged by the standby system pump supplied pressure to wheel-brakes for parking. All pipe-lines were clearly labelled green, blue, red or yellow, according to the part of the system they served.

The main components of the hydraulic system - e.g. fluid reservoirs, accumulators, cut outs, ground test valve etc. - were conveniently grouped together in the forward equipment bay. Hydraulic system functioning tests could be carried out on the ground by the use of the aircraft's 'red' system, operated by an aircraft electric pump, or by the use of an independent ground test-rig.

Controls. Flaps and Brakes - the flying controls were power-operated by completely duplicated hydraulic boosters with a duplicated source of power through two entirely separate systems as described above. A

Smith's SEP1 automatic pilot was fitted.

Split flaps were fitted over the inboard section of the wing and plain flaps outboard. Flap control was by means of a pre-selective lever on the control pedestal.

Air brakes were fitted to facilitate deceleration, to provide a high rate of descent without forward speed in emergency, and to provide a means of altitude regulation during the stand-off phase of the flight.

Undercarriage - the tricycle undercarriage was fitted with twin nose wheels and had a four-wheeled bogie unit on each main leg. There were two separate hydraulic power systems for retracting and lowering the undercarriage, backed up further by a hand pump for emergency lowering only, as described above. The steerable nose wheel was controlled by the Captain through a wheel on his control column. The wheel brakes were twin disc, hydraulically operated with a completely duplicated operating system.

Provision was made for towing the aircraft on the ground, and to prevent inadvertent retraction of the undercarriage on the ground.

The Fuel System - all fuel was carried in the wing. Bag tanks were fitted in the centre-section and the out-board tanks were integral.

The fuel system was designed for pressure refuelling at a rate of 150 gallons per minute and for normal over-wing refuelling. With this system the aircraft could be completely re-fuelled in about 25 minutes. To safeguard the tanks against excessive pressure when they were full an automatic fuel cut-off valve was provided and, as an added safety measure, refuelling blow-off valves were fitted. Waymouth capacity type fuel-contents gauges were employed; in addition, drip-sticks were fitted in the underside of the tanks for a visual capacity check on the ground. Fuel mass flow indicators also were carried.

Normal over-wing refueling was also possible. A control panel was positioned in each wheel-well for controlling the operation of the refuelling valves. Fuel off-loading was also controlled from this panel.

Normal fuel feed was by immersed booster-pump pressure. Two pumps were fitted in each tank. Provision was made for suction feed from each tank in, case of booster-pump failure. Each pump could be removed from the under surface of the wing without draining. Access to the centre-section bag tanks and all integral tanks was provided through removable manholes in the wing under-surface.

Fuel could be jettisoned from the centre-section tank and the two inboard tanks on either side; this was done by blowing the fuel out by ram-air pressure from the leading-edge intake.

The Cabin Air System - the cabin pressurisation system was designed for a maximum working differential pressure of 8.25 pounds per square inch, to give a maximum cabin altitude of 8,000 ft. when the aircraft was flying at 40,000 ft.

The method of pressure control was designed to provide for the selection of any desired altitude up to 8,000 ft. and any desired rate of change of cabin altitude up to the equivalent of 1,000 ft./min. at sea level, provided that the permissible range of differential pressure was not exceeded.

The cabin pressure-control equipment was designed to limit the maximum differential pressure to 8.25 pounds per square inch and was fully duplicated, each section being capable of functioning independently. In addition, a safety valve was fitted, which was designed to limit the differential pressure to 8.5 pounds per square inch. Two inward relief valves limit the negative differential pressure to 0.5 pounds per square inch.

Fresh air for the cabin was tapped from the compressors of each of the four main engines, and

The Flight Engineers station, showing the operational controls and equipment. *(DH Hatfield)*

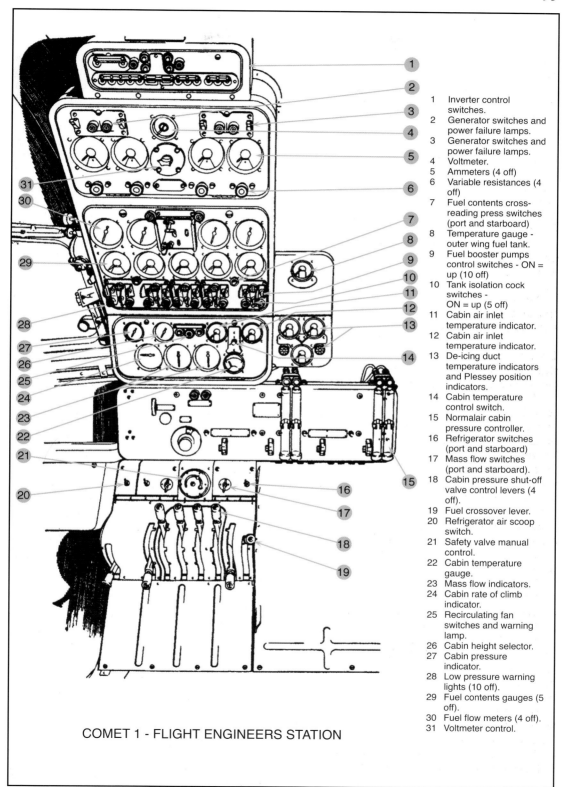

1 Inverter control switches.
2 Generator switches and power failure lamps.
3 Generator switches and power failure lamps.
4 Voltmeter.
5 Ammeters (4 off)
6 Variable resistances (4 off)
7 Fuel contents cross-reading press switches (port and starboard)
8 Temperature gauge - outer wing fuel tank.
9 Fuel booster pumps control switches - ON = up (10 off)
10 Tank isolation cock switches - ON = up (5 off)
11 Cabin air inlet temperature indicator.
12 Cabin air inlet temperature indicator.
13 De-icing duct temperature indicators and Plessey position indicators.
14 Cabin temperature control switch.
15 Normalair cabin pressure controller.
16 Refrigerator switches (port and starboard)
17 Mass flow switches (port and starboard).
18 Cabin pressure shut-off valve control levers (4 off).
19 Fuel crossover lever.
20 Refrigerator air scoop switch.
21 Safety valve manual control.
22 Cabin temperature gauge.
23 Mass flow indicators.
24 Cabin rate of climb indicator.
25 Recirculating fan switches and warning lamp.
26 Cabin height selector.
27 Cabin pressure indicator.
28 Low pressure warning lights (10 off).
29 Fuel contents gauges (5 off).
30 Fuel flow meters (4 off).
31 Voltmeter control.

COMET 1 - FLIGHT ENGINEERS STATION

was passed through coolers and, when necessary, through a refrigerator before entering the fuselage. The supply system in each wing, with the exception of the refrigerator, was independent of that in the other wing and either wing independently could supply adequate air for pressurisation. Temperature control on the coolers was automatic with manual override, but the refrigerator was switched in and out manually as required. Heat necessary for warming the cabin was supplied by the compression of the air in the main engines.

Humidifiers were provided to increase the humidity of the air in the cabin when necessary. In addition to the fresh-air supply, a fan sucked air from the cabin for recirculation at the rate of approximately 1,200 cubic feet per minute and this air was mixed with the fresh air before distribution round the cabin.

The air-conditioning system was not designed for use on the ground and provision was made for the connection of a conditioned air supply from an external source.

As much of the equipment as possible associated with this system had been grouped in the forward equipment bay e.g. the humidifiers, the re-circulating fan, the front discharge valve and the safety valve. The pressure controller in the control cabin could be switched to 'ground test' for ground functioning of the system, which could be carried out from a special attachment at the rear pressure dome.

The De-icing System - thermal de-icing for engine air-intake, wing leading edge, tail-plane and fin leading edges was fitted. Hot air for this purpose could be bled direct from the engine compressors whenever it was required.

Windscreen de-icing was by external fluid spray. There was a dry-air sandwich for insulation, and a hot-air spray internally for de-misting. A lamp was fitted to illuminate the starboard leading-edge and air-intake for ice detection at night.

Radio Aerials - were suppressed into the structure. The main fin was insulated from the stub and used as the High Frequency (HF) aerial; Very High Frequency (VHF) and Instrument Landing System (ILS) aerials were housed in dielectric tips on fin and tail-plane, and the grid aerial was mounted in the nose-wheel doors behind a dielectric flush panel. Automatic Direction Finding (ADF) loop aerials were installed in the top fuselage behind flush dielectric windows, and ADF sense aerials in the underside of the fuselage. The ILS glide path was behind the windscreen and the remaining ILS marker and Distance Measuring Equipment (DME) behind flush dielectric panels in the underside wing-root fillet.

The Radio Operator's station showing the operational controls and equipment. *(DH Hatfield)*

The Electrical System - was operated at 28 volts D.C. Power was provided by four engine-driven 8.5 KVA alternators and the three-phase out-put of each was rectified by a Selenium- type blast-cooled rectifier. The output was parallelled after rectification. Total output per alternator/rectifier was 250 amps. less a varying amperage up to 50 amps. for excitation of the alternator. Field regulation was by carbon pile regulator and was maintained at 28 volts. Pre-flight power with engines running could be obtained up to 150 amps. per alternator/rectifier. Pre-flight power without engines running was obtained from ground equipment.

Alternating current at 115 volts 400 cycles 3-phase and 26 volts 400 cycles single-phase for auxiliary power was provided by D.C. motor-driven inverter sets.

The rectifiers were mounted in pairs in the wing leading-edge between the engine air-intakes, while cooling air was drawn from a leading-edge air-intake. The voltage regulators were also mounted adjacent to the rectifiers. Batteries were mounted immediately inside the access door convenient for servicing and removal. The main fuse and circuit-breaker panel was located in the bulkhead behind the navigator's station

COMET 1 - RADIO OPERATOR'S STATION

1   Top Support Mounting.
2   Localiser and Marker SR.14.
3   Glide Path and Receiver SR.15.
4   Support member.
5   Intercooler Power Unit.
6   Power Supply Units.
7   ADF Receiver Units.
8   Spares Box.
9   Regulator Units.
10 HF Amplifier Units
11 HF Drive Units.
12 Bearing Indicator and Loop Controller.
13 Master Receiver Controller.
14 Communication Receiver Units.
15 Morse Key.
16 Radio Operator's Table
17 Jack Box.
18 Bottom Support Mounting.
19 Oxygen Regulator.
20 Jack Box.
21 Side Table.
22 Intercom Station Box.
23 Bottom Support Mounting.
24 Radio Switch Panel.
25 Top Support Bracket.
26 Radio Crate.

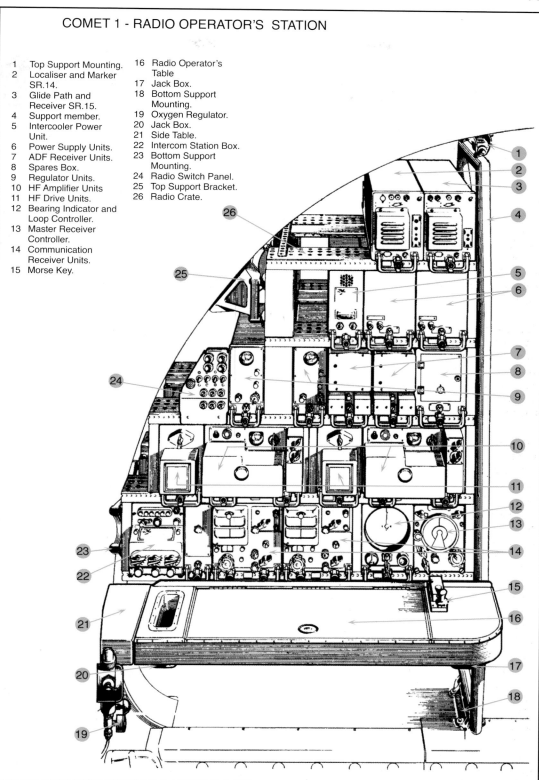

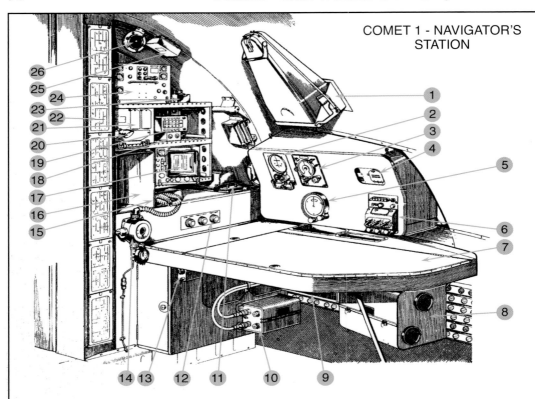

COMET 1 - NAVIGATOR'S STATION

1	Periscopic Sextant Stowage.	10	Condenser Unit.
2	Bearing Indicator and Locp Controller.	11	Stroboscope Tuning Fork
3	Master Receiver Controller.	12	Dimmer Switches.
4	Gyrosyn Compass Amplifier.	13	Intercomm Jack Box.
5	Gyrosyn Compass Master Indicator.	14	Oxygen Regulator.
6	Intercomm Station Box.	15	Oxygen Mask Stowage.
7	Navigator's Table.	16	Manual Rack.
8	Autopilot Amplifier Unit.	17	Rebecca Indicator Unit.
9	Autopilot Junction Box.	18	Rebecca Generator Power Switches.
		19	Rebecca Control Unit.

20	Flood Lamp.
21	Zero Reader.
22	Junction Box Circuit Breaker Panels.
23	Stroboscope Induction Coil.
24	Rebecca Transmitter/Receiver.
25	Flasher Unit for Navigation Lights.
26	Booster Pressure Warning Horn.

Right: the Navigator's station showing the operational controls and equipment used by BOAC. The equipment differed somewhat in Canadian Pacific Comet IAs (below) with the No. 2 A.D.F. controller and indicator and the two

bearing indicators of the C.L.2 gyro-magnetic compass. A Loran set was mounted on the bulkhead, and there was an air position indicator beneath the instrument panel on the chart table. *(both DH Hatfield)*

in the control cabin; thus all fuses and circuit-breakers were readily accessible to the crew for replacement and resetting.

Engines - the engines were housed in the wing root between the main spars. The mountings were specially designed for rapid engine changing and include quickly detachable air-intake and tail-pipe connections, and special disconnect joints in engine-control connecting-rods.

The complete under surface of the wing in the area of the engines was in the form of hinged panels which when opened up completely exposed the whole installation, Further access panels were provided in the top surface for servicing accessories and engine slinging.

The installation was split into three temperature zones, each zone being separated by steel fireproof bulkheads and having its own ventilation and fire-extinguishing system.

A mechanical 'wipe-off' lever was fitted to the underside of the engine cowling, this being the lowest part of the aircraft which would, when operated, cut off fuel supply at all four engines, operate fire-extinguishing systems and cut off electric power in the event of a wheels-up landing.

The maintenance scheme for the engines was based upon inspections in three categories;- (a) between-flight inspections (b) daily inspections (c) minor inspections.

By 1952, experience with the Comet had shown that between-flight inspections, which were purely visual checks, took one man about ten minutes per engine. Thus the Comet engines could be inspected by four men well within the minimum time likely to be spent at a refuelling halt.

The daily inspection took one man about twenty minutes per engine, plus a further five minutes for a ground run from cold. There was no waiting for cylinder-head and oil temperatures to rise to a

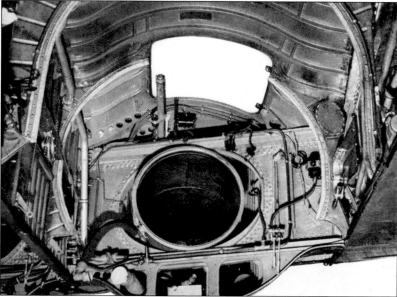

Above right: Routine testing of the electrical system through an inspection door on the upper surface of the nacelle.

Above left: This engineer is fitting a hydraulic pump. He is able to work while standing on the hangar floor; the manner in which inspection platforms could be largely dispensed with afforded material saving of time and of expenditure on ground equipment.

Left: looking up into an empty engine bay once the Ghost had been removed.(*DH Hatfield*)

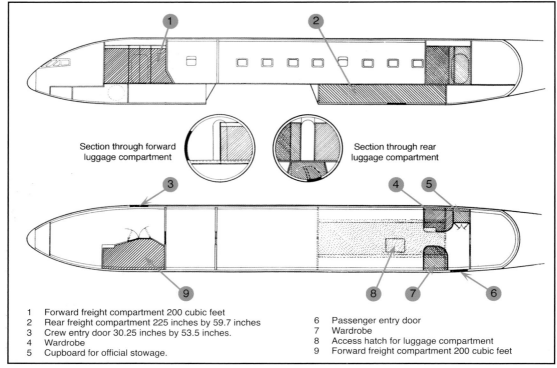

1 Forward freight compartment 200 cubic feet	
2 Rear freight compartment 225 inches by 59.7 inches	6 Passenger entry door
3 Crew entry door 30.25 inches by 53.5 inches.	7 Wardrobe
4 Wardrobe	8 Access hatch for luggage compartment
5 Cupboard for official stowage.	9 Forward freight compartment 200 cubic feet

Comet 1 freight and luggage accommodation. *(DH Hatfield)*

minimum figure; a run up to full power would be made immediately.

In current airline practice a minor inspection of airframe and engines was carried out every 50 to 100 hours, or at the end of a round trip of roughly that duration. To arrive at a comparative appreciation, the jobs to be done on the Comet's engines at such inspections could be classified under the conventional headings used in planning piston engine maintenance, but there the similarity ends.

De Havilland's made much of the simplicity of the turbine engine: *'Consider, as an example, the inspection of the ignition system. For the piston engine: change up to as many as 56 sparking plugs (which may be inaccessible and may involve removing baffle plates), check magneto, contact breaker gaps and the insulation and continuity of the plug leads and switches. For the Comet; inspect the igniter plugs, which were used for starting only, and make a function check.*

Such a minor inspection for one engine (including, of course, a daily inspection as described above) requires about two man hours, so that approximately eight man-hours suffice to complete a minor inspection of all four. The ideal practice was to employ a crew of three for each pair of engines, so completing the task in under 90 minutes. The economic *implications of these figures were self-evident to any airline engineer with trunk route experience'.*

In 1950 development of combustion chambers and flame tubes gave very good promise that at about the time the Series 2 Comet was planned to enter service, the flame tubes were expected to survive the complete overhaul life of the engine, which was expected to be 500 hours. Progressive development of the engines would undoubtedly lead to a longer overhaul life, and it was hoped to more than double this. During initial operations of the Series 1 Comet ideas concerning engine maintenance and overhaul were based on the only experience then available, namely military operation, which was the severest test to which any type of engine can be put. It became apparent that the more careful handling which a jet engine received in civil use resulted in the longer life of all its components. For instance, slow opening and closing of the throttles avoids rapid changes in temperature in combustion chambers, turbine and jet pipe.

Changing an engine in the Comet was a quick and simple operation. The engine mounting of the Series 1 Comet was similar in respects to that of the Series 2 aircraft, consisting of two trunnion bearings with a single steadying tie-bar, all secured by single bolts, and all the control, pipe-line and electrical

Real accessibility : the starboard underside of the Comet's port inner Ghost engine. Fuel-system components and all other accessories are mounted forward of the fireproof bulkhead and, when the front cowlings are exposed conveniently at shoulder height. The rear cowlings, also lowered in this picture, cover the tailpipe and tailpipe extension and need be opened only for routine inspections. *(DH Hatfield)*

couplings were designed for quick release and connection. The throttle controls, for example, could be coupled up after an engine change without adjustment. The jet pipe was held to the engine by four clamp fastenings, which, when disconnected, allowed it to slide aft on runners, and the engine was released from the air intake duct by a single toggle fastener.

The cost of maintaining an piston-engined airliner in 1950 terms amounted to some 40 per cent of its total operating cost. In addition to this there was the cost of unscheduled maintenance, nearly all of which was due to engine trouble. The experience gained with the Comet, and the encouraging progress that was made in the gas turbine field, was expected to lead to the achievement of the airline operator's ideal - the elimination of all unscheduled maintenance.

Fire Precautions - Fire warning lights and switches were mounted on a central panel in front of the pilots. In addition, a fire warning light was mounted behind each throttle so that there could be no doubt which engine to shut down in the event of an engine fire.

A master fire warning bell rang when any fuselage or engine fire zone warning had operated.

A methyl bromide fire-extinguisher system protected the engine fire zones, the wing leading-edge equipment bay and de-icing bay. The fuselage fire-extinguisher system comprised a semi-portable 12.5 pound carbon dioxide bottle, which could be plugged into built-in sockets in the under-floor zones, and which, through a trigger-control, discharged carbon dioxide at will. A portable two-pound carbon dioxide bottle was stowed in the control cabin and two one-and-a-half pound water glycol bottles were stowed in the main cabin and one in the galley. All fuselage under-floor zones were fitted with access hatches and small observation windows; freight and luggage compartments above the floor were readily accessible in flight.

Maintenance - the gas turbine made possible a fresh approach to aircraft design. Apart from the improvements in performance brought about by the increased power available, it provided an opportunity for the aircraft designer to cut away from the growing complexity of the modern airliner. In the Comet the basic simplicity of the jet engine was reflected throughout the aircraft; the simple cockpit and the absence of auxiliary cabin blowers and heaters for thermal de-icing were particularly notable. It was this factor, coupled with the absence of vibration, which paid dividends in increased serviceability and reduced maintenance costs.

The Comet Airframe.
The low-wing layout of the Comet made the buried engines and the refuelling points readily accessible from the ground, without the need for steps. The short undercarriage made possible by the absence of propellers made the utmost of the low-wing layout in this respects. Control cables, hydraulic pipes, electric cables and equipment etc, were all run or grouped under the cabin floor so that they were accessible for

One little known event occured on Wednesday, February 27, 1952 when the future arrived unexpectedly at Luton. John Cunningham brought G-ALYP into the then grass airfield at Luton for an unscheduled landing when Hatfield Aerodrome became smog-bound. John Cunningham landed and took off from Luton without problems - even on Luton's grass runways.

inspection and maintenance through doors in the underside of the fuselage, thus obviating the need to work in the cabin or disturb the cabin upholstery.

The 'handing' of components was avoided as far as possible in the Comet; power plants, tailplanes, elevators and brakes, for example, were all interchangeable. Careful attention had been given to the easy removal of all components without, as far as was possible, the disturbance of the structure or pipe runs and cables and the minimum number of attachment bolts was used.

Because it was undesirable in a large pressure-cabin aircraft like the Comet to provide many access doors, a large equipment bay, accessible during flight as well as from the ground, was provided beneath the floor of the flight deck. This bay housed most of the equipment associated with the cabin air conditioning, hydraulic and electrical systems, separated for easy access as far as possible, and it was roomy enough to allow two or three people to work in it at a time.

Instrument panels in the control cabin were all hinged for rear access, a convenient and, especially in the case of a pressurised aircraft, a necessary feature.

In the Comet remote control was effected by mechanical linkage or by cable whenever possible. A significant proportion of airline maintenance costs was devoted to maintaining electrical and electronic services, and an effort was made in designing the Comet to keep this type of equipment to a minimum. Though often convenient and effective, it was likely to give trouble in service, whereas mechanical linkages, once properly installed, needed very little maintenance and were a reliable means of operating vital systems without the chances of failure so often associated with small electrical units.

Ground Handling - Ground locking pins, with red pennants attached, were provided for insertion in the undercarriage lock mechanisms to prevent inadvertent retraction when the aircraft was jacked. Ground locking was automatic when the oleo legs were taking the weight of the aircraft.

The tractor towing arm was normally fitted to the nose leg but should the aircraft become, for instance, bogged, provision was made on the main-wheels for towing gear attachment.

There were three jacking points; one under each rear spar behind the main undercarriage legs and one on the starboard side of the fuselage near the nose leg. Thirty-ton hydraulic jacks were normally used; those under the wings had ball-end heads and the nose jack a cranked adaptor. Jacking adaptors were also provided on each wheel leg for wheel-changing.

An intercommunication socket was provided in the nose-wheel bay to enable ground to aircraft contact to be maintained while the engines were started.

The Flying Control System - To enable the control cables to be identified and to facilitate inter-cabin connections, labels carrying a printed code were fixed round the ends of each cable.

Rigging pins were used extensively to align pulleys, levers, etc. in their neutral positions to facilitate the tensioning of rods and cables. With maintenance platforms in position it was possible to remove the control surface manually.

Cabin Toilet and Galley Servicing - waste from the toilets and the galley was disposed of from outside the aircraft. Suitable coverings which were easy to wash down were provided in the washrooms, toilets and galley.

Chapter Seven

INTO SERVICE

In the afternoon of 2 May 1952, the British Overseas Airways Corporation Comet G-ALYP - 'Yoke Peter' in the parlance of the day - took off from London's Heathrow Airport bound for Johannesburg, on the world's first jet-airliner service. Operating as Flight number BA113, the aircraft arrived at its destination 23 hours 37 minutes later, at twenty-three minutes to four local time on 3 May, three minutes ahead of the scheduled time. It left again at nine o'clock local time on 5 May on the first north-bound service and arrived at London Airport two minutes early at 07.48 on the morning of 6 May.

An indication of the special operating technique employed by high-speed jet airliners was apparent even at the start from London Airport on 2 May. At a 14.45 the last passenger embarked and the door was closed; at 14.58 the engine-starting routine commenced. Promptly at 15.00 the Comet moved off from the apron and taxied direct to the duty runway, a distance of nearly three miles. At 15.10 the aircraft was lined up on the runway, the four Ghost engines were opened up to take-off power, the brakes were released and twenty seconds later, at exactly 15.12, the Comet was airborne en route for Rome.

On board that afternoon were crew members Captain A. M. Majendie, First Officer J. G. Woodill, Engineer

Officer W. I. Bennett and Radio Officer R. W. Chandler. In the cabin was Steward E. W. Charlwood, and Stewardess J. P. Nourse.

The passenger list for the Heathrow departure was Mr. Alex Henshaw, Mr. J. S. Crossley, Mr. D. Carter, Brig. G. Ross, Mr. A. O. Cookman, Mr. P. F. Knight, Mr. R. D. Gwyther, Mr. E. T. Pinkney, Mr. J. Garlick, Mr. W. K. Peters, Mr. P. Sraffa, Mr. D. P. Bertlin, Miss D. Hannaford, Mr. S. C. Brealey, Dr. J. M. Brown, Col. E. P. J. Ryan, Mr. W. E. Lawson. Mr. G. N. Wright, Mr. B. I. D. Jackson, Mr. L. Morris, Mr. R. Brook, Mr. C. H. Brigish, Alderman J. H. Wemsley, Mr. D. Willis, Mr. Fraser Wighton, Mr. G. W. Pearson, Mr. W. A. Walker, Mr. G. Movshon, Mr. E. C. Bailey, Mr. O. Garlick, Miss A. Coleridge-Taylor, Mr. T. West, Mr. A. C. Hales. Mr. B. Hardy, Mr. L. Orton and Mr. S. Naude.

At Beirut, there was a crew change: Captain J. T. A. Marsden, First Officer K. Emmott, Engineer Officer T. W. Taylor, Radio Officer G. L. Coutts, In the cabin was Steward A. C. McCormack and Stewardess E. P. Courtney.

Khartoum saw another crew change for the flight

Captain Geoffrey de Havilland (left), John Cunningham and members of the BOAC and De Havilland Boards 'see away' the world's first jet airliner passenger service. *(DH Hatfield)*

M.C.A. Form No. 958

UNITED KINGDOM

MINISTRY OF CIVIL AVIATION

CERTIFICATE OF AIRWORTHINESS

No. A.3215

NATIONALITY AND REGISTRATION MARKS	CONSTRUCTOR AND CONSTRUCTOR'S DESIGNATION OF AIRCRAFT	AIRCRAFT SERIAL No. (CONSTRUCTOR'S No.)
G-ALYS	The de Havilland Aircraft Co. Ltd. Comet D.H.106 Series 1.	06005

CATEGORY :	Normal
SUBDIVISION :	(a) Public transport for passengers (b) Public transport for mails (c) Public transport for goods (d) Private (e) Aerial work (h) Demonstration (i) Crew familiarisation

This Certificate of Airworthiness is issued pursuant to the Convention on International Civil Aviation dated 7th December, 1944, and the Air Navigation Order, 1949, the Air Navigation (General) Regulations, 1949, and the Air Navigation (Radio) Regulations, 1949, in respect of the above-mentioned aircraft, which is considered to be airworthy when maintained and operated in accordance with the requirements of the above-mentioned Order and Regulations, and the pertinent Flight Manual.

John S. Maclay.

~~Secretary~~ Minister of Civil Aviation.

Date 22nd January, 1952.

This certificate is valid for the period(s) shewn below			Signature, Official Stamp and Date
From 22nd January, 1952	to	21st January, 1953.	
From	to		
From	to		
From	to		
From	to		

No entries or endorsements may be made on this Certificate except in the manner and by the persons authorised for the purpose by the Minister of Civil Aviation.

If this Certificate is lost, the Secretary, Ministry of Civil Aviation (R.L.2) should be informed at once, the Certificate Number being quoted.

Any person finding this Certificate should forward it immediately to the Secretary, Ministry of Civil Aviation (R.L.2), Ariel House, Strand, London, W.C.2.

(9158. Wt. 9786 J93s 900 4 49 C.& Co. 745(8)

Above: the 'waving off' party as Comet Yoke Peter leaves London Airport for the inaugural flight to Johannesburg.

Left: Captain Alastair M A Majendie, MA, FRAeS boards G-ALYP for the world's first jet passenger service.

Opposite page: issued by the Ministry of Civil Aviationon 22 January 1952, the Certificate of Airworthiness for Comet G-ALYS allowed commerical services to commence. *(all DH Hatfield)*

to Johannesburg : Captain R. C. Alabaster, First Officer D. T. Whitham, First Officer B. A. Arterton, (flying as supernumerary crew) Engineer Officer J. A. Johnson and Radio Officer. R. J. Dolman. In the cabin was Steward T. D. Irwin and Stewardess A. Cartmell.

Sir Miles Thomas had gone on ahead with the last training flight and joined the service at Livingstone - there was no trunk-line airport at Salisbury at that time - and went on with the aircraft to its destination at Palmietfontein airport as Jan Smuts airport was not then built. Two days later he left in the Comet on the first northbound jet service from South Africa to London, arriving on schedule - the culmination of countless hours of devoted effort by thousands of people in Britain and other parts of the world.

Reading through the documentation of the time, it is impossible not the hear in your mind the clipped, precise tones of the BBC newreader explaining to his listeners the dawning of a new Elizabethan age as he described the scene at London Airport and the following journey down to Johannesburg. It was all so '... frightfully British old chap':

Airliners of many nations throng the busy parking apron, their cabin tops white against a threatening sky, and the spectators crowding the terraces and public enclosures are a jostle of precautionary raincoats and umbrellas. But the weather flaunts British ceremonial tradition with a brilliant dazzle of sunshine as, promptly at three o'clock, the shrill scream of turbines cuts suddenly across the heavy background hum of the airport.

BRITISH OVERSEAS AIRWAYS CORPORATION

AIRWAYS TERMINAL BUCKINGHAM PALACE ROAD LONDON, S.W. 1

Phone VICtoria 2323 Telex: VICtoria 3126 Telegrams: Speedbird Wire London

B·O·A·C

SSE.8C.78.   24th March, 1952.

Dear Sir,

The Comet Jetliner

       Following the general announcement this afternoon, it is with pleasure that I now attach for your further information the timetable of the world's first commercial service by Jetliner, to be introduced by B.O.A.C. on Friday 2nd May.

       The Comet means yet more effortless and comfortable flying with B.O.A.C., and with it our renowned standard of passenger service - but this time at super-speed.

       With the introduction of the Comet on our route between London and Johannesburg, passengers will be able to fly:-

LONDON to ROME	in	$2\frac{1}{2}$ hours
LONDON to BEIRUT	in	7 hours
LONDON to ENTEBBE	in	16 hours
LONDON to JOHANNESBURG	in	$23\frac{1}{2}$ hours

       The Comet Jetliner flys high above the weather at nearly 500 miles an hour, in air so clear and smooth that all feeling of motion is lost and there is a complete absence of vibration.

       In view of the already heavy demands for seats on our Comet flights, please let us know your requirements as far in advance as possible. Further information and reservations can be obtained from your B.O.A.C. Appointed Agent or our Passenger Booking Offices at this address or at 75, Regent Street, London, W.1. (MAYfair 6611). Intending passengers in Scotland should apply to their local Agent or to our Passenger Booking Office at Prestwick Airport telephone Glasgow Central: 1244/5.

                          Yours faithfully,

                          M.D. Morrissey,
                 Sales Manager, U.K. & Europe.

All eyes turn to where Yoke Peter, its full complement of thirty-six waving, chattering passengers embarked amid a fusillade of flash-bulbs, is swinging out on to the taxiway. Standing with the little send-off party of BOAC executives are Sir Geoffrey de Havilland, Ronald Bishop and John Cunningham: and their feelings can well be imagined as a few minutes later a wash of thunderous sound comes rolling back from the runway and the Comet climbs swiftly away, heading east on the world's first commercial jet service.

In command for the first part of that historic trip was Fleet Captain Alistair Majendie, whose flair for mathematics had enabled him to contribute much towards devising BOAC's new jet operating technique. Strong headwinds over the Alps made them nine minutes late arriving at Rome to refuel, but they made up time on the next leg, and in the gathering dusk swept in low across the surfbound coast of the Lebanon, to land fifteen minutes ahead of schedule at Beirut.

While the clattering kerosene bowsers once more disgorged their thousands of gallons into the great wing tanks. Captain Majendie handed over to the slip crew who were to take the service on through the night. And so to Khartoum, silvery in the waning moonlight. More fuel, another fresh crew. a stroll for the yawning passengers, and they were off again, the brazen sun tipping the rim of the desert as the Comet winged southwards to Entebbe on the edge of Lake Victoria; then on to a last refuelling stop in the midday furnace heat of Livingstone. Climbing away over the Victoria Falls, there were still a few minutes in hand and they dawdled along the last leg of the journey, making wide turns to kill time. When Yoke Peter finally touched down at Johannesburg, twenty

Once BOAC had the Certificate of Airworthiness for the type, they could go ahead and plan, then announce the world's first commerical jetliner service, which they did on 24 March, as this classically understated invitation letter opposite shows. The timetable, below, was even more understated - being just a simple, single typewritten sheet.

BRITISH OVERSEAS AIRWAYS CORPORATION

FREQUENCY:- ONCE WEEKLY   **AIRCRAFT:-** COMET JETLINER

	BA.113 LT				BA.114 LT	
Fri.	1500	dep.	LONDON	arr.	0755	
	1735	arr.	ROME	dep.	0510	
	1835	dep.	ROME	arr.	0410	
	2310	arr.	BEIRUT	dep.	0110	
Sat.	0010	dep.	BEIRUT	arr.	0010	Tue.
	0355	arr.	KHARTOUM	dep.	2025	
	0455	dep.	KHARTOUM	arr.	1925	
	0900	arr.	ENTEBBE	dep.	1725	
	1000	dep.	ENTEBBE	arr.	1625	
	1245	arr.	LIVINGSTONE	dep.	1155	
	1345	dep.	LIVINGSTONE	arr.	1055	
	1540	arr.	JOHANNESBURG	dep.	0900	Mon.

EFFECTIVE:-   BA.113 EX LONDON 2.5.'52.
  -"-   BA.114 " JOHANNESBURG 5.5.'52.

three and a half hours after leaving London, it was just two minutes ahead of schedule'.

The clockwork precision of this 6,774-mile flight did more than thrill the crowd of 20,000 who were waiting to greet the Comet on its inaugural schedule; it impressed the whole aviation world. Long after the South African service had settled down into the normality of simple routine, there remained a widespread general interest in this revolutionary mode of travel.

During May the Comet service was to operate once weekly in each direction, leaving London on Fridays and Johannesburg on Mondays, but because of the great demand for seats an extra service was operated, leaving London on 24 May. The frequency increased to three services a week from June.

The Comet service was operating on the Springbok route in conjunction with the Constellation services of BOAC's partners, South African Airways.

The Corporation's Hermes services, which flew three times a week between London and Johannesburg on the west side of Africa, would be withdrawn progressively as the Comet frequencies are increased.

In the original time-table the actual flying time of the service was eighteen hours forty minutes southbound and eighteen hours fifty-five minutes northbound. Later, when formalities at the transit points were accelerated, the journey time was reduced. Plans were in hand, depending on the political situation in Egypt, to re-route the service through Cairo instead of Beirut, which would bring a saving of 450 miles, thus cutting nearly an hour off the schedule time.

Sir Miles Thomas, DFC, MLMechE, MSAE, Chairman of the British Overseas Airways Corporation, was understandably proud: '*The introduction of the Comet into regular airline service as the world's first civil jet- propelled aircraft is*

Above: the world's first fare-paying jet-liner passengers board the Comet at London Airport for Rome and points south to Johannesburg *(DH6291M photo)*.

Left: amongst the thirty-six passengers on the 2 May flight were Miss T Coleridge-Taylor, daughter of the famous musician, who was herself a noted conductor and composer, and Miss D. Hannaford, a 22-year-old London policewoman. *(DH62911 photo)*

Above: Charles Sims, who had been photographing aircraft for *'The Aeroplane'* for more than 25 years, records the scene at London Airport as the Comet is prepared for its inaugural flight at lunchtime on May 2 1952. *(DH6283Y photo)*

Right: passengers' luggage is manhandled into the pressurised freight compartment of the Comet before departure. *(DH6291J photo).*

indeed a memorable and historic event. Moreover, it is an event in which Britain can well take pride. Not only does it mark the fulfilment of the aims which inspired British initiative and enterprise at the close of the last war; it justifies the faith which the manufacturers and the British Overseas Airways Corporation placed in this remarkable product of the De Havilland factory, where the labours of skilled workers have been crowned with such striking success.

When the war was over we were convinced that a jet airliner was practicable both for its flying qualities and from the maintenance point of view. One of the problems that exercised us most was the question of operating cost. As a result of exhaustive investigation, however, it became apparent that this new type of air transport should be competitive economically and from that moment we had no doubt but that the pure-jet aircraft would become a British achievement.

The inauguration of the Comet into passenger service on a great British trunk route in little more than five years from the decision which set in motion the whole machinery of detailed design and manufacture, test and development, is deeply gratifying to everyone who has been engaged in the task - and the confidence felt at the inception of the project has gained force during the intervening period.

The Comet certainly heralds a new era in international travel. It will in effect halve the size of the world, and passengers will appreciate in particular the high standard of comfort and the smooth-riding qualities of an aircraft in which the lack of vibration is so notable a characteristic. Furthermore, the Comet introduces a form of powerplant which is basically simple and unmistakably offers much scope for development.

The British manufacturers and the British airline operator, in their close working harmony, together

have the ability to retain the ascendency that has now been established for our country in the world of civil aviation.

The Comet was instantly fashionable, exclusive and futuristic. Its essential up-to-dateness was reflected in a load factor of 89% on the South African route - 32 seats filled out of 36 on every single flight - throughout the first few months of operation. On 11 August, it had begun flying a regular schedule between London and Colombo, and on October 14 the service was taken on from Karachi through to Singapore.

Again the load factors jumped to record levels while slower competitors lost business, and travel agents' waiting lists for each new service became longer and longer as the fashion spread.

More royal attention

John Cunningham borrowed brand new Comet G-ALYR from BOAC to take the Queen Mother and Princess Margaret on a 1.800-mile jaunt during the afternoon on 23 May. Luncheon and tea were served to the Royal Party during the flight, which extended down to Switzerland and northern Italy, embraced the south coast of France and the Pyrenees to Bordeaux and thence home. Before embarking The Queen Mother and The Princess Margaret spent a little time at Hatfield, where they saw Comet manufacturing operations. In the style of the day it was reported that

One hour out of London and the Comet passengers gaze down on the 15,000 feet Alps of Switzerland - the Savoie and Rhone Valley are under cloud. At the time this was a scene viewed by only military pilots, but one that was set to become commonplace. By lunchtime the next day, 5,000 miles from England, the Comet is refuelled and revictualled at Livingstone .

'Her Majesty and Her Royal Highness expressed great pleasure and enjoyment in the flight, in the course of which each of them spent considerable periods in the control cabins'.

Not to be outdone, Prince Philip flew back from the Helsinki Olympic Games in one; Pandit Nehru looked down on Mount Everest from the flight deck of another which was making a series of route-proving runs to Ceylon, Singapore and Tokyo. Two months after the ratification of the Peace Treaty between Japan and the Allied Powers, De Havilland announced orders placed by Japan Air Lines for two Comet Series 2 jet airliners. JAL, an independent company which had taken the lead in the first stages of the Japanese revival in the air wanted the Comets for the first external service then being planned to extend westward to India and Europe and eastward across the Pacific. They were planning to start with the most modern equipment available.

Around the same time an 'improved' Comet was due to make its maiden flight in time for exhibition

Right: refuelling at Livingstone Airport, Rhodesia.

Above: arrival at Johannesburg.

at the 1951 SBAC Display at Farnborough, the first of the Comets for Canadian Pacific Airlines marked an important stage in the continuing programme of development of the Comet jet airliner. Designated the Series 1A, the Canadian Comet CF-CUM incorporated Ghost engines with water-methanol injection and increased fuel capacity, whilst the all-up weight was increased to 110,000 lb. By the use of water-methanol injection, the dry thrust of the Ghost engine was increased by 10% under ICAN conditions. At higher temperatures the proportion rose to approximately 12% as the dry thrust of the engine fell off. In terms of Comet take-off performance the injection of water-methanol in tropical conditions had the same effect as lowering the ambient temperature by about 10°C.

The fuel capacity of the Comet Series 1A was increased to 7,000 gallons. This enabled the Series

In the clear air of the high veldt at Palmietfontein Airport, on the Rand near Johannesburg, two Comets of the world's first jet airline are being serviced. *(DH Hatfield)*

1A Comet to operate over stage lengths some 20% longer than the Series 1 which has a fuel capacity of 6,000 Imperial gallons. All the extra fuel in the Series 1A was accommodated in the wing structure.

The Comets for Canadian Pacific Airlines, which had accommodation for 44 passengers, were due to go into service on the Sydney, Honolulu, section of the trans-pacific route. Based at Sydney, the Comets were to fly a twice-weekly service to Honolulu, one service via Fiji and Canton Island and another via Auckland, Fiji and Canton Island.

The improved performance of the Series 1A further enhanced the revenue-earning capacity of the Comet, which, as announced by Sir Miles Thomas, had already enabled BOAC to show a profit of £3,000 on the operation of Comets during the month of May on the Johannesburg route.

Another announcement was that Linea Aeropostal Venezolana, known briefly as L.A.V., had ordered two Series 2 Comets with Rolls-Royce Avon engines. Venezuela thus became the seventh country to select Comets. At that time L.A.V. operated a fleet of 26 aircraft, consisting of Constellations, D.C.3s and Martin 202s, and flew approximately 7,000 route miles on the services between Caracas, the capital of Venezuela, and the USA, Peru and Brazil.

It was the intention that the Comets operated a direct, non-stop express service across the Caribbean between Caracas and New York, a distance of 2,410 statute miles, in a scheduled time of four and a half hours. At the time LAV ran a thrice-weekly non-stop service between the two cities, employing

Constellations which are scheduled to cover the route in eight hours.

Delivery of the two Comets was expected in the middle of 1955. At a later stage LAV proposed to operate additional Comet services to destinations in South America.

BOAC scheduled services had started modestly enough on with a once-weekly service to Johannesburg, a route mileage of 6,724 miles. In June, following the delivery of the fifth aircraft the previous month, the Johannesburg schedule was increased to three services per week. By August the ground organisation on the route was beginning to run so smoothly that at Khartoum and Livingstone the transit time was cut from sixty to forty minutes - the first time that a BOAC aircraft had been scheduled for so brief a stop. This reduction in ground time and the re-routing of the flight through Cairo enabled elapsed time for the journey between London and South Africa to be reduced from 23 hours 40 minutes to 21 hours 20 minutes. The delivery of the sixth and seventh aircraft by July was followed on 11 August by the introduction of the service between London and Ceylon to be flown once weekly, 5,961 miles in an elapsed time of 20 hours 35 minutes. Until April, 1953, this service worked under a severe handicap because the Ceylonese Government refused permission to uplift passengers from Colombo, which made it necessary for the homeward bound aircraft to fly empty as far as Bombay.

On 14 October a weekly service between London and Singapore was started covering 7,833 miles in

Her Majesty Queen Elizabeth The Queen Mother and Her Royal Highness The Princess Margaret alighting from the Comet G-ALYR after a four-hour flight from Hatfield on 23 May.

The aircraft was piloted by John Cunningham (extreme left), and Mr. Peter Bugge, Accompanying the Royal visitors were Lord and Lady Salisbury (right) Air Commodore Edward H. 'Mouse' Fielden, Captain of the Kings Flight, Group Captain Peter Townsend, Sir Miles Thomas, Sir Geoffrey and Lady de Havilland and Mr F. E. N. St. Barbe.

Below: Canadian Pacific Airlines Comet 1A CF-CUN

25 hours 30 minutes, and on the last day of October this was stepped-up to twice weekly. On April 3, 1953, London was linked with Tokyo by once-a-week Comet service scheduled to cover the 10,380 miles, reaching halfway round the world, in 36 hours 20 min. elapsed time. Ten days later, on April 13, the frequency of the service was doubled.

Thus within eleven months of the inauguration of the world's first jet service, Comets were flying 122,000 miles a week on a network of routes with an unduplicated mileage of 20,780. During the year the Comets flew 9,443 revenue hours and carried nearly 28,000 passengers thus achieving 104,600,000 revenue passenger miles.

So much for the bare record. In assessing the scale of the achievement it must be remembered that the Comet in use by BOAC during the inaugural year, the Series 1, was the undeveloped Comet and that the fleet of eight consisted of the first Comets off the production line.

As Sir Miles Thomas said: *'If there was scepticism about the practicability of a jet air service within the industry, the public did not share it. As was to be expected the early services were fully booked for months ahead and bookings for the first service itself were being received by BOAC over a year before the start and before the applicants knew where the inaugural flight was to be routed. There is always a large number of people anxious to be 'first' and it was recognised that the novelty factor which led to the heavy bookings achieved during the first weeks of operation could not be considered as necessarily representative of the normal demand. In the event, however, there has been no detectable falling off in the high load factors, and, if anything can be said to have been proved by 12 months of service, it is that the Comet has become firmly established as a favourite medium of travel with the public, who have quickly come to appreciate not only the value of the speed but the unprecedented degree of leisureliness and comfort, which enables them to reach their destination unfatigued and even refreshed by the experience'.*

'Statistically the figures are remarkable: from the start of the service until the beginning of January, 1953, the average passenger load factor over the entire network was no less than 87 per cent. and the overall load factors including passengers, mail and freight have been nearly 80 per cent. Individual route figures show up even better. During February, 1953, for instance, a total of 1,116 stage-seats were offered outbound between London and Singapore and of these seats 1,028 were occupied, representing a passenger load factor of over 92 per cent. In practice it is hardly possible to improve on this figure. On a long trunk route some concession must be made to passengers who require to travel only part of the way and it is not always possible to fill the seats thus vacated. Another reason which prevents every seat from being occupied is the passenger who having booked a seat just does not turn up. This 'no-show' problem, the solution for which has defied the best brains in the air-line business, can affect load factors by as much as six percent, although for the Comet the figures are not so high'.

Passenger appeal

In common with all major airlines, BOAC provided each passenger with forms on which they were invited to make comments about the quality of the service. This facility was widely used on the Comet services and, as was expected, the vast majority of passengers who turned in comments were full of praise for the comforts of jet travel — however, the gentleman from across the Atlantic who stated that he could detect no improvement in noise and vibration must be considered as having been 'got at' by the opposition! A lady passenger evidently more friendly disposed towards the Comet, wrote that from her own experience she was able to assure the Corporation that there was no truth in the rumour that the high cruising altitude disintegrated nylon stockings and underwear. For the most part, however, the comments were eulogistic, and sensible.

Sir Miles Thomas: *'Notable among the few criticisms which have been made is a general dislike of the seats in the forward cabin. Unlike the seats in the main cabin of the Comet 1, which are adjustable through a range of positions from upright to reclining, the fore-cabin seats are fixed and thus do not provide the same degree of comfort for sleeping. This feature was, in fact, dictated by the position of two structural bulkheads which limit the length of the cabin. Because of the justifiable criticism alterations have been made in the Series 2 Comets which will permit the eight seats in this compartment to be of the same adjustable type as in the main cabin. In the Series 3 Comet, too, all the seats will be adjustable. Another criticism, and more difficult to correct, concerns the toilet facilities. With passenger loads which are predominantly male the equal provision of toilets for both sexes inevitably leads to congestion in the men's room, particularly at shaving time. Until the British traveller becomes more continental in his outlook there does not seem to be any answer to this complaint in an aircraft the size of the Comets 1 and 2'.*

During the year's operation a great deal of flying time

Then as now, BOAC never missed a trick in the publicity stakes. This special Air Mail envelope is one of a series that was sent to different sales managers 'down the route' on the occasion of the first London to Singapore service - this one being from the Cairo - Karachi leg.

had been occupied in crew training and proving flights. Sir Miles Thomas went into some detail. *'Since the regular services began in May, 24 proving and training flights covering 381,700 miles have been completed prior to the opening of new routes and this is additional to the 248,600 miles covered during 28 similar flights before May 2, 1953. These figures take no account of the local training flights* covering *general familiarisation, landing practice including three-engine wave-off approaches and approach-pattern procedure.*

Each BOAC captain, before taking a Comet on regular service, has completed at least 60 hours of flying on the aircraft, about 10 hours of which consists of local flying followed by at least two trips under supervision over the route he is to operate. In addition all pilots undergo a nine-weeks' course of instruction covering the technicalities of the airframe, the engine and the theory of cruise control. Under Captain Rodley, who is in charge of Comet flying training, there are five of the fleet captains who are qualified as instructors and after qualification each captain has a check-flight of two hours or more every six months. The training syllabus of first officers, flight engineers (both of these groups must complete at least three route trips before qualification), radio operators and the cabin crew varies in detail according to their duties, but is equally thorough.

At the year's end the target of 40 operational Comet crews was achieved, but even before then five captains and ten first officers were undergoing ground courses and initial flying training in anticipation of the introduction of the Comet Series 2 into service.

Operational Lessons

After a complete year of operation the overriding lesson was that many of the expected troubles did not materialise and that the Comet had a much greater degree of operational flexibility than was indicated by theoretical considerations.

Sir Miles Thomas again: *'As is well known, the jet's fuel consumption is high during taxying and ground manoeuvring, although a considerable saving can be achieved if stopping and restarting can be avoided and the aircraft kept moving fairly fast. For this reason a novel take-off routine has been adopted at London Airport and other points where traffic congestion might cause delay.*

In the case of the Comet clearance to take off is obtained from traffic control before the engines are started so that it is possible to taxy without stopping to the duty runway and then take-off without interruption. This procedure, which is made possible by the rapidity with which the Comet engines can be started and the fact that no warming-up or full-throttle checks are required, has worked very smoothly in practice and has not in itself led to any serious take-off delays.

After take-off it is desirable, for fuel-

B·O·A·C

Comet
Jetliner

. . . part of the modern

Speedbird Fleet

planned for

extra service

and comfort

in the air.

economy reasons, to make an uninterrupted climb to cruising altitude. The Comet's climb is more rapid and the air speed is higher than in the case of a piston-engined aircraft and the resultant climbing angle is rather better.

Although since the start of the Comet service there has been no case of an engine failure during take-off, such a condition is simulated frequently during training and it is well established that the three-engine rate of climb with full load leaves an ample margin of safety and is much superior to that of a comparable piston-engined aircraft.

The cruise technique adopted by BOAC consists of flying at a constant angle of incidence which is achieved in practice by flying at an indicated air speed selected in relation to the weight, alterations in speed being made at half-hourly intervals as the weight decreases.

This procedure results in a gradual climb. Depending on load and the length of the stage and to some extent on the ambient temperature, the cruising height will vary from about 35,000 ft. to 42,000 ft'.

On the score of punctuality the Comet service has acquitted itself well, and has indeed already put in a record which compares favourably with that of the well-established types of the BOAC fleet—no mean achievement for the first year of operation of a new type of aircraft.

During the course of the year the standard of punctuality has steadily improved, mainly due to an improvement in mechanical reliability resulting from the increasing knowledge of the aircraft and the growing experience of the engineering staff. The mechanical reliability of the Comet is considered below in greater detail and here it is enough to say that the troubles experienced have been of a nature such as might be expected when a new aircraft is put into service. The proportion of time lost due to mechanical trouble during the period showed a marked improvement, but the overall picture showing a reduction of about 44 per cent. in time lost was not so favourable because of the exceptionally high incidence of fog in London from October through to

With the control tower at London Airport in the background an outward-bound Comet stands ready to embark its load of passengers, mail and freight. Throughout the first year of Comet operation, the passenger load factors averaged 87%. *(DH Hatfield)*

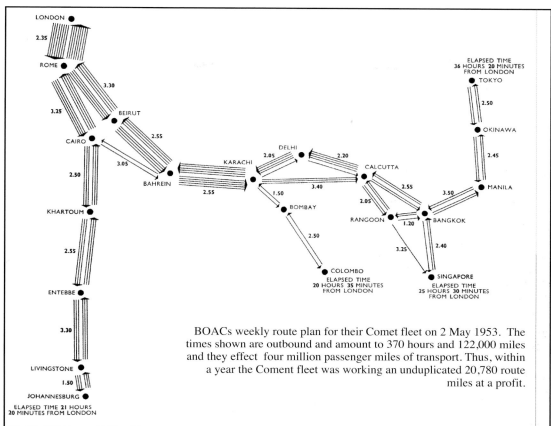

BOACs weekly route plan for their Comet fleet on 2 May 1953. The times shown are outbound and amount to 370 hours and 122,000 miles and they effect four million passenger miles of transport. Thus, within a year the Coment fleet was working an unduplicated 20,780 route miles at a profit.

the end of February. During this period London Airport was on many occasions closed, sometimes for days at a time, with a consequent disruption of all air services. Other factors which contributed to delay, although only to a small extent, were concerned with traffic control and ground services, passenger service and late connections. In the final reckoning the record shows that 33 per cent of the services arrived on time - or early - and 61 per cent. were within 2 hours of schedule.

A glance at the BOAC route network operated by eight Comets gives an indication of the increasing rate of utilisation being achieved. During May, 1952, when the service started, the total utilisation was in the order of three hours per day, of which only just over one hour was revenue earning. With the gradual introduction of new services and the stepping-up of service frequencies the rate of utilisation steadily improved. By October, 1952, the figure for the total had reached 4 hours and, with the start of the service to Tokyo, five hours. The increase in the Tokyo schedule to two services a week, ten days later, raised it to 6.5 hours per day.

As already mentioned, the normal basis of statistical reckoning tends to penalise the Comet and this is particularly so in the case of utilisation because the great reduction in stage time which has been accomplished cannot be matched by a proportionate reduction in transit time at intermediate stops. If one considers a future aircraft in which, for the sake of argument, the stage time is reduced to one hour and the transit time is also one hour it then becomes obvious that the maximum possible utilisation, without taking maintenance into account, which could be achieved with such an aircraft, could never exceed 12 hours a day. Thus it can be appreciated that a figure of 6.5 hours' daily utilisation is one that can be considered as a good beginning for the Series 1 Comet, with its comparatively short stage lengths, when the work-done factor is taken into account. More scope for improvement will be available with both the Series 2 and 3 Comets which will offer progressively longer operating stages.

Serviceability
Closely linked with the rate of utilisation was the degree of mechanical reliability achieved. Some

degree of mechanical trouble was to be expected in a completely new type of aircraft and, in addition, however efficient the pre-delivery instruction of engineers may be it is inevitable that in the early stages of service with a new aeroplane the factor of unfamiliarity and even, perhaps, over-caution, would affect the serviceability standard. As was expected, mechanical delays were fairly prevalent at the start of the Comet service and during the first month the average arrival time at the terminals was behind schedule to an amount equal to nearly 40% percent of the journey time. The standard of serviceability quickly improved and the final figure showed that time lost by mechanical delays was reduced to 9%.

Most of the troubles which were encountered at first were of a type which could quickly be eliminated as each aircraft became 'bedded-down' in service.

One of the most serious faults and one which nearly led to the temporary grounding of the fleet was the misting of the windscreen, which without any previous warning suddenly started to occur in June 1952, when the aircraft were on the final approach to Beirut and Khartoum airfields. This phenomenon occurred only in certain conditions of temperature and humidity The cure, simple enough in principle but involving a fair amount of engineering, was to increase the flow of warm air across the inner face of the screen. Needless to say this modification had a high priority and was incorporated in every aircraft within a very short period.

Of a similar but less serious nature was the trouble encountered with the early type of windscreen wiper, which having given every satisfaction during the test-flying period proved to be not up to the job on service. Its replacement by a more satisfactory type— hydraulically driven—was achieved only after a considerable amount of development work. In spite of the many hours of flying, many of them fruitless, which were spent in searching- out icing conditions, it was again not until the aircraft encountered service conditions that some mal-distribution of the hot-air in the de-icing system was discovered.

Finally, there was some evidence of cracking in the elevator skin, which called for its replacement in certain areas by a heavier gauge of metal. In the case of the Ghost engine two main problems occurred. After some months of trouble-free running, cracks

A cross-section of the Comet Fleet personnel on parade at London Airport. In the centre of the front row is Captain M. J. R. Alderson, Manager of the Fleet. On the left is Captain E. E. Rodley, Officer in Charge of Training and on the right is Mr. R. A. V. Dismore, the Fleet Maintenance engineer. Immediately behind Captain Alderson is a Comet crew headed (from left to right) by Captain T. B. Stoney, First Officer P. A. Wilson, Engineer Officer J. H. Kingston, Radio Officer I. M.Clark, Steward E. A. Johnson and Stewardess Miss J. Todd. Flanking the crew to the left are representative members of the administrative staff and to the right representative members of the engineering staff. In the back row are representatives of the ground services including an M.C.A. Air Traffic controller and a Tarmac controller. Captain A. M. A. Majendie in charge of Comet operations was abroad when this photograph was taken. *(DH Hatfield)*

began to appear in the centrifugal compressors, the cause of which was finally traced to high- frequency vibration. The cure was to crop the impeller blades by a small amount, not enough to affect the efficiency but sufficient to shift the frequency nodes outside the critical range.

The other fault which developed on a number of occasions soon after the service started was a failure of a small ball-bearing supporting the shaft driving the generator cooling fan. This fan was required only during ground running and its failure would not necessarily have rendered the engine unserviceable had it not been for the risk of the engine oil being contaminated by the damaged bearing.

Sir Miles Thomas: *'In summing up the record of serviceability for the first year of operation it can be stated that the Comet and its Ghost engines have earned unstinted praise from the engineering department of BOAC. The incidence of faults with the first production aircraft and engines has been considerably below that which was expected by the engineers, a point which is fully borne out by the unprecedented increase in hours which has been found possible between the check 4 inspections. Starting off at 200 hours - admittedly representing a cautious approach - the check 4 period has been progressively extended to 1,040 hours. This rate of increase represents a record, which has not been approached by any other aircraft in the history of the Corporation'.*

The first full year of operation has shown that the Comet is a mechanically sound aircraft capable of operating in a normal manner with regularity at unprecedented speeds on the world's air routes, but what of the economic picture? In spite of authoritative statements to the contrary there are those who without grounds assert that the Comet 1 has proved uneconomic and that the BOAC services are being run at a loss. Even if this were true the operation of the small fleet of Series 1 Comets by BOAC would still have proved worthwhile because of the invaluable experience which has been gained in jet operation, experience which can be obtained in no other way and which has enabled BOAC to establish the commanding lead which it enjoys today among the world's airlines. But it is definitely untrue.

In considering the matter of airline economics and the break-even loads for a given aircraft, a large number of factors which vary route by route must be taken into account. First, the rate of revenue for each route is fixed by the fare structure and the differing proportion

between passengers and mail loads over different air routes and different stages has a great influence on the revenue figures. The cost of fuel varies considerably from place to place mostly because of local duties and taxes, whilst the cost of maintaining the line stations naturally differs considerably according to location. All these important considerations greatly influence the break-even load factors which consequently vary considerably from route to route irrespective of the type of aircraft

B·O·A·C

introduces

the newest,

fastest airliner

in the world

THE *Comet*

JETLINER

BRITISH OVERSEAS AIRWAYS CORPORATION

---

employed. Taking all these factors into account it has been established that on the routes on which BOAC have been operating Comets (connecting London with Johannesburg, Colombo, Singapore and Tokyo) an average load factor of 75% shows a profit.

When considering the profits made it must be borne in mind that eight Series 1 aircraft operated by BOAC represent only the first stage in Comet development. No more of this type will be built and already the Comet 1A with an improved performance is in service. At the present time the Series 1 aircraft are benefiting by high load factors, and this advantage can be expected to last for some years, as there will be no other jet airliners during this time to challenge their monopoly of the travelling public's preference. On this basis, therefore, it is reasonable to suppose that the Series 1 Comets will have gone far to pay for themselves by the time the progressively more profitable Comets 2 and 3 are put into service by BOAC and this takes no account of the value of accumulated experience.

In the final analysis the year's operating figures have shown that the eight Series 1 Comets, which have been operating at an overall load factor of nearly 80 per cent., have made sufficient profit during the period to cover the interest on the capital expenditure. This calculation is on a realistic costing basis, exactly as is applied to all the Corporation's fleets, and includes the cost of route proving and training flights spread proportionately over the life of the aircraft.

The Corporation can thus look back with justifiable satisfaction on the record of their first year of Comet operation in which they have shown the world that the spirit of the British merchant adventurer is vigorously alive today, and in which they have gained a lead that their competitors will be hard put to recover. But once having assimilated the varied experience gained they do not look back. The Members of the Board of the British Overseas Airways Corporation and the small team, under Captain Alderson, who bear the responsibilities for the day-to-day operation of the Comet fleet are farsighted men - actuated by the enthusiasm of crusaders - who more than most can visualise the future in store and who even now are laying plans for the long-range operation of the bigger and better Comets to come.

By Jet Airliner to Japan

Sir Miles made mention of the BOAC service to Japan - the opening of the Comet service of the BOAC between London and Tokyo, with a weekly departure each way from 2 April- that became twice

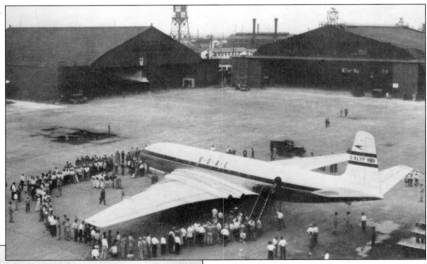

Above: BOAC Comet G-ALYP at Naneda Airport Tokyo on 8 July 1952 at the end of a proving flight to Japan.

Left: Captain A.M. A, Majendie of the Comet Fleet, who piloted the Comet on its flight to Japan, and A. C. Campbell-Orde, Operations Development Director of BOAC are here seen with the ladies of the Takarazuka Opera Company who greeted the aircraft at Tokyo airport. BOAC planned to start a Comet service between London and Tokyo early in 1953. (both DH Hatfield) weekly from 13 April - demonstrated with fresh force the facility of jet travel. Even the Series 1 Comet, working relatively short stages, was able to cut the timetable on this line from the 86 hours taken by the Corporation's twice-weekly Argonaut service to a mere 36 hours.

The eastbound traveller left London at 09.00 and, flying against the sun, passed the first short night between Beirut and Karachi, and the second between Bangkok and Tokyo, by way of Manila and Okinawa, reaching Tokyo for breakfast - only 36 hours after departing from England.

Westbound, with the sun, take-off from Haneda Airport, on Tokyo Bay, was at about midnight and after a long day flight between Manila and Karachi, arrived in London for early breakfast the next morning.

One weekly service was via Rome, Beirut, Bahrein Karachi, Calcutta, Rangoon, Bangkok, Manila, Okinawa and Tokyo. The other weekly service called at Cairo instead of Beirut, at New Delhi both ways instead of homeward only. One service called at Rangoon outward, the other homeward. The Comet flying time for the whole journey was scheduled at $28\frac{1}{2}$ hours, against 44 hours for the Argonaut.

With typical thoroughness BOAC spent nine months proving the Comet route to Tokyo before opening it to traffic. Between 4 July 1952, and 9 March 1953, eleven trial flights were made with

Comets between Bangkok (on their Comet twice-weekly line to Singapore) and Tokyo, and many captains and crews were thus familiarised with every feature of the natural and the contrived aids on the last three legs. Hong Kong, served by the Argonauts, was not available for the Comets because of the lack of a suitable alternative airport, so the jets flew from Bangkok to Manila and then to Okinawa and Tokyo.

The editor of the *De Havilland Gazette* was on the last proving flight: '*...we confess to being surprised at the size and resources of Okinawa. It is 70 miles long and has 600,000 inhabitants, and the American forces have constructed two fine air bases, Naha for civil and Kadena for military operations, both comprehensively equipped. We must admit also to a suppressed flutter at the turnout of bomber crews with their trousered wives, jean-clad juniors and bright Cadillacs, and at the footage of Kodachrome which they expended on the Comet as it taxied in. They are enthusiastic and generously co-operative, and manage their heavy air traffic well. Operating along with jet fighters, as well as many lumbering transports and bombers, the Comets ask for no favours, only efficient handling, and that they are accorded.*

The same may be said of Tokyo, where the military and civil air traffic can only be described as intense—it is up to 600 in-or-out movements a day. The BOAC crews have experienced tremendous winds in this region— 180 and 200 knots at Comet

Comet G-ALYP on the apron at Kadena Field, Okinawa, Saturday 28 February on the last of the proving flights. The Okinawans in the foreground are gathering painful pebbles and packing-case nails in order to prevent damage to aircraft tyres but unfortunately for the Comet they missed one and a puncture resulted.(*U.S. Air Force photograph by Robert Coiner*)

At Haneda Friday March 6, important passengers on a Comet demonstration flight around the Japanese islands in superb spring weather. Left to right: Mr. N. S. Roberts, Minister, British Embassy; Mr. Eric Watts, Managing Director, Jardine Matheson & Co. (Japan) Ltd. Mr. M Ishil, Japanese Minister of Transportation; Mr E. G. Price, Managing Director, Butterfield & Swire; Mr. G. W. Denny, Manager, BOAC Tokyo ,Mr. J Holland, Tokyo Evening News.The Princess Takamatsu ; Mr. Lewis F. Bush, Manager, British Commonwealth Film Corporation: Sir Esler M. Dening, H.M. Ambassador to Japan, Grand Master of Ceremonies, Imperial Household ; Mrs. K. Okumura; Mr. M. Kumashiro, Commissioner, Ministry of Finance ; Mr. K. Okumura, Vice Foreign Minister, Mr T. Onizawa, Chief of Haneda Airport Post Office : Mr. K. Ohno, Vice-Minister of Postal Services (in dark overcoat) and three others.

height—and believe that the velocities off the Asiatic seaboard at high latitudes are the greatest in the world, even 400 knots and above in rare jet streams. But with seasoned experience they remark that it is all a matter of fuel reserves and frequent fixes, and readiness to take advantage of every favourable element.

Arriving over Honshu in moonlight and four-eighths cloud late in February, circling Tokyo's seven-million population and landing at Haneda to be greeted by cheerful ground crews, gloved and muffled against the wintry weather, is an experience for an occidental.

French Operations...

Seven times each week a Comet of Union Aeromaritime de Transport (UAT) left Paris or Marseilles with passengers bound for French Africa. UAT was second to BOAC among operators of jet airliners, having had Comets in service since 19 February 1953, this private French company quickly establishing a fleet of three Comet lA's on its routes between La France Metropolitaine and La France d'Outre Mer.

UAT was the largest private airline in France, and

it was not without some pride that the Company became the first in France and the second in the world to employ the Comet.

UAT decided in 1951 to order a fleet of Comet lA's for the *lignes primaires* to West and Equatorial Africa, with an option on four Comet 2s, and nine DH Herons to feed the Comets.

A contract for two Comet lA's was signed on 1 May 1951, a further one being ordered on 30 October.

It was a bold step for a private company to re-equip on such a scale with new types of aircraft but one that gave promise of great competitive advantage. After nearly two years of thorough technical planning and the training of selected crews and engineers the first aircraft was delivered to Paris from Hatfield on 17 December 1952. The captain was the director, M. Loubry, who subsequently carried out all the route-proving nights. The aircraft was 'baptised' at UAT's Le Bourget base on 23 December 1952, by Madame Jacqueline Auriol, daughter-in-law of the French President, who at that time held the Women's International Speed Record with a Vampire.

The second captain on the delivery flight was the

company's chief pilot, M. Jean-Pierre Villaceque. He and four other captains, including M. Tony Veillard, assistant director in charge of operations, had taken familiarisation courses on the Comet at Hatfield, and at the invitation of BOAC had accompanied crews on passenger services to Johannesburg and Singapore. Crew training was continued in France after delivery of the first aircraft, the instruction of five captains and five first officers being carried out by M. Villaceque, assisted for a time by Mr. Peter Bois of De Havilland. All pilots received a minimum of fifteen hours' instruction, and the full training syllabus was completed in each case without difficulty.

Each member of UAT's ten Comet crews, whether pilot, radio officer or engineer, was trained as a navigator, although in practice the crew-member licensed and responsible for navigation was the first officer. Two senior captains had attended the BOAC navigation school at Middlebank to study Comet navigation techniques, and afterwards undertook the training of other personnel in France.

Four radio officers trained at Hatfield and returned to instruct six others. The chief flight engineer and nine others spent 12 weeks in the Comet school and similarly undertook the instruction of other engineers on their return.

Route-proving flights totalling 90 hours to Casablanca, Dakar, Abidjan, Algiers, Marseilles, and Toulouse were carried out before the start of passenger services. During the course of these tests the Comet was granted formal certification for S.G.A.C.C. (Secretarial General a l'Aviation Civile et Commerciale) by pilots and engineers of the Centre d'Essais en Vol, and Veritas. No difficulty was experienced by UAT in the ratification by the French authorities of the ARB certificate.

A number of small improvements in design were carried out by UAT - typical of the natural French

aptitude for making life more convenient and pleasant for everyone. Pitot covers - which with jet pipe and air intake covers were always put in place a few seconds after the engines were stopped - were attached to long poles to avoid the need for steps. A public address system was fitted to each aircraft to enable the captain or the hostess to talk to the passengers in flight, and - an important item not thought of by the makers - special fittings were made to enable infants' carry-cots to be slung from the luggage racks.

When UAT inaugurated its Comet service on 19 February 1953 with the departure of F-BGSA from Le Bourget on the first of a twice-weekly return service to Dakar by way of Casablanca, the schedule - three hours to Casablanca and six hours forty minutes to Dakar - cut the then fastest times by nearly a half. On the same day the second Comet, F-BGSB, was delivered, and on 14 March an extra twice-weekly return service to Casablanca was started.

A month later, on 14 April, operations were extended to include two services a week to Abidjan, via Casablanca and Dakar. The third Comet, F-BGSC, was delivered on 30 April, and on 6 May it was possible to open a once-weekly service to Brazzaville, capital of French Equatorial Africa. At first, this route was by way of Casablanca and Abidjan; the schedule of eleven hours twenty minutes from Paris cut existing times by four hours. From 3 July the time was further reduced by an hour by re-routeing via Tripoli and Kano.

A good record of punctuality achieved by UAT was due to efficient maintenance at base and to the careful way in which operations were built up. It should be recorded that BOAC co-operated with the French company, enabling them to draw for their flight planning upon existing Comet airline experience. Fuel reserves, for example, were based

F-BGSB of UAT rests between services. *(DH Hatfield)*

upon those used by BOAC for their Comet 1s, and were strictly adhered to.

Just as with BOAC, curiosity was aroused by the first arrival of a Comet at the airports which it was to serve. At Abidjan practically the whole town went to greet the Comet's first visit on 15 April 1953. Two thousand five hundred people, Africans and Europeans, filed through the aircraft during the day, and caviare and champagne filled the tables of the Customs hall. At first fare - paying passengers were comparatively few because the seasonal peak of leave traffic was yet to come, and the first-class fare which was charged for Comet travel - 20 per cent higher than competitive tourist-rate - mitigated against the 40 or 50 per cent reduction in travel time offered.

The Comet 1A and its Ghost engines received unqualified praise from all departments of UAT -from crews, planning staffs, and engineers. The small fleet was operated with enthusiasm, and the company was confident of its revenue-earning ability. As operations of the Comet 1A built up and experience accrued, keenness to introduce the Comet 2 increased. UAT had three of these aircraft on order for delivery in 1954-55, and they intended to improve on the Comet 1A services by increasing frequencies, reduce the number of stops and to open up new world routes.

Comet 1A routes gave an indication of the improvements the Comet 2 could bring about with its better range and, in particular, better take-off performance. Direct services between Dakar and Marseilles, or Dakar and Paris were probabilities and undoubtedly Douala could be joined with Paris with one halt at Algiers. The confidence that operation of the Comet 1A gave UAT made possible an immediate expansion of operations.

American interest at last!

In the United States, aircraft operators had until then been far too engrossed in developing bigger and better piston-engined airliners to pay much attention to the Comet. They had believed, for a number of reasons, that the time was not yet ripe for jet transports; that when these were needed, their own industry could probably supply them almost overnight; and that anyway Britain was hardly likely to be able to pull such rapid construction and development out of its war-torn bag. It was not surprising that BOAC's inaugural jet service should cause more than one American airline executive to sit up and start taking a keen interest in Comet affairs, although it is doubtful even then if any of them would have been prepared to back the comparatively uneconomical Series I in the way BOAC had done.

It was BOAC's announcement that they intended to put Series 2 Comets on their South Atlantic route in less than 18 months, that finally shocked the U.S. into the realization that Britain had stolen a clear five-year lead over them in prestige travel. It was not long before Pan American and a number of other leading airlines placed orders for the Comet 3, a 'stretched' version of the Series 2, with still more powerful Rolls- Royce engines, a longer fuselage seating up to 78 passengers, and additional nacelle-like fuel tanks near the wing tips that increased the range by something like 60 per cent as compared with the Series I.

Captain Eddie Rickenbacker, president of Eastern Air Lines, after a trip in the Comet 2X development aircraft was quoted as saying *'It was all I expected— plus.'*

The American press was generous in its tribute; as the influential Christian Science Monitor put it, "*A good competitor knows how to congratulate a winner as well as how to carry off trophies himself.*' The New York Daily Mirror was brief and to the point with the headline *"Britain Out-Jets Us'*

An out-of-the-way appreciation came during a teenagers' discussion on television when a 16-year-old asked what experience she would most like if she had only 24 hours to live - she replied that a flight in the Comet was the most exciting thing she could think of. Sir Miles Thomas, who happened to be watching the programme, promptly gave orders that she should

Comet 2E G-AMXK seen at a very wet Hatfield before the application of

be given a ride during a crew- training flight!

Finally, on 20 October 1952, De Havillands were able to announce the purchase of three Comet Series 3 jet airliners by Pan American World Airways. Thus for the first time in history a British main-line transport aircraft had been chosen by an American airline operator.

'The contract just signed calls for delivery of the three Comets in 1956 and includes an option on seven additional aircraft for delivery in 1957. The advanced delivery date was made possible because Sir Miles Thomas, Chairman of the British Overseas Airways Corporation, agreed to release three of the 11 Comets Series 3 which have been earmarked for BOAC.

The historic importance of this event to the British aircraft industry becomes apparent when it is realised that not for 20 years have American operators found it necessary to go beyond their own borders for equipment. It may be recalled that 95 per cent. of all the American production of aircraft for the 1914-18 war were to de Havilland design, and that American- built D.H.4s were used to carry United States mails in the years between 1919 and 1927. Thereafter, while British air transport developed under a policy of minimum subsidies and struggled to pay for itself with specialised aircraft, American civil aviation thrived in its naturally favourable circumstances and yielded in the early 'thirties the Douglas DC-2 and a succession of fine American airliners. Just when British manufacturers were beginning to see broader

opportunities the war broke out in 1939 debarring the British industry from further civil developments. British wartime progress with jet engines opened the way for the Comet.

Now, with the advent of the Comet 3 and its forthcoming entry into the United States airline system, comes a fresh opportunity for Britain to become established in the airline markets of the world. With a payload capacity and a cruising range in tune with the expected requirements of the early 1960s and with a speed of travel and a degree of passenger comfort marking nothing less than a new era in world communications, the Comet Series 3, backed by many thousands of hours of route- operating experience with the Series 1 and 2, shows every promise of international success.

Pan American World Airways will now become the first American operator to put jet liners into service. Since before the war Juan Trippe, the President of Pan American, has been a leading advocate of the low-fare tourist- class air service. In 1948, alone among the world's airlines. Pan American instituted a tourist-class service between New York and Puerto Rico, but it was not until late in 1951 that the principle of the tourist fare was generally accepted, to go into effect internationally on May 1, 1952. Pan American's enthusiasm for tourist-class air travel emphasises the fact that the Series 1A and Series 2 Comets, seating 44 passengers, were not large enough for operation on

Below: the Comet sale to Pan American was fittingly celebrated in London on October 21 by a party to Franklin Gledhill, Pan Am vice-president, also Jackson Kelly, regional director for Western Europe, and Mr. Sturtevant, CAA representative in England. Rolls Royce, BOAC, M. of S. and SBAC joined the toast. Fourteen stayed on to dinner. L. to R. : Messrs. Lloyd, Sharp, St. Barbe, Kennedy, Burke (all of D.H.); Sir Miles Thomas, Mr. Hinkley (R R), Mr. Dunnett (M. of S) Mr. Hill (R R), Mr. Campbell Orde (BOAC); in the centre Mr. Gledhill;

Mr. Clarkson (DH); Mr. Musgrave (M. of S.); Mr. Sturtevant, Mr. Hearle (D.H. chairman), Mr. Jackson Kelly, Mr. Bowyer (SBAC), Mr. Bishop. Along with the announcement came a typical De Havilland 'artists impressions' is this picture of a Comet 3 in Pan American livery.*(DH Hatfield)*.

their system; the Comet 3, with a capacity ranging from 58 to 78 seats, allows full scope for a service combining high-density traffic with high-speed operation. The Comet's ability, by reason of its speed, to cover more miles for a given rate of utilisation increases its work capacity far above that of piston aircraft of comparable seating capacity. In a statement issued by Pan American, Juan Trippe pointed out that the Series 3, capable of carrying a full payload of passengers, mail and cargo for about 2,700 miles against a headwind of 50 m.p.h. with adequate reserves, will be the first jet transport able to operate efficiently over the principal routes of the Pan American system. Plain business reasons brought about the American purchase of the Comet and it is to be hoped that plain technical satisfaction will bring about its airworthiness certification by the USA'.

That same month Trans World Airlines chief pilot, Paul S Fredrickson, and TWA Vice-President Robert W Rummel - acting on behalf of the secretive American billionaire Howard R Hughes - visited Hatfield and Frank Lloyd, the Commercial Sales Manager.

Here they were briefed on the programme about the Comet I and 1A, the building of the Mk II, work being done on engineering the Mk III and the plans for the Mk IV. Frank Lloyd told them that the Mk IV, powered by Rolls-Royce Conway engines, would be larger and fully competitive with anything that the American market would offer in eight to ten years time.

As with many comments from the Americans, Rummel was privately dismissive and disparaging about de Havilland's efforts: *'By American standards, de Havilland's production tooling seemed meager and rudimentary. Wings were being constructed in an inefficient horizontal position over pits rather than with the wing chord (the line between the leading and trailing edges) vertical, as was customary in the States. Production was very slow. Only nine Mark 1s had been delivered. De Havilland planned to establish additional production lines at Chester and Belfast rather than expand the Hatfield facility. Frank Lloyd explained that this would make use of existing factory facilities. It was necessary to move the work to the workman rather than the opposite because of the housing shortage and the extreme reluctance of workmen to move. He said, 'They refuse to leave their homes, which in many cases have been in the family for generations."*

Rummel also raised one other point - that of certification. United States certification of the Comet was considered a major problem, for the authorities were already putting obstacles in the path of the new airliner. Lloyd said De Havilland wanted complete reciprocity to permit automatic certification in the United States without need for the aircraft design to comply with U.S. Civil Air Requirements (CAR).

While Britain and the United States had agreed to reciprocal certification during the 1944 Chicago Convention, which resulted in the formation of the International Civil Aviation Organization, the United States held the view that this was limited to piston engined powered aircraft only - because U.S. turbine aircraft certification requirements had not then been written then, and still had not been written by 1952.

Rummel expressed the view that the expectation of automatic certification was an unrealistic, and that he thought it would be more constructive for De Havilland and the British authorities to assist the Americans in establishing appropriate U.S. turbine-powered aircraft certification requirements that would have to be complied with.

'I considered the Comet program to be a superb pioneering venture that quite obviously required pressing the state of the art of airplane design in nearly all significant technology areas to achieve the barest minimum acceptable overall efficiency. In the earlier models this produced marginal structure, minimal operating weights, and borderline performance. For example, the thin fuselage skin of the Comet had been stretched during manufacturing to increase strength at the expense of ductility; every pound of empty weight was critical re payload or range; higher-thrust engines were clearly needed. The limited range, sluggish takeoff at high rotation angles, and the ability to stop after landing on slippery runways were also important concerns.

Except for the lack of reverse thrust, I did not think any one of the marginal conditions ruled the airplane out, but the combination of them gave me serious pause. I thought it likely that the anticipated march of progress could lessen or erase these concerns in succeeding models, possibly in the Mark IV, which was years away.

I had evaluated potential TWA Comet operations several times and recommended each time to Hughes that none be procured because of borderline design and performance or because of program timing with respect to the clearly superior U.S. jets. My early negative recommendations, which Howard accepted, generated considerable high-echelon TWA criticism after BOAC's initial operations proved the extreme popularity of the Comet. One TWA board member even commented, "Bob, you could have been a hero."

Two weeks later, a Comet crashed at Rome Airport.

Chapter Eight

DISASTERS - INVESTIGATION - INQUIRY

The Comet was the focus of the hopes of many in the aviation industry - it had been delivered on time and lived up to its specification. Then a series of disasters that rivalled the loss of the RMS *Titanic* struck the design – disasters that had worldwide implications.

G-ALYZ - Rome

On 26 October 1952 BOAC's G-ALYZ, operating on a London-Johannesburg flight with intermediate stops, was readied for take-off from Rome-Ciampino Airport. It was taxied to runway 16 and lined up; all pre-take-off checks were made and the elevator, aileron and rudder trim were set at the neutral position. The Captain's estimation of runway visibility was five miles but with no horizon. The flaps were lowered to 15 degrees and the windscreen wipers were operating. The engines were opened up to full power; RPMs were checked at 10,250 on all engines; fuel flows, engine temperatures and pressures were reported to be correct.

The brakes were released and the aircraft accelerated normally. At an airspeed of 75-80 knots, the nose wheel was lifted off and a slight tendency to swing to starboard was corrected. At 112 knots the aircraft lifted from the ground by a backward movement of the control column and when he considered that the aircraft had reached a safe height Captain Foote called for 'undercarriage up'. At that moment the port wing violently dropped and the aircraft swung to port; the controls gave normal

response and lateral level was regained. Foote realised that the aircraft's speed was not building up, although he made no reference to the airspeed indicator. A pronounced buffeting was felt suggesting the onset of a stall and in spite of two corrective movements of the controls, the buffeting continued. Before the First Officer had time to select undercarriage up, the aircraft came down on its main landing wheels and bounced. It was now evident that the aircraft's speed was not increasing and Foote was convinced that there was a considerable loss of engine thrust. He was also aware that the aircraft was approaching the end of the runway and so the take-off was abandoned. The undercarriage struck a mound of earth as he was closing the throttles and the aircraft slid for some 270 yards over rough ground. The main undercarriage units were wrenched off, the port wing and tailplane smashed into two of the airport's boundary lights, and the aircraft finally slid to a stop on the muddy ground. Mercifully, though fuel poured from a ruptured tank, no fire broke out and the occupants, though badly shaken, all escaped injury.

36-year-old Captain Foote was an experienced pilot. He had flown for 5,868 hours, including time as an instructor on Avro Yorks, Lancastrians and Handley Page Hermes. Now he was being criticized by both the public and his fellow pilots; for had he not injured national prestige and betrayed the Comet?

The Italian Government investigated the incident,

Above, original caption: *'The delivery of Comet G-ALYZ from Hatfield to London Airport on September 30 completed BOACs first fleet of Comets, The Corporation now has nine Series 1 aircraft to serve the routes to Johannesburg, Colombo and Singapore. During the ensuing months Comet 1As will be delivered to Canadian Pacific Air Lines, Union Aeromaritime, the Royal Canadian Air Force, and Air France.' (BAE Hatfield)* Left: Captain Harry Foote of BOAC, who was blamed for the loss of the aircraft at Rome. *(Hugh Jampton Collection)*

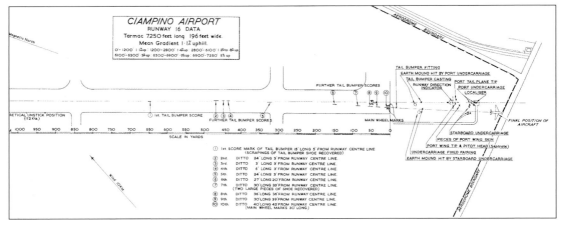

Above: A diagram from the AAIB Report CA.147, showing the sequence of events and runway contact points during the aborted take-off. *(AAIB)*
Left: G-ALYZ at the end of the runway at Rome Ciampino. The damage caused by the broken undercarriage is clearly visible. *(Hugh Jampton Collection)*

with a British accredited representative in attendance in accordance with International Law. An official enquiry by the Italian Authorities found that the tail of the Comet had made contact with the runway stretching over 650 yards in a series of scrapes, each varying from three to forty feet long.

Air Commodore Sir Vernon Brown, Chief Inspector of Accidents, wrote in his report: *'An error of judgement by the captain in not appreciating the excessive nose-up attitude of the aircraft during the takeoff'.*

The report quoted BOAC's Comet manual: *'At 80 knots the nose should be raised until the rumble of the nose wheel ceases. Care should be taken not to overdo this and adopt an exaggerated tail-down attitude with consequent poor acceleration'.*

It also quoted De Havillands, who found that rotating the aircraft through six degrees caused the wing - which had a symmetrical section aerofoil for the new high-speed cruise regime - to stall. Their tests showed that if the aircraft was tilted to nine degrees there would be a partial stalling of the wing, which would cut acceleration and bring on a low-frequency buffet - the judder that Captain Foote felt and tried to

correct; and with an eleven and a half degree tilt, the tail would hit the ground. Today this phenomenon os known as 'over-rotating'.

Foote was blamed and transferred to York freighters; a conclusion that was disputed by the British Air Line Pilots Association and the International Federation of Airline Pilots Associations.

Tests by John Cunningham established that if the nose of a Comet was raised too high while taking off, the induced drag from the high angle of attack would prevent the aircraft from accelerating to flying speed and would bring on a low frequency buffet - pilots were briefed on a revised takeoff technique, *'...the nosewheel must not be raised from the runway until a speed is attained 5 knots below the unstuck speed. The nose is then raised so that the aircraft leaves the ground at the unstuck speed'.*

1953 started badly - in January another Comet, flying from London to Johannesburg, landed short at Entebbe. Again the flaps and undercarriage were damaged. But, more serious, an airport worker was knocked down and killed.

The second major calamity came about four months after the Rome crash.

CF-CUN – Karachi

Production of Comets continued at Hatfield and by February, Comet 1A *'Empress of Hawaii'*, carrying Canadian registration CF-CUN, was ready for delivery to its new owners, Canadian Pacific Airways (CPA). A CPA delivery crew, led by Captain Charles R Pentland, the company's Director of Overseas Flight Operations, arrived at Hatfield to undergo endorsement and engineering training, with the delivery flight planned for the end of the month.

Not surprisingly many commentators over the years assumed that given the owners and aircraft's country of registration that it would be based in Canada. However, the *De Havilland Gazette* for August 1952 stated that '…the Comets for CPA, which will have accommodation for 44 passengers, are due to go into service next year on the Sydney to Honolulu section of the trans-pacific route. Based at Sydney, the Comets would fly a twice-weekly service to Honolulu, one service via Fiji and Canton Island

and another via Auckland, Fiji and Canton Island'.

This was due to Grant McConachie, CPA's CEO, who had been forced to compromise the first jet service across the Pacific due to the Comet 1A restricted range. He conceded he would have to base the jet airliner in Australia and operate it up the line as far as Honolulu to connect with the piston-powered DC-6B for the long flight to Vancouver. The *'Empress of Hawaii'*, the first of the two CPA Comets, would be ferried from England to Australia to start the service. This was not going to be a simple delivery flight - McConachie ballyhooed it as a record-setter - the Comet and CPA was to establish a new elapsed-time air record from England to Australia. The proposed flight was widely reported and many Australians looked forward to seeing their first jet airliner literally a little more than a day after its departure from England.

Alongside Captain Pentland on 3 March 1953 during the take-off for Rangoon at 03.00 hrs after a

Right: Captain Charles Pentland and the remainder of the Canadian Pacific Airways flight crew in front of the ill-fated *'Empress of Hawaii'*.

Below: CF-CUN outside the new, unfinished flight test hangar at Hatfield in early 1953 before departure on the fateful delivery flight. The '422' on the top of the fin is thought to be the CPA fleet number. *(both BAE Hatfield)*

quick refuelling stop at Karachi, Pakistan was Captain North Sawle, CPA's chief overseas pilot. Also on board was Radio Operator/Navigator Mr R J Cook, P D Roy, CPA's Chief Navigator, and J H Smith, their Chief Mechanic. There were also a number of De Havilland people on board: D H Edwards, DH Chief Liason Engineer, H Waters. senior DH Service Engineer, D Morgan-Tripp, DH Field Service, B Rees, DH Flight Engineer, J Wilson, DH Engine Field Service and N H Gardner of Smith Instruments (Australia).

Although there was a ground haze obscuring any horizon, CF-CUN was seen to assume an abnormally nose-up attitude early in the takeoff run. After using up the entire length of the runway and its overrun without becoming airborne, the Comet's undercarriage struck the culvert of a perimeter drainage ditch. The aircraft swung, lurched, and then plunged into a dry canal bed beyond the airport boundary, exploding violently into flames on impact.

The steep nose-up attitude of the aircraft would not have been visually apparent to the pilots. It was also the first night take-off in a Comet by the pilots. The aircraft was at maximum permissible take-off weight, with two pilots, plus four crew, six passengers, Comet spares, and full fuel tanks.

Contributing to the cause of the accident was Captain Pentland's very limited experience on Comets. Though a highly experienced airline pilot, he had little jet experience and had not previously attempted a night takeoff in a Comet. During his conversion course at Hatfield, John Cunningham briefed him on the Rome accident and demonstrated the revised take-off technique. It was also thought that the Comet's powered hydraulic flying controls, with no 'feel' that provided feedback to the pilot, could easily contribute to over control, especially when no external visual reference was available.

In addition, eyewitnesses who said the aircraft's nose was abnormally high for almost the whole takeoff run, marks on the runway showed that the Comet's tail bumper had come in

contact with the ground a number of times. Unlike the Rome accident, there was nothing to indicate that the crew had made any attempt to abandon the takeoff. There was evidence that the nose high attitude was corrected towards the end of the runway and the Comet was about to become airborne when the undercarriage hit the culvert.

The attempt to break the record for the flight from London to Sydney put pressure on the two-pilot crew. They were flying east, with a five-hour time difference between London and Karachi, producing jet lag, then a little known phenomenon. Fatigue was a contributory cause of the accident.

Superficially, it appeared exactly the same as the Rome incident, but there were significant differences. Captain Pentland was short on Comet experience, having flown one for less than ten hours. The *'Empress of Hawaii'* was heavier than G-ALYZ, and the night air at Karachi was hotter – and therefore thinner - than the air at Rome.

Again there was an inquiry, this time conducted by the government of Pakistan, with representatives present from Canada, the Air Investigations Branch and De Havillands with a probable cause that the '... *accident was caused by the fact that the nose of the aircraft was lifted too high during the takeoff run, resulting in a partially stalled condition and excessive drag. This did not permit normal acceleration and prevented the aircraft from becoming airborne within the prescribed distance. The pilot appears to have realised that the nose was excessively high and took corrective action, but this was done too late to prevent the aircraft striking an obstruction*

Canadian Pacific Air Lines Comet 1A CF-CUM seen at London Heathrow as the support crew are about to board just prior to departure on 2 March 1953. *(BOAC)*

immediately beyond the perimeter fence before it became airborne'.

The inquiry stated that a contributory cause was: *'...the pilot, who had only limited experience in the Comet aircraft, elected to takeoff at night at the maximum permissible takeoff for the prevailing conditions. The circumstances required strict adherence to the prescribed takeoff technique, which was not complied with'.*

For whatever reason, the lesson from the Italian incident had not been learned. It seems that a new phenomenon, determined as 'ground-stall', had been discovered in the Comet. The report was not published by the Pakistan government, which issued only a press release. Neither the Canadian nor the British government published a report, and again IFALPA disputed the findings.

The Karachi accident was a blow to both Canadian Pacific and De Havillands. The repercussions were not just limited to the Comet's future in Australia: CPA promptly cancelled orders for a further two Comets.

In an effort to understand the phenomenom of ground stall John Cunningham made numerous attempts to learn more about it by scraping the tail of CF-CUM along the runway at Hatfield.

The Comet's symmetrical aerofoil was best for Mach number and avoidance of 'pitch-down'. Leading-edge slats had been fitted to the prototype as an insurance against wing-drop, but they had made little difference to stalling speed and their mechanical complexity was dispensed with early in flight trials. With hindsight perhaps with more angle they might have prevented the ground stall.

Bishop decided to droop the aerofoil leading-edge to maintain lift should the wing find itself abused again in such a manner. The prototype was modified using wooden frames and wood screws – it worked well, with only a small penalty in cruising speed so the fitment became standard.

G-ALYV - Calcutta

On 2 May 1953 - the first anniversary of the aircraft type's inauguration of jet passenger services - Comet 1 G-ALYV, under the command of Captain Maurice W Haddon, landed at Calcutta's Dum Dum Airport for refuelling at the conclusion of the leg from Rangoon. The weather was fine, with three eighths of cumulus cloud, but it was the monsoon season and scattered cumulo-nimbus build-ups to 35,000 feet were likely. Following an in-flight message from an Indian aircraft operating to the northwest of Calcutta, an airfield weather report had been issued just before the Comet landed, warning of a thunderstorm approaching with squalls reaching 50 knots. The thunderstorm was reported to have '…very strong vertical updraughts'.

Soon after arriving from Rangoon, Captain Haddon went to the meteorological office to discuss the approaching weather and was personally briefed by the duty forecasting officer. Clearly the captain did not consider the approaching storm warranted a major diversion from track and elected to continue the flight on to Delhi as planned.

At 1620 the Comet taxied out. On board, in addition to the crew of six, were 37 passengers, most of them Britons resident in the Far East. They included the Leader of the Opposition in the Victorian State Parliament, Trevor Oldham and his wife, on their way to London to attend the Coronation of Queen Elizabeth II. Ten minutes later the aircraft lifted from Dum Dum's Runway 19 and set course to the northwest. The surface wind was south-westerly at 13 knots

Contacting Calcutta Area Control at 1632, the Comet reported that its ETA Delhi was 18.50 and was '…*climbing to 32,000 feet'*. At 16.53 the Comet was heard calling Delhi, but when Delhi's Communications officer told the Comet to go ahead with its message, there was no response. At around 16.53 workers in paddy fields near Jagalgori, some

Comet G-ALYV had been in service with BOAC for less than a year when it crashed near Calcutta.

20 miles west of Calcutta, heard a loud report during the passage of an unusually severe thunderstorm and saw '...a blaze of fire' in the sky. Pieces of aircraft wreckage, some burning, then fell to the ground over a wide area.

Ground and air searches were launched and the following morning a BOAC York - by an ironic coincidence flown by Captain Harry Foote, who had been involved in the earlier Rome accident - was the first to spot the missing aircraft. The wreckage lay scattered over eight square miles, and villagers told of having seeing a wingless machine coming down in a blaze of fire through severe thunderstorms and rain. The main wreckage, consisting of the forward fuselage, stub wings and engines, were found lying inverted in a watercourse about 24 miles from Dum Dum Airport and right on the aircraft's planned track. The rear fuselage lay in paddy fields 250 yards away, and a wreckage trail of smaller components extended for nearly five miles in a south-westerly direction. It was clear that the aircraft had disintegrated in the air, the separated tailplane exhibiting evidence of having failed under excessive downloading.

The Indian Government set up an inquiry, conducted by Shri Ram Malhotra, the Indian Inspector of Accidents. The UK ARB representative was T R 'Bob' Nelson, who had also represented UK interests at the previous two incidents, assisted in Calcutta by Jimmy Lett. The investigation was upgraded to a public inquiry conducted by N S Lokur, an Indian High Court judge. K M Raha, Director-General of Civil Aviation, Engineer N Shrinivasen and Bob Nelson were appointed technical assessors. This time, the findings of the public inquiry were published in India and in England.

The remains were collected and sent back to England for detailed examination by the Royal Aircraft Establishment (RAE) at Farnborough. Run by the Ministry of Supply, this organization has long served as the centre of British aviation research and development; and here, in a special hangar set aside for the purpose, a group of the country's leading technicians began the task of examination and reconstruction.

Study of the wreckage by ARB and RAE specialists established that the tailplane had failed through excessive downloading, probably caused by the combination of a severe gust load and a heavy manoeuvring load. The thousands of pieces of wreckage were identified and laid out on trestles on the floor in their correct relative positions, every one having been labelled and plotted on a huge chart showing the way it had probably fallen, taking into account the height and wind, and the speed of descent of each fragment according to its shape. From this laborious process and from an analysis of all the scratches, dents and the various blistered paint and smoke marks, the scientists were able to deduce the order in which the parts had broken away, gradually tracing the process of destruction back to its source to see if there was any inherent weakness in the design. They found none. They did, however, discover that the port elevator spar had failed due to excessive loading.

The Indian report detailed the condition of all major components and pieces among the wreckage. The undercarriage and flaps were retracted; the throttle levers were broken and jammed in the half-open position; fuel cocks were on; the flying-control system change-over levers were in their normal position; elevator and aileron trim was normal; the cabin was being pressurized; the fire extinguishers had not been operated, nor was there any evidence of any emergency procedures.

Some extracts from the statement of damage revealed that both outer wings had failed at a station outboard of rib No. 7, and both tail planes had suffered impact damage in the air. There was no structural damage to the fin panels. The lower fin and

Two pictures showing the shattered remains of G-ALYV that crashed not far from Calcutta Dum Dum Airport on 2 May 1953. The upper picture shows the rear pressure dome and part of the tail structure that was severely damaged by fire.

rudder had suffered extensive impact damage, the port elevator had been cut in two pieces, and the spar showed bending failure at a station in between No. 3 and No. 4 hinge brackets. It indicated a compression failure on the top flange and a tension failure at the bottom, due to downloads. The starboard elevator spar had failed in bending, significantly at the same point as on the port elevator.

The deduction of Shri N. Srinivasan from the design department of Hindustan Aircraft Ltd contained the following passages:

'A close examination of the spar in either elevator shows a bending failure at a station in between the No. 2 and No. 3 outboard hinges. It is a download bending with compression at the top flange and tension at the bottom. It is significant that this failure is of a localized nature with no damage over the surrounding area either in the tailplane or elevator skin, in spite of the subsequent impact damage observed on other portions of the structure. This elevator down-load failure may have been due to a 'pull-up.' The download on the tail-unit seems to have caused a fuselage failure in bending at bulkhead No. 26. The top panels have failed in tension and the bottom panel in compression.

'It is understood during the investigation that the wing was subjected to a static test by the manufacturing firm during the development stage of the aircraft. On one test-piece static and fatigue tests were conducted alternately. The wing failed in fatigue test and after modifications was subjected to a static test. The wing failed again at 90 per cent of the ultimate load. The failure was attributed to the fatigue test conducted before. Modifications were carried out again, and without a re-test, it was found satisfactory for the ultimate load on theoretical considerations. The fatigue failure during static test occurred at Rib No. 7 where the cross-section changes from two heavy spars to an outboard shell construction. In this accident, again the wings have significantly failed at Rib 7. Whatever the load may be the failure at Rib 7 may indicate the lack of proper diffusion of the wing loads on to the two spars at Rib 7. In the absence of design data, no definite comments can be made on the wing failure, but a further investigation on the above subject of load transfer at Rib 7 will be helpful.

'It is extremely difficult during this short period of investigation with limited facilities and data to substantiate the primary failure with all details, but there are strong indications on the wreckage to suggest the primary failure of the elevator during a 'pull-up.' The Comet has got an elevator control system operated with booster power with no feed-back arrangement for pilot feel. It is quite probable

that the pilot, who is accustomed to a sort of 'feel' on the controls during manoeuvres, had over-controlled the aircraft beyond the limit that would impose the design loads on the aircraft'.

The report concluded that the probable cause was *'Structural failure of the airframe during flight through a thunder squall. In the opinion of the Court, the structural failure was due to overstressing which resulted from either:- (1) Severe gusts encountered, or (2) Over-controlling or loss of control by the pilot when flying through the thunderstorm'.*

The Court's report was released simultaneously in New Delhi and London in December, followed by a joint statement by De Havillands and BOAC, saying that until expert tests decided what part of the aircraft actually had failed, it was not possible to do more than theorise. The statement dismissed as unlikely the suggestion that over-control or loss of control by the pilot caused the accident.

Meanwhile, another Comet - G-ALVG - was undergoing a full-scale programme of fatigue tests for general research purposes. Metal fatigue, long regarded as merely an interesting subject for academic study, had suddenly assumed a major significance in the light of one or two recent accidents, and the problem had begun to receive priority attention on both sides of the Atlantic.

Fatigue occurs in any metal that is repeatedly subjected to stress. A piece of wire such as a paperclip, for example, will snap if it is bent backwards and forwards often enough and sharply enough, the metal 'remembering' how many times it has been strained, until quite suddenly it loses resilience and fails. On an aircraft, the most critical component is usually the wing, which flexes up and down in flight as it meets the wind gusts, alternately stretching and compressing its surface skin and supporting structure until eventually - if it flies for long enough - a fatigue failure of some part will probably occur. Thus, although a structure may stand one application of a load quite satisfactorily, or even many thousands, it may not stand many millions of applications, and break under a load it could easily have withstood when new. The time taken to reach this dangerous condition is known as the 'fatigue life' which must nowadays be measured on all new transport aircraft so that they may be withdrawn from service when their 'safe life' - set at a much lower number of hours - has expired.

Other incidents

Meanwhile Comet services with BOAC and UAT continued as usual. The aircraft had flown more than 7,000,000 miles in service and the accidents that it

The immedate aftermath of the G-ALYR's taxi-incident in Calcutta.

had suffered were no more than had been experienced by many other well-known but less highly publicized British and American airliners during their introduction into service. Then, on 23 June 1953 Comet 1A F-BGSC of UAT, operating a scheduled passenger flight into Dakar-Yoff airport, overshot the runway and crossed a wide, sandy culvert. As a result it came to rest 120 feet later with a sheared off undercarriage. None of the passengers was injured.

A month later, on 25 July, BOAC's G-ALYR was attempting to taxi at Calcutta. Because taxi lights were too dim to use at night, the crew had to use the landing lights while taxiing. Both lights had to be alternated left and right to avoid a meltdown by using a switch behind the captains seat. In a left hand turn the captain took his left hand off the steering wheel to select another landing light. The steering centred, and the right wheel bogies ran off the paved surface. Engine power was applied on the two right engines, causing the bogie struts to be forced up and into the wing structure, causing much damage.

By the end of 1953 De Havilland had delivered all 21 Comet Is and 1As - nine of them to BOAC, three to Air France, and nine to other airlines. There were 35 Comet 2s on order, of which BOAC were expecting to take delivery of twelve in 1954; and eleven long-range Comet 3s had been ordered - five by BOAC, three by Pan American, and two by Air India. As 1953 closed, jet propulsion had been firmly established in the world, by one aircraft only, the Comet, of which there was an accumulated experience exceeding 30,000 hours. The Comets were then flying 177,000 miles a week.

It was shortly before Christmas that the first tiny cracks began to appear in the wing structure of 'VG, which by this time had 'flown' the equivalent of some 6,000 hours on its test rig at Farnborough. Although this was well in advance of the life reached by their leading aircraft, BOAC lost no time in putting into action a regular inspection procedure, so as to be sure of spotting the defect in their own machines the moment it showed up. But the question of whether the Comets should be taken progressively out of service for wing modifications never had to be answered, for it was overtaken by a calamity that led to the withdrawal of the entire fleet.

After it's taxi-accident in Calcutta, G-ALYR was shipped back to the UK and is seen here partially dismantled and partially cocooned at London Airport in the mid-1950s.

G-ALYP - Elba

Tragedy struck again on 10 January 1954. Comet G-ALYP left Rome-Ciampino Airport at 09.31 UTC on a flight to London from Singapore under the command of Captain Alan Gibson DFC using the callsign Speedbird 781. Gibson was regarded as such a good Comet man within BOAC that he had been listed to become an instructor. After taking off, the aircraft was in touch with Ciampino control tower by radio and from time to time reported its position.

It was a calm winter's morning, with only thin, broken layers of middle level cloud which the Comet quickly surmounted as it climbed towards its cruising altitude. Tracking via the Ostia NDB on Italy's west coast, thence north-west up the coast, the Comet reported passing through 26,000 feet over Orbetello, 44 nautical miles south east of the island of Elba, at 09.50. A minute later, Captain Gibson called Captain J Johnson, the pilot in command of BOAC Argonaut G-ALHJ, which had taken off from Rome 10 minutes ahead of the Comet, apparently to enquire about an in-flight weather report he had transmitted a few minutes before. *'George How Jig from George Yoke Peter did you get my…'* and then broke off. At that time, approximately 09.51, the aircraft was probably approaching a height of 27,000 feet.

The transmission cut off in mid-sentence and down below, fishermen stopped hauling their nets to look up as a series of shattering explosions echoed across the sky. Then they saw aircraft wreckage, some of which was on fire and streaming smoke, spiral down into the sea, midway between Elba and the smaller island of Montecristo, sixteen nautical miles to the south.

The alarm was given throughout Elba. It reached Colonel Giuseppe Lombardi, the Harbour Master of Portoferraio on the northern shore of the island. He alerted the Italian mainland authorities, and search aircraft were ordered out. He also alerted the island's fishermen, and soon a small armada sailed towards the wreckage. The Colonel was the last to leave, but he had taken over a fast motor-boat and soon was leading the search.

It was 16.20, more than five hours after the crash, when the trawler *Francesco Guiseppe* lifted the first of the dead from the water. In all, 15 bodies were recovered, nearly all half-naked, and the severity of their injuries was plain to see. Nets were spread, and they snared the flotsam of disaster. As darkness fell the vessels returned to Porto Azzurro, where the fishermen laid the bodies to rest in a chapel.

In London, Sir Miles Thomas, Chairman of BOAC, hurried from his home in Virginia Water to London Airport. There he held almost non-stop conferences, first with Captain Johnson of the Argonaut, and then presided over a conference attended by Sir Victor Tait, BOAC Operations Director; Ronald E Bishop, chief designer and a director of De Havilland Aircraft Company; Mr R E Hardingham, chief executive of the Air Registration Board; Captain M J R Alderson, manager of the BOAC Comet fleet; Captain G S Brown, head of the corporation's accidents investigation department. At midnight on 11 January Sir Miles suspended Comet services. French airlines immediately followed suit.

The official BOAC announcement said: *'As a measure of prudence the normal Comet passenger services are being temporarily suspended to enable minute and unhurried technical examination of every aircraft in the Comet fleet to be carried out at London Airport. Sir Miles Thomas has decided to devote himself almost exclusively to probing the Comet mishap, with Sir Geoffrey de Havilland and the highest authorities in Britain. His decision is based on a desire to retain the good name of the Comet.'*

BOAC issued a full casualty list: at Singapore, J.P. Hill, J. Steel boarded. At Bangkok F.J. Greenhouse, R. Sawyer-Snelling (14), Captain R.V. Wolfson boarded. At Rangoon Chester Wilmot boarded. At Karachi Mrs D. Baker, Miss E. Fairbrother, T. Moore, H.E. Schuchmann boarded. At Bahrain Mr and Mrs J.M. Bunyan and child, B. Butler, J.B. Crilly, B. Crilly (believed a child) boarded, In Israel Miss R. Khedouri (13), Miss N. Khedouri (15), Miss L. Yateem (17) boarded. At Beirut Mrs R.E. Gerald, Master M. Geldard, Miss C. Geldard, A.D. Leavat, S.F. Naamin, E.S. MacLachlan, J.V. or J.Y. Ramsden, A. Vrisa boarded. Finally, at Rome Captain C.A. Livingstone boarded. The crew were Captain Alan Gibson DFC. (31), First Officer William J. Bury,(33) Engineer Officer Francis C. McDonald, (27) Radio Officer Luke P. McMahon, (32) Steward Frank L. Saunders, Stewardess Jean Evelyn Clark.

It was not long before Sir Miles addressed himself to a theory which, in the early days, was widely suspected: sabotage. Rumours abounded that explosives might have been put on board the aircraft, either at Rome or Beirut. The UK Government also considered sabotage. A week after the disaster, Alan Lennox-Boyd, Minister for Transport and Civil Aviation, took off for Rome to interview the people on the spot. In the two days he was away, he took a ferry to Elba to attend the funeral service for the victims. Returning to London Airport, he made a quick comment to the waiting press before going straight to the House of Commons. He was joined there by the Prime Minister, Sir Winston Churchill.

The unique position of the Comet at the cutting edge of airline equipment was shown as much by the

G-ALYP - the aircraft that disappeared off Elba on 10th January 1954 - it had previously suffered a heavy landing in August 1952.

restrained way in which the world press dealt with the disaster, as by the widespread publicity it attracted. Many other theories were advanced as to its cause, including turbine wheel fracture, and clear air turbulence. Some wondered if the Comet had broken up in a jetstream - one of the invisible currents of upper air that move at very high speeds relative to the surrounding atmosphere and which could impose destructive loads on an aircraft crossing it. It must be remembered that the Comet was the first of its kind and even as recently as 1954, little was known about stratospheric weather conditions.

For weeks the remaining seven aircraft in BOAC's Comet fleet were checked. Some were specifically examined for signs of structural trouble - not the basic weakness that the Farnborough experts had been looking for, but faults which might have developed in service; others for the functioning of their electrical, hydraulic and control systems, in addition to a detailed study of their general condition.

G-ALYP was exactly three years old the day before the accident and had flown a total of only 3681 hours - about 1200 flights. Fatigue testing by De Havilland's during the development of the Comet up to twice the cabin's designed operating pressure differential of 8.25 pounds per inch had shown the fatigue life of the pressure cabin to be of the order of at least 18,000 flights.

A group of specialists, which became known as the Abell Committee after Charles Abell, the Deputy Operations Director of BOAC in charge of engineering - decided that fifty modifications must be made. Many were routine improvements which would have been made anyway at the next opportunity. Others, such as the fitting of armoured shields between the turbines and the fuel tanks, were made because it was thought better to be over-cautious rather than run the slightest known risk of any further trouble. Comets re-entered service on 23 March. It was all that could be done, for no one had any idea of what had gone wrong with YP. But

confidence returned and the Corporation, which was losing £50,000 a week on its Comets, prepared to send them into the air again.

The first aircraft took off from London nearly nine weeks after services were suspended. It was bound for Johannesburg with 34 passengers - only two short of a full load, for accident had not made the British public afraid of Comets. The BBC's television cameras was at the airport for the take-off. So were dozens of Press photographers - and four policemen.

It seems that the sabotage theory - even if it did not convince the specialists - had won a victory to allay fears. As Captain Peter Cane lifted the aircraft into the air, hopes of the nation, as well as BOAC, were high. Sir Miles Thomas told reporters: '...*the Comet's all right.*'

The Italians set up a board of inquiry, with an air force general, two colonels, and two majors. Bob Nelson was again appointed UK accredited representative and a meeting was held on 11 January in the conference room at the Italian Ministry of Defence.

The meeting began with the General expressing his condolences to the relatives of those killed, and also to BOAC and the British government. He then outlined the circumstances of the accident, the search and the recovery of floating wreckage, including the corpses, ten miles south of the coast of Elba.

This caused Bob Nelson to raise the point that the accident had occurred 'over the high seas' so, the responsibility for conducting the investigation, in accordance with international law, rested with the United Kingdom as the state of registry. The General consulted his board members and then announced an adjournment to consider the point.

After about an hour the board re-convened and the General announced that the question of territorial waters was to be settled by higher authority. Evidence was collected about the departure of the aircraft from Rome, air traffic reports of the short flight, emergency procedures etc. On Elba they inspected the recovered flotsam which Bertram Morris took over for detailed inspection.

Eyewitnesses were interviewed and post mortem examinations were made on the recovered bodies, the Italian pathologists making a careful search for any metallic fragments that might be embedded in the bodies from the reported explosion. None was found, indicating that explosive decompression of the pressurised cabin had probably occurred.

One of the important early reports came from Professor Antonio Fornari, assistant to the Director of the Institute of Forensic Medicine, University of Pisa. His findings were added to later by Dr. D. Teare, the London pathologist, who examined four of the 'YP victims at Uxbridge mortuary four days after they were killed. He had hurried to Elba as soon as the alert was given on the crash, and at Porto Azzurro made a post mortem on 15 of the 35 victims. Death was no stranger to the Professor, but on Elba he found something unique. *'I have made an examination of the hearts of a very great number of people who have died in the most extraordinary circumstances, but I have never come across anything like this before.'* The Professor submitted that death came quickly *'… By violent movement and explosive decompression'*

He found that most of the victims fractured their skulls in life - that is to say a fraction of a second before they died. He considered that they hit their heads suddenly against either the sides or roof of the cabin. Their lungs were damaged. They also had severe rib injuries in nearly all cases. The victims also suffered a second series of injuries which included broken limbs and severe internal damage. None died by drowning - they were all dead before they struck the water. He noted that all had disturbed clothing. Some had lost only a shoe, whereas others were nearly naked.

Some discoveries were puzzling. A few of the deceased had limbs torn away, although their end was obviously violent. None of them showed signs of having been in a fire in the air, although witnesses saw at least part of the Comet falling in flames. But on all but one of the bodies the Professor found signs of skin damage caused by scalding. On thirteen of them, these marks were on the back; on one, the marks were on the chest and abdomen. Three had these marks on their faces. This damage, he decided, after microscopic examination, was received after death; and most of it was on parts covered by clothing. The clothes in these areas carried a strange yellowish stain.

Professor Fornari and Dr. Teare's reports posed several problems: What caused the fractured skulls? What had torn their lungs so badly? What caused the internal injuries and broken limbs? Why were clothes missing? And what was the cause of two completely different types of burns?

The specialists theorized that something must have happened suddenly inside the cabin, either to throw the passengers forward hard against backs of seats in front of them, or catapult them up to the roof. At the same time the pressurization must have instantly failed so as to damage the lungs.

Recovery

On returning to Rome Bob Nelson telephoned the Chief Inspector of Accidents, Gp Capt Tweedie. Recovery of the wreckage, scattered over the seabed in water around 500ft deep, was essential.

The Minister of Transport and Civil Aviation Alan Lennox-Boyd took immediate action. He sought and was granted assistance by the Royal Navy from Malta to help with the wreckage. The Admiralty in London signalled Admiral Lord Louis Mountbatten, Commander-in-Chief of the Mediterranean, in Malta: 'Endeavour to locate and

The funeral ceremony at Porto Azzuro on Elba for the bodies recovered from G-AYLP.

salve crashed Comet.' The difficulties were immense, but Lord Mountbatten mobilized his ships at top speed. The first ship ordered into the hunt was the fast anti-submarine frigate HMS *Wrangler,* equipped with the most modern devices afloat at the time for plumbing the depths of the sea. *Wrangler's* commander, Captain C. Morris Parry CVO CBE, arrived at Elba within a week of the crash and was placed in charge of 'Operation Elba Isle'.

On arrival he met with one piece of good fortune - Colonel Lombardi, who organized the initial hunt for the bodies of the Comet victims. After the initial search all Lombardi's work was aimed at solving this single problem - where exactly did the aircraft go into the sea?

Colonel Lombardi talked to everyone who saw the tragedy. First he questioned the fishermen who sailed with him to recover the fifteen bodies from the sea. Together they worked out that Elba's Calamity Point was north-north-east of the spot where they found the dead. And it took them two hours to sail back to Porto Azzurro. Their boats did about six knots, so, on simple reckoning, Colonel Lombardi was able to put the first of many crosses on a chart. He marked that cross thirteen and a quarter miles from Porto Azzurro. Then he questioned everyone on Elba's shore who saw anything of the crash. He took them to the spot where they had been standing and

got them to point where they thought they saw the aircraft go in. He took a compass reading of the direction their arms pointed, and plotted those lines on his chart, too. He visited witnesses on the Italian mainland; he heard that an old man on the island of Pianosa, south-west of Elba, and a teenage girl on tiny MontiCristo, an island due south of Elba, both had seen the Comet come down. At the end his chart was covered with crosses.

It was this chart that Colonel Lombardi unrolled before Captain Parry aboard *Wrangler.* They inspected it together, Captain Parry questioning, Colonel Lombardi answering. When they finished Captain Parry had something to work on - an area of about one hundred square miles. Somewhere inside that square were the remaining bits of the Comet.

Wrangler set sail to find them, and as he steamed out of Porto Azzurro, Captain Parry said: 'I don't know how long it will take. But we are going to stay until the Comet is found, or until the Admiralty is convinced there is no hope of finding it.' It was ten days since the Comet crashed. *Wrangler* was not operating alone. A fleet of five local trawlers had been contracted and the Navy's *Sursay,* a Danlayer vessel of 545 tons. A danlayer was a small trawler assigned to minesweeping flotillas fitted for the purpose of laying dans. A dan was a marker buoy which consisted of a long pole moored to the seabed and

Right: the Danlayer *Sursay,* (M427).

Below: *Wrangler* (R48) was an W-class destroyer of the British Royal Navy that saw service during World War Two. The vessel was later converted into a Type 15 fast anti-submarine frigate, with the new pennant number F157. *(both Rusell Plummer Collection)*

fitted to float vertically, with a coded flag at the top.

Captain Parry worked out a procedure which was above all else monotonous, but which held the only hope of success. The only method of doing that was to sweep up and down the search area in lanes, one after another, until the one hundred square miles of sea had been sounded. This technique today is known after the patterns the lanes make – 'mowing the lawn'. *Wrangler* and the trawlers made these sweeps, while *Sursay* stayed at one end of the lanes, marking the right line.

The trawlers dragged wires along the sea bed, hoping to snag something. Aboard the *Wrangler* the hunt was more scientific. It centred round the room housing the asdic apparatus. ASDIC - an acronym from A(nti-) S(ubmarine) D(etection) I(nvestigation) C(ommittee) – is a measuring instrument that sends out an acoustic pulse in water and measures distances in terms of the time for the echo of the pulse to return. The Americans called the same device SONAR from SO(und) NA(vigation) R(anging).

Captain Parry ordered his crew to stand one-hour watches, so that their senses remained fully alert. Three of the ratings in these crews - Able Seamen John Worsey, Edward Saxton and Trevor Thomas - knew well the strain of such tense jobs. Advised by aviation specialists, and given the equipment of the day, the operators did not expect to find any piece of the Comet much bigger than thirty square feet. The first things located - mainly by the trawlers - were of the smallest; passenger seating cards, an overnight bag, a pair of children's shoes, and items of lingerie. *Wrangler* was getting plenty of targets located on her ASDIC, each of which was marked on charts. If a series of targets were located close together, *Sursay* marked it with a marker buoy. Those chart marks and sea flags sign-posted the places for the salvage ships preparing to depart Malta.

The main salvage vessel was the 1,440 ton RFA *Sea Salvor*, and its first assistant was the *Barhill*, a 750-ton boom defence vessel. In Valetta Harbour they took aboard all the paraphernalia of salvage: wire mooring lines, ropes, buoys and shackles. *Sea Salvor* stowed on her deck the two most important instruments of all—an underwater television camera and a diver's deep-sea observation chamber. Also prepared was a steel grab with ten foot jaws, which would clutch any pieces found from the sea bed. *Sea Salvor* and *Barhill* reached Elba only fifteen days after the tragedy.

Commander Gerald Forsberg RN (some sources say Charles) was the Mediterranean Fleet's Boom Defence and Salvage Officer. The Navy had ships and manpower, but no foreign currency - in 1954 British Exchange Controls were still in force. Bob Nelson was given an imprest account of £5,000 to help cover the cost of local expenses on the salvage before joining Bertram Morris in Porto Azzurro.

'There was no bank in Porto Azzurro, so Bertram and I went over to Portoferraio to collect some cash from my imprest account. We travelled back to Porto Azzurro by taxi (through bandit country!), carrying

Above: the television camera inside a sealed container is lowered over the side of *Sea Salvor*. The rig was equipped with floodlights and a power supply.

Left: RFA *Sea Salvor* (A503). She was launched on 22 April 1943 and remained in service until April 1971 when it was broken up. *(Rusell Plummer Collection).*

A couple of stills taken from a 16mm film taken as a diver climbs into the Observation Chamber about to be lowered onto the wreck site from RFA *Sea Salvor*.

several million lire in cash — banknotes so big that we could have used them as wallpaper.'

The trawlers set to work under Navy control. The salvage operation went on; the wreckage, as it was recovered, was air-freighted to Farnborough for detailed examination.

By 23 January 1954 HMS *Wrangler* was acting as Headquarters Ship when *Barhill, Brigand* and *Sursay* joined forces at the scene. *Striker, Wakeful* and *Whirlwind* arrived later.

Other salvage specialists came to the scene including Captain J B Pollard from Risdon Beazley Ltd and a member of the Admiralty Research Laboratory with underwater television cameras. In addition members of the Italian Navy assisted, including Lt Col Lombardi, Port Commandant of Elba and Commander Todaro.

Wrangler was relieved by *Wakeful,* with Captain Parry being replaced by Captain C W McMullen DSC and it was the latter vessel which, on 12 February, reported that a piece of Comet wreckage had been sighted by television despite high winds and rough seas.

As well as television, *Sea Salvor* carried an oxygen-fed observation chamber in which a man

could be lowered. Mooring in exactly the required position, and retaining that position, was one of the problems. Cmdr Forsberg: *"When salving the ship would have to moor securely with at least six wires leading in different directions. The Italians, who have become rather expert in deep-sea salvage, use eight mooring wires at forty-five degree spacing'*.

'Naturally, the television camera - or the observation chamber - needed another one of each. Likewise a heavy weight must be lowered into the vision of camera or chamber for otherwise, the observer cannot ascertain the direction into which he is looking. That makes eight cables in the water so far! Then there is two more for the grab and one for the derrick topping-lift'.

'As it happened, we were lucky. There was thrill after thrill - sighting after sighting. The only annoying thing was that really big pieces seemed non-existent: The bottom looked as though someone had up-ended a waste-paper basket. Therefore, we did not lay out our moorings immediately; for had we done so it would have meant either playing hide-and-seek round our own anchors and cables, or simply stopping further search for a quarter-mile or so all round us.'

More stills taken from the film of the salvage operation.

G-ALYY - Naples

It was not long before disaster struck again - Comet G-ALYY was leased to South African Airways by BOAC. It was flown by SAA crews between Johannesburg and London with several intermediate stops. The aircraft had been grounded in January 1954 following the in-flight structural breakup of G-ALYP. Special checks were carried out and a number of modifications were made affecting the airframe, the controls and the fire detection and protection at the engines. On 15 February 1954, the fuselage was subjected to a proving test to 11lb/sq. in. The aircraft returned to service on 24 February.

G-ALYY arrived at Rome-Ciampino on 7 April from London and was due to depart the same evening. However, on completion of refuelling it was discovered that the centre tank contents gauge showed no reading although the tank was full. The fault was traced to a co-axial cable for which a replacement had to be flown from England and the departure of the aircraft was consequently delayed for 24 hours. However, there was another reason for this delay - an engineer, investigating the fuel system fault, found 22 quarter-inch bolts rolling about in the port wing. They were from a removable panel that had been taken off at London Airport nine days earlier and not put back properly. A further 30 bolts were not done up tightly.

SAA Flight 201 departed Rome in the hands of Captain Wilhelm K Mostert at 18.32 UTC. Alongside him was First Officer Barent J. Grove, who had been married in London a few days earlier. The other crew were Navigation Officer Albert E. Sissing, Radio Officer Bertram E. Webbstock, Flight Engineer Officer August R. Lagesen, Air Hostess Pamela Reitz and Steward Jacobus B. Kok. In the cabin were fourteen passengers; Mr O. L. Anderson, Mr & Mrs A. B. Brooks, Miss D. M. Eady, Mr F. H. Harbison, Mr M. A. Lamloum, Dr J. Staurt, Mr R. L. Wilkinson, Miss N. Young, Capt.

J. A. Collings, Mr J. F. Murray-White, Mr E. S. Hack, Mr J. Rosenburg and Mr Salzman.

G-ALYY climbed through three layers of cloud. After taking off the aircraft from time to time gave its position to Rome ATC and at about 18.57 reported that it was abeam Naples and climbing to 35,000 ft. At 19.05 Cairo received a signal from the aircraft reporting its departure from Rome and giving its estimated time of arrival at Cairo. No further message was received from G-ALYY. The aircraft crashed off the coast of Sicily, near the island of Stromboli.

As in the case of the accident to 'YP, the assistance of the Royal Navy was invoked and on the 9 April, HMS *Eagle* and HMS *Daring* proceeded to search for 'YY. Avenger aircraft from HMS *Eagle* were used to assist in the search as were a number United States aircraft. Six bodies as well as some aircraft seats and other wreckage were identified in the water and later recovered. The depth of water at the site varied between 520 and 580 fathoms and the evidence established that at that depth the prospect of further recovery was hopeless.

There were similarities between accidents - both occurred at about the same altitude; and both aircraft had about the same airframe life. The coincidence was too obvious to ignore, and the British Certificate of Airworthiness was withdrawn on 12 April.

A reappraisal of the entire structural integrity of the Comet was made. Within days all the aircraft had been ferried back to London Airport by volunteer crews, flying in short stages and light weights, keeping below 20,000ft. Two were immediately turned over to De Havilland Hatfield for examination and three more joined 'VG at the RAE, whose scientists had been asked to give absolute priority over all other work to solve the Comet mystery.

On 24 April, the C in C Mediterranean, Lord Mountbatten of Burma, issued high praise for the efforts in a Special Order of the Day: *'The skill, initiative and tenacity of purpose displayed by all in*

G-ALYY in predominently BOAC markings, but with the South African Airways 'Springbok' emblem on the nose and tail. The aircraft is believed parked on the north side of London Heathrow airport.

Office of the Commander-in-Chief,
Mediterranean,
Malta.
24th April, 1954

Special Order of The Day

Shortly after leaving Rome on 10th January 1954, Comet YP crashed into the sea south of Elba; and six days later I was ordered to locate and salve it. For this it was initially decided to use an A/S frigate, which could also act as headquarters ship, a salvage ship, a boom defence vessel and a dan layer.

2. On 20th January 1954, Captain C. M. Parry, c.v.o., o.b.e., Commanding the 5th Frigate Squadron, arrived in H.M.S. Wrangler at Elba to take charge of operations. The first requirement was to attempt to establish the area of wreckage by investigation and analysis of the many and conflicting eye-witness accounts. By 23rd January 1954, H.M.S. Wrangler had been joined by H.M.S. Sursay (Lieutenant-Commander H. Stern), H.M.S. Barhill (Lieutenant S. C. Smith) and R.F.A. Sea Salvor (Captain J. Hayward). In charge of the boom defence and salvage vessels was Commander C. G. Forsberg, Boom Defence and Salvage Officer, Mediterranean; Mr V. Campbell, M.B.E., Senior Admiralty Salvage Officer, Malta was in H.M.S. Barhill. On board R.F.A. Sea Salvor were Captain J. B. Pollard of Messrs. Risdon Beazley, a salvage expert, and Mr. G. Macniece, who had been flown out from the Admiralty Research Laboratory with an underwater television camera. Later Lieutenant-Commander M. G. Fowke, the Captain of H.M.S. Chameleon, was sent to Elba while his ship was refitting at Malta, in order to take charge of Italian trawlers which were chartered to assist in the search.

3. Having analysed the information available A/S search was started and the trawlers began to sweep the area. When an object was detected by asdic or a trawler sweep engaged an obstruction the position was marked by danbuoy. H.M.S. Barhill then laid moorings so that R.F.A. Sea Salvor could identify the object concerned with the underwater T/V camera and the observation chamber, and lift it if it was found to be part of the aircraft. Operations were hampered by bad weather; made difficult by the depth of water sometimes up to 600 feet; and complicated by the fact that the water being disturbed reduced the visibility at this depth to about 10 feet and that wreckage was spread over a very large area.

4. On 4th February 1954, H.M.S. Wrangler was relieved by H.M.S. Wakeful (Commander J. G. B. Morrow, D.S.C.) with Captain C. W. McMullen, D.S.C., Commanding the Mediterranean Minesweepers, on board. The latter assumed command of the operations until 13th March 1954, when the duties of Senior Officer (Salvage) Elba were assumed by Commander Forsberg until completion of operations. H.M.S. Wakeful was fitted with a second T/V camera which had been sent out from England by Messrs. Pye, Limited. On 12th February 1954, H.M. Tug Brigand (Lieutenant-Commander E. Turner, D.S.C.) arrived to assist. On 22nd February 1954, H.M.S. Whirlwind (Commander A. R. Evans) relieved H.M.S. Wakeful; and on 25th March 1954, the former was relieved by H.M.S. Striker (Commander C. T. B. Tibbits). H.M. Tug Brigand sailed for Malta on 2nd March 1954, with some pieces of recovered wreckage on board; and H.M.S. Sursay sailed on 4th March 1954.

5. Operations continued with small pieces of wreckage being recovered daily until 15th March 1954, when a large section of the front of the aircraft and part of the wings were recovered and two engines sighted. By 19th March 1954, all four engines had been recovered and on 24th March 1954, H.M.S. Whirlwind sailed with them for Gibraltar. By 9th April 1954, over 80 per cent of the aircraft had been recovered and R.F.A. Sea Salvor and H.M.S. Barhill sailed for Malta after 11 weeks at Elba. The remainder of the wreckage which included the tail unit, was left to trawlers to recover. In this operation the Royal Navy was greatly assisted by Lieutenant-Colonel Lombardi, Port Commandant at Elba, by Commander Todaro (late Italian Navy) as Second-in-Command of the trawlers, and by local Italian trawler captains whose willingness and skill were major contributions to the success of the operations. The British salvage firm Risdon Beazley were also of the greatest help. Representatives of the Ministry of Transport and Civil Aviation, including Mr. Newton, of the Accident Investigation Department, were present throughout the operations.

6. The skill, initiative and tenacity of purpose displayed by all concerned in the operation were most praise-worthy; they were faced with locating many pieces of wreckage, mostly fairly small, scattered over a very large area in a considerable depth of water; and although they met with many disappointments in the first weeks of the operation all showed unflagging zeal and determination in their efforts to locate and salvage the wreckage. In these circumstances the efficiency with which such a large part of the aircraft was located and recovered in what was a comparatively short period reflects the greatest credit on all concerned.

Mountbatten of Burma

Lord Louis Mountbatten's Special order of the Day praising all those involved in the recovery of Comet YP.

the operation were most praiseworthy; they were faced with locating many pieces of wreckage, mostly fairly small, scattered over a very large area in a considerable depth of water; and although they met with many disappointments in the first weeks of the operation all showed unflagging zeal and determination in their efforts to locate and salvage the wreckage. In these circumstances the efficiency with which a large part of the aircraft was located and recovered in what was a comparatively short period reflects the greatest credit on all concerned'.

Investigation

A high-level committee of specialists from the ARB, De Havilland, BOAC, RAE and the AAIB had been set up to study all information available on the Elba accident, to attempt to locate factors and to introduce modifications to the Comet in the hope of eliminating future accidents.

RAE Farnborough undertook a thorough investigation under the direction of Professor Arnold Hall, a brilliant engineer with a flair for marshalling scientific facts and presenting them in their true perspective. His painstaking report, the size of a telephone directory, was later to become one of the most historic in the annals of civil aeronautics.

Arnold Alexander Hall was born in the North of England on 23 April, 1915. When he was eighteen he won a scholarship from Alsop High School at Walton, Liverpool, to Clare College, Cambridge with an ambition to become an electrical engineer. While there he came under the influence of Melvill Jones, the Professor of Aviation. After graduation, Hall went to Farnborough in 1935, but he did not stay long. He was soon back with Melvill Jones at Cambridge. In 1938 he felt that war was inevitable, and he retraced his steps to Farnborough, to work there as a Principal Scientific Officer. Soon after war's end Hall was offered the chair as Zaharoff Professor of Aviation at the University of London, and once again he left Farnborough. At the same time he became head of the Department of Aeronautics at the Imperial College of Science and Technology in Kensington. Both of these were high-prestige posts. Then one Sunday morning in 1951, the Director of the Establishment at Farnborough passed away and Hall was asked to take the job.

With the Comet, a pressing problem was to get the wreckage back to England. Sixty per cent of the Comet had been raised from the seabed by the second week of the investigation. A number of large sections had been brought up intact and these were now in Rome awaiting transport home. In the normal way they would have come by sea, and would not reached

Farnborough for several weeks, but due to the urgency, this was not good enough. Hall decided that those sections must be moved by air. But there was only one aircraft in Britain with freight space large enough to take the bigger pieces. This was an American Fairchild C-119 cargo aircraft, nicknamed the Flying Boxcar, thought to be C-119C 51-2611, that was sitting on the perimeter of Farnborough's airfield on loan to the Royal Aircraft Establishment by an arrangement made through NATO. But could he use it? No. For the NATO agreement stipulated that the aircraft was not to fly outside the United Kingdom. Hall knew that the C-119 was the only aircraft suitable for ferrying the Comet's wreckage, so he took direct action and cabled the Pentagon in Washington. Supposedly, his cable said that unless he received word to the contrary, the Boxcar would take off for Rome the next morning at 06.30.

Somewhere along the line his message received diplomatic attention, but not from the Pentagon, from Whitehall. A worried telephone caller wanted to know why he was trying to upset the NATO agreement. The diplomatic hubbub was considerable, and by midnight he had received no word from the Pentagon. Nevertheless, Hall instructed the crew to be ready to fly in the morning as planned. Soon after dawn all was ready. Then, at 06.00, 30 minutes before take-off time Hall was handed a signal from Washington. It said 'Okay'. Down Farnborough's runway roared the Boxcar, away on its ferry flight.

This red tape cutting action by Hall set the tempo

Arnold Hall, who as Director of the Royal Aircraft Establishment at Farnborough, was to head the Comet investigation.

for the Farnborough operation. All four engines arrived in England towards the end of March, a centre-section of wing in early April, and the front part of the cabin in mid-April. All this came under the Accidents Section of the RAE and the Principal Scientific Officer of the Structures Department, Eric Lewis Ripley.

Ripley began poring over the YP wreckage. Most of it was ferried from Rome by air, but the biggest piece of all - the centre wing section - was delivered on the deck of the battleship *Vanguard*. Ripley flew to Italy to shepherd some of the more important sections home. And someone was always on hand at London Airport or Farnborough to see the precious bits through Customs – every piece of Comet wreckage had to be inspected.

His first task was to unscramble the world's most complicated jigsaw puzzle; to sort out all the bits of wreckage and decide where they fitted. He had men sent over from De Havillands to help, along with all the records on 'YP. A canvas Bessoneau hangar was erected at Farnborough to give them covered space to work.

'YP's hull number was 06003. It first flew on 9 January 1951. De Havillands handed 'YP over to BOAC in August 1951 - nine months later it opened the Corporation's first commercial service. There were two incidents in its life. The first was in August 1952, when its undercarriage and flaps were damaged during a heavy landing in wet weather at Khartoum. The second came fourteen months later at Bahrein in the Persian Gulf. There was an explosion in the trailing edge of the wing during take-off, and fire broke out in one engine. Repairs involved taking out the engines and replacing all the flexible piping. Then came Elba.

The team identified each piece of wreckage as it reached Farnborough. As the number of pieces grew, carpenters built a wooden skeleton to the exact proportions of the aircraft so that members of the Structures Section could wire the pieces to this outline; some bits were large and therefore easily set in position, others were less than six inches square - hard to identify and difficult to wire on. Slowly a true picture of 'YP was recreated.

Each piece of wreckage, particularly the edges, added to Ripley's knowledge of the crash, for, as he said ' Fractures talk their own language'. Some were bent downwards, indicating that they had broken off that way. Others were torn. There were tension breaks, indicated by the ángle of the edge. Some were corroded. Only a few could be definitely classified by the naked eye; most had to be examined under the microscope.

The early parts of 'YP to be recovered was not valuable as far as detecting the cause of the disaster went, but it gave many leads. At the end of the fuselage, under the root of the tail fin, there was a collection of wreckage from the cabin. They had all been driven back there by the force of the impact into the sea. Clearly the rear fuselage broke off in one piece in the air, but was shattered into lesser bits by the force of hitting the water open end first.

Ripley also found blue marks on the stub of the sliced off port tailplane. A marked piece was sent to the laboratory for test to identify the blue - it matched the material of the cabin seats. Ripley decided that one of the seats, falling through the air, had collided with the tail and cut a piece of it off.

The engines were also of interest. It was suggested in some aviation circles soon after 'YP crashed, that an engine was the culprit; that some

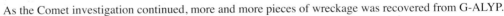

As the Comet investigation continued, more and more pieces of wreckage was recovered from G-ALYP.

The wreckage of G-ALYP was cleaned and then assembled inside a canvas hangar at Farnborough.

All four engines had been recovered - as had many large sections of the aircraft, which were mounted on specially constructed wooden trestles in their correct relative positions.

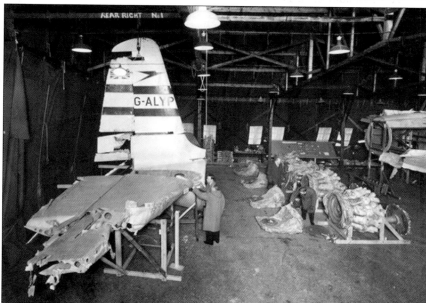

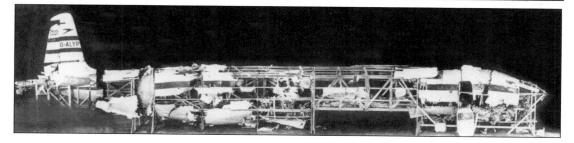

small part of the turbine had broken off and been fired into the passenger cabin, wrecking the aircraft. The Navy recovered three of the engines intact and both RAE and de Havillands gave them a clean bill of health. But the fourth, the port inner engine, was salvaged without its turbine disc. When this engine was hauled up from the deep, some observers immediately reported that this missing disc had indeed broken free in the air and triggered the disaster. Ripley was not so sure.

The wing wreckage was laid out on the hangar floor and examined. Ripley found that the top of it, over the port inner engine, had been slashed through. The turbine disc did not enter the cabin; the centre section of the wing landed on the sea upside down, and this particular turbine disc kept right on going, cutting its way through the engine casing and through the wing. The upside-down theory was confirmed by the wing itself. Impact with the sea had forced the top skin inwards, throwing into sharp relief the ribs and spars which supported it.

The wing yielded something else: a fatigue crack in the skin at the edge of the port undercarriage bay. It was similar to the crack produced under test on the prototype 'VG, and confirmed the unease felt about the wing strength. But Ripley was emphatic that this fatigue failure had nothing to do with the crash.

By the time nearly two-thirds of the fuselage wreckage was wired to its wooden skeleton, and about half the wing was fitted together on the hangar floor, Ripley and his Structures team were confident enough to make the first major analysis of what happened to 'YP when it blew itself to bits in the air. They were not sure of the sequence or why, but following the first failure - which was thought to have occurred somewhere in the front of the passenger cabin –the rear fuselage and tail broke off downwards from the main cabin section; so did the nose, with the cockpit and galley. Then the outer parts of the wing broke off, also downwards. That left only parts of the fuselage and the centre section of the wing together; this was the part that caught fire.

Ripley found a series of blue, yellow and white marks, scrapes and rubbings on the inboard stubs of the wing that were apparent to the naked eye in several places. The wings and lower half of 'YP's fuselage were polished metal. Above that, and running full-length along both sides of the fuselage was a broad band of blue edged with yellow, the airline's colours; above that, all the fuselage, except for the blue and gold letters BOAC was painted white. Clearly the marks on the wing were made by pieces of the cabin brushing over the wing - probably having been blown outwards by an explosion.

Did the explosion come first? The only way to be sure was to check the outboard tips of the wing, which were somewhere on the bed of the Mediterranean. If the paint marks crossed the major wing fractures, that was proof that the explosion happened before the wing tips broke off; if there were no paint marks on the ends of the wing, then the wing must have failed first.

There was still the question of the fire. Ripley called in the fire experts to examine the centre section. They calculated from the damage done to the metal that it had burned for at least three minutes. But Hall's team questioned the finding. Some said that the fire would have been put out at the instant the wreckage hit the water, and therefore three minutes was much too long. The fire experts, equally puzzled by the time factor, stuck to their three minute reckoning.

Ripley had to have 'YP's wing tips – the Navy salvage vessels had long since left the scene, and only trawlers were still on the job, so some clue was needed to put them on the right trail. Hall decided that the only way to solve both problems was to launch a fresh series of tests, this time with flying models.

Craftsmen created over 50 model Comets; some roughly finished for preliminary tests, others exact replicas of the airliner. They were one-thirty-sixth scale, with a wingspan slightly over three feet, and weighing about five pounds. They were designed to come apart in flight in a pattern deduced from VP's

The great airship sheds at Cardington near Bedford, from the roofs of which the Comet models were fired.

wreckage - the tail, nose and wing falling from the centre fuselage. The break-up was started by a length of cord attached at one end to the catapult which launched the models, and at the other to a set of pins in the models - when the cord tightened with the models' flight, the pins pulled out.

The tests were done at Cardington in Bedfordshire, once the home of the ill-fated R101 airship. The first tests were made from the roof of one of the hangars, 160 feet above the ground, and were catapulted away at about sixty miles an hour. They were caught in a 110 feet long by 30 feet wide net so as to prevent damage. These hangar tests were a preliminary to more conclusive ones conducted from a barrage balloon gondola.

The tethered balloon swayed over the field at 835 feet. As each model was catapulted away it was followed by a battery of high-speed movie cameras; one in the balloon, the others on the ground.

Here was the answer to the three-minute fire poser – a careful stop-watch check was made on the models' fall and the times recorded, then scaled up to represent the true times if the models had been full-sized aircraft falling in bits from thirty thousand feet. It was found that the model pieces took the equivalent

of nearly three minutes to reach the ground. Only a few pieces in a few of the tests hit in under two minutes, for the wreckage dallied on the way, doing strange time-consuming gyrations in the air. This confirmed the findings of the fire experts, but there was still the need to trace the wing tips.

The observers carefully logged the pattern the pieces made on the ground, charting the results of several tests and found that the major parts fell within a tight circle. When these distances were scaled up, the radius of the wreckage circle varied from a third to three quarters of a mile. This agreed with the chart the Navy kept of where 'YP's wreckage was actually found. So Farnborough radioed the trawlers still in the hunt, suggesting where to look for the wing tips. Two days later the trawlers signalled that they had found some wreckage at the places suggested, but not the wing tips. The Farnborough men crossed their fingers and waited.

In the middle of the investigation there was a pause – the day was 10 June, the Queen's birthday. In her Birthday Honours List Arnold Hall was gazetted as a Knight Bachelor. Several 'Comet Honours' came six months later, in the 1955 New Year's Honours, when the Investigation was finished.

The fuselage of G-ALYU is trucked by Pickfords heavy haulage from Hatfield to Farnborough.

Once there, the aircraft was re-assembled, to be surrounded by steel plates as the tank is assembled at Farnborough. The aircraft still carried the briefly worn 'large' BOAC titling.

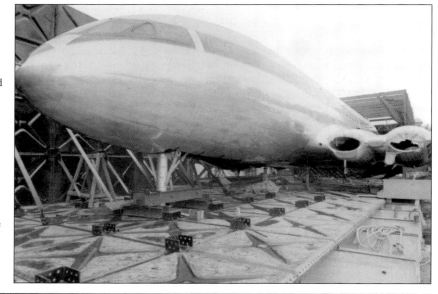

G-ALYU sits inside the tank at Farnborough on 25 May 1954 as the remainder is constructed around it.

The completed tank, with the Comet fuselage inside it, along with the water storage tank and associated buildings surrounding it.

One was particularly well earned. On Eric Ripley the Queen conferred the Order of the British Empire.

Full Size Tank Tests

Hall and Walker decided to test both the cabin and the wings at the same time, something never attempted before. They had in mind a cabin test made by De Havillands to find out how much pressure it could stand. In this case, the manufacturers used only a section of the cabin.

To make the test they needed a specially built very large tank. The tank had to be so constructed that the Comet's wings could stick out from either side, in order to use the hydraulic jacks to bend them.

To make such a tank was a big engineering job in itself, and the largest single experiment of the whole investigation. Hall gave orders that the tank must be ready to start operations in six weeks!

Braithwaite and Co were contracted to build a tank 112 feet long, 20 feet wide by 16 feet high out of four foot square steel plates, and for an additional reservoir alongside which would hold the water when the test tank was emptied.

Construction workers toiled around the clock on a site sheltered by a thicket of trees at the end of the main runway. Ministry of Works men, who were doing another job at the Establishment, were switched over to lay the stubby concrete piles which formed the tank's foundations.

At the same time Comet G-ALYU - which was midway between YP and YY in flying age - was, according to some reports - flown to the Establishment from London Airport. In fact, it appears that the aircraft was flown from Heathrow to Hatfield on 10 April 1954, the day after G-ALYY crashed. It was stripped of interior fittings and had its tailplane removed to allow De Havillands to conduct further static and fatigue testing on it throughout the remainder of April and into May.

As fitters were stripping it of its engines and all its cabin upholstery and interior equipment, Dr. Walker considered how could the places where the wing projected out of the sides of the tank could be sealed in such a way as to be watertight, and at the same time allow the wing to move as it was waggled by the hydraulic jacks? The solution was a fat pneumatic tube, made out of vulcanized layers of the fabric used in making balloons. It was tested to see if it would crack under repeated pressures, and found satisfactory.

On 7 May, after de Havillands had fitted the required pipework inside the aircraft, G-ALYU started to make its way by road from Hatfield to Farnborough.

When the floor and one end of the tank were built a tractor hauled Yoke Uncle to the site. It was wheeled up a ramp and rolled into the tank, tail first. It still wore its BOAC titles on the top curves of the fuselage, and the word 'Comet' glistened on its nose. The remainder of the tank was bolted up round YU until all the fuselage was out of sight, and the tank looked like a winged shoe box - a very big shoe box, one hundred and twelve feet long, twenty feet wide and sixteen feet deep.

Workmen placed lengths of metal ballast on the cabin floor to represent the normal weight of passengers and equipment. Water gushed in filling the cabin and tank, a quarter of a million gallons in all. The machinery was readied for action, and the testing could now begin. The job had taken exactly six weeks.

But there was a hitch. Water was leaking from the tank, not through the wing seals, but through the inside of the wing itself, where it bolted on to the fuselage. Water poured on to the ground. The answer was more farmyard than laboratory. They stuffed the wing full of straw, and for good measure installed a pump which sent any water that did seep through back to the tank. At the end of the seventh week the project was again ready for action.

The test was continual: additional water was pumped into the inside of the cabin, raising its pressure from zero - or equal to that of the tank water surrounding it - to 8.25 pounds per square inch; this meant the injection of about one hundred gallons extra, and the effect produced was the same as when the Comet was flying normally pressurized at forty thousand feet. That pressure was to be held for a while and then lowered again to zero. At the same time the electrically-controlled hydraulic jacks were to waggle the wings. Each filling - holding - and emptying action on the cabin was to represent a three hour flight, with half an hour climbing, two hours cruising, and half an hour coming down - like an average BOAC passenger flight.

The time taken on the test for each 'flight' was about five minutes. During this time the wing lifts reproduced twenty-five gust cycles, again the number measured by BOAC in actual flight conditions when Comets were in service. The only variation to this was to come every thousand 'flights' when the cabin pressure was pumped up to the equivalent of eleven pounds per square inch. These represented proving tests - special pressure checks made periodically by BOAC on its operational Comets.

A twenty-four hour watch was set over the tank as the machinery started, and everyone settled down to wait and see what happened.

To Fly, To Test…

Preparations were made for the most hazardous part of the investigation, actual flying tests in a Comet. Sir Arnold was not at all happy about exposing his staff to such risks, but he knew that it was absolutely necessary.

The scientists wanted to know if bad flying by the pilot would have imposed loads on the aircraft sufficient to start its break-up; or whether continuous vibrations could have caused disastrous failure. They were concerned about the effect of the jet effluxes - the air rush pushed backwards by the engines - on the skin of the rear fuselage. Fuel leakage from the tanks at take-off and in the air was another worry.

Preliminary tests were made on the ground in a Simulator. This was a Gloster Meteor cockpit, fitted out with Comet controls, and correctly loaded to represent Comet responses when flying at 200 knots and at 30,000 feet. A TV screen was set up in front of the cockpit to show pilots a pseudo horizon, and the effect of atmospheric gusts and bumps which their 'aircraft' was flying through. The idea was to test the reaction of the pilots and calculate from them the strains put on the aircraft.

The pilots were drawn from BOAC and the RAF. The ten BOAC men all had Comet experience, ranging from the 1,255 hours flown by Captain Ernest E Rodley, Captain of the Comet Fleet, to the 441 hours flown by a First Officer. The RAF pilots were Squadron Leader Roger Topp and Flight Lieutenant Bob Ross, the men who later took the test Comet into the air.

The simulator tests showed that the pilots were inclined to 'ride the gusts' fed into the television screen; they did not try to correct each little bump, being happy to adjust their controls to keep the general trim of their aircraft steady. They gave no sign of over-controlling, and thus straining the aircraft. Later they were asked to 'chase the gusts' – that is to correct the aircraft's trim with each bump. This was translated into terms of loads on the tail. Even then the biggest load produced was less than half the ultimate strength of the tail. So the scientists felt there was no danger there.

CF-CUM was built for Canadian Pacific, but with the loss of CF-CUN was taken over by BOAC as G-ANAV as their sole Mk.1A. It is seen being extracted from the assembly hangar at Hatfield tail first and down - a standard practice until it was decided to install cut-outs in the roof for vertical fin clearance

The interior of G-ANAV as seen on 17 June 1954, just before test flying began, showing some of the test equipment installed. Incongruously, BOAC managed to keep the main cabin curtains!

The scientists made other checks on the ground. They satisfied themselves that the power controls were not prone to dangerous defects or fire. They paid attention to the autopilot, which was normally engaged once a pilot has completed the take-off. The autopilot was suspect because of five minor incidents in Comets, highlighted by an experience reported by the Captain of 'YX on its last flight home to London Airport after the Comets were forbidden to carry any more passengers. Climbing from Cairo, the Captain engaged the autopilot and at once the aircraft started to roll. He disengaged it for a few minutes, then tried again; another roll. It happened again after refuelling at Malta. RAE men who went to London Airport and discussed this with BOAC technicians learned that the fault had already been traced to a loose connection.

The dangers of flying the Comet were obvious, and Sir Arnold insisted that all possible precautions be taken. The cabin would not be pressurized; the crew and scientists wore oxygen masks instead. Extra fire detectors were fitted and a Canberra bomber shadowed the Comet on every flight, so that it could warn the airliner if anything odd developed. Finally, Comet AV was selected as it had only about half the flying age of YP with 1,255 hours. Although a different variant (1A) it was considered to be similar enough not to influence the results of flight-testing. The RAE started negotiations with BOAC during April to acquire the aircraft to conduct flying investigations and research and by the end of the month the use of G-ANAV had been confirmed.

The Comet was prepared for flying tests by BOAC at London Airport. who removed all the seats, floor coverings and upholstery and fitted additional oxygen supplies, airspeed indicators. altimeters and power supplies into the main cabin. They also installed flying seats with full safety harness for the scientists. Then Haydn Templeton the head of the Flutter and Vibration Division of the Structures Department took over. They attached more than 200 strain gauges, 24 vibration pick-ups and 24 thermometers. All were wired to banks of recording instruments set up in the passenger cabin.

Templeton selected seven of his people to fly in AV. They included thirty-eight-year-old Anne Burns, a Scientific Officer, whose husband Dennis also worked at the Establishment.

Peter Bois, one of the De Havilland test pilots, arrived from Hatfield to fly as co-pilot with the RAF men. This was necessary because of a regulation that said a pilot must have ten hours' experience in a Comet before he could take it up unsupervised. Topp and Ross were not qualified.

All was now ready for AV to fly. At the last moment Sir Arnold had misgivings, for no real clue had yet been found which pointed to the Comet's basic fault, but on 23 June he gave his permission. This was the first of fifty flights; the Farnborough team flew AV for one hundred testing hours in all, and travelled the equivalent of twice round the world.

All this time men watched over the tank test, listening to the gurgle of water and checking the pressure gauges. Sometimes they drained the tank to see how YU was standing up to it all; otherwise they talked, and waited.

Already the expected wing fatigue had developed. The watchers detected it first after 5410 hours, 3539 of which were logged during the aircraft's operational life. Inspection revealed small cracks at the rear of both the port and starboard undercarriage bays. After the equivalent of another 130 flying hours one of the unchecked cracks on the starboard side had grown to 8.25 inches - having spread 2.5 inches in the last six flying hours, or ten minutes of tank operation. This crack was so serious that the scientists had to halt the test.

The advent of wing fatigue in YU confirmed the earlier fears, and showed that this could have wrecked the Comet, even if nothing else went wrong. That said, it must be remembered that as a result of earlier Farnborough tests, BOAC had already introduced a wing inspection programme; and Ripley was sure that wing fatigue did not cause 'YP's crash, although the wing did have small fatigue cracks.

YU's wing was repaired and the scientists on duty at the tank continued their watch. Pressure was pumped into the cabin and the hydraulic rams waggled the wing, compressing into hours the flights of days.

In order to make sense of all this study and gained data required carrying out some intricate calculations - a task perfect for the Pilot ACE (Automatic Computing Engine), a computer which had been designed by computer scientist Alan Turing at the National Physical Laboratory (NPL) in the early 1950s. Turing had been the key figure in breaking the German's Enigma code at Bletchley Park during World War Two.

It was a preliminary version of the full ACE, which had also been designed by Alan Turing. After Turing left NPL (in part because he was disillusioned by the lack of progress on building the ACE), James H. Wilkinson took over the project and Harry Huskey helped with the design. Although originally intended as a prototype, it became clear that the machine was a potentially very useful resource, especially given the lack of other computing devices at the time. After some upgrades to make operational use practical, it went into service in late 1951, and saw considerable

Alan Turing (left) and his 'pilot' ACE, or Automatic Computing Engine. This was one of the first electronic 'universal' computers. Its fundamental design was by Alan Turing, who wrote the specification in 1945 while working at the government's National Physical Laboratory. It was completed in 1950.

service over the next several years, including providing many answers to calculations for the Comet investigations.

Early on the morning of 24 June it was time for one of the periodic proving tests, in which the cabin pressure was raised to 11 per square inch, instead of 8.4. The scientists adjusted the pumps and watched the cabin pressure gauges mount; at 10.4 the needle stopped – then dropped away. The cabin had burst.

The scientists could not see where the rupture was, so they began to drain the tank. Sir Arnold Hall was called - he came out to the tank just as it was nearly dry. By chance he had an appointment that day with Sir Geoffrey de Havilland and Ronald Bishop – they joined him at the tank as at least part of the Comet truth unfolded.

What became visible was a break eight feet long and three feet deep on the port side over the wing. It included the forward escape hatch with its inset window. Such was the strength of the water forcing it out that the frames and stringers were sliced through. The break was what was expected and it proved that the cabin was weaker than calculations and other tests had even hinted.

Three questions had to be answered:
1   Was it fatigue?
2   If so, why did it not develop earlier? YU's cabin did not fail in the tank until after the equivalent of 9,000 flying hours - more than double YP's flying age, and treble that of YY.
3   Could anyone be certain that the cabin was the first thing to fail in YP and in YY?

The first was easy. Dr. Walker and his men examined closely the hole blown in YU's side, had their attention caught by the discolouration of the skin at a rivet hole at the lower rear corner of the escape hatch. All the other breaks ran away from this spot, and it certainly looked like fatigue.

Metallurgists were consulted, who confirmed that it was fatigue. Inspection revealed another crack, 1.25 inches long, at the top rear corner of the first window on the port side forward of the wing's rear spar. This was also a fatigue crack and the starting point of another major failure in the cabin.

The question of time was more involved. Dr. Walker was able to resolve it by delving into his

G-ALYS seen at London Airport in June 1952, wearing the early BOAC titles

G-ALYS

B·O·A·C

earlier esoteric researches on metal fatigue. These showed that, after testing a number of specimens, it was possible to get an average 'fatigue life' for a particular grade and type of metal; and having found the average, the shortest life – what became known as the 'safe life' of the metal type would be set at one-third of the average; and the maximum life would be three times greater than the average.

This could be directly applied to the Comet. YU failed in the tank at 9000 hours. Disaster overcame YP at 3681 hours, and YY at 2703 hours. Assuming that the average fatigue life of the Comet cabin fell somewhere between YU, on the one hand, and YY on the other; the three aircraft came well within the nine-to-one life scatter reached by these calculations. So the scientists suggested that a fatigue cabin failure was the cause of the two Mediterranean crashes.

Ripley continued to pore over the wreckage of Yoke Peter, marrying piece to piece to complete his picture. All the flight controls were looked at, and found to be satisfactory. The cabin pressurisation system was also looked at and cleared of blame.

It was July before the trawlers working off Elba had any success in their search for the outer wings of YP when they found a section of the port aileron. It was flown to Farnborough, and Ripley went to work on it. He could not see paint with the naked eye, but there were scratches, and they might contain fragments of paint which were not visible. He called in the chemists to make tests. The chemists knew that the blue and yellow paint on the sides of YP's cabin contained a dark grey metallic element called titanium. So they tested for titanium and got a positive reaction. It looked as if the paint definately scratched. Then someone pointed out that titanium is common, and occurs in many things, perhaps even in the sand of the Mediterranean.

RAE sent a request to Elba for a sample of sand. Back it came by air and, sure enough, it was full of titanium! The chemists devised a fluorescent test that could trace elements in the BOAC paint which were not common to the sand or anything else in the picture. Again the test was positive and conclusive. Sir Arnold, Walker and Ripley were able to say for sure that the first thing to fail in YP was the pressure cabin.

This was an important discovery and encouraged a theory that had been evolving: that the Comet cabin was considerably weaker structurally than De Havillands, the ARB or BOAC suspected. This view was reinforced by later tests on YU in its tank. After the first cabin failure, the aircraft was

The eight foot long structural failure of G-ALYU in the tank at Farnborough on 19 May 1954, seen from both the outside and inside. The damaged section was removed for analysis, being replaced by a new section to allow the tests to continue.

A further failure occurred on 24 June 1954, when a fifteen foot length towards the rear of the aircraft split apart from frames 26 to 34.

G-ALYS in the short-lived 'large' BOAC titles seen at Farnborough after it was requisitioned by the RAE. The aircraft was subjected to fuel overfilling and leakage testing using a Dorset fuel bowser.

repaired and strain gauges were put on the skin near some of the windows and the test continued.

These gauges demonstrated that at certain points of the fuselage the load on the skin reached a peak stress that was 70% of the metal's ultimate strength - nearly twice the load that either De Havillands or the ARB estimated. What is more, the load was reached two or three times on each flight!

Now RAE was able to say that in general, the skin at probably all corners of cut-outs - windows, hatches, and the like – were vulnerable to fatigue. They had not yet proved that fatigue caused YP's cabin to blow up, for the vital top section of the cabin was still at the bottom of the sea.

Meanwhile, almost every day in July AV was flying from Farnborough. Sometimes Topp or Ross took off only once a day; on other days it was twice, three, or even four times. Every time the guarding Canberra went too.

Every night the Comet was put away in a hangar to keep all the electrical contacts attached to the fuselage dry. Most of the flying was done early in the morning, soon after dawn, when conditions were the best for testing. One take-off was nearly disastrous. AV was well down the runway when a workman drove a fuel tanker on to the far end. Topp slammed on the brakes and stopped just in time.

For safety AV kept below 38,000 feet, and this ceiling was later lowered to 35,000 because of the risk of danger from the hydraulic system. Even so the strain on the people aboard was considerable as the aircraft was not pressurized.

AV came through most of these purely technical tests well. But it did not do so well when the effect of the jet effluxes on the rear fuselage was examined. The position of the engines in the Comet produced one serious problem - damage to a section of the rear fuselage. BOAC had already discovered this, for

when AV arrived at Farnborough there was already several small patches on the fuselage.

The scientists attached gauges and thermometers. They discovered that at the moment of take-off, when the nose was raised, the efflux from the engines hit the runway and bounced up again, breaking against the fuselage. This hot air attacked the skin and weakened it. The specialists calculated that one hour of this buffeting - which in reality was hundreds of take-offs - would produce fatigue in the fuselage just forward of the tail. This was a specific fault in the aircraft, which De Havillands tried to overcome in the design of their later Comets by angling the engines' jet pipes away from the fuselage.

Topp and Ross made their own survey. Throughout the flying tests they made a careful log of the aircraft's handling characteristics, and at the end they wrote their opinion, which was embodied in the Establishment's overall Comet report. They found many good features: AV's almost silent cockpit, its speed and ease of climb, and its cruising speed that could not be matched by any airliner in the world. But they criticized the apparently large time lag between moving the stick and response by the aircraft. They thought this was due to the large 'break out' force which had to be overcome in the elevator circuit. Here they referred to the spring which the manufacturers built in to give the stick some 'feel.' They reported: *'The break out force gave the effect of high stick forces for very small stick movements, so that when trying to maintain an accurate air speed and height there was a tendency to move the stick quickly in jerks and to over-correct.'*

This led to a more general finding: 'The aircraft was not easy to fly accurately in rough air'. Topp and Ross also found that the aircraft's directional stability was poor. They had something to say about the take-off technique laid down in the BOAC operating manual. The take-offs from Rome and Karachi were caused by the hazards of taking the aircraft off the runway at night, when it was easy to get the nose too high and thus lose speed and bring on a stall. To avoid this, a new rule was drawn up and included in the Manuals. It said they must keep the nosewheel down as long as possible. This led the Farnborough pilots to comment: *'The take-off technique of not raising the nosewheel until five knots below unstick speed is felt to be undesirable, mainly due to the' hammering' from the nose-wheel at high speed.'*

They had something to say about landing, too. *"Even when using a final approach speed felt to be the minimum for adequate control, there was a marked tendency to float during the hold-off. When making a fairly ' tail down' landing, the aircraft would balloon easily... In a crosswind landing, it was difficult to get rid of drift just before touchdown, due to lack of rudder effectiveness and slow response."*

The problems with fuel…

Soon after 'YP crashed off Elba there was much talk about the possibility of faulty refuelling at Rome's Ciampino Airport. This talk increased when 'YY crashed after taking in fuel at Ciampino.

Most people in Britain were anxious to find out that 'something unimportant' caused the accidents; the national temptation was to blame the Italians.

Questions were raised about the Comet pressure refuelling due to the high speed and high pressures required. One of BOAC's aircraft had significantly damaged tanks, and nearly all the others of the fleet were modified with steel replacing light alloy bolts.

The two outboard tanks were damaged, which were integral parts of the wing, the skin forming the

roofs and floors of the tanks. When these were to be filled, the operator fitted a bowser hose into a socket which automatically opened the tanks, and pumped in fuel till an automatic switch cut off intake. This meant that the tank would take only a hundred gallons more. The operator suppressed that switch and continued pumping till a second automatic switch cut off — when the tank was filled to within twelve gallons of its capacity. That was considered a full tank, and he disconnected the bowser.

This was the correct method of refuelling. Unfortunately it was not always used. An operator could ignore the two safety switches by using the 'offload' switch, which was really designed for emptying the tank, but which did permit fast uninterrupted loading—loading at too high a pressure, which endangered the tank.

Two types of bowsers were used on the Comet. One was British made called the Dorset. The other, used at Ciampino, was the Italian Viberti. Widespread suspicion fell on the Viberti. So to check it properly, RAE had one brought to Farnborough. Then they tested it in comparison with the British Dorset. They found that the Dorset, operating flat out, could pump in 200 gallons a minute with a bowser pressure of 40 psi. However, the Viberti, working flat out, pumped in only 120 gallons a minute with a bowser pressure just half that of the Dorset.

The scientists decided to blow up a couple of fuel tanks to see exactly what they could stand. The first damage test was done with water on the prototype VG, the Comet used for the first wing fatigue tests. Water was pumped into the port outer tank until something happened. It did - with a thump - when the pressure in the tank was 6.5 psi. Light alloy bolts—

The scene at Ciampino Airport, Rome, during the course of route-proving trials carried out by BOAC with the second Comet in June, 1951. In March, 1950, the Comet set up a new international speed record by flying the 900 miles from London to Rome in just over two hours. It was from Rome Ciampino that most of the Comet disasters transpired. The Shell refueller in the foreground is a Viberti which came under suspicion as to being a contributory factor in causing the accidents. *(De Havilland Hatfield)*

the ones replaced in operational Comets—sheared off in the ribs and rib connections.

The other Comet tested was G-ALYS, the one flown to Farnborough for examination when the investigation began. Helped by crews from the Shell Company, the investigators pumped fuel into the port tank at rising pressures inside the tank until it, too, gave a thump and gave way at some of the ribs and skin attachments. The pressure was nine psi.

Apart from the thumps, only two things indicated failure: a quick fall on the pressure gauges and slight leaking from the bottom of the wing. The untrained eye, looking at the damaged wing, could notice nothing wrong.

From these tests to destruction, the experts worked out that fuel pumped in at speeds up to 120 gallons a minute could not produce a critical pressure inside the tank, because the escape vent could cope with any over-filling. If the fuel were pumped in at between 120 and 190 gallons a minute there was a chance of switching off the bowser quickly enough to avoid serious damage. But if the fuel went in at 200 gallons or more a minute, and all parts of the tank were not operating in first class order, there was little hope of avoiding damage to the tank.

These tests showed the dangers of the unofficial 'off-load' method of taking on fuel, which was procedure abuse on the part of the fueller. They also cleared completely the Viberti bowser.

It was known that some fuel overflowed from the tanks when Comets took off and started climbing. De Havillands did have one fire in the air, so the question was: How dangerous, from the fire point of view, was this overflow?

The normal way of tracing fuel overflows in aircraft was to paint the suspect sections of the aircraft white and then 'label' the fuel with a dye, so that it left a coloured outline where it spilled out of the tank. The Farnborough scientists tried this method, but they found it almost impossible to reach the right places in the wing to paint them white. So some new method was necessary. The one suggested was revolutionary in the aircraft industry. Why not 'label' the paraffin with a radio-active isotope, and then go over the wing with a geiger counter, the hand-held detector which clicks when exposed to radio-active material ?

Sir Arnold called Sir John Cockcroft, the head of the Atomic Research Establishment at Harwell, in Berkshire. Sir John's men cooked up some isotopes which would radiate beta rays, a type not dangerous to metal and a Harwell technician hurried over to Farnborough. The first test was not successful. So a radioactive mixture ten times stronger was prepared

the next night. The following morning AV took off with the tanks loaded with nicely radio-active fuel. Geiger counters were run over the wing the minute the Comet landed, and this time the counters clicked like machine guns!

The scientists discovered that when the fuel overflowed from the top of the tanks, it ran down and re-entered the wing, finally collecting at the rear edge in the area of the flaps. The geiger counters showed that fuel spilled to within a few inches of the rear shrouds of the jet engine pipes, where the heat was intense. If the fuel came in contact with those pipes, said the scientists in something of an understatement '...it could constitute a serious fire hazard'.

Almost by accident the geiger counters did an unexpected job. One started to click as it was taken past the engine bay. The clicking intensified at a combustion chamber. It was discovered that the chamber had a crack, too small to be seen by the naked eye, but sufficient to trap the radio-active gases. Here was a new way of finding cracks in metal.

What really happened inside the cabin?
Certain that the cabin was the first thing to fail, Sir Arnold wanted to discover exactly what happened inside when the failure occurred. There was a way to find out - reproduce the explosion in miniature.

A series of stills taken from the footage shot from two angles of the 1/10th Comet model showing the effects of catastrophic depressurisation. Aircraft seats, dummies and luggage are catapulted all around and the cabin breaks up. What the stills fail to show is that it all happened in the blink of an eye.

The RAE built a one-tenth scale model of the main part of a Comet fuselage out of Perspex, a transparent plastic. It was fitted with bulkheads and twenty-eight miniature seats; and in six of those seats, scattered throughout the cabin, the scientists placed dummy passengers.

They cut a hole in the top of the Perspex fuselage, and then sealed it again with a separate piece of plastic. This piece was anchored by cables firmly fixed on one side and connected to an electrical bomb-release mechanism on the other.

The model was placed in a pressure chamber designed for testing pilots' reaction to very high altitudes. Pressure was reduced until it represented the atmosphere at a height of 40,000 feet, and air was pumped into the model to the pressure found at 8,000 feet. This difference in pressure – 8.5 pounds – produced the conditions of a high-flying Comet. Then the bomb release was fired.

High-speed movie cameras recorded what happened. The films, shot from several angles, were a record of chaos. The inside of the cabin looked as if it was swept bare by a mighty hand, and the Perspex itself was torn to shreds.

The timing in the film sequence, would have been in a full-scale Comet.

0.003 second: the backs of the passenger seats, all except those in the back row, snapped forward— dragged that way by the force of air rushing out. The cabin starts to break up.

0.009 second : a camera trained on the front half of the cabin just underneath the primary hole, shows things in a shambles - seats ripped up and flying through the air, dummy bodies twisting along the cabin floor.

0.25 second: the cabin furnishings are piling up under the hole, some of them flying out through it. One dummy can be seen in the flying wreckage being lifted feet first towards the hole.

0.6 second: a dummy flies upwards out of the model. Another hits its head against the roof.

When the high-speed exodus was over, only two of the dummies remained in the cabin. They lay twisted on the floor. No seat was in its proper place. No seat was undamaged. Round the shattered model inside the altitude chamber lay the scattered wreckage. One dummy and a seat were six feet away from the cabin. Below it, on the floor, were one dummy, seven smashed seats, a dozen back rests.

Key wreckage arrives
Late in August, three rather dull-looking bits of YP wreckage were delivered to Farnborough. They raised the total recovered to 70% of the whole aircraft. And this final delivery was more important than everything before. For here was the top of the centre section of the fuselage—the part that was blown sideways over the wings in the first instant of the explosion; the part of YP which failed first.

Ripley focused all his attention on it. This special section formed the roof and top half of the sides of the forward passenger cabin. It stretched forward for about five feet from the 'B' of the BOAC painted on the port side, or the 'C' painted on the starboard side. At the top of this section were the two square-cut Automatic- Direction Finding - or ADF - 'windows', which were not really windows at all for one cannot see through them. They are dielectric, non-metallic squares of fibre glass, made so that electricity can be transmitted through them without being conducted to the surrounding metal.

The ADF windows were placed dead centre in the roof. And it was round them in YP that Ripley found the clue which clinched the solution to the Comet riddle.

On two sides of the rear ADF window and one side of the front one, he saw that the rivets holding down the skin were placed too close to the edge, closer than the designers' specifications allowed. Then he saw another series of manufacturing faults. The first of these was in the reinforcing plate which was riveted in to strengthen the skin round the forward

This high camera vantage point of the prototyope Comet shows the position of the ADF aerials - the two black areas - in the fuselage roof. It was crack in the vicinity of these that ultimately led to the structural failure and the loss of a number of Comet 1s.

ADF window. When the aircraft was built a small crack was made in this plate, and a workman had drilled a hole at one end to stop it spreading further – a perfectly acceptable standard workshop practice at the time. This sort of workmanship was not limited to YP, for men working on the tank test found a similar drilled crack near YU's rear ADF window.

Ripley now concentrated his attention on YP's rear ADF window, for he found that all the breaks in the skin of this part of the fuselage ran away from that small square—some were tension breaks, others were tears. It was clear that this was the source of all the other failures.

All the broken edges in this area were examined under the microscope for characteristic signs of fatigue. At the rear starboard corner of the window, centred round a bolt hole, he found the tell-tale crystalline discolouration. Here was where YP failed. Here was fatigue.

The RAE's work was done. The investigation had cost at least £2,000,000, certainly the most expensive aviation enquiry ever undertaken. YU had been destroyed in the tank; VG, the prototype, was written off; YS had its fuel tanks blown up, was no longer airworthy; and AV needed plenty of work done on it when the flying tests were over to restore it to the luxurious aircraft it once was.

By mid-September the scientists began to write their report. Sir Arnold and his deputy, Morien Morgan, wrote a synopsis, leaving each department head to fill out his own section. Sir Arnold then wrote the opening six-page summary of the whole investigation, and Morgan and Ripley edited the rest. By early October a draft was ready and Sir Arnold

went into a series of conferences to make sure that nothing was muddled, inaccurate, or left out. Finally, 380 pages of typescript and more than 370 illustrations were sent off to Farnborough's printers, and by mid October - five months after YY crashed - the fruits of this mammoth investigation were ready to be laid before the Government's Comet Inquiry.

Before the Court…

The Public Inquiry, held in Church House, Westminster, London – a dignified building that overlooks Deans Yard in the shadow of Westminster Abbey - opened on 19 October before Lord Cohen, Commissioner. His 'bench' was the Bishop's Throne, carved with an episcopal coat of arms and set on a raised dias. Lord Cohen had Sir William Farren, CB, MBE, FRS, Professor W. J. Duncan, CBE, DSc FRS and Air Commodore Alan H. Wheeler, OBE as his assessors. Sir Lionel Heald, Q.C., Mr. J. P. Graham, Q.C, and Mr. P. J. Stuart Brown appeared on behalf of Her Majesty's Attorney-General, while the Ministry of Transport and Civil Aviation, the Ministry of Supply, the British Air Line Pilots' Association, British Overseas Airways Corporation, South African Airways, the Air Registration Board, the De Havilland Aircraft Co. Air Research, Ltd, British Thomson-Houston Co. Ltd., the Navigators and Engineer Officers' Union, Normalair, and the personal representatives of a number of the deceased crew-members and passengers, as interested parties, were represented by counsel Mr J M Shaw. Accredited representatives of the Governments of Italy and of the Union of South Africa were also present, and a watching brief was held on behalf of

Union Aéromaritime de Transport.

As the press of the day recorded: *'The Assembly Hall was strangely decorated. On an easel, almost as if in flight, hung a white picture of a Comet. Behind the Commissioner stood a second easel, with diagrams and photographs, and two mysterious hulks shrouded in white sheets—parts of the Comet Yoke Peter salvaged from the Mediterranean. Overhead was a muddle of hanging wires and microphones, twenty-two in all, controlled from a switchboard in the gallery. That gallery was the microphone for the world. There press and public crowded in to hear and spread the news of each day's evidence.'*

The enquiry was told that four separate lines of enquiry were initially followed by the staff of RAE in their investigation. Firstly, there was a study of the wreckage. As the amount of this was uncertain at that time, however, their primary line of inquiry depended on general theoretical considerations. The third line of research at RAE was that of comparative tests of other Comets, both on the ground and in the air, and the fourth was that of experiments with models, test pieces and special apparatus.

The explanation of what was believed to have happened to Comet G-ALYP was given by Sir Lionel Heald in his opening for the Crown. He traced the history of the accidents and of the events which followed them, with reference to the technical investigation performed by the RAE. The techniques used were detailed, and also the process of elimination which led to the opinion that metal fatigue was the only possible cause, consistent with all the facts of the Elba accident.

Eric Newton, the chief investigating officer of the Accident Investigation Branch (Civil Aviation), MTCA, produced formal aircraft documents relating to G-ALYP, with Mr C M Mack and Mr M R Ovenden, BOAC inspectors confirmed that they had signed the airframe and engines sections respectively on the aircraft's Certificate of Maintenance. Mr A A Elliott the MTCA, stated that all the aircrew licences of the crews concerned in the accident were valid, with the exception of that of the flight engineer, which had expired on 11 December 1953.

Capt. E E Rodley of the BOAC Comet 2 fleet, gave evidence concerning the flight experience of the crew of YP. Capt. Alan Gibson was above average as a pilot and as a commander and had shown himself extremely capable of dealing with any emergencies that might arise he said. The other crew-members were First Officer Bury, Radio Officer Macmahon, Flt/Eng. F C Macdonald, Steward F L Saunders, and Stewardess Jean Evelyn Clarke.

Day Two saw a picture being built up as to the events leading up to the accident, with spoken evidence given by flight and ground crews based at Ciampino and from eye witnesses on the isle of Elba.

'Ninuccio Geri was a sailor who was ashore on Elba at the time: *'I was busy working when I heard a heavy roaring noise, like thunder. I turned in the direction of the noise which came out to sea. I saw a globe of fire rotating as it came down into the sea. I saw it plunge into the sea, leaving a cloud of smoke over the air. My watch said 11.03'.*

Vasco Nomellini was spending the morning out shooting in the Collee Rescio area behind Elba's Porto Ferrario: *'I was on a small hill where the gun emplacements used to be. I heard a noise of an aircraft but I did not pay attention to it. Suddenly, however my attention was caught by a roaring sound in the air in the direction from which the aircraft was coming, and I distinctly noticed in that direction, two pieces of an aircraft, the smaller in flames falling in almost parallel lines into the sea'.*

Lorry driver Leopoldo Lorenzini: *'I suddenly heard a number of explosions and a great roaring noise. I turned in the direction from which the noise was coming and saw a red flame falling into the sea, followed by a wake of smoke in the form of a spiral'.*

Day Three focused on the evidence of Sir Arnold Hall, concerning the Establishment's comprehensive and thorough investigations into the Comet accidents, which was the main feature of this day's proceedings, amplifying the outline given by Sir Lionel Heald on the opening day. In addition, details were given of the Royal Navy's search for wreckage of G-ALYP, and of the available medical evidence.

Professor Antonio Fornari, of the Institute of Forensic Medicine at Pisa University, who examined the bodies of 15 of the victims of the Elba accident, was next witness. Speaking through an interpreter, he gave his evidence.

Sir Arnold Hall explained that the RAE approach in the early stages of its Comet investigations was that *'We clearly wished to satisfy ourselves on the structural integrity of the aeroplane and therefore initiated certain tests on the cabin, tail, and reviewed certain other tests done by the De Havilland Company on other parts of the aircraft. We clearly also wanted to satisfy ourselves about the possibility of explosion in the pressure cabin due to either ignition, for example, of hydraulic fluid, or any other causes. We wanted to satisfy ourselves about the possibility of explosion in the fuel tanks. We needed to satisfy ourselves about any possibilities of loss of control due to either aerodynamic cause or other cause. We wished, of course, to satisfy ourselves about the cause of any particular phenomenon we noticed on the wreckage as it came in, and that involved a great deal of metallurgical, chemical and physical testing of parts as they were produced'.*

Sir Arnold told the court that their souces of information - apart from the wreckage - included Comet G-ALYU which was subjected to fatigue tests, and Comet G-ANAV which was used for flight tests. *'Those flight tests in our mind at the beginning were particularly concerned with the possibilities of vibration and flutter, though the aircraft was used subsequently for certain aerodynamic tests and fuel venting tests. . . . We operated it at all times in company with a Canberra aircraft which flew behind it in order to keep general observation on it'.*

The Establishment's report on the Comet investigations, which was before the court, was an account of the results of all the lines of inquiry which had been pursued. Running to 380 pages of closely typed foolscap and as many diagrams and photographs, it was the key document.

22 October: Day Four - most of the day was discussions on fatigue to which the cabin failure of YP was attributed. Sir Arnold Hall and Dr. Percy B Walker, head of the Aircraft Structures department at Farnborough, both gave evidence. The existence of cracks in G-ALYP, formed during manufacture and drilled to prevent their propagation, was revealed.

Sir Arnold Hall gave his conclusion that the probable cause of the primary failure of the pressure cabin was *'...a phenomenon known as fatigue. The essence of the phenomenon is that whereas the structure will stand one application of the load quite satisfactorily, it may not stand many hundreds, thousands or millions of applications of the load satisfactorily, and may in the end fail under a load which it is well capable of bearing when new'.*

To find out what caused the first failure, BOAC donated G-ALYU for testing. A huge steel water tank was erected around 'YU, allowing the entire fuselage to be submerged while the water pressure in the cabin was raised, held and lowered to represent climb, cruise and descent conditions; each five-minute cycle was equivalent to a typical three-hour flight. At the same time the wings, which stuck out somewhat incongruously through seals in the sides of the tank, could be heaved up and down by hydraulic rams to simulate the wind gusts in flight.

After six weeks of feverish round-the-clock activity by relays of workmen, the tank was ready for action. Engineers opened the sluice valves, a quarter of a million gallons of water flowed in over the aircraft, and the pumps and rams were set in motion. Then one morning towards the end of June, the needles on the big pressure gauges outside the test tank slipped back to zero. The cabin had failed from fatigue, after the equivalent of 9,000 hours service.

Describing experiments with 'YU in the water

tank at Farnborough, Sir Arnold said that when failure occurred near the forward escape hatch the structure had reached a peak stress, and it was deduced that the stress was reached two or three times per flight. Calculations deduced that the ultimate static strength of the material was such that the failure occurred at 70 per cent of the ultimate load.

'The decree of stress concentration at the forward escape hatch' Sir Arnold said, *'was of the same order of magnitude as that at the ADF window, although the two structures were different. We examined the fractures in the area of the rear ADF window (of G-ALYP) which we had already decided was the origin of the failure, and we found what we believe to be evidence of high-level fatigue at one particular point'.*

After examination of the area round the windows Sir Arnold said, *'We observed certain cracks which had, I believe, been formed during the process of manufacture of the aeroplane, because they had been drilled at their ends to stop their propagation... The presence of these cracks does rather suggest that the manufacturing process used was one capable of cracking the material. Although you may see a crack which is formed by such a process, one is always a little worried as to whether there are some you do not see... The inference I put on these cracks is that I cannot totally eliminate that they might have accelerated the onset of fatigue in this aeroplane... it might have brought the accident a little forward in time; it certainly was not in any sense a primary cause.'*

Sir Lionel Heald read from the RAE report the outline of the investigation, and a discussion on the Elba accident. The cabin tests on G-ALYU at Farnborough demonstrated that the fatigue life of the cabin was relatively short. In reply to Sir Lionel, Sir Arnold said, *'If we take YD as unity, YP was 2.4 times younger and YY was 3.4 times younger... these ratios are those of a kind that we find reasonably normal. At the time of the Elba and Naples accidents, both aircraft had flown longer than the safe fatigue life we could give in the light of the evidence obtained from YU'.*

In describing what may have happened aboard YP, Sir Arnold Hall explained that he formed a view that the Comet must have broken up at a great height, somewhere about 30,000ft, and come down in a series of certain quite dearly defined paths. As the wreckage continued to accumulate, an informative picture of the accident built up. After giving examples of the type of indications and processes used, including the medical evidence after the examination of the bodies. Sir Lionel said *'It was quite clear that there had been an almost instantaneous and tremendously powerful forward force generated inside the pressure cabin which had thrown most of*

Two Italian fishermen explain what they saw when the Comet came down near Elba.

the passengers and their seats forwards and upwards against the roof. But it must also have driven some of them right clear out of the aircraft without touching anything at all, because in the case of some of the bodies it was clear that they had an initial impact and in other cases that they had not.'

Experiments with a one-tenth scale model of the pressure cabin had led to the belief that "*...within one-third of a second of the accident taking place the cabin was apparently empty.*' There was evidence of decompression of the lungs in the bodies of the victims consistent with sudden loss of pressure in the cabin. "*It is clear on general principles that if a fracture of any substantial size (not a mere perforation or something like a bullet hole) occurs in the wall of a tube or vessel which is under 8 lb pressure, a large hole will immediately open up and the tube will at once become what the layman might describe as a compressed-air gun. A terrific blast of air will force anything and everything out of the hole and will tend to throw the aircraft into violent contortions and so tear the whole of the fuselage to pieces.*"

Using a specially constructed Comet model, Sir Lionel next indicated the sequence in which, according to the RAE report, the Elba Comet had broken up. '*The first thing that happened was a violent disruption of the centre part of the pressure cabin. The next thing that happened was that the fuselage aft of the rear spar, the nose and the outer port wing fell away under what are called downward forces. Thirdly, the main part of the wing separated and caught fire. Next, Sir Arnold says, the fuselage aft of the rear spar, with the tail unit still attached, fell into the sea with the open end first and the tailplane last. Last of all, the main part of the wing, still on fire, hit the water in an inverted position.*

'*The apparent cause of the disruption was obtained by a process of elimination. The possibility of an internal explosion, abnormally high tail-loads, insufficient tail-strength, an abnormal increase in atmospheric pressure, failure of the powered control system or the pressurization control, and inefficiency*

of the pilot had in turn been eliminated. Sir Arnold Hall told the court that there was only one thing left: 'There is what is called fatigue—metal fatigue. Everything in Sir Arnold Hall's investigation supports the theory that this was the cause of the failure of the cabin, and nothing contradicts it.

The word 'fatigue' is not an accurate technical term. It tells you nothing about the cause, and therefore scientists do not like it. But to the layman it does seem quite apt to describe in ordinary language the effect which actually occurs, What fatigue failure means is that a structure which had an ample reserve of strength when it was new might fail under its normal working load after a certain length of time'

The Inquiry continued with a visit to Farnborough to view the wreckage and review the methods used by the RAE investigation team.

It was revealed that other avenues were investigated: strength-testing the tail unit; purposely damaging the skin of the outer wing tanks by refuelling too quickly; checking what happened when high-pressure hydraulic fluid escaped in a fine, inflammable mist near to electrical equipment; photographing the whirling chaos of uprooted seats and flying passengers inside a transparent model cabin, a split second after it had burst; testing impact damage - after a fresh study of the medical evidence at the inquests - with fully clothed dummies tipped out of aircraft flying at various altitudes; checking whether the flight engineer could accidentally set too high a cabin pressure on the automatic control; checking whether the pilot could unintentionally mishandle the aircraft to the extent that it broke up under the strain, or whether the powered controls themselves could run amok; checking the behaviour of a Comet at high altitude and top speed, flown without cabin pressure by test crews wearing oxygen masks and shadowed always by a Canberra bomber acting as observation aircraft just in case.

All the breaks in the fuselage seemed to run back to a single point in the forward cabin roof where one of the two ADFs - automatic direction finders - had been fitted; and there were marks made on the wing by parts of the cabin as they had been blown violently sideways across the slipstream.

Initial examination and reconstruction of the wreckage of G-ALYP revealed signs of inflight break-up. Shreds of cabin carpet were found trapped in the remains of the Comet's tail section; The imprint of a coin was found on a fuselage panel from the rear of the aircraft; and smears and scoring on the rear fuselage were tested and found to be consistent to the paint applied to the passenger seats of the Comet.

It became more than ever vital to recover the missing piece of cabin, but the problem was where to look for it. The experimentation with the Comet models at Cardington were described, that brought about a re-orientation of the search, that in the third week of August it produced the rear ADF window.

When the wreckage was recovered, investigators found that fractures started on the roof, a window then smashed into the back elevators, the back fuselage then tore away, the outer wing structure fell, then the outer wing tips and finally the cockpit broke away and fuel from the wings set the debris on fire.

After the equivalent of only 3,000 flights investigators at the RAE were able to conclude that the crash had been due to failure of the pressure cabin at the forward ADF window in the roof. This 'window' was in fact one of two apertures for the aerials of an electronic navigation system in which opaque fibreglass panels took the place of the window 'glass.' The failure was a result of metal fatigue caused by the repeated pressurisation and de-pressurisation of the aircraft cabin. Another worrying fact was that the supports around the windows were only riveted not glued, as the original specifications for the aircraft had called for. The problem was exacerbated by the punch rivet construction technique employed. Unlike drill riveting, the imperfect nature of the hole created by punch riveting may cause the start of fatigue cracks around the rivet.

The Comet's pressure cabin had been designed to a safety factor comfortably in excess of that required by British Civil Airworthiness Requirements of the day (2.5 x P as opposed to the requirement of 1.33 x P and an ultimate load of 2 x P, 'P' being the cabin 'Proof' pressure) and the accident caused a revision in the estimates of the safe loading strength requirements of airliner pressure cabins.

A number of high-profile witnesses were called before the court. Possibly the 'star' was Lord Brabazon of Tara, Chairman of the Air Registration Board. He addressed the Court in words that rang around the world. *'You know and I know the cause of this accident. It is due to the adventurous pioneering spirit of our race. It has been like that in the past, it is like that in the present, and I hope it will be in the future.*

'In this inquiry there is nothing to be ashamed of; much more to be proud of. Here was a great imaginative project, to build a machine with twice the speed and twice the height of any existing machine in the world. We all went into it with our eyes wide open. We were conscious of the dangers that were lurking in the unknown. We did not know what fate was going to hold out for us in the future.

"Of course we gave hostages to fate, but I cannot believe that this Court, or our country,

The overall scene in the main hall of Church House during the Comet Inquiry.

will censure us because we ventured. You would not have the aeronautical people in this country trail behind the world in craven fear lest they be censured in such a Court as this for trying to lead the world. Everything within the realm of human knowledge and wisdom was put into this machine.

'When we gave this Certificate of Airworthiness to these machines they were airworthy. True, they deteriorated in a way no one on earth at the time could foretell, and they deteriorated, so I am led to understand, by a slowly developing molecular metallurgical fault. It is metallurgy, not aeronautics, that is in the dock.'

'My Lords, I have now had fifty years connected with aviation, and if I may say something about it, I would like to say this. That in every step in progress, we have paid for it in blood and treasure, and God knows that in this case we have paid in full.

'Finally, I do hope that the threat of having to face an inquiry such as this, with all its publicity, if anything goes wrong, will not stop adventurous spirits pioneering in the future."

Mr. Shaw, council for the deceased, commented almost as an aside that Lord Brabazon's speech might have been good advocacy on behalf of the aircraft industry, but it was not of great comfort to the public. Lord Brabazon told the court that the ARB did not ground the Comet, BOAC did. '*.. And I think it wise to let you know straight away, that if you grounded every aeroplane that had an unexplained accident, you would scarcely have a machine in the air to-day ... we saw nothing in that accident which justified grounding it.'*

From the evidence that was placed before the enquiry, it seems that on 19 February 1954 the Chairman of BOAC forwarded the report and papers to the Minister of Transport and Civil Aviation, Alan Lennox Boyd stating in his letter that, on the assumption that no further indication of the cause of the accident emerged prior to the completion of the inspection and modification work, BOAC considered that all such steps as were possible before putting the aeroplanes back into service would have been taken.

The position was also considered by the Air Registration Board. On 4 April 1954 the Minister

was advised that although no reason for the accident has been established, modifications were embodied to cover every possibility that imagination has suggested as a likely cause of the accident. When these modifications were completed and satisfactorily flight tested, the Board saw no reason why passenger services should not be resumed.

In the meantime, the Minister had asked the Air Safety Board, under the Chairmanship of Air Chief Marshal Sir Frederick Bowhill, for advice on the resumption of the Comet passenger services. On 5 March 1954 the Minister was told that the Board had considered all the information resulting from the recent investigations and had noted the nature and extent of the modifications planned as a result. This being so, the Board saw no justification for imposing special restrictions on Comet aeroplanes. The Board therefore recommended that Comet aeroplanes should be returned to normal operational use after the current modifications had been incorporated and the aeroplanes had been flight tested.

Acting on this advice, the Lennox-Boyd gave permission for flights to be resumed, and the first Comet aeroplane to resume passenger service took to the air on 23 March 1954.

Lord Brabazon recalled that two Avro Tudors had mysteriously disappeared. The ARB had made tests but could find nothing wrong. So they went through the aircraft with a fine toothcomb and made every modification which might be useful. The result: they never found the cause of the accidents, but no more occurred. The Board did the same thing with the Comet, made every possible modification, and recommended that they should fly again.

So the questioning went on. Each facet of the Farnborough report was examined, each theory probed, each responsible party called to account.

In America, the interest in the Comet riddle was as intense as it was in Britain—for it was the American rule of the air which the Comet challenged. To the quest for truth the Americans paid generous tribute. The *New York Herald Tribune* said: 'Full

The vital piece of the wreckage of YP, preserved to this day by the Science Museum in London.

G-AYLS seen at Heathrow North Side in happier times.

marks to Britain for its brutally honest and frank inquiry into the Comet.'

Time magazine reported: *'British science has told the world, without excuse or cover-up, what happened to Britain's proudest airliner, the ill-starred jet Comet."*

When Sir Hartley Shawcross gave his summing up for De Havillands, he stressed the point that the manufacturing cracks discovered in YP had nothing whatever to do with the crash. In view of the publicity this matter had received, he said, he thought it should be clearly understood.

Then, on the day before the Inquiry ended, Sir Hartley issued a statement on behalf of de Havillands, setting out, point by point, their proposals for the future.

On the pressure cabin: The problem of high-level fatigue had been recognized, and de Havillands would take adequate measures to deal with the problem, in full consultation with the ARB. There would be thicker gauge materials in the pressure cabin area: the windows and cut-outs would be re-designed (made round instead of square) to lower the stress levels around rivets and bolt-holes; there would be no more manufacturing cracks if they could prevent it, and if there were any, they would make sure that no repair scheme would be allowed unless it was perfectly safe.

On the wing: They were re-designing the wing structure, where fatigue had been shown, and would probably use thicker skin, and reinforce certain areas.

The fuel system: They had modified the fuel system to prevent leakage, and to make sure that if there were any leakage the fuel would be discharged clear of the aircraft.

Fuel tanks: they were working on the problem of damage to the tanks during refueling and they planned to advise operators to put a flow meter into the refuelling unit.

Flying controls: they were considering a modification of the controls to reduce the 'break-out' force which had worried the pilots.

Hydraulic fluid: they were working on a non-inflammable hydraulic fluid.

Jet buffet: they had already reduced the jet buffet on the underside of the fuselage by altering the angle of the jet engines, and the thicker fuselage skin would lessen any risk of damage.

Accidental damage: they planned to reinforce areas, such as doors and hatches, where accidental damage could occur during loading of freight or passengers.

The Court had heard 68 witnesses and looked at 145 exhibits. The official transcript had stretched to 1,600 pages.

The Report is published

Three months later Lord Cohen made his report. *'The accident was not due to the wrongful act or default or to the negligence of any party or of any person in the employment of any party."*

His report was clear, detailed, precise; 28,000 words that gave a clean bill of health to everyone who built, licensed, and operated the Comet. He accepted the RAE finding that the accident at Elba was due to structural failure of YP's pressure cabin in the region of the ADF window, brought about by fatigue.

On the question of responsibility, he said: *'No suggestion was made that any party wilfully disregarded any point which ought to have been considered, or willfully took unnecessary risks'.*

He dealt carefully with the work of De Havillands, and their methods of testing, which had been criticized during the inquiry as inadequate. *'The primary object of De Havillands was to lay the foundation for extensive tests which they regarded as the soundest basis for the development of a project, rather than to arrive at a precise assessment of the stress distribution at the corners of the cabin windows. I do not think that they can justly be criticized for this approach to the problem.'*

'I am also satisfied that in the then state of knowledge de Havillands cannot be blamed for not making greater use of strain gauges than they actually did, or for believing that the static test that they proposed to apply would, if successful, give the

necessary assurances against the risk of fatigue during the working life of the aircraft."

Nevertheless, he included a memorandum from his three assessors, which pointed out that static tests were made on two parts of the pressure cabin which were incomplete, and therefore had to be supported on stiff bulkheads - thereby altering the accuracy of stresses portrayed.

As far as the manufacturing cracks were concerned, Lord Cohen said he had been advised that most aircraft experience cracks, and all witnesses agreed that 'crack stoppers' by drilling was a reasonable means of dealing with them.

Throughout the design of the Comet, he said, De Havillands relied on well-established methods. In the testing they followed what was believed, at that time, to be good engineering practice. The drilling of cracks would have been appropriate if the stresses had been as low as De Havillands thought they were.

Neither did he have any criticism to make of the ARB. He quoted the order under which the Board operated, and stated that he believed the existing system of inspection was essentially satisfactory.

As to allowing the Comets to fly again after the Elba crash: *'I am of the opinion that no blame can be attached to anyone for permitting the resumption of the services.'*

Lord Cohen referred to the controls of the Comet, criticized by some of the pilots for excessive break-out force, and by one of the assessors at the Indian Court of Inquiry into the Calcutta crash for lack of 'feel'. *'As advised by my assessors, I am satisfied that the characteristics of the control system of the Comet should be reconsidered by De Havillands and by ARB in the light of both the criticisms which have been made.'*

The report produced no jubilation at De Havillands, but it did bring a sigh of relief for reputations was at stake.

The Government was equally relieved, for it was involved almost as much as De Havillands, through BOAC and the Ministry of Supply. The airline had staked everything on its Comets; flight schedules and all future plans were geared to Comet development. Ministry of Supply funds not only bought two Comets outright, they helped to develop the engines and much of its equipment, and paid the bill for the £2,000,000 Farnborough investigation. The Government and BOAC quickly went into action to rebuild public confidence and try to regain some of the national prestige unavoidably lost through the Comet disasters.

There was activity again at Hatfield. The job facing De Havillands was not an easy one. To come out of the Court of Inquiry unscathed was one thing.

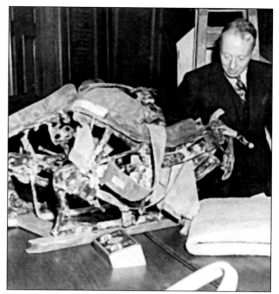

A twisted and distorted Comet seat recovered from the sea is placed before the enquiry.

To obtain a new Certificate of Airworthiness was quite another. First they had to carry out the strengthening modifications announced during the Inquiry, and repeated in the Court's report, without making the aircraft so heavy that it would be uneconomic to fly. Then they had to carry out the even more important schedule of testing evolved as a result of the Farnborough investigation.

De Havillands were also spurred on in their fresh efforts by a race against an American competitor. Across the Atlantic, Boeing were pressing on relentlessly with the Boeing 707 – their third attempt to enter the jet airliner market via the KC-135 Stratotanker for the US Air Force that was based their experimental Model 387-80.

So ended what was undoubtedly and probably still is the most intense and costly accident investigation in the history of aviation. The transcript of the formal Court of Inquiry created a document 10 inches thick.

The proceedings had developed into a frank and open commentary on manufacturing methods and techniques, many of which came in for their share of criticism, and to some it seemed that British aviation gained little and suffered much from the spotlighting of the shortcomings among its many achievements. But the Court found no one to blame for the accidents. Throughout the design and testing of the Comet, De Havillands had relied on well-established principles and had followed what was considered at the time to be sound engineering practice. Now many

The diagram showing the items of the airframe recovered from Yoke Peter.

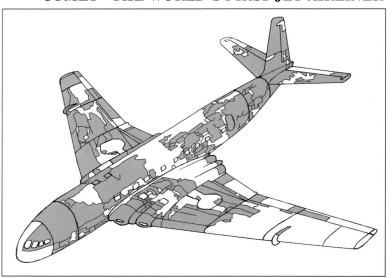

of the techniques were to be drastically revised, and the Court gave its approval to the measures announced by de Havillands to correct the Comet's weaknesses.

Some commentators speculated that the three Comet disintegrations did not involved two different causes, or that cabin failure was the primary cause. They believed that the tail failed first and that the rest of the airframe failed in rapid sequence - almost too rapidly to measure. There was also a belief that all three Comets suffered jet upset, a phenomenon which was not investigated until the Boeing 707 and Douglas DC-8 era, and that crews, in attempting recovery, overstressed the airframes. This would have been consistent with tail failure, because tail unit failure would overstress the wings and fuselage, whereas a fuselage primary failure would be unlikely to cause a tail failure.

The official inquiry report did not refer to the Comet G-ALYV after take-off accident from Calcutta on 2 May 1953, but in retrospect, Senior Inspector of Accidents T R Nelson, who participated in the Indian investigation, privately believed that its basic cause was probably similar to the Elba and Naples accidents. However, John Watkins, Director of Engineering for Trans Australian Airways and a distinguished Australian aeronautical engineer, who was seconded to the Indian investigation as an observer, had an entirely different theory which never came out in the official report. Watkins had a keen professional interest in the future of the Comet at the time, believed the precipitating factor in the Calcutta accident was a lightning strike in the cumulo-nimbus cloud of the monsoonal squall line.

At Calcutta when G-ALYV was re-fuelled, the wing tanks were filled to capacity, but only a small amount of fuel was pumped into the Comet's empty belly tank. As it happened, the tanker vehicle which refuelled the Comet had been standing in the hot Calcutta sun for two and a half hours before the aircraft arrived. Also, the Comet's belly tank contained a relatively small quantity of hot kerosene - and by the time of takeoff, a large quantity of highly explosive vapour. In these circumstances, John

Watkins thought, a lightning strike could have touched off the vapour, creating an explosion that initiated the structural failure. Watkins examined the wreckage himself and was convinced the remains of the belly tank exhibited evidence of such an explosion.

Indeed, it was another belly tank explosion – set off by an electrical short circuit, not a lightning strike in a tank that contained little more than very hot fuel vapour - that brought down a Boeing 747 operating as Trans World Airlines flight 800 on 17 July 1996.

Throughout the world, new design standards for the structural safety of airframes and pressure cabins were adopted, and the spectre of metal fatigue became an ever-present consideration in the minds of designers. Manufacturers were alerted to the fact that even the smallest fatigue crack resulting from repeated pressurisation of a fuselage had the potential to lead to a disastrous structural failure.

The investigation also pointed out the problems inherent in designing cut-outs in pressure cabins. The result is that today's pressurised jet airliner fuselages have heavier skinning and smaller windows. Their design also incorporates a cross-webbing type of fuselage wall structure intended to stop any crack extending unimpeded along the cabin skin. The resulting gain in design knowledge and safety is plain to see - since the Comet disasters, no other airline jet has exploded in flight as a result of a pressure cabin fatigue failure.

The scandal of Channel 4's 'Comet Cover-Up'.

Worldwide, lessons had been learned from the terrible tragedies, and there the matter would have rested if it were not for a UK television company's programme broadcast in 2002.

Made by Principal Films and forming part of Channel 4's 'Secret History' series, the programme makers had invited De Havilland veterans to help them mark the 50th anniversary of jet passenger transport. Past editor of *Flight International*, J. M. (Mike) Ramsden worked on the Comet 1 as a De Havilland apprentice, and was one a many invited to assist the production company.

'Director and interviewer Steve Ruggi, producer David Coward and sound and cameramen met us in our homes and other locations around Hatfield, birthplace of the jet airliner. John Cunningham, retired De Havilland director and chief test pilot, agreed to meet them in the De Havilland Museum's Comet 1 cockpit. Ralph Hare, retired Comet structures engineer, also met them on location and gave hours of his time and expertise.

Their smilingly deferential questions ranged over the whole history of the Comet project. One or two questions seemed rather suspicious. Was de Havilland arrogant? Well, we had made some very good aeroplanes, but arrogant? Sir Geoffrey de Havilland drove a Morris Minor and would hold doors open for lowly apprentices.

We knew that the programme was going to be about tragedy as well as triumph questions and sent them photographs, films and documents without charge.

They set the scene truthfully enough. One after the other in 1954, two BOAC Comet 1s broke up over the Mediterranean with the loss of more than 50 lives. The world-beating British jetliner fleet was grounded while the Royal Navy, the Royal Aircraft Establishment and a public inquiry painstakingly investigated and established the cause. They found that window or hatch frames in the Comet's pressurised fuselage had failed from fatigue.

We had made manufacturing and design mistakes, and these mistakes - all in Lord Cohen's thorough published 1955 report - were splashed on every newspaper front page. Well, we had been pioneering jet passenger transport, solving problems never posed before, and there were no excuses. We got it wrong.

When the programme was aired it showed a different perspective. Now titled 'Comet Cover-Up' the main allegation was that De Havilland's had neglected to fatigue-test the Comet 1. The whole programme was riddled with many mendacious quotes: 'Senior de Havilland executives knew that the plane was susceptible to metal fatigue, yet so desperate were they to be the first to fly a jet airliner that they chose to ignore repeated warnings and postponed crucial safety testing'.

'The secret compromise by the Government, De Havilland and BOAC to postpone full-scale fatigue tests is recorded for posterity in the confidential letters we have discovered'.

'None of the executives involved in the Comet ever went on record about the secret fears they shared before the accidents, and the relatives of the passengers who died in the accidents were never compensated'.

'Secret letters' are cited in support of these grave allegations.

Secret letters from whom, dated when, saying what exactly? Fleeting glimpses of old files and lingering close-ups of the word 'fatigue', accompanied by doom-laden music and voice commentary, created a dark, menacing atmosphere, but proved nothing.

Use of the video pause and replay buttons caught a bit of a 1951 Royal Aircraft Establishment internal memo about fatigue-testing the Comet's wing.

The documentary's core allegation, said to be proven by the secret letters, was that de Havilland was warned that the fuselage would fail from fatigue but refused to fatigue-test it. Mike Ramsden again: *'We explained all these tests in filmed interviews with Mr Ruggi and Mr Coward. Too technical and boring, perhaps. They edited it all out. But then to state as fact that De Havilland refused to fatigue-test the Comet 1 is just wilful untruthfulness. It makes you wonder how much you can believe of any Channel 4 documentary.*

Yes, the Comet 1 window frame failed catastrophically from fatigue. Why, if it had been fatigue tested so thoroughly? Because, as we explained on camera, the production window frames were riveted to the fuselage skin hand-made test section.

Bishop had agreed to riveting, which would be stronger than Reduxing if heavier, because the production people could not get consistently good glued joints on the production line. Forty years later Bishop called that 'my biggest mistake'. But it was a perfectly sound engineering decision, and still would be. All 15,000 jetliners built since have had riveted window frames.

There was another 'causal factor' test section used for fatigue-testing had been toughened by the 2.5P load applied to it before its 16,000 'flights'. That was a new structural discovery. Engineers who try to do things that have never been done before will sometimes make mistakes. Bishop accepted complete responsibility. A lesser man would have blamed the production or structures departments, or both'.

Many former De Havilland employees were furious at such allegations. A G T Peters FRAeS and D R Newman FRAeS also went on record listing some of the programmes inaccuracies: *'We were part of the Comet design team from its inception, through its troubles and on to operation as the successful Comet 4 and finally as the Nimrod maritime reconnaissance aircraft still in RAF service. The Channel 4 programme was deeply distressing, portraying a completely false impression of the atmosphere and motivation of the De Havilland company. No one who knew the De Havilland directors of the day (as we did) would ever associate them with a 'mad race for profit'.*

Detail inaccuracies abounded. To name but a few: The contract for the initial batch for the BOAC and BSAA was placed by the airlines themselves, not the Ministry of Supply. MoS bought only the first two examples.

The Ghost engines were the only ones available which were capable of certification for civil use at the time. They performed consistently and reliably in service. The Rolls-Royce Avon engine was not even cleared for civil certification when the fleet was grounded in 1954. It was wrong to say that lack of Ghost power led to extreme weight reduction - reduction of airframe weight to the minimum practicable is basic to the aircraft design process.

There was no mention of the ARB, which was then the authority responsible for framing requirements, overseeing design and testing and recommending to the Ministry of Civil Aviation that aircraft should be certificated for public transport.

It was not made clear that the concern raised by the RAE on the subject of fatigue was related to the wing, not to the fuselage. No mention was made of the extensive fatigue tests conducted by the company before the aircraft flew, involving fuselage sections and many individual critical components.

It is incredible to claim that the Court of Inquiry was unaware of all the facts or that it should have connived at covering up the true situation.

The senior people who carried the responsibility for the Comet in de Havilland, BOAC and the ARB are no longer able to defend themselves against the charges implied by this programme and it is regrettable that Channel 4 should stoop so low to denigrate their efforts without recognising that they were stretching the state of knowledge at the time. The Comet, after its problems were corrected, introduced jet transport to a wide variety of airlines and enjoyed a successful career for many years. The Nimrod, which in many respects was still a Comet, continued to give good service in the RAF until 2011.

As an illustration of the mutual interest in safety issues between manufacturers, the Boeing company sent senior representatives to Hatfield and offered their help after the first pressure cabin failure. They were subsequently fully informed of the outcome of the inquiry.

Such was the fury at the programme, the failure to produce the so-called 'secret' letters and the failure to respond to Mike Ramsden's and others letters of complaint, the matter was eventually upheld - that is that it being in agreement with the complainers - by The Broadcasting Standards Commission who eventually made a judgement: *'The Broadcasting Standards Commission has upheld overall a complaint of unjust or unfair treatment from Mr Ian F Burns, Mr Anthony John Heath, Mr John Loader on behalf of Hatfield Aviation Association, Mr John Martin, Mr Mervyn Nixon and Mr John Michael Ramsden, about Comet Cover-Up, broadcast by Channel 4 on 13 June 2002. The programme concerned the development of the Comet jet aircraft and the reasons for the Comet 1 crashes.*

The Commission considered that, on the evidence before it, the impression given by the programme that The De Havilland Aircraft Company ('De Havilland') had defied warnings and postponed recommended tests to the fuselage which would have saved passenger lives, was misleading. The Commission was also not persuaded, on the evidence before it, that considerations of speedy production or commercial advantage had led to De Havilland acting culpably in the manner alleged in the programme.

In the light of Channel 4s acknowledgement that relatives were paid compensation in accordance with the requirements of the Warsaw Convention, the Commission considered that it was misleading for the programme to state that relatives had never been compensated for the loss of life.

The Commission considered that the programme treated the subject unfairly in these respects. Taking into account the negative impact of this on the individual complainants and members of the Hatfield Aviation Association, who were involved in the design or production of Comet 1 or De Havillands management at the time, the Commission found this was unfair to the complainants.

The Commission did not find unfairness to any of the complainants in respect of omission to mention the Air Registration Board in the programme, representations made about the nature of the programme or editing of the interview with Mr Ramsden. However, it considered that the aspects on which it did find unfairness represented the major issue in contention and, accordingly, upheld the complaint overall.

The Commission directed Channel 4 to broadcast an approved summary of the Commission s findings on Channel 4 on 11 December 2003. It also directed that it be published in The Daily Telegraph newspaper'.

Chapter Nine

COMET 2, 3, AND MILITARY SERVICE

Before the series of accidents beset the Comet 1, the capabilities of the Series 2 began to emerge. Confidence in the practicability and economic value of jet propulsion in public transport became solidly established, and interest in the Comet became much more serious.

Only 21 of the Series 1 and 1A (including the two development aircraft) were built, and already production of the Series 2, fitted with Rolls-Royce Avon engines, got under way. Larger sales of the Series 1 had never been expected, for a number of reasons; it was known that improved versions were likely to be available at a relatively early date, airlines were fairly well stocked with new fleets after the war, and because operators needed convincing of the merits of jet propulsion.

Now that the airline's confidence had started to grow they were faced with the problem of whether to purchase the Series 2 Comet, a 44-passenger airliner for delivery in 1954 and onwards, or to wait for a 58-78-passenger Series 3 Comet in 1957.

Furthermore, they were aware that De Havilland developments would not stop with the Series 3. The introduction of improved versions had to be balanced against operator requirements - trunk-route airliners in the early 1950s cost more than half a million pounds apiece, and operators were shrewd. They could not introduce Comets to replace good existing piston-engined machines unless assured of sufficient extra profit from the Comets to make good the premature write-off of their earlier investment. On the other hand, world traffic was increasing and fleets had to expand, and operators began to see the wisdom of gaining experience in jets with the Comet 2, which, by reason of its 500 miles an hour speed, was able to achieve more work than a much larger piston-engined liner while giving the travelling public the convenience of high-frequency service, in addition to much greater speed and comfort. They knew that the Comet 2 would have a good innings before it was superseded. They knew that the Comet 3, like the Comet 2, would outclass still larger liners that were

Comet 2X G-ALYT was the original Comet 2 prototype and is seen here on one of its many test flights. One of its many claims to fame was that on 30 April 1952 it carried Brigadier General Albert Boyd and a number of other USAF officers. At the time General Boyd was commander of the Wright Air Development Center, ARDC, at Wright-Patterson Air Force Base, Ohio.

After completion of BOAC route work, G-ALYT was handed back to the Ministry of Supply and then underwent various trials associated with the Avon engines, including trials on the reverse thrusters, which were to be fitted to the Comet 4s. During one such test the thrust reverser to one engine was locked in the reverse position. The reverser engine was started but remained in idle and a normal take-off and circuit was completed on three engines. On touchdown the reverser engine was engaged and the results assessed. *(DH Hatfield)*

not jet-propelled.

De Havilland, in direct touch with the world operators during this period, developed and held in readiness schemes for rapid expansion when the orders justified them. Thus, when an operator spoke of 50 Comet 2s in the year 1955, de Havilland undertook to supply that quantity in addition to orders already taken, provided a contract was placed without delay. They also offered to commence deliveries of the Comet 3 late in 1956.

One such order came from Panair do Brasil, who placed a firm order for four Series 2 Comets for delivery commencing in 1954, and at the same time took an option for two series 3 Comets for later delivery. Both Series were to be powered by Rolls-Royce Avon axial-flow jet engines.

Panair's Comet 2s were to be standard 44-seaters, capable of operating stage lengths exceeding 2,000 miles when carrying their capacity payload of over 13,000 lb. The Comet 3s were intended to be furnished as first-class mainliners seating 58 passengers, but the same type could be equipped as a 78-passenger tourist-class coach. The first-class version could carry its capacity payload of about 17,300 lb, over stages of about 2,600 miles, and the coach version could carry 20,000 lb, over stages of about 2,400 miles.

Not long after that, British Commonwealth Pacific Airlines announced on January 26, 1953 an agreement to purchase three Comet Series 2 for use on their trans-Pacific service linking Australia and New Zealand with the North American continent. It was also made known that further orders for either Series 2 or Series 3 Comets were under consideration.

Delivery of the three Series 2 Comets was expected to take place towards the end of 1954. British Commonwealth Pacific Airlines was 50% owned by the Australian Government, and the New Zealand and British Governments with 30 and 20% holdings respectively. The company operated in parallel with Pan American Airways and Canadian Pacific Airlines on the 7,500-mile Pacific air route connecting Sydney and Auckland with San Francisco and Vancouver by way of Fiji,Canton Island and Honolulu.

As a first step towards the opening of a BOAC Comet service to South America, a proving fight to Rio de Janeiro was carried out in September using the Comet Series 2 prototype G-ALYT. The aircraft was flown by BOAC crews headed by Captain A. P. W. Cane and Captain A, M. A. Majendie, and among the nine passengers were Sir Miles Thomas, Chairman of BOAC, and Dr. Paulo Sampaio, President Director of Panair do Brasil, who also planned to operate Series 2 Comets between Brazil and Europe.

Although this was the first time a jet airliner had flown to South America no attempt was made to put up spectacular times. Long ground stops were planned ahead because of the unfamiliarity with the Comet of the ground staff and refuelling crews. On many of the stages practice approaches were made and in some cases short demonstration flights were given before landing.

The Comet left London Airport on Sunday, 13 September at 17.29 GMT and flying via Lisbon, Dakar and Recife, arrived at Rio de Janeiro at 14.35 GMT on 14 September - an elapsed time of 21 hours and six minutes, which could be compared with the normal BOAC piston-engined airliner schedule of 30 hours 45 minutes. The flying time for the 5,850-miles journey was 15 hours 49 minutes.

The return flight was commenced on 17 September and was via Dakar, Casablanca and Madrid. After a 24-hour stop over there, the aircraft arrived back at London Airport at 14.37 GMT on 19 September after a flight lasting 2 hours 10 minutes.

All along the route tremendous interest was displayed, especially at those places where the Comet was appearing for the first time, namely Madrid, Recife, Natal and Rio de Janeiro. At Natal the military had to be called out to disperse the crowd thronging round the Comet and at Rio similar scenes of enthusiasm were seen. Before landing at Rio`s Airport the Comet flew several times round the town, finishing-up with a low fly-past along the famous Copacabana beach.

The first production Series 2 was seen as the first definitive variant, coming complete with Rolls-Royce Avon engines, modified intakes and reconfigured wing leading edges. Twelve of this version were ordered by BOAC and the first, G-AMXA, was built at Hatfield.

It made its maiden flight on 27 August 1953, making a public appearance at the SBAC show at Farnborough the following month.

'XA then undertook a series of route-proving and production-test flights, the first of which began in January 1954 when the Comet was flown from Hatfield to Khartoum in a time of 6 hours 30 minutes over a distance of 3,080 miles. Aboard for this flight were John Cunningham and Peter Bugge from De Havilland, while BOAC was represented by Captains A. Majendie and H. Field; other organizations with representatives aboard included the Air Registration Board and Rolls-Royce. The purpose of the trip was to carry out tropical trials at Khartoum and high altitude take-offs and landings from Jan Smuts airfield, Johannesburg. After visits to other airfields in the region the Comet finally returned to Britain on 6 February.

The came the Comet disasters. Unsure of the safety status of its potential Comet 2 fleet, BOAC decided to adopt a conservative course and reject the aircraft.

The summer of 1954 saw all work cease on the Comet 2s, and production of the Comet 3 had also been put off pending the outcome of the Farnborough investigation, but the company had wisely decided to

G-AMXA was built as a Comet 2 for BOAC, and was seen here taking off from Hatfield on an early acceptance flight.

Colonel Charles Lindbergh, American aviator, author, inventor, explorer, and social activist and a technical advisor to the United States Government, visited Hatfield in September 1953. Accompanied by Mr. A. A. Priester (second from right), the Vice-President and Chief Engineer of Pan American World Airways, and Mr. V. A. F. Taylor (extreme right), a director of the same company, Colonel Lindbergh flew in the Avon Comet G-ALYT. The Colonel and his companions are seen at Hatfield with John Cunningham and Frank Lloyd of the De Havilland Aircraft Company. Colonel Lindbergh described his flight as *'...enjoyable and most impressive'* *(both DH Hatfield)*

Left: The Comet at Rio seen through an archway of the terminal building at Galeao Airport. The Comet covered the 5,850 milesfrom London in 15 hours 49 minutes flying time. The outward and return flights were completely 'snag-free'.

Below: Light at the end of a dark tunnel - Comet 2E G-AXMD in the foreground with the sole Comet 3 G-ALNO in flight behind.

press on with its programme on the nearly completed Comet 3 prototype, and its maiden flight duly took place on 19 July in the hands of John Cunningham and Peter Bugge.

Despite the uncertainty that surrounded the future of the aircraft, its dramatic appearance at the Farnborough Air Display in September did much to dispel the gathering despair among Britain's air-minded public, who had so recently seen their country's aviation prestige shattered by the failure of the first Comets. A month later came de Havilland's heartening announcement of the steps they were taking to overcome the faults in the design. In addition to using a thicker and stronger skin, there were to be extensive modifications to a number of points - such as the clumsy feel of the pilot's elevator

control - that Farnborough had criticized in the course of their tests; and the entire structure was to be redesigned in the light of the latest knowledge to improve the fatigue characteristics, especially at the vulnerable 'cut-outs' round the hatches and windows, where the stress concentrations were highest. In fact, de Havilland's were virtually setting out to build an entirely new aeroplane, and it wasn't long before someone started calling it the 'New Comet'. Over the past few years it has often been suggested that it should have been given a new name as well, if people were not to associate it with an unfortunate early history. But de Havilland's felt there was nothing about the Comet to be ashamed of; the name had never ceased to be a proud one, and they stuck to it.

There remained the problem of what to do with

the multi-million pound fleet of existing aircraft. They were mostly brand new and too valuable for the scrap heap, but could not economically be rebuilt to the advanced standards required for the Comet 4. In the case of the few Comet Is that remained intact - a number had been wrecked during the Farnborough tests - it was obvious that the modifications needed to make them fit for any sort of further passenger service would be far too extensive. They were accordingly stripped of their luxurious furnishings and turned over to the Government for experimental work.

The Comet 2 proved a much better proposition.

Comets for the military

It was to the Royal Canadian Air Force that the honour of introducing the first Comet to the North American Continent, having been ordered in November 1951 - the aircraft being unusual at the time, for they were to be fitted with Ekco weather radar in the nose that resulted in the metal nosecone being replaced with a fibreglass one.

While the aircraft were being built at Hatfield sixty air and ground crew drawn from 412 Squadron RCAF were sent to De Havillands for training in October 1952. On 14 March 1953 the first Comet IA, 5301, was handed over to the RCAF in Britain, the second machine being handed over on 13 April before the crews started an intensive flying training course under the supervision of BOAC, during which they covered over 60,000 miles on the routes to South Africa, India and Singapore. On 9 May one of the Comets established an unofficial record by flying non-stop the 2,250 miles from London to Beirut in 5 hour 10 minutes, and on June 5 the other flew non-stop in the reverse direction in 5 hours 20 minutes.

The historic arrival in Canada did not occur until 29 May, when 5301 landed at Uplands Airfield, Ottawa, at precisely 15.00 local time, after completing the flight from England via Iceland and Labrador in an elapsed time of 14 hours 34 minutes.

The Comet took off from London Airport at 04.23 GMT and flew against strong headwinds to Keflavik, a distance of 1180 statute miles, in about four hours flying time. The next stage of 1,495 statute miles to Goose Bay in Labrador was covered in a flying time of 4 hours 5 minutes and the final stage to Uplands, Ottawa, 870 statute miles, in just over two hours. The total flying time for the journey was 10 hours 20 minutes.

The Royal Canadian Air Force's first Comet at Uplands aerodrome, Ottawa, on 29 May shortly after arrival from London. The flight by way of Keflavik and Goose Bay, was accomplished in 11 hours 20 minutes flying time. The second Comet, (below) following the same route, flew to Ottawa on 16 June in 9 hours 23 minutes flying time, and arrived on schedule after an equally trouble-free journey. The RCAF was the first air force in the world to operate jet transports. *(DH Hatfield)*

The highly polished RCAF Comets were seen all over Canada and in Europe.

On arrival at RCAF Uplands, the Comet was welcomed by the Hon. Brooke Claxton, Minister of National Defence in the Canadian Government, and by Air Marshal Roy Slemon, CB, CBE, CD, BSc, Chief of the Canadian Air Staff.

Having had a tumultuous welcome at Uplands, the Comet then departed on a cross-country tour to show off the aircraft's speed and sleek lines. Initially 412 Squadron would remain at Rockliffe while five new hangars were constructed at Uplands, partly to accommodate the Comets. 412 Squadron moved to their new premises on 1 September 1955.

On 16 June the second RCAF Comet, 5302, flew over the same route from London to Ottawa, cutting by very nearly one hour the time taken by her sister ship. On this occasion the flying time was 9 hours 23 minutes and the total elapsed time was 14 hours.

The two RCAF Series IA Comets were to be operated by 412 Squadron, under the command of Wing Commander Howard Morrison, DSO, DFC, AFC. 412 Squadron employed the Comet on VIP flights - those over short distances were reduced in time by one third while longer range flights were reduced by up to 50%. In between these trips the Comets were used in the high-speed target role to test the abilities of the CF-100 force that made up the bulk of Air Defence Command, and of the ground-based air-defence radar chain.

As well as flying VIP and air-defence flights the two RCAF Comets were employed in transporting personnel to 1 Wing, based at Marville, France, which served as part of NATO. When the flights from Ottawa were undertaken the aircraft would have a maximum take-off weight of 117,000lb of which 50,000lb was fuel. This load gave the aircraft an endurance of 6 hours, plus 45 minutes' diversion time, this being calculated at a consumption rate of 8,000lb per hour. The normal passenger load for each of these flights was thirty-seven persons.

The Comets were grounded in January 1954 in the wake of the crashes that overtook the BOAC aircraft and were placed in storage at De Havilland's Downsview. Investigations were made regarding the possibility of having the aircraft modified, which was eventually agreed and the aircraft were flown - unpressurised - to Boughton, Chester during May 1956 to undergo structural repairs which involved the fitment of heavier-gauge fuselage skins, oval windows in place of the original rectangular examples and uprated Ghost engines. After modification to Comet Mks IXB standard both aircraft were returned to the RCAF in November

1957 to resume service. The cost for modifying both these aircraft was £142,000. Both Comets resumed their previous range of duties, which continued until they were withdrawn from service and placed on the disposal list at Mountainview on 30 October 1963.

Into RAF service.

The second air force to acquire the Comet was the RAF, which came about through the cancelled BOAC order. Thirteen Comet 2s were transferred to the RAF on 18 March 1955, of which ten were reworked with a new, stronger structure complete with oval windows capable of safe pressurization so that they could attain a Certificate of Airworthiness. This made aircraft suitable for use by Transport Command. As an added precaution, a limit would be set on its flying life.

But before it went into service, it was decided that it should obtain a full commercial passenger-carrying Certificate of Airworthiness - a unique step in the case of an RAF aircraft - and no one expected that this certificate would lightly be handed out. Under the stringent new regulations drawn up as a result of the Inquiry - and since adopted by the other major aircraft-producing countries of the world - two complete and fully representative airframes had first to undergo structural testing, one for static strength and the other for fatigue. This work occupied De Havilland's throughout 1955 and the early part of l956. Several thousand individual tests on

components and fuselage specimens were carried out before a fully modified Comet 2 was submitted to full-scale fatigue tests in the newly built Hatfield tank, and showed itself to have a safe life comfortably in excess of the RAF's requirements.

The Certificate of Airworthiness programme also called for precise measurements of the aircraft's behaviour under the full range of temperate and tropical conditions. Thus, although full trials had already been carried out on an earlier Comet 2, they now had to be done all over again, because the strengthened aircraft were naturally a bit heavier than their predecessors. There proved to be very little change in performance, however, the increased power of the latest Rolls-Royce Avon engines, which developed 7,300 lb thrust for take-off, easily compensating for the extra weight.

On 18 March 1955 G-AMXA was transferred to the Ministry of Supply for conversion to Comet R1 standard for use by the Royal Air Force. A similar fate befell the second Series 2, which had also been rolled out at Hatfield in BOAC colours as G-AMXB. Having made its maiden flight on 3 November 1953 the aircraft was allocated to the airworthiness clearance programme. Peter Bugge was the pilot in command for these flights and also for the stall tests that were undertaken in December 1955. As the performance and the behaviour of the aircraft was satisfactory it was subjected to C of A testing which was completed in May 1956.

Left: The clean lines of XK671 - the former G-AXMG - seen in flight.

Below: the same aircraft looking somewhat weather-stained at RAF Waterbeach in 1963.

As with 'XA', this aircraft was sold to the MoS and pursued a further career with the RAF. The third Series 2, G-AMXC, made its first flight from Hatfield on 25 November 1953. It was soon delivered to BOAC and undertook route-proving flights. These ended at the beginning of 1954 with the aircraft being purchased by the MoS for further use by the RAF. A similar fate befell the fourth Series 2, G-AMXD, which made its first flight from Hatfield on 20 August 1955, before a public appearance at that year's SBAC Farnborough show. This was followed by various flight trials for clearance purposes, which kept De Havilland's and the aircraft occupied until 1957. Having completed its various trials the Comet was flown from Hatfield to Chester where it was put through an extensive modification programme to allow it to be flown pressurized.

Changes were made to the engines, with Avon Mk 504s at positions two and three (the inboard positions) while Avon Mk 524s were installed in positions one and four (outboard). In its new form the aircraft was designated the Comet 2E and was issued with a C of A to that effect on 23 July 1957. Although intended to be used as an engine test bed it was seconded to BOAC for engine-performance trials in

anticipation of the airline accepting the Comet 4. In September 1957 G-AMXD was flown to Beirut and Nairobi to undertake 'hot and high' performance trials, these lasting until May 1958. During this period over 3,000 hours were flown by the crews allocated to the programme. Having left the Middle East, the Comet 2E began route-proving trials to New York in anticipation of Comet 4 services that were intended to start in October 1958.

Upon completion the Comet 2E was allocated permanently to RAE Farnborough for various trials and evaluation work, a task it performed admirably until withdrawal in 1973.

The remaining Comet 2s intended for BOAC were still on the production line at Hatfield in various stages of completion when the order came to cease work while investigations were undertaken into the crashes that had overtaken the earlier machines.

One of the outcomes of the crashes was the cancellation of various orders which in the end would affect seven airframes due to be built at Hatfield, while a further thirty scheduled to be built at Chester were also cancelled and their already-built sections scrapped. A further fallout was that a production line created to build Comets at Shorts Brothers in Belfast

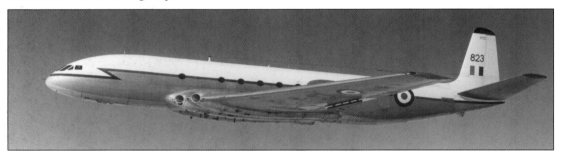

The Royal Air Force's XM823 was a Mk1A, originally delivered to Air France as F-BGNZ. It was grounded following the Comet 1 accidents, returned to Hatfield, strengthened, and modified as a Mk.1XB and returned to the air as G-APAS. It was transferred to Hawker Siddeley Dynamics and used on a number of trials programmes. It was finally transferred to the ownership of the RAF Museum and is preserved. *(DH Hatfield)*

The cockpit of the aircraft, now on display at Cosford. *(author)*

in 1954 in a 500,000 square foot factory, production was started in 1953, but was soon shut down after just two fuselages and other assorted components were built. These, and other components were shipped across the Irish Sea aboard the *Empire Cymric,* in late October 1955, docking near Chester where they were taken by road to the Chester site by Pickfords Removals and were eventually scrapped.

Finally in May 1956, after a number of setbacks and delays that provoked a certain amount of unfavourable and mostly unfair press comment, the Comet 2 was granted an unrestricted Certificate of Airworthiness and ten of them subsequently entered service with the RAF. In the years that followed, they earned an enviable reputation for their reliability, speed and comfort. Their roles were high-speed transport, VIP transport and medical evacuation. The final three airframes remained unconverted, with their pressurization disabled: their role was that of electronic intelligence gathering, the crew having to wear oxygen masks above 10,000 feet.

The first reworked Comet C.2 made its maiden flight in December 1955, deliveries being made to 216 Squadron at RAF Lyneham in 1956. Initially the first few Comet C.2s were designated as trainers for use in the crew conversion role, for which purpose they had dayglo bands on the nose and tail. These bands also served as high visibility marks for when the Comets were flown into and out of Berlin along the East German air corridors that were regularly monitored by Soviet MiGs.

The first two of a batch of ten Comet Mk. 2 aircraft were delivered to the RAF on 7 June and 8 1956, forming the equipment of 216

Squadron, operating from Lyneham in Wiltshire.

The first operational flight of the Comet Mk. 2 in squadron service timed for two weeks or so later was of historic interest, for a British Minister and his staff were conveyed to Moscow, and in the first British jet-engined aircraft ever to visit Russia's capital.

This first flight was made on Saturday 23 June. The aircraft landed at Moscow Airport carrying Mr. Nigel Birch, PC, OBE, MP, Secretary of State for Air in Her Majesty`s Government and other senior Royal Air Force officers who had been invited by Mr, Bulganin, the Russian Prime Minister, to attend the Soviet Union Air Display held at Tushino Airport on 24 June. The Comet left London Airport at 11.20 British Summer Time and landed in Moscow some four hours later, having flown non-stop by an obligatory indirect route via Berlin and Warsaw, a distance of about 1,700 statute miles. The Comet returned to London Airport on 29 June, bringing back Mr Birch and part of the delegation.

On 3 July, a second Comet of Transport Command returned to Moscow to pick up the remainder of the British party, which was now headed by Air Marshal Sir Thomas Pike, Deputy Chief of Air Staff. The outward and return flights on this occasion were made on the same day, and while in Moscow the opportunity was taken to give a 'full house' of Russian officials a flight in the aircraft; this

The two Shorts Brothers-built Comet 2 fuselages aboard the *Empire Cymric* ready shipping across the Irish Sea to Chester from Sydenham. Both aircraft has been laid down for the French airline UAT, but were never completed.
(DH Hatfield)

Above: XK715 - a genuine Comet C.2, not a conversion - seen in RAF Transport Command marks, with high-visibility daygo bands on the nose and tail.

Left: A view of the forward cabin of a Comet 2. In common with all other aircraft of Transport Command, RAF Comets were fitted with rearward-facing seats of a standard pattern.

About to leave for Malta! During the Suez Crisis of 29 October – 7 November 1956 the RAF's Comet 2s maintained a regular service between the UK and Allied Headquarters Middle East Command in Cyprus.

RAF Comets were used to 'show the flag' all over the Empire!

Ghana's celebrations on achieving independence within the British Commonwealth provided the occasion for two Comet 2s of Transport Command to support Bomber Command Valiants on a goodwill mission. During the visit, three special Comet flights were made. Passenger lists included no fewer than twelve Chiefs, some of whom are seen boarding here.

RAF Transport Command Comets were also regularly used by royalty. Here Her Majesty The Queen, accompanied by HRH Prince Phillip, Duke of Edinburgh is seen arriving at London Airport after a flight from Leuchars, where she presented a standard to 43 Squadron.
(all DH Hatfield)

Mr Nigel Birch, PC, OBE MP, Secretary of State for Air is seen in the company of Air Chief-Marshal Sir Ronald Ivelaw-Chapman, KCB, KBE, DFC AFC, Vice Chief of the Air Staff before their departure for Moscow. On the Air Marshal's right and with his back to the camera is Air Vice-Marshal A McKee, CB, CBE, DSO, DFC, AFC, Air Officer Commanding-in-Chief Transport Command

RAF Comet 2 XK670 visits Moscow - the first western jet to do so.

would have taken place during the first visit but for an internal fault in one of the aircraft's batteries. On this second journey to Moscow the Comet took off from Hatfield and had on board Lady Hayter, the wife of the British Ambassador to the Soviet Union.

Following the 70-minute demonstration flight, during which many Russian officials commented favourably on the aircraft and its handling qualities, the Comet left for Hatfield, where it arrived four hours later at 19.30. During the flight the Comet was intercepted over Germany at 40,000 feet by Hunters and Venoms of the 2nd Tactical Air Force.

On both occasions the Comets were flown by Wing Commander B D Sellick as Captain of the aircraft, with Squadron Leader P Bois, DFC, RAFVR, as his second pilot.

Comet Casevac

Casualty evacuation during peacetime was usually a scheduled operation and it was possible to give more attention to comfort, for the maximum use of payload was not the prime consideration. The Comet 2 proved to be an ideal aircraft for this duty, flying at between 38-42,000 feet to be above the weather, with high performance over a satisfactory range. The introduction of the Comet in this new role revolutionised the whole concept of aeromedical flights, and the effect on the morale of patients was considerable. In the early 1950s the flight from Singapore (Changi) to England (Lyneham) took seven days, and the journey from Cyprus (Nicosia) took two days. By 1956 by Comet, the flying time from Singapore was nineteen hours (with stops at Aden, Katunayake and El Adem). From Cyprus the journey was a direct run of some five hours.

The Cyprus and Singapore flights were, as mentioned earlier, scheduled services. In addition there were many 'mercy' flights and Comets brought back individual cases to the UK from as far afield as Australia and Christmas Island.

The normal medical 'crew' on the Comet was four, consisting of two flight sisters from RAF hospitals in England, and two male nursing staff, one fully trained and one under training, known as air ambulance attendants. Only if a patient`s condition demanded it, was a medical officer also carried.

Up to 36 patients could be transported by one Comet. There were six stretchers in three pairs in the forward cabin of the aircraft for the seriously ill and in the rear cabin were eight reclining seats for the most needy of the ambulatory patients. The remainder travelled in trooping seats together with the medical team and other passengers. Because of the lightness of the forward load represented by six stretcher cases, baggage and freight were also put into the front compartment.

A typical Comet 2 'casevac' flight in the 1956 was when a number of patients needed to be evacuated from the British Military Hospitals in the Near East, with the British Military Hospital in Nicosia being the central clearing station for all Middle East flights.

Flight SP2044 left Lyneham in Wiltshire on time at 08.00 GMT. The aircraft followed normal Comet flight patterns by climbing steadily at 230 knots and reaching 37,500 feet when 180 miles out. It then levelled off. As the fuel load steadily reduced the aircraft climbed further at Mach .73 to 41,800 feet.

On the outward journey the Comet was flying in a normal passenger-freight role. The 36 passengers included a medical team of four, a Hastings slip crew, men of the Royal Suffolk Regiment, two RASC NCOs, a driver from the RAOC and the wife of a senior Royal Air Force officer based in Akrotiri.

Comet XK 671 arrived at RAF Nicosia at 13.20 GMT having flown nearly 2,500 miles non-stop in 5 hr. 20 min. at an average speed of more than 450 mph. On arrival the seats were removed from the forward cabin of the aircraft and preparations were

made for the accommodation of three stretchers which would be in position on the return journey. Meanwhile the nursing staff had left for the British Military Hospital to see the patients who would be travelling next day and to ascertain their in-flight requirements.

The aircraft was put under armed guard from the time of arrival and the following day an early start was to be made, scheduled take-off time being 07.30 GMT. There were patients from all three services and they were transported from the hospital to the aircraft in their respective ambulances. The RAF was responsible for all patients when they were moved by air. They were always seen by an RAF medical officer prior to flight. Being an ambulance patient did not preclude one from security arrangements then in place on the island.

The stretchers with the patients on were loaded in the forward cabin of the aircraft direct from the ambulance. Loading was carried out through the crew entry door and the change in the level of vehicles was accommodated by means of a portable covered ramp which was man-handled into position. The stretchers were lashed to the floor of the aircraft and the patient made comfortable.

The make-up of the patient load was typical - one seriously ill driver from the Grenadier Guards had a fractured skull and jaw. The only way he could be fed was through a polythene tube inserted through his jaw splints, and on the journey he was given warm milk. Comet speed and smoothness meant much to him. The two other stretchers carried National Service men who were less ill.

In the reclining seats were seven patients including a six-year-old boy travelling home with his father. The remainder of the patients were mainly convalescent and were being repatriated to the United Kingdom for convalescence and sick leave.

The flight from Nicosia to Luqa, Malta, a distance

Six hours before this photograph was taken, XK671 was in Cyprus; now, after a brief stop in Malta the patients are in England and will be en route to the RAF Hospital at Wroughton within minutes of landing.

Left: three stretchers are gently moved from an Army ambulance onto a covered ramp by the crew door of XK671. The covered platform is used to adjust the height, and provide the patients with some shade.

Below: Flight Officer Dawson of the Princess Marina Royal Air Force Nursing Service from the RAF Hospital at Wroughton talks to two National Service men being evacuated from the Middle East.

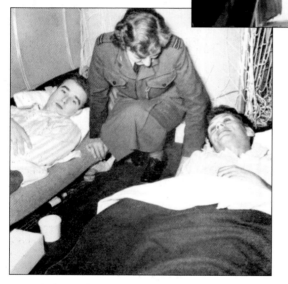

experts; it would also save dollars. Past visits-made once yearly - by RAF navigation specialist students to America had been undertaken in several aircraft navigated by the students. By travelling in one group in the Comet both time and money should be saved. Extra time in America can be devoted to intensive studies and discussions with the specialists of the USAF and RCAF, The flight entailed a 12,000 miles journey via Goose Bay, Labrador,and Keflavik, Iceland, outward. The return was via Bermuda and the Azores arriving back at Lyneham on 3 June.

Stops on the tour included the RCAF Central Navigation School at Winnipeg on 20 May, the USAF Air Development Centre at Wright Patterson AFB; Mather Air Force Base, California, where the USAF course equivalent to the RAF Specialist Navigation Course was located; and Eglin AFB, where the USAF Armaments Centre and Air Proving Ground was based. Passenger as far as Washington on a liaison mission to the USAF and the Pentagon was Air Marshal Sir Richard Atcherley, Air Ofiicer Commanding-in-Chief Flying Training Command, who was accompanied by Group Capt D. L. Amlot, CBE, DFC, AFC and Director of Flying Training, Air Ministry, and Wing Commander G. McKenzie, DFC, of Headquarters, No. 23 Group.

Comet spies

The Comet R.2 ELectronic/SIGnal INTelligence (SIG/ELINT) aircraft were delivered to 51 Squadron at RAF Wyton in 1957, the flight-deck crews having been trained by 216 Squadron. Conversion work was carried out by Marshalls of Cambridge and continued until the aircraft were rolled out in February 1958. The aircraft were supplied without engines but with a guaranteed minimum fatigue life of 2,000 hours. The engines now installed in them were Rolls-Royce

of nearly 1,100 miles, took 2.75 hours. There more service personnel joined the aircraft during the one-hour stop and the Comet was soon on its way on the second hop of its journey to England, a 1,400-mile stage which took a mere 3.25 hours.

On 10 May 1957 it was announced that an RAF Transport Command Comet had been selected by Flying Training Command for a 17-day tour of RCAF and USAF units in North America, starting from RAF Lyneham on 17 May for specialist navigation students of the RAF Flying College, Manby, Lincolnshire. This was the first visit to America by a RAF Comet.

Sponsored by Air Vice-Marshal G. D. Harvey, the Assistant Chief of the Air Staff (Training), the flight was designed for economy as well as prestige. It not only enabled a Comet to show its wings in both the USA and Canada before audiences which mainly comprised of high-ranking service officers and

In the hangar at Lyneham a Comet undergoes inspection after returning from Cyprus. The rate of servicablity was regarded as good, averaging around 80 hours a month not long after the type entered service.

The arrival of the first RAF Comet 2 at Changi airfield, Singapore on 23 October 1956. This was the first of several proving flights to the Far East.

Avon 504s rated at 7,330lb thrust each.

The decision to equip Comets as SIGINT platforms goes back to a US/UK ELINT conference of December 1952. An English Electric Canberra was soon delivered but the Treasury dragged its heels on Comet for about a year. Three airframes were converted at CSE Watton by the Special Radio Installation Flight (SRIF). Work began in the spring of 1957 but one airframe was destroyed in a hangar fire on 3 June 1959. Two years elapsed before GCHQ could persuade the Treasury to release funds to replace it.

The first two examples were delivered to 192 Squadron at RAF Watton who soon re-numbered to 51 Squadron and moved to RAF Wyton. Eventually a total of seven Comet R Mk 2's were delivered and

they took over the ELINT role from the venerable Lincoln and RB-29A Washington. With 4 jet engines, the performance of the Comet was considerably better than its piston engined predecessors.

The Comet R Mk 2 was frequently deployed on so-called 'ferret' sorties over the Barents Sea north of Norway, along the Baltic and even detached to Cyprus where it could easily monitor activity along the border of the Black Sea – an area of particular interest. These activities were described as 'Radio Proving Flights', the purpose of which was to allow the intelligence community to build up a picture of Soviet Air Defences, upon which RAF Bomber Command could then base their operational plans.

The flights all took place over friendly or neutral territory or over international waters – no penetration of Warsaw Pact airspace was involved. The Prime Minister was sent a copy of the proposed monthly programme of flights for his approval. Once this was obtained for the overall monthly programme, Ministry of Defence and Foreign Office officials carefully planned each individual flight and final authorisation rested with the Secretary of State for Defence.

The principle rules governing RAF 'radio proving flights' were that the aircraft approached no closer than 30 nautical miles to Soviet or Satellite territory. Except in the case of West Germany, aircraft were not permitted to overfly the territory or territorial waters of friendly or neutral countries whilst engaged in these operations without the concurrence of the competent authorities in the countries concerned. No more than four aircraft were

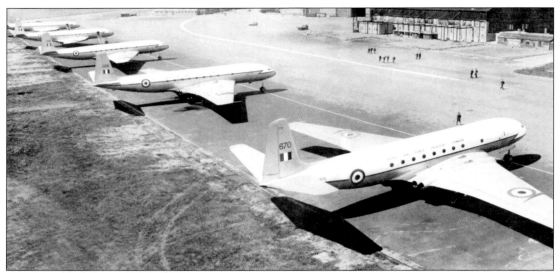

Above: 216 Squadron at Lyneham.

Left: Air Chief Marshal Sir Dermont Boyle is greeted by Major-General Homer L Saunders, Vice-Commander CONAC at Floyd Bennett Field - this was the first time a Comet had visited New York.

Below: A pair of RAF Comet 2s and one of the Valiant V-bombers on the apron at Pinecastle AFB, near Orlando in Florida. The Comets were used to ferry over Bomber Command ground crews.

Comet C.2 XK697 'Cygnus' at the 1970 RAF Honington 'Battle of Britain' Open Day before the public were let in! This aircraft had been used for some SIGINT work with 51 Squadron at RAF Wyton and was fitted with a long nose-probe for a time. *(author)*

used together in the same operating area. Daylight operations were limited to single aircraft and single aircraft operating by day or night were not permitted to make a direct 'provocative' approach to the coast or border and had to fly broadly parallel to the coast line. Operations involving more than one aircraft had to be normally flown in conditions of total darkness and in any case under conditions of the light than 'half moon'.

The American intelligence community also ran their own electronic intelligence gathering operations using, during the same period, the RB-47. The American government submitted a monthly list in advance to the British government detailing when an RB-47 intelligence gathering flight was planned to operate from a British base, such as Brize Norton. A copy of the RAF monthly programme was also

forwarded to the American government. Radio Proving Flight Co-ordination Meetings also took place on a regular basis between British and American officials.

RAF flights were usually conducted with two aircraft, a Comet R.2 and a specially equipped Canberra also from 51 Squadron. Typically, the Canberra would fly a profile that would attract the attention of the Warsaw Pact radar defences, allowing the Comet to record the transmissions. This would usually involve the Canberra flying at low-level below radar cover towards the target area and then, as the aircraft neared the minimum distance, they could approach the Warsaw Pact boundary, it would suddenly climb rapidly into radar cover alerting the air defence radars. Meanwhile the Comet would sit back at higher altitude, flying parallel to the

The differences between the C.2 and Comet 2R were not immediately obvious.

Right: C.2 XK715 in flight.

XK695 seen at RAF Wyton with at least two pods under its fuselage. This machine went for removal of its secret equipment before being flown to Duxford for supposed preservation - it was scrapped there in 1992

XK659 had first flown on non-passenger carrying proving flights in BOAC colours, but was later converted into a Comet 2R. It was never converted to oval windows and thus would never fly with pressurisation. It is seen above with assorted 'lumps and bumps' under its fuselage, including one aerial that looks suspiciously like some form of sideways looking radar!

At some point in the aircraft's career whilst at RAF Wyton it gained this smoke-ejecting duck emblem - clearly a variation of 51 Squadrons 'droopy goose' badge - on its vertical fin, the meaning of which has been lost in the mists of time. *(both Warrant Officer Paddy Porter BEM)*

boundary, listening in and recording the frequencies and transmissions of the radar and radios used by the air defence forces. Direction finding equipment on-board the Comet would also enable the location of the radar and transmitters to be determined.

Flights were conducted throughout in strict radio silence, to maintain an element of tactical freedom and surprise whilst concealing the identity of the aircraft from the Russian defences. Radio silence was only broken in an emergency or to recall the aircraft. As far as it can be ascertained, no RAF aircraft conducting a 'radio proving flight' was ever lost, although a number of American aircraft were shot down whilst engaged in these activities.

In addition to the front crew of two pilots, two navigators and a flight engineer, up to ten specialists were carried in the main cabin of the Comets where they operated the monitoring and recording equipment, much of which was manufactured in the USA.

Because of a long-standing agreement to share intelligence, the Comet R Mk 2 often operated in conjunction with USAF RB-47s.

The decision to replace the Comets was made

perhaps as early as 1961. A secret group, the Technical Committee of London Signals Intelligence Committee began looking into future ELINT research in November 1961. This group had been behind the development of the 'Airborne Rafter' programme hunting for KGB agent's radio transmissions over Britain. The committee reported back that tactical elint collection over the Eastern Bloc borders was a future need and in 1962 Plessey was awarded a development contract for a 'experimental sideways-looking ELINT system'. This system was covered under Air Staff Requirement 817 'Sideways Looking Airborne Search Reviewing System.' It has been claimed by some sources that this was the offical start of the what became the Nimrod R.1 programme.

The Comet R.2s were eventually replaced by 3 Nimrod R.s in 1974.

The Comet 3

By the middle of 1952 the Series 3 Comet was in an advanced stage of design - to a point where it was publically revealed at the SBAC airshow at Farnborough in September. It was an enlarged version of the original configuration, incorporating all the lessons of experience gained with the earlier versions.

Initially, the Series 3 Comet was to have an all-up weight of about 145,000 lb. The four -Royce Avons of 9,000 lb. static thrust provided a cruising speed of at least 500 m.p.h.

Interior accommodation was to provide alternative seating arrangements for up to 58 first-class passengers or for up to 78 passengers in the tourist class.

The practical stage length, taking into account fuel reserves for climb, descent, headwinds, stand-off and diversions, meant that it was about 60% greater than that of the Series 1 Comet and the specific cost of operation was appreciably lower.

The prototype Series 3 was expected to fly early in 1954, and the first production aircraft was scheduled to appear late in 1956. In December 1953, BOAC announced that it was to order five Comet 3s to form the airliners initial express transatlantic fleet. A contract was signed on 1 February 1954. However, just as with the Comet 2, the incidents involving the Series 1 aircraft had a great impact on the Comet 3.

Only a single Comet 3 was built - G-ANLO, actually owned by the Ministry of Supply - and this aircraft served as a development machine for the Comet 4. Rolled out in May 1954, it took to the skies

for the first time on 19 July. The first public display was at the 1955 SBAC show, when it appeared in BOAC colours. After Farnborough the aircraft was readied for a series of development flights, even though the investigations into the Comet crashes were still ongoing. The Series 3 was a completely different machine and so the authorities had no hesitation in clearing the aircraft for these flights.

Around the world!

28 December 1955 saw the return home of G-ANLO, the Comet 3 development aircraft, at the completion of a round-the-world proving flight. The purpose of the flight, as conceived, planned and executed by de Havilland, was twofold - to operate and prove the aeroplane in a wide variety of atmospheric conditions simulating as far as possible actual airline operations and to check the performance of the aircraft against the basis used for calculating the brochure performance figures of the Comet 4.

The outward configuration of the Comet 3 closely resembled that of the Comet 4 but the Rolls-Royce 10,000 lb. thrust Avon R.A.26 engines fitted were not so powerful as the 10,500lb. thrust Avon R.A.29 that were to be installed in the Comet 4. The total fuel capacity of the aircraft was less but the specific consumption would be appreciably improved.

In spite of these limitations it was possible

Above: the sole Comet 3 G-ANLO seen at Hatfield not long after roll-out in May 1954.

Right: now with full BOAC markings, the aircraft is displayed at the 1955 SBAC Farnborough display.

Above: With a partially complete fuselage on a ground handling trolley in the background, Comet 3 G-ANLO awaits another test flight.

Right: being a development aircraft, things constantly changed with G-ALNO. Here, in what was obviously a posed photograph, test pilot John Cunningham 'inspects' one of a pair of Rolls Royce thurst reverser units fitted to the outboard Avons as standard equipment for all future Comets.

throughout the flight to simulate very closely the Comet 4 operating technique.

Frank Lloyd, Commercial Sales Manager and Contracts Manager of The De Havilland Aircraft Co. Ltd., was the executive in charge of the business aspects of the flight and John Cunningham, Chief Test Pilot of the Company, commanded the aircraft. Peter Buggé was second pilot.

As the *De Havilland Gazette* said '...*John Cunningham and all aboard were very pleased to fly in BOAC colours and greatly appreciated the decision of the Corporation to send Captain Peter Cane, who headed the pilots of the Comet fleet in 1952-54, to accompany the aircraft as a member of the crew throughout the tour.*

The Company is most grateful for the assistance given by BOAC at ports of call, and likewise by QANTAS Empire Airways, Trans-Australia Airlines, Australian National Airways, Tasman Empire Airways, Canadian Pacific Air Lines, Trans-Canada Airlines, the Shell Company and its associates, the Royal Air Force and the Royal Australian, New Zealand and Canadian Air Forces, as well as the airport and airway authorities throughout the world. Efficient help all round was received from the airway organisation, and the many who contribute to it with

ground handling, maintenance, refuelling, meteorology, radio and communications, customs, immigration and other services'.

The Company took fullest advantage of the opportunity to demonstrate the aircraft to operators, technical authorities, the Press and public, and this aspect of the flight has of proved of the utmost value. Apart from the circuiting of cities to give as many people as possible a good view of the Comet, the aircraft was flown strictly in accordance with airline technique. The Sydney-Melbourne stage (circling Canberra) and the Toronto-Montreal stage were too short for representative flying, and the Melbourne-Perth was made unrepresentative by circling Adelaide.

Airline pilots, familiar with their respective respective sectors, who were carried as supernumerary members were as follows:- BOAC pilot, Captain Peter Cane who flew all round the world; QANTAS pilot, Captain I. D. V. Ralfe, who flew London-Sydney QANTAS Pacific pilot, Captain W. A. Edwards TAA, ANA, and Australian Department of Civil Aviation pilots CPA pilot, Captain W. S. Roxburgh CPA Director of Flight Operations, Captain B. Rawson TCA Flight Superintendent of Western Division, Captain A. Rankin who flew Sydney-Honolulu Melbourne - Perth - Sydney Honolulu - Vancouver then Vancouver - Toronto and Vancouver-Toronto.

The aircraft was equipped with elaborate recording instruments and, in addition to flight and engineering crew, carried observers including a senior aerodynamicist from Hatfield.

A specific flight procedure was adopted in order to create standardised performance

1 - Climb. Immediately after the undercarriage was retracted the engines were throttled to the cruising rating of 7,100 RPM. The aircraft was accelerated at this power to reach 240 knots indicated air speed below 5,000 feet, and this speed was held until 30,000 feet altitude was achieved. At 30,000 feet the RPM. were increased to the maximum continuous rating of 7,300 RPM and the speed reduced by 3 knots per thousand feet above 30,000 feet.

2 - Cruise. The normal cruising technique was to fly the aeroplane at a constant incidence at 1.2 times the speed for minimum drag, varying the RPM to keep the true Mach number at 0.74. This implied that the indicated air speed was reduced by 3 to 4 knots about every 30 minutes and that the RPM were adjusted according to the outside air temperature. It was found helpful to use the air speed indicator lock on the auto-pilot to keep the air speed at the required setting.

3 - Descent. Initially the descent was made at the cruising Mach number until the indicated air speed reached 220 knots. Then this speed was maintained, using the air speed indicator lock. The RPM on the outer engines were adjusted in steps to pre-determined settings to maintain the required flow of pressurising air into the cabin, while the inner engines were idling throughout the descent. Below 23,000 feet all engines were idling. In certain cases when the descent was inadvertently commenced too late, the air brakes were found to be extremely useful in providing a higher rate of descent.

4 - Holding. When it became necessary to hold this was done with two engines idling, with the other two at a sufficient R.P.M. to give an indicated air speed of 180 to 200 knots.

For the world flight it was necessary to lay down special supplies of fuel at most of the calling points. In a few cases turbine fuel was available at diversion aerodromes, but on most of the sectors it was necessary to carry sufficient reserve fuel in the aircraft to enable a return flight from the alternative to the destination to be made should diversion become necessary.

Every flight was planned on a take-off weight with tanks full and this gave a maximum take-off weight available of from 140,000 lb to 142,000 lb depending upon the number of people carried.

The fuselage of the Comet 3 prototype had not been fully modified as a result of the Comet 1 investigation. To do so would have needlessly delayed the aeroplane's test programme, and the cabin was therefore pressurised to a differential of only 4lb./sq. in. This gave a cabin altitude of from 16,000 to 20,000 ft. on the cruise and therefore a special oxygen system was installed. For this reason passengers were not carried on the long en-route flights, and on short flights and demonstrations the altitude was restricted to 20,000 ft. giving a cabin altitude of 8,500 ft.

Technical results of the flight were completely satisfactory. The performance which the aircraft had achieved had shown that the basis used for the calculations of both the brochure performance of the Comet 4 and the flight planning data for the prototype Comet 3 were correct.

In exterior form and drag the Comet 3 was identical with the Comet 4 that was going into production. The Comet 4 differed in having slightly larger wing-nacelle tanks than the Comet 3, but the form and installation of these larger nacelles hadalready been developed on the Comet 3, and the only difference in the nacelles 'worn' by the Comet 3 on the world flight was an internal one - their actual fuel capacity was less. This created a difference of 450 Imperial gallons, so that the total usable Comet 4 tankage would be 8,750 Imperial gallons.

The capabilities of the Comet 4 had thus been established in the De Havilland trials of the Comet 3 during 1954 and 1955, and the brochure on the Comet 4 was compiled with full confidence that it would be borne out in the production aircraft. This brochure was circulated to world carriers at the time of the SBAC Display in September, 1955.

A great deal had been said about 'brochure-manship', where extravagant claims were made - for the purpose of serious sales negotiations - regarding the performance, economy and 'controllability and airfield behaviour' of a large jet airliner that had not yet been built, tested and developed.

Those on board G-ANLO from Hatfield to Sydney (left to right on the ground): P F Mouritz (Technical Sales); P F L Hall (Senior Assistant, Aerodynamics Department); P O Buggé (Second Pilot); J Cunningham (Chief Pilot); F H. M Lloyd (Commercial Sales Manager); Capt. A P W Cane BOAC); Capt I D V Ralfe (Qantas); R W Chandler (Radio Navigator). On the steps, reading upwards: E Holley (Rolls-Royce); H Davies (Inspector), S F Borrie (Flight Development Engineer); J Hamilton (Flight Engineer); J A Marshall (Flight Observer); E Brackstone Brown (Chief Flight Engineer), R V Ablett (Flight Engineer). *(DH Hatfield)*

In the case of the Comet 4 the brochure problem did not occurr, for the Comet 3, on which the brochure was based, was a developed and measured aircraft.

The world voyage gave the chance - at an early stage in the marketing phase of the Comet 4 - to verify the capabilities publicly along world routes for which it was suited, for which it was designed, and with the great benefit of having on board skilled senior pilots familiar with the stages flown.

One aspect of operation which the flight brought out was the small effect of winds upon the punctuality of a jet airliner. With this may be mentioned the more realistic weather forecasts due to the shorter period of forecast.

The performance, fuel consumption and all-round economics of the aircraft on every stage of the world flight were within very close tolerances of the flight planning data. The complete figures were discussed with operators and the whole system and detail of calculation were available to them.

At the end of the Cairo-Bombay stage of 2,710 statute miles, 2,900 Imperial gallons of fuel remained in the tanks, sufficient for a further three hours flying. At the end of the Fiji-Honolulu 3,210 mile stage, 1,250 gallons of fuel remained, sufficient to fly a further 1.25 hours. At the end of the Montreal-London 3,350 mile stage on December 28 enough fuel remained in the tanks to circle London for an hour at low level and then, if diverted, to fly to Prestwick, 330 miles away, and there safely circuit and land.

English winter fog baulked the 30-hour proving flight from Hatfield to Sydney. The fog which prevented a pre-dawn departure seemed likely to reoccur several mornings. Therefore, when fog lifted a little towards noon, John Cunningham seized the chance to get off. But the crew, having been busy for about 10 hours before take-off; could not safely work the 30-hour flight without sleep so an overnight halt was made at Cairo - which proved to herald a popular Sunday afternoon arrival in Sydney. The picture shows the aborted 05.00 departure on Friday 2 December. *(DH Hatfield)*

Now, if the first technical asset of the world flight was performance, the second certainly was serviceability. The De Havilland and Rolls-Royce Companies had expected that the aircraft and its engines would demonstrate a higher standard of serviceability than any other airliner in the world. On the airframe side it was because of the vast amount of development work put into the Comet design before the first flight and in the years since then, including 30,000 hours of airline service.

On the engine side it was because of the enormous amount of development that has gone into the Avon engine, including 500,000 hours of service experience, and because the essential characteristics of the continuous-burning turbine made for an altogether new standard of reliability.

This expectation was fully borne out in the course of the world flight. In the 27,000 miles of route flying from London to Montreal (plus a few thousand miles of local demonstration flights) there were no flight snags or hold-ups whatever; and in the course of the inspections, the normal schedule of which was strictly adhered to, all that had to be done was to change a fuel-pipe seal which was seeping slightly due to having been cut on assembly, and to change a refuelling actuator. Each engine used about two pints of lubricant in some 75 hours and 35,000 miles, Except that the fog in London on 2 December had set the programme back by just one day, as far as Montreal no departure had to be made from a schedule which had been drawn up before leaving Hatfield. The technical fault, to do with the attachment of the jet pipe of No. 3 engine, which prevented the Atlantic flight on the night of 21 December was a small one which could be easily corrected. It need never recur, either on the production Comet 4 or even on this development Comet 3 aircraft. The fault was rectified without recourse to any of the spare parts which as a precaution had been sent from England.

The third aspect of the Comet which has at last been made plain to the world as a direct outcome of the flight was its airfield behaviour.

The crew on this flight were surprised to find that in some parts of the world, notably Hawaii, the public and even the aviation community seriously thought that a jet airliner would need a long runway, would climb at a flattish gradient over the city of departure, causing a noise nuisance, would circuit, approach and land rather fast, would be unbearably noisy when standing and manoeuvring in front of the terminal building, and might even scorch the paving!

Original caption: 'Sydney; 24 hours 24 minutes' flying time from Hatfield. Twenty thousand happy Australians greeted the Comet at Mascot (Kingsford Smith Airport) on Sunday afternoon, December 4. Enthusiastic children led a break-through onto the field and the Comet, when on finals, was asked to circle Sydney again while the runway was safely cleared. The crowd surged around the aircraft as it came to rest. To get a gangway and vehicles through, a water hose was used as a last resort, but the uniformed operator really hadn't the heart to spray those pretty frocks. Everyone laughed and cheered. Australians want jets, and would like British ones - but on merit only'.

Technical people in Honolulu really thought that special regulations might be needed to keep people a considerable distance away from the jet engine intakes and effluxes during ground running. One newspaper referred to the efflux as '...*a blast as hot as a blow torch*', and said that '...*the danger-point behind a jet engine is 100 yards*'.

The De Havilland Company had always stated that the Comet was designed to use runways and airport facilities as they exised, and had emphasised that a low wing loading was specified so as to be sure of a short take-off and steep climb and a low landing speed with a short landing run. The sight of the Comet landing on the short 7,000 foot runway at Honolulu - this was in the days before the reef runway - pulling up within 3,000 feet and turning off at the intersection, impressed the observers of the Hawaiian Aeronautics Commission. They were also horrified to see ground staff standing and walking quite close behind the aircraft's tail while all four engines were running fast enough to start the wheels rolling away from the parking bay. They were also astonished to learn that the fully loaded Comet 3 or 4

could climb out after take off far more steeply than modern piston-engined airliners.

It seemed to those on board the Comet that many had been misled deliberately or otherwise by Press accounts, especially in USA, during the previous two or three years, and they were pleased to dispel some of the myths and legends that were starting to grow.

As part of this, a great many people were given rides in the Comet, in local flights of 60 to 90 minutes from Sydney, Melbourne, Perth, Auckland, Honolulu, Vancouver and Montreal; parties were also carried from Sydney to Melbourne, circling Canberra, and from Toronto to Montreal. In all about 600 people were given passenger rides.

Another misunderstanding which the world voyage tried to eliminate concerned the purpose for which the aircraft had been designed - a 'misapprehension' that is still around to this day. As the *De Havilland Gazette* reported: '*At every port of call the crew have had to explain that the Comet 4 was complementary to rather than competitive with the American conception of a jet airliner. It was smaller than the American jet airliners which are*

The Comet gets lei'd! The South Sea interlude saw leis showered on aircraft and crew alike, and there was time for a swim on Waikiki beach, Honolulu during refuelling before a dawn take-off to cold Vancouver, Canada.

From the *De Havilland Gazette*, December 1956. 'This picture of the Comet 3, taken at Honolulu Airport on December 13 1955, as it taxied in after flying the 3,250-mile stage from Nandi, Fiji in 6 hours, 40 minutes, is offered a Christmas time reminder of the contribution which the Comet can make to the facility of trade between the producing and manufacturing countries of the world. Trade is the peacemaker'.

promised. Those aircraft, arising from a US Air Force requirement for a flight-refuelling tanker, are aimed at long-range operations with high traffic density, especially the coast-to-coast service across the United States and the non-stop connection between New York and European capitals.

De Havilland designers had as their main aim the other trade routes around the world. On these the traffic was less dense and most of the centres of trade and industry are 2,000 to 3,000 miles apart. Designed to fit these conditions, the Comet has a world-wide suitability. It is, in fact, universally useful on world routes except for the one case of the non-stop service between New York and European capitals, on which it will need to make one halt on the westbound flight.

This North Atlantic route is exceptional in two respects: it has exceedingly heavy traffic, especially in the summer months, and it experiences strong westerly winds, especially in the winter months. These conditions call for an exceptionally large aircraft if the flight is to be made without ever stopping between European capitals and New York.

Let us glance at some of the other regions crossed by the Comet 3 in its recent circuit. It has shown that the journey between London and Sydney (nearly 12,000 statute miles) can be made within 30 hours, including four halts at important traffic junctions. Only 24 hours would be spent in the air and no stage would be much longer than 5 hours. It has demonstrated the usefulness of the Comet on trans-Australian routes, for instance by bringing Perth and

Sydney (2,045 miles) within about 4 hours of each other. The Pacific Ocean, with its vastness, is well suited to the Comet 4. A full load can be carried between Vancouver and Honolulu (2,750 miles) in 5 or 6 hours, between San Francisco and Honolulu (2,420 miles) in less time. Honolulu and Tokyo (4,280 miles) are connected in less than 10 hours of flying time, with a halt at Wake. The long stage between Fiji and Honolulu (3,220 miles) can on many occasions be flown non-stop.

The Comet 4 is excellent for trans-Canadian or trans-American non-stop services. By covering the short stage from Vancouver to Toronto (2,185 miles) in 4 hours it has even shown that a Toronto businessman could make a day return trip to Vancouver without hurry or fatigue and have some hours in Vancouver city. It will cross Canada between Vancouver and Montreal (2,290 miles) with full load in 5 hours westbound, 4.5 hours eastbound. It is equally suitable for linking Canadian cities with South American cities.

Contemplating the world routes on which traffic is not so dense as it is from coast to coast across U.S.A. or across the North Atlantic, it may be expected that as the traffic builds up over the years operators will prefer to increase the frequency with a moderate-sized airliner rather than to employ larger vehicles less frequently.

It is well known in the airline business that frequency means almost as much to travellers as speed. Later still, when end-to-end traffic eventually becomes heavy enough to justify a larger airliner flying with minimum refuelling halts, those intermediate centres of trade and traffic will still need to be served, affording a continued employment for the 3,000-mile vehicle, capable of carrying 60 to 80 passengers, for many years to come.

Even on the North Atlantic crossing, with its special conditions, the Comet 4, which should be in service before larger jet airliners, will provide the most comfortable and speedy operation despite its necessary one-hour halt on the westbound flight. At the present pace of British jet engine development specific consumption may well improve, yielding the opportunity for a superior capability on the North Atlantic without recourse to a very large aircraft.

Indeed the remarkable progress which has been made by British jet engines is one of the outstanding facts in the whole outlook of air transport, and great confidence is derived from the development history of the Rolls-Royce Avon engine which powers the Comet 4. It is employed in many of the latest aircraft types and has half a million hours of operational service behind it.

Likewise a wealth of hard-earned experience, the only experience of a jet passenger liner in public service, is built into the new Comet.

The Comet has had six years of continuous development flying, including 30,000 hours or 13 million miles of airline duty. There is no short cut to such invaluable knowledge as De Havilland and the British Overseas Airways Corporation have gained during these years, and all of it is built into the new Comet 4.

Without doubt jet propulsion is about to revolutionise the standards of world travel. Its two outstanding qualities are speed and comfort. Its speed of over 500 miles an hour virtually halves the journey time. Its comfort arises from the fact that the jet airliner flies extremely high, in the region of the smoothest passage, and it employs virtually vibrationless power. A long inter-continental journey is cut down to a very few hours, and the comfort and

Summary of Performance Figures over the tour

Sector	Flight Plan Distance N. miles	Time Hrs Mins		Fuel kgs	Actual Time Hrs Mins	Fuel kgs	Difference from Flight Plan Time Mins	Fuel kgs	Fuel %	Outside Air Temp	Remarks
Hatfield - Cairo	1,946	4	32	17,650	5 03	18,470	+31	+820	+4.7	-61C	Actually flew 2076 N miles.
Cairo - Bombay	2,532	5	15	19,280	5 08	19,120	-7	-160	-0.8	-53C	
Bombay - Singapore	2,110	5	13	19,800	5 13	19,730	+2	-70	-0.4	-55C	
Singapore - Darwin	1,817	4	33	17,690	4 36	17,900	+3	+210	+1.2	-53C	Climbed to 44,000 ft. Fuel heaters operated satisfactorily.
Darwin - Sydney	1,819	4	06	16,100	4 08	16,320	+2	+220	+1.4	-50C	Landing at Sydney delayed by crowds.
Perth - Sydney	1,777	4	10	16,500	4 05	16,380	-5	-120	-0.8	-49C	High OAT throughout cruise.
Sydney - Auckland	1,166	2	46	11,420	2 43	11,290	-3	-130	-1.1	-52C	
Auckland - Fiji	1,153	2	46	11,230	2 52	11,590	+6	+360	+3.2	-51C	
Fiji - Honolulu	2,791	6	41	23,650	6 44	23,500	+3	-150	-0.6	-56C	Longest air distance flown. Climbed to 43,650 ft.
Honolulu - Vancouver	2,408	5	37	20,620	5 40	21,120	+3	-500	-2.4	-56C	Fuel heaters used to remove ice from fuel filters.
Vancouver - Toronto	1,898	4	13	15,780	3 56	15,550	-17	-230	-1.5	-52C	Temperature rose 11C after 1.5 hours. Strong tail winds. 69 kts forecast, 85 kts encountered
Montreal - London	2,907	6	27	23,350	6 09	22,150	-18	-1,200	-5.1	-53C	Again strong tail winds. 108 kts forecast, 161 kts encounted.

Notes

The distances, times and fuel quantities are from take off to arrival overhead at 1,000 feet at the destination and do not include en route allowances.
Outside Air Temp is mean cruise temp.
On Hatfield - Cairo leg, ATC routed aircraft via Zifta, costing 830 kgs of fuel.
On Montreal - London leg, tailwinds over 50 kts stronger than forecast saved 1,200 kgs of fuel and reduced flight time by 18 minutes.

The contrast beween Hawaii and Canada could not have been more extreme. Montreal, 20 December and minus 15 Fahrenheit. Some of the crew posed, to show off their English-designed cold weather gear. From left to right: Messers E Brackstone Brown, H Davies, J Hamilton, E Holley and R V Ablett.

quietude and perfect air-conditioning of the aircraft make the journey seem even shorter still. One arrives without the sense of having travelled.

During the early months of 1956 G-ANLO was employed on further trials work before being placed on loan to De Havilland in April for demonstration to potential customers, including UAT. Further trials and demonstration flights occupied the aircraft until it was grounded in June 1956 after it returned to Hatfield, where the experimental department reworked the aircraft to represent as closely as possible the Comet 4, although certain fatigue and loading restrictions would apply to the airframe.

De Havillands then turned their attention to the engine bays, where the Avon 521 engines were removed and the bays modified to accept the uprated Avon 524. Other modifications included the ability to change the outer wing panels so that different configurations could be tried out, upgrades to the electrical supply and distribution system, and the installation of automatic pressurization and a much improved 'artificial feel', or 'Q', system.

All this required extensive flight testing, which kept G-ANLO fully occupied until 16 April, when it was diverted to carry out fixed-airbrake trials on behalf of the design team. The development trials, though, were occasionally interrupted to provide demonstration flights for interested customers, one such flight taking place on 26 July 1957 for the Mexicans. After a two-year absence G-ANLO reappeared at SBAC Farnborough in September, this time wearing the latest revised BOAC colour scheme. Following the show the Comet was flown to Johannesburg for further 'hot and high' trials. Upon returning to base the Comet was subjected to additional noise-suppression trials - having undertaken similar flights at Stockholm-Bromma the preceding June - a task that was becoming important as airports around the world increased their noise-suppression requirements. The aircraft was then flown to Khartoum on 16 October to face the joys and delights of tropical rainstorms.

Departing Khartoum the Comet flew on to South Africa for further 'hot and high' trials, which took until 11 November to complete. Twenty-four hours

A truly stunning picture of the sole Comet 3 as it banks away from the camera.

Cranfield, and Richards at Southampton; it was put on a sound theoretical basis by Lighthill and the results have been developed into full-scale hardware by Rolls-Royce.

In the United States similar work has been done by the NACA and by Boeing and Douglas. As a result of all this work the number of different nozzle shapes that have been tried out must run into thousands, but the ones that we have developed in this country have all been a variant of the 'corrugated' nozzle of which the one on the Comet 4 is an example.

later the Comet left Hatfield for Zurich, where the directors of Swissair were given demonstration flights. Having completed these flights the Comet was employed on 'before and after' approach noise-assessment sorties before and after the installation of noise suppressors in January 1958.

The art of noise... and water!

Noise suppression of aircraft engines was becoming more and more important, in the practical, environmental and political sense, as Ferdinand Basil Greatrex MA, FRAeS, AMIEE, the Manager of the Rolls Royce Flight Development Establishment at Hucknall explained: *'Some time ago there appeared in Flight a sketch of two people cowering under the wing of a jet aircraft obviously enveloped in a raging storm of noise, and one saying to the other, " Now let's hear it without the silencer! " Fortunately the art of silencing of jet engines has since developed considerably beyond this stage, and the Comet is the first aircraft in the world fitted with silencers to be given permission by the Port of New York Authority to use Idlewild Airport.*

Work on jet noise and on methods of reducing it - largely sponsored by the Ministry of Supply - started in this country with model testing at universities by such people as Lilley and Young at

It has been realised for some time that, although a good idea of the relative merits of various silencing nozzles can be obtained from model tests and from static tests on engines running on the ground, the actual amount of silencing achieved by any nozzle in flight can be measured only by means of a direct flight test. We at Rolls-Royce have therefore carried out quite a large amount of carefully controlled flight testing, measuring on the ground the noise from the aircraft flying overhead fitted with various nozzles.

At typical climbing conditions of 7,100 rpm and 160 knots speed the relative jet velocity is about 1,350 ft./second and the amount of noise reduction given by the silencer is 35 db. At higher relative jet velocities it is about 5 db. This is by no means the limit of what can be achieved in the way of silencing. Obviously the tests carried out for the Port of New York Authority show that the smaller amount of silencing of the Comet nozzle is sufficient.

The other factor which helps to keep the noise of the Comet down to a reasonable level is the fact that it has a much better climb-away performance than comparable piston-engined aircraft. By the time the Comet crosses the airfield boundary it is at a height of around 1,000 feet, whereas the piston-engined aircraft are only at about 500 feet. This difference in altitude is equivalent to 6 db reduction in noise.

The net result of all this is that the Port of New York Authority is able to draw the conclusion that the noise of the Comet as it flies over the airfield boundary is about 8 or 9 db lower than that of a DC.7 or a Super Constellation. However this has to be qualified a little when the frequency response of the human ear is taken into account, because jet noise has more of its energy in the high frequencies, which people find more disturbing, than has the piston engine. When this is taken into account the noise from the Comet is judged to be effectively about 3 or 4 db quieter than that from a DC.7 or Super Constellation.

On the other hand it is these higher frequencies which are more reduced by walls or windows so that if the noise inside a house is being considered the Comet would be effectively better by about 6 db.

It is difficult to give an understanding of the value of these numbers to the average person but some idea can be obtained from the fact that a reduction of about 8 db is equivalent to giving the impression of having halved the noise.

There is one further difference between the noise from the Comet and that from piston-engined aircraft -it lasts longer, and is therefore rather more disturbing on that account.

The final conclusion then, in the words of the Port of New York Authority report, is that "...the noise of the Comet jet airliner is subjectively comparable to the noise of large present-day four-engine propeller-driven airliners."

Clearly it is very satisfactory to know that the Comet, with suppressors fitted to its four Rolls-Royce Avon engines, will be acceptable, on grounds of noise, at any of the world's airports which to-day accept the larger piston-engined airliners'.

In September 1959 De Havillands used the aircraft - along with Comet 2 G-ALYT - to investigate methods of preventing water ingestion into the engines by modifying the nosewheels and the undercarriage legs. Water ingestion into compressors could cause extensive damage to the blades, and should too much enter the intakes the engine could stall, neither set of circumstances being good for a heavily loaded airliner attempting a take-off.

The purpose of the installation was to carry out extensive tests on the ice protection systems on both engine and intake and to demonstrate their effectiveness under a wide range of conditions.

To achieve this, a grid was mounted forward of the air intake to spray water at the required concentration on to the air intake and engine inlet guide vanes, and to provide maximum icing. Distilled water from two 96-gallon Vampire fuel tanks situated in the main passenger compartment was supplied to the rig, and temperatures down to minus 30°C provided most severe icing conditions.

The control panel for the system, situated to the left of the crew entrance door, occupied the former galley position. Water was delivered to the panel by the tanks' booster pumps; a converted fuel heater, using hot air from the port engines and fed to the spray grid, heated the water as required, the temperature being maintained by running hot air and water pipes together inside a lagged fairing. Both hot air and water were released through finely calibrated nozzles on the spray grid, preventing any tendency of the water to freeze prematurely.

A Bar and Stroud CL.9 periscope mounted at the control panel station enabled the physical process of ice accumulation and removal to be observed. The wing leading edge adjacent to the engine intake, the intake itself and the front portions of the engine (inlet guide vanes, starter fairing, and bearing struts) could all be seen.

Two electrically-operated robot miniature cameras recorded these conditions. One was mounted in a heated box on the spray grid structure facing aft towards the engine; this covered the leading edge, intake and part of the engine. The other, also in a heated box, but mounted on the side of the intake and operating through perspex windows, covered the intake and the lower part of the engine (inlet guide

Rolls-Royce Noise Suppressors became standard equipment on all Comets after the Comet 3.

The design and construction of the spray grid and supporting structure are apparent from this view of G-ALYT. The Robot camera mounted on the grid operates at selected time intervals during icing tests; the periscope for visual observations can be seen ahead of the rig.

The flow of water to the spray grid was controlled from this panel so as to give continuous or intermittent delivery. The large pipe at the bottom of the photograph contained hot air for heating the water and runs alongside the water pipe out to the grid. The water heater (lower centre) and the periscope (left centre) can both be identified.

vanes, etc.) on a larger scale. Since both the periscope and the observer/operators were in a good position to monitor events, control for the robot cameras was provided at both stations.

To assess the efficiency of each method of de-icing and the effect on engine performance, it was necessary to obtain comprehensive data on pressures, temperatures, valve positions, etc. relative to outside conditions of altitude, air speed, temperature and water concentration.

In order that instantaneous records of a permanent nature could be obtained, two recording media were used: the photographic observer's and the transient trace recorder. The observer instruments, more than 60 in all, were grouped on an illuminated panel and photographed by a single shot F.24 camera. Exposures could be made at will by the observer/operator or the control panel operator, or at definite time intervals during icing conditions by means of an automatic camera control.

The photographic record was not in itself sufficient, since instantaneous values only were obtained. In order therefore to obtain records of transient conditions, certain data were recorded on a continuous trace recorder operated by the observer/operator throughout all phases.

To photograph the engine and intake, lighting was introduced to the front of the engine; this consisted of three electronic flash tubes suitably housed and equally spaced round the intake; the windows in the intake were fitted with special filters allowing only

The auto-observer panel included Avon RA.29 engine instruments as well as those required for the icing tests. An F.24 camera (right fore-ground) photographed the panel at intervals of 30 seconds. The balanced bridge thermometer (to the right of the panel) indicated outside temperature over the operating range of altitudes.

The air intakes of a pair of RA.29 engines as fitted to the Comet. The central scoop - the upper half which fed cooling air to the recifiers while the lower half fed air to the heat exchanger for the cabin air conditioning system.

infra-red radiation to pass through; the Robot cameras, loaded with infra-red sensitive film, produced an image in a similar manner to ordinary light-sensitive material, experience being that infra-red penetration of the spray was much better than normal photographic light. The electronic flash (synchronised to both the grid and intake cameras) operated automatically from the Robot camera switches.

Floodlights were also fitted to the intake adjacent to the flash tubes for use when viewing through the periscope; control for these was provided at the control panel station subject to an override fitted at the auto-observer position; this ensured that the floodlights were not left on when pictures were being taken with Robot cameras loaded with infra-red film. The auto-observer, tailored to fit in the eight-seater compartment forward, enabled four technical observers (including the observer/ operator and the control panel operator), to have an uninterrupted view of the instruments.

The spray grid and the spray grid structure, both of which were of tubular design, carried the robot camera box; they also stabilised the outboard end of the periscope by means of spherical bearings. The spray grid itself could be mounted in either of two positions fore and aft and was transferred from one to the other with a minimum of time and effort. The forward position was used for the tests on the leading edge and air intake, while the aft position was used for tests to be carried out on the engine. In view of the high drag loads and the distance to the outboard intake the fuselage was strengthened considerably by means of external reinforcing.

Internally, long brackets picking up the eight-seater compartment bulkhead absorbed the high compression load at the rear pick-ups.

The project was the result of close co-operation between the Rolls Royce Flight Development Establishment at Hucknall and De Havilland, Rolls-Royce having a special interest in the efficiency of the engine anti-icing system and De Havilland in the proving of the air intake ice prevention system as it would affect the Comet 4.

For this, Rolls-Royce made the auto-observer, the water control panel, electronic flash equipment, transient recorder and the spray grid structure, together

with the grid itself; they also made the Robot camera box and the hot air and water pipes, etc. De Havilland then installed it all.

The electronic flash units, flood-lighting equipment and intake robot camera and box were fitted first to a mock-up intake at Hucknall where trial photographs were taken; later these items were transferred to the production intake by the experimental department, the work being the responsibility of a senior Rolls-Royce designer attached to Hatfield for the purpose.

The latter was able to follow through the air intake and nacelle work involved and supervise the installation of the equipment manufactured at Hucknall.

In March 1958 G-ANLO was grounded again, this time for modification to Comet 3B standard representing the requirements of British European Airways (BEA). To this end the extended outer wing panels and wing fuel pinion tanks were removed and replaced by shorter panels which reduced the span by 7 feet. Other modifications incorporated while the aircraft was grounded included an improved weather radar and definitive thrust reversers. The first flight in this new guise was undertaken on 21 August 1958, after which an appearance at that year's SBAC show at Farnborough was made.

At the completion of these trials G-ANLO made a final appearance as a civil aircraft at the Hatfield Open Day in July 1960, after which it was struck off the civilian register on 25 January 1961 and transferred to Ministry of Supply trials fleet as XP915 on 20 June.

Although G-ANLO was the only registered Comet 3, at least one other airframe was completed at Hatfield in 1954. BOAC cancelled its order for this version as the forthcoming Series 4 was more to its taste, so it was decided to use this airframe as a structural test and for cabin-pressure testing.

The Avon RA.29 being 'offered up' to the engine bay of the Comet 3. It was supported at four points and the mounting had quick-release joints for all fuel and electrical connections to facilitate changing, which could be accomplished in about one hour. The mounting of the engine tail pipe made full provision for the fitting of reverse-thrust mechanism.

The Avon RA.29 showing the slinging points and the two forward mounting spigots. The two large pipes on either side conduced hot air from the rear of the compressor for engine de-icing purposes. The air-intake support struts and the variable inlet guide vanes are clearly visible in the photograph.

Once these tests had been completed the fuselage was used for interior mock-up trials and layout demonstration purposes for potential customers. Having finished its role with the Comet, the airframe was then employed in Nimrod development work, after which it was broken up in August 1966. Apart from these two completed airframes, ten more Series 3s were in various stages of construction when they were cancelled during the Comet crash investigation.

Orders had included eleven for BOAC, two for Air India and Pan American with three on order plus seven on option.

Chapter Ten

THE COMET 4

The sole Comet 3 G-ANLO was a development aircraft for the Comet 4, which allowed the rapid development of the production versions - the result of the continuous and intensive development of De Havilland's jet transport aircraft.

This continuious planned development put the Comet years ahead of other jet airliners both in terms of manufacturing and operation.

During its two years in service with BOAC, UAT, Air France and the Royal Canadian Air Force, the Comet 1 flew on the airlines for over 30,000 hours, or, putting it another way, it covered over 12,000,000 miles, which is equivalent to roughly 500 times round the world. The major part of this experience was obtained on the BOAC routes between London, South Africa, Singapore and Tokyo.

When the Comet capabilities were compared, the Comet 1 was an aircraft of 107,000 lb. all-up weight, with four de Havilland Ghost engines each of 5,000 lb. thrust. It had an average practical stage length of about 1,500 nautical miles including generous stand-off and alternate fuel allowances, and carried a payload of 11,000lb.

The Comet 2 had an all-up-weight of 120,000 lb. and was fitted with four Rolls-Royce Avon engines of 7,000 lb. thrust. lt could carry a payload of 13,000lb. on a stage length of about 2,000 nautical miles.

The Comet 4 was to have an all-up-weight of 152,500 lb. and has four Avon engines of 10,500 lb. thrust. The capacity payload of the 60-passenger first-class version was 16,500 lb, and that of the 76-passenger tourist version was 19,300

Comet 3 G-ANLO in flight, photograhed against a typically impressive cloudscape.

lb. With these capacity payloads the stage lengths were approximately 2,600 nautical miles for the first-class version, and 2,350 nautical miles for the tourist version, In both cases the figures included full airline reserves and were based on a 45-knot headwind.

Taken all round, the aerodrome performance of the Comet 4 was impressive. On the Comet 3 world tour, airline pilots and airport officials alike were surprised at the short take-off and landing distances required and at the low landing speed. The stalling speed was a little higher than that of most propeller- driven aeroplanes then in service but generally speaking the Comet was able to operate into and out of almost all important airports without extension or runway strengthening.

Structurally, there was very little difference between the Comet 3 and 4. The fuselage was of conventional construction, being a semi-monocoque structure of stressed skin and stringers supported by transverse frames. The whole fuselage from the nose to the rear pressure dome, but excluding the wing centre section, was stressed and sealed for pressurisation. All doors, hatches and emergency exits were inward-opening and the cabin windows were of double Perspex construction, the outer panel being the load-carrying member. The two equipment bays housing and separating most of the electrical and hydraulic systems were situated fore and aft of the forward freight hold.

All floors were of metal construction, stressed for freight and were easily removable where necessary for access to under-floor equipment.

The wing was of cantilever construction comprising a centre-section, two stub wings, and two extension wings. The centre-section was a two-spar structure integral with the fuselage incorporating pick-ups for the attachment of the stub wings. It was not pressurised and accommodated four flexible fuel tanks. The stub wings, also two-spar structures, carried the engines and the main undercarriage, and incorporated integral and bag-type fuel tanks and de-icing leading-edge ducts. Engine bays were separated by stainless steel bulkheads.

Extension wings were attached to the stub wings by fore-and-aft bolt-plates extending between the spars. They carried the ailerons and the outboard section of the flaps, the flexible fuel tanks, nacelle-type fuel tanks, and de-icing ducts.

The fin and tailplane and the associated control surfaces were of conventional construction.

The passenger cabin was in two parts: a forward cabin about 25 ft. in length, and a rear cabin of about 30 ft. Width was a constant nine feet, and the headroom 78 inches. Standard De Havilland chairs were mounted on permanent seat tracks, enabling different arrangements to be achieved easily and quickly in service. All seats were forward of the jet pipes; noise was thus kept to a minimum.

A feature of the cabin – carried over from the

The Comet 4 Structure

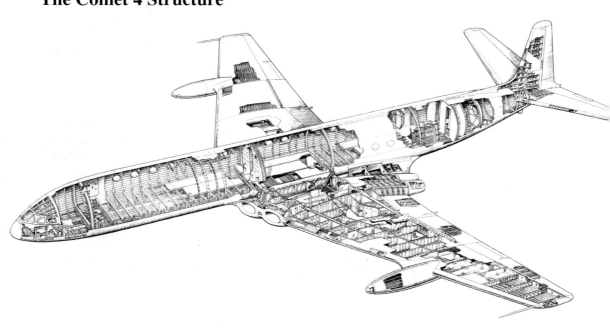

Comet 1 – was that the passenger door opened into a roomy and well illuminated vestibule, an arrangement of some convenience to the cabin crew during the embarkation of passengers. Passenger lists could be checked with the minimum of delay, and light baggage and coats were quickly stowed in the cloakroom leading off the vestibule. This area also, opened on to the comprehensively equipped ladies' and gentlemen's dressing-rooms and toilets.

The galley was designed for the compact but accessible accommodation of the whole of the ship's food stores and associated utensils. Features included two ovens, spacious working table-tops, cold-boxes, sink, and a tip-up seat for the steward.

Stainless-steel galley fittings were used, the floor being of heavy-duty washable plastic.

Additional amenities which could be made available in the passenger cabin included a bar, a drinking-water fountain, and a library. A special amenity was the convertible lounge, which could be offered as a special extra to enable operators to convert the forward end of the cabin into a luxurious bar-lounge.

The flight-deck, cabin and luggage compartments were pressurised to a maximum differential of eight pounds per square inch, giving a cabin height of 8,000 ft. when the aircraft is flying at 45,000 ft. Fresh warm air was tapped from the compressors of each of the four engines

The Comet 4 Layout

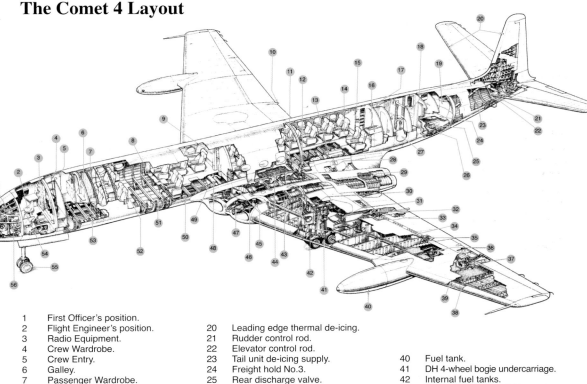

1	First Officer's position.	20	Leading edge thermal de-icing.	40	Fuel tank.
2	Flight Engineer's position.	21	Rudder control rod.	41	DH 4-wheel bogie undercarriage.
3	Radio Equipment.	22	Elevator control rod.	42	Internal fuel tanks.
4	Crew Wardrobe.	23	Tail unit de-icing supply.	43	4 Rolls-Royce Avon RA29 engines.
5	Crew Entry.	24	Freight hold No.3.	44	Centre-section flexible fuel tanks.
6	Galley.	25	Rear discharge valve.	45	Rectifiers.
7	Passenger Wardrobe.	26	Elevator and rudder servo unit.	46	Cold air unit.
8	Air conditioning supply grills.	27	Passenger entrance vestibule.	47	Heat exchanger.
9	Structural bulkhead containing supply and recirculating air ducts.	28	Dingy stowage (port and starboard)	48	DH double chair
10	Fuel jettison outlet.	29	Jet pipe support rails.	49	Forward discharge valve.
11	Aileron servo unit output.	30	Fire extinguisher bottles.	50	Hydraulic equipment bay.
12	Flap servo.	31	Undercarriage door servo.	51	Freight hold No.1.
13	Freight hold No.2	32	Flap servo.	52	DH double chair
14	Stewardess position and bar cabinet.	33	Flap linkage.	53	Electrical equipment bay.
15	Library and water fountain (wardrobe behind).	34	Air brakes.	54	Radio and Navigation station
16	Hat rack each side of cabin.	35	Air brakes jacks.	55	Steerable nosewheel
17	Emergency exit.	36	Fuel booster pump.	56	Captain's position
18	Toilets and dressing rooms - Ladies port, gentlemen starboard.	37	Aileron operating mechanism.	57	Pressure bulkhead
19	Rear pressure bulkhead.	38	Flexible outer wing tanks.	58	Space for search radar.
		39	Leading edge thermal de-icing duct.		

eliminating the need for mechanically driven blowers, auxiliary blowers and combustion heaters. Adequate heat for warming the cabin was available from the compression of the air and humidifiers and De Havilland cold-air units are incorporated in the circuit to regulate the humidity and the air temperature for maximum comfort.

The Comet 4 series of airliners were developed to make jet travel, with its unparralelled standards of speed, comfort and convenience, available in practical and economical form to the airways of moderate traffic density – and in 1958 that meant nearly all the airways of the world.

This, coupled with the flying qualities of the Comet - especially its ability to use airports of moderate size - were in harmony with its operating economics; putting it bluntly, de Havillands stated that the Comet could '*...go everywhere, and pay its way*'.

A whole new level of fatigue test

As soon as it had been established that pressure-cabin fatigue was the cause of the Comet 1 accidents and that compliance with a static load factor did not guarantee an adequate fatigue life, De Havilland's adopted the following philosophy. Thicker gauge materials would be used in the pressure cabin area, and windows and cutouts would be re-designed so as to lower the stress level to such an extent that cracks would be most unlikely to occur during the life of the aircraft. Should, however, cracks occur due to manufacturing error - or due to damage in service -then the rate of propagation of the cracks would be so slow that they would readily be seen before they could possibly reach a dangerous magnitude.

The aim was to demonstrate by suitable test

The Hatfield Assembly Hall was jigged for Comet 4 and 4A production in 1956, which was fed with aircraft components from other factories within the De Havilland Enterprise. One of those components being machined from a solid billet of aluminium(left) then a very new process which not only saved work in making what used to be made from 20 individual items, but also saved weight and added strength!

Above: The nose section and canopy ready for testing. This sample completed 118,000 pressure reversals, equivalent to 354,000 hours of flying - a 'safe life' of more than 60,000 hours or more than 20 years on intensive airline flying.

Above right: One of a number of Comet 4 fuselage test sections about to be placed in the water tanks at Hatfield. This particular sample completed the equivalent of 360,000 flying hours and in a further test in which a 3 inch crack was deliberately introduced a further 6000 'hours' of flying occured before the crack grew singificantly.

Right: The failure of the Comet fuselage was exactly where expected and at 104% of its fully factored design load.

Below: A centre-section test sample is loaded into a pressure tank at Hatfield. *(all DH Hatfield)*

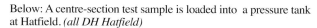

specimens that no cracks would occur before a minimum of 60,000 reversals, and that any cracks subsequently appearing would not propagate seriously before another 60,000 reversals. If each reversal is assumed to be equivalent to a 3-hour pressurised fiight, the apparent life is 180,000 hours, but to this must be applied a scatter factor of six which gives a safe life of 30,000 hours. To this end a test programme was embarked upon.

Six full-scale representative specimens of each main type of cutout were fatigue-tested under water. Typical of the results obtained from these tests was a panel in which cracks started at 68,000 reversals but did not propagate quickly until 164,000 reversals had been reached.

An important part of the series of tests was a 28-foot long fuselage section containing representative Comet 4 cutouts, comprising three cabin windows, an escape hatch, a passenger-entry door, a freight door, an escape door, a luggage-bay door, two toilet drains and a de-icer pipe outlet. This specimen had up to the beginning of April 1956 completed 85,000 reversals of pressure equivalent to 255,000 flying hours without failure of any sort.

A further 27-foot-long test piece representative of the fuselage section centre was also constructed and was tested in the water tank. In this test, in

A complete, but non-flying Comet 4 was built alongside other airworthy Comet 4s for BOAC as a test airframe, being allocated construction number 06402.

The fuselage was mated to the wing spars in 1957, and was built as a fully representative aircraft - to the point that it was finished in BOAC livery.

After testing at Hatfield, it was later moved by road to Woodford for Nimrod testing.

06402 is placed in the large water-tank at Hatfield for pressure testing.

Other tests were more of a shipyard nature. The Comet 4 fuselage, 111 feet long and weighing four tons in its bare state was fixed into as massive rig by its wing-root fixings and then bent fore and aft under loads totalling more than 90 tons. This test was designed to simulate the ultimate designed landing load, a figure that was safely in excess of any stress expected in regular service. It was a test to destruction - the break occurred under a load almost exactly equivalent to the designed figure. *(both DH Hatfield)*

addition to internal pressure loads, the effect of gust loads from the wing was included.

Exhaustive testing was also carried out on the wing spars, and the main tension booms particularly came under close investigation with a view to achieving more than adequate fatigue life. Similarly many tests were conducted to ensure a satisfactory fatigue life for the skin on the bottom surface of the wing. In addition to these components many hundreds of tests were carried out on examples of seam joints. It was confidently anticipated that the many thousands of tests such as have been described would establish beyond doubt the structural integrity of the Comet 4. The culmination of the test programme consisted of fatigue-testing a complete Comet 4 in the water tank for the purpose of providing final confirmation of the design philosophy.

Differing types of Comet 4

The intercontinental Comet 4 was designed for stages up to about 3,000 statute miles carrying,

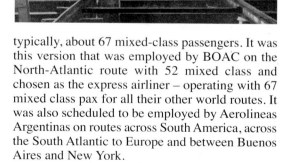

typically, about 67 mixed-class passengers. It was this version that was employed by BOAC on the North-Atlantic route with 52 mixed class and chosen as the express airliner – operating with 67 mixed class pax for all their other world routes. It was also scheduled to be employed by Aerolineas Argentinas on routes across South America, across the South Atlantic to Europe and between Buenos Aires and New York.

The Continental Comet 4B, with longer fuselage and clipped wings was intended for inter-city networks with stages from about 400 to 2,500 statute miles, carrying about 86 mixed-class passengers. It had a higher maximum speed than the Comet 4 and less fuel tankage. This version was selected by, amongst others, British European Airways and Olympic Airways for their fast services across the continent of Europe.

The Intermediate Comet 4C combined the longer fuselage of the Comet 4B with the larger wing and fuel capacity of the Comet 4. It carried substantially more payload than the Comet 4 at the cost of a small reduction in maximum range, and was most suitable where neither very long nor very short stages were the main consideration.

Thus the three versions met the requirements of almost every airway system, typical exceptions being the few domestic routes within the United States of America where the traffic was many times heavier and called for a larger vehicle.

De Havillands freely admitted that they thought that outside the United States only the North Atlantic route could justify the large jet. Here the traffic was considerably lighter and more than a dozen airlines competed for it, but an increased frequency would not of itself yield further traffic growth, so the large jet could be filled. Also, because the stage was exceptionally long - about 3,000 statute miles - and because of strong westerly winds, an airliner with a somewhat longer range than the Comet would be better suited - although the Comet 4 had long operated an excellent and profitable service on the route.

It was the Comet's low operating cost per aircraft mile that made its introduction economically sound wherever traffic was moderate – a situation that prevailed everywhere outside the United States at the time. Compared with 28,000 seats per week each way across the USA only 1,000 to 4,000 seats were needed on most of the world's other routes.

For example, nine airlines operated 23 flights per week each way between Europe and South America, providing 1,400 seats each way, or an average capacity of 60 seats per aircraft.

In 1958 De Havillands assumed that the Comet 4 was the right size for the traffic, and if the rate

In 1957 De Havilland produced a series of maps showing flight times that could be achieved by the long-range Intercontinental Comet, carrying its full payload on some typical sections of the world air routes. The times included five minutes for circuit and landing.

London - Lisbon = 978 miles 2 hrs 17mins
London - Dakar = 2708 miles 5 hrs 40mins
Lisbon-Dakar = 1737 miles 3 hrs 45 mins
Dakar - Rio de Janeiro = 3126 miles 6 hrs 30 mins
London-Tripoli = 1469 miles 3 hrs 25 mins
Tripoli-Leopoldville = 2560 miles 5 hrs 28 mins
Leopoldville-Johannesburg = 1732 miles 3 hrs 45 mins
London-Cairo = 2195 miles 4 hrs 25 mins
Cairo-Nairobi = 2199 miles 4 hrs 40 mins
Nairobi-Johannesburg = 1811 miles 4 hrs 2 mins.

New York-Miami = 1091miles 2 hrs 25 mins
New York-Trinidad = 2211miles 4 hrs 37 mins
New York-Caracas = 2117 miles 4 hrs 30 mins
New York-Bogota = 2486 miles 5 hrs 15 mins
Vancouver-Mexico City = 2449 miles 5 hrs 28 mins
San Francisco-Mexico City = 1882 miles 3 hrs 50 mins
Mexico City-Lima = 2647 miles 5 hrs 42 mins
Lima-Santiago = 1530 miles 3 hrs 17 mins
Santiago-Buenos Aires = 695 miles 1 hr 30 mins
Buenos Aires-Rio De Janeiro = 1232 miles 2 hrs 33 mins
Rio De Janeiro-Lima = 2339 miles 4 hrs 40 mins
Rio De Janeiro-Bogota = 2803 miles 5 hrs 50 mins
Rio De Janeiro-Caracas = 2814 miles 5 hrs 50 mins
Rio De Janeiro-Trinidad = 2613 miles 5 hrs 25 mins

Beirut-Karachi =1995 miles 3 hrs 52 mins
Beirut-Bombay = 2509 miles 5 hrs 50 mins
Nairobi-Aden = 1124 miles 2 hrs 35 mins
Aden-Karachi = 1666 miles 3 hrs 30 mins
Aden-Bombay = 1896 miles 4 hrs 10 mins
Karachi-Singapore = 2942 miles 6 hrs 10 mins
Karachi-Bangkok = 2300 miles, 4 hrs 40 mins
Bangkok-Hong-Kong = 1077 miles 2 hrs 25 mins
Hong-Kong-Tokyo = 1787 miles 3 hrs 35 mins
Jo'burg-Mauritius = 1905 miles 3 hrs 45 mins
Mauritius-Cocos = 2651 miles 5 hrs 37 mins
Cocos -Singapore = 1051 miles 2 hrs 30 mins

Bangkok-Singapore = 891 miles 2 hrs 7 mins
Singapore-Perth = 2429 miles 5 hrs 5 mins
Singapore-Darwin = 2092 miles 4 hrs 35 mins
Cocos Island-Perth = 1827 miles 3 hrs 45 mins
Cocos Island-Darwin = 2296 miles 4 hrs 50 mins
Darwin-Sydney = 1960 miles 4 hrs 5 mins
Sydney-Perth = 2036 miles 3 hrs 50 mins
Sydney-Auckland = 1341 miles 2 hrs 40 mins

of traffic increase continued at it's present rate, then there would be no justification for a larger airliner than the Comet 4 for at least the next eight to ten years.

Likewise on the continental inter-city networks, operators almost everywhere required an aircraft which seated fewer than 100 passengers - which was the policy of British European Airways - the largest passenger air carriers outside the United States - for the next ten to fifteen years.

It was known that frequency of service sooner than time taken for the journey mattered greatly to air travellers. Passengers travelled by the airline whose service took them to their destination at the convenient time on the right day. Frequency enhanced an airline's competitive appeal as against other air operators who have larger aircraft, and as against surface transport. The thinking here was that the Comet, having only a moderate number of seats to fill, could be operated at an attractive frequency even on routes where the traffic was far from heavy, without the fear of uneconomically low load factors. And the frequency could easily

be built up as the traffic grew. On seasonal routes, because of its moderate size and its competitive appeal, the Comet was unlikely to experience load factors below its break-even point.

The Comet 4B especially was designed to be virtually independent of ground services at intermediary non-refuelling halts, so that the aircraft need not be on the ground more than a few minutes-
the aim being to secure a quick turn-around in keeping with its speed of nine miles a minute.

To accomplish this, De Havilland planned to have the Comet 4B equipped with a built-in power-operated stairway - or 'air-stairs' - that emerged from under the main floor under the rear door the moment its wheels have come to rest. It was to have a built-in auxiliary power unit for electrical services and for cabin air conditioning and refrigeration while standing, also for re-starting its engines to pull out again.

With its low costs per aircraft mile, however, the Comet could pay its way even with a considerable proportion of seats unoccupied. BOAC was on record of stating that after tests using the Comet 3, the Comet 4 when flown on the Atlantic and Europe-Far East routes could make a profit with less than half the seats filled. In

Artwork in the 1957 brochure for the Comet 4 revealed a longer, sleeker aircraft that had integral airstairs fitted.

The art was very much 'of the time' - revealing chic elegance, gentlemen in suits, waistcoats and ties, ladies with wasp-waists, fur stoles, hats and handbags. Only a few years later it would be Beatles, Mary Quant bobs and mini-skirts.

practice, of course, the Comets on these routes were so popular that three-quarters and more of their seats were occupied. Higher passenger load factors than 75 per cent. were difficult to achieve on the Far East route because so many travellers book for only part of the 10,000-mile journey: on the simpler North Atlantic operation the moderate-size Comet steadily recorded 90% of seats filled.

The jet will always draw the traffic away from slower and less comfortable aircraft, so airlines that were early to adopt the Comet immediately took the major share of the traffic offering, and secured an enduring lead.

The Comet's moderate size had certain advantages to passenger comfort. No first-class traveller by Comet was ever asked to put up with five-abreast seating. Also the more personal and less 'busy' character of the cabin service on an airliner of this size was appreciated, while the smaller passenger complement means faster passage through customs and other formalities.

BOAC buys Comet 4s

It was Sir Miles Thomas who in February 1955 had given De Havilland an Instruction to Proceed with the manufacture of nineteen Comet 4s for delivery in 1958 and 1959 but it was December 1956 before Basil Smallpeice was able to outline the main features of a draft contract with de Havilland. The price subject to escalation was to be £1.16m per aircraft and delivery dates were to be phased between September 1958 and December

1959; BOAC was to receive the first four aircraft delivered to any airline and De Havilland would be entitled to a bonus if they were able to give the Corporation eight months notice that delivery dates of all the nineteen aircraft would be advanced. On the other hand BOAC would be entitled to damages if the aircraft had not been delivered within six months after the planned delivery dates. Also included in the draft was a 'most favoured customer' clause which provided that if De Havilland sold Comets at less than £1.16m per aircraft or on more favourable terms than those in the BOAC contract within two years after delivery of the nineteenth aircraft, the price to BOAC was to be reduced accordingly and any more favourable terms substituted for those in the BOAC contract.

In February 1957, the Board approved a sum of $35,437,566 to cover the nineteen Comet 4s and one Comet 2E, with spare RA29 Avon engines, provision for escalation and change orders, and spares, equipment etc, and on 4 April 1957 the contract was formally signed.

In contrast to BOAC's experience over the Bristol Britannia - which was plagued with problems, mostly from the Proteus turbo-props - progress of the Comet 4 was unhindered by any serious problems.

Sir Basil Smallpeice: *'We had started Britannia services with the 102 to Australia in March, only a month after putting it into service to South Africa. On the route to Sydney it earned*

Three of the new Comet 4s at BOACs maintenance facility at London Heathrow.

The delivery of Comet 4s to BOAC was a great occasion, well covered by national and international media.

Right: Notables on a notable occasion! On September 30, when the first two Comets were formally delivered, Sir Gerard d'Erlanger, Chairman of BOAC, shakes hands with Sir Geoffrey de Havilland, as he alights at London Airport. To the right of Sir Geoffrey are Sir Basil Smallpeice, Managing Director of BOAC, Mr. W. E. Nixon. Chairman of Havilland Holdings Ltd., and The de Havilland Aircraft Co. Ltd., and Mr. Aubrey Burke, Deputy Chairman and Managing Director. Mr. A. S. Kennedy, de Havilland Financial Director, is between Sir Gerard and Sir Geoffrey. On the left are Sir George Cribbett, Deputy Chairman of BOAC, Mr. John Cunningham, de Havilland Chief Test Pilot, and Mr. C. T. Wilkins, de Havilland Chief Designer. *(both DH Hatfield)*

a very bad name for irregularity and unpunctuality due to repeated mechanical troubles. By August, Charles Abell reported that certain provisos we had made in accepting the aircraft from Bristol at the end of 1956 had not been met.

We had stipulated that we should never encounter engine damage through ice ingestion so that it was necessary to shut down engines in the air and that that the engine relighting system provided by the glowplugs would never require manual operation by the crew. We also stipulated that the aircraft could be used over all our routes without temperature or altitude limitations.

Capt Trevor Marsden,[Deputy Britannia Fleet

Comet 4s at BOACs maintenance facility at London Heathrow. In the middle is G-APDB. *(DH Hatfield)*

Manager] *held a meeting of pilots to consider the matter. It was agreed that, until mid-October, we must accept a height limitation and operate at low level between Karachi and Hong Kong, and between Karachi and Darwin; after mid-October, operations on all sectors would have to be reviewed in the light of experience and information gained.*

Meanwhile, Captain Rendall [Britannia Fleet Manager]reassured his pilots that 'the whole matter is being pursued at the highest possible level. The Prime Minister has asked to be kept informed at short intervals of how things develop, and to this end a combined report by MOS, MTCA, BACI and BOAC is submitted twice every week to the Minister of Transport and Civil Aviation and the Minister of Supply.'

The long-range Britannia 312 also ran into trouble, but of a different kind, after a promising start. At the end of June 1957 our first 312, G-AOWA, made the first ever non-stop flight from London to Vancouver, taking 14 hours 40 minutes to cover the distance of 5,100 miles. But on a proving flight which took off at 24.00 hours on

Friday, 27 September, our second aircraft, G-AOVB, had two engines fail almost simultaneously after flying for about four minutes in cloud at altitude. Bristols thought that the quenching effect ofthe moisture in cloud caused a contraction in the compressor casing which resulted in the stator blades rubbing on the spaces between the rotor blades and causing destruction. This had not happened in the 102 engine; so what had gone wrong? It transpired that the stator blades in the 312 engine were made of a different material, which expanded more under heat.

No other airline in the world was liable to encounter such snags in aircraft recently delivered by the manufacturers. The matter was so serious - particularly against the background of the 102's history - that l felt I had to report personally to the Minister, Harold Watkinson.

The first production Comet 4, G-APDA, flew on 27 April 1958 The crew for this flight was John Cunningham as captain, assisted by Pat Fillingham, E. Brackstone-Brown, J Johnston and J Marshall. This aircraft was then used for extensive flight testing between 12 June and 10

G-APDR appears in the Hatfield sunshine. This aircraft had been allocated the registration G-APDL, but it was not taken up. *(DH Hatfield)*

July. The pilots involved with these flights included John Cunningham, Peter Bugge, Pat Fillingham and John Wilson, and they accumulated sixty-nine hours during twenty-five flights. During these sorties the complete flight envelope was explored and confirmed, while the onboard systems were given a thorough check-out.

After completing basic flight trials the Comet was flown to Khartoum to conduct a full range of tropical trials which kept the aircraft and crew occupied until the end of July.

A full C of A was issued to 'DA on 29 September 1958. The first aircraft to be delivered to BOAC was G-APDB on 12 September 1958 with a limited C of A but together with G-APDC the two aircraft were officially accepted by the Corporation on 30 September, the actual date

provided in the contract. From then on deliveries proceeded according to plan with the nineteenth and last aircraft handed over on 11 January 1960. De Havilland had done an exemplary job in meeting contract dates.

Entry into service was smoothed as a result of the extensive trials the Corporation had carried out with Comet 2Es fitted with the Rolls-Royce Avon engines which were to be in the Comet 4s. These trial flights took place over a period of eight months between September 1957 and October 1958 over the London-Beirut stage and subsequently across the North Atlantic to gain experience of engine performance and with the object of introducing the Comet 4 first on the North Atlantic to compete with the Americans.

Chapter Eleven

'BOAC INAGURATE THE FIRST ATLANTIC JETLINER SERVICE'

Sir Basil Smallpeice: *'As we moved through the first half of 1958, reports on the Comet 4 from Hatfield were more and more encouraging. In the light of the Comet 1 explosions, its airframe had been submitted to rigorous static tests under the supervision of the RAE at Farnborough. It passed satisfactorily. In other respects, too, production was well up to schedule and it looked as though de Havilland would repeat its 1952 performance and deliver the aircraft on time.*

But then we ran into difficulty over the Comet 4 with the authorities in New York, who would not authorise us to land the aircraft because of the noise it was alleged to create. We produced evidence that the noise level in 'perceived noise decibels' was not materially higher than that of large piston-engined aircraft and was lower than that of the French Caravelle. But the Caravelle had never flown in New York, which was unimpressed by that particular evidence. We brought as much pressure to bear on the Port of New York Authority as we could, through the Ministry in London and the British Embassy in Washington. As a first stage we succeeded in getting approval for Comet 4 training flights but not - repeat not, they emphasised - for commercial service flights'.

It was thought that these 'objections' on the grounds of noise from the Port of New York Authority were both a political and commercial excuse – just as they were years later when the Europeans tried to introduce Concorde into the USA. The Americans were still smarting that the United Kingdom had been the first to fly at jet airliner in 1949 and the first to put a jet airliner into service in 1952. They were damned certain that the Brits were not going to be the first to operate passenger services into and out of the USA!

Sir Basil again: *'The Port of New York Authority's willingness to meet us to this extent was, I feel, greatly influenced by the fact that Juan Trippe's Pan American Airways were also hoping to put the new Boeing 707 jet into service in the autumn of 1958.*

Clearly Americans would not stand in the way of Pan Am or a Boeing product. The Port Authority in New York also feared that, if they were too difficult, Pan American might encounter retaliatory action from London. The New York authorities were also aware that the jets - both Comet and Boeing - would be welcome at Boston.

Thinking about New York's reluctance to admit the Comet 4 on noise grounds, I was certain they would never keep the Boeing out. They would be bound to give way on our Comet 4 application in due course - but probably not until the fifty-ninth minute of the eleventh hour. So we went full speed ahead with our Comet 4 pre-service flight-training and other preparations as though there were no obstacles in our path.

Aubrey Burke from de Havilland's told me that they would be delivering our first aircraft on Tuesday 30 September, ahead of schedule. When the day arrived, de

Crew of the first BOAC Comet 4 crossing: According to airline custom a flight with Press representatives and others was made a couple of days before the frst regular London-New York passenger service. Here are the crew at London Airport, Thursday 2 October, before departure on the pre-inaugural crossing in G-APDB. Left to right: Captain E. E. Rodley, Captain T. B. Stoney, Captain C. Farndell, Steward J. Miller, Steward A. C. J. McCormack, Stewardess Barbara Jubb and Stewardess Peggy Thorne.

Havilland delivered not just one aircraft but two - a great achievement.

I was already determined to get to New York in our first aircraft as soon as possible. I wanted to see what l could achieve with the Port Authority with a BOAC Comet 4 actually sitting on the ground in New York - previous Comet 4 visits having been made with aircraft still belonging to de Havilland. The Ministry did not rate very high my chances of success in getting early Port of New York Authority permission for scheduled public services, but I decided to go all the same. Aubrey Burke and Captain James Weir of BOAC would come with me.

On the Wednesday we alerted the press and took them across on Thursday, 2 October. For their purpose we dubbed our westbound training flight to New York that day a pre-inaugural flight. The next morning, I met the Port Authority. After the meeting, there was nothing to do but return to our office on Fifth Avenue, and try to possess ourselves in patience until we heard the results.

On the Thursday before leaving my home in Esher, I conceived the idea that, as we now had two aircraft, we could inaugurate the world's first transatlantic jet service with a flight in both directions on the same day, passing one another in mid-Atlantic. Gerard 'Pops' d'Erlanger liked the idea, and said he would

BOAC took great advantage of the publicity to be gained from the first transatlantic jet service - and rightly so!

Right: Captain Roy Millichap below the nose of G-APDC.

Below: G-APDC on the North side of London Airport. *(both BOAC/DH Hatfield)*

accompany the westbound flight.

While waiting in New York on the Friday for the Port Authority decision I was turning over in my mind the organising complexities of a double inaugural, when suddenly, about 5 o'clock, word came that a letter was on the way. It was 10 o'clock at night in London. There was still time to alert them for a possible flight next day.

Shortly afterwards, waving the Authority's letter in my hand, I stood on a chair in the Speedbird Club and told everybody that we could at last start New York services with the Comet 4 - and would do so next morning.

At midnight British Summer Time on 3 October - the Port of New York Authority publicly authorised

jetliners to use the International Airport at Idlewild (now John F Kennedy International). Permission was subject to a number of restrictions, all of them designed to safeguard the amenities of the neighbourhood.

That the Comet was able to easily meet all the restrictions imposed by the Port of New York Authority - which represented one of the most noise-conscious communities in the world - and the fact that it did so without loss of range or payload were obvious sources of satisfaction to potential Comet operators throughout the world; most of them faced similar problems to a greater or less extent.

The actual wordage of the restrictions placed upon jet airliner operations by the Port of New York Authority was thus:

1. *The Comet would use Runway 25 as a mandatory preferential runway for take-offs in zero wind conditions and for all wind conditions which will produce a headwind component during take-offs on this runway, provided the crosswind component does not exceed 20 knots.*

2. *Runway 22 may be used for take-offs in lieu of Runway 25, in which case the pilot will make a right turn as soon as practicable after take-off sufficient to avoid flying directly over the communities which are in a direct line with the runway.*

3. *In the event that take-offs could be made on Runways 25 or 22 under the conditions set forth in (1) and (2), then, and only in that event, Runways 13R, 3lL and 07 will be used under the following conditions:*

   (a) For take-offs on Runway 13R, the pilot will make a turn to the right as soon after take-off as practicable, such turn to be made with

Left: BOAC's promotional material advertising their 'Monarch Luxury Service' to New York on the Comet 4.

Below: One of BOAC's Comets is caught by the camera on a proving flight through Gander in Newfoundland.

approximately 15° bank. In addition, taking into account wind and temperature conditions, take-offs from Runway 13R will be so planned and conducted that the aircraft will not fly over any community underlying the flight path at an altitude of less than 1,200 feet and the pilot will observe the piloting procedures set forth in (5) below.

(b) Take-off's on Runway 31L will be so planned and conducted, taking into account wind and temperature conditions, that the aircraft will not fly over any community underlying the flight path at an altitude of less than 1,200 feet and the pilot will observe the piloting procedures set forth in (5) below.

(c) For take-off's on Runway 07, the pilot will make a turn to the right as soon after take-offs as practicable, such turn to be made with approximately 15° bank. In addition, taking into account wind and temperature conditions, take-off's from Runway 07 will be so planned and conducted that the aircraft will not fly over any community underlying the flight path at an altitude of less than 1,200 feet and the pilot will observe the piloting procedures set forth in (5) below.

4. No take-offs will be made on any other runways without specific permission.

5. All take-offs in 3 (a), (b) and (c) above will be made using the following piloting procedures:

Initial take-off will be made with a power setting of 8,000 r.p.m. and 20° flap.

Aircraft will be allowed to accelerate to V2 +15 knots during climb, and the pilot will maintain

Right: British journalists arriving at Idlewild: well-known aviation writers of the British daily and Sunday papers and the news agencies, together with Mr Freddie Gillman, the efficient public relations officer of BOAC sfter the pre-inaugural flight from London on 2 October.

this speed to the best of his ability until he has reached the communities adjoining the airport.

Just prior to or upon reaching the nearer boundaries of communities adjacent to the airport, as defined on Chart No. NYA-5967, the pilot will efect a power reduction to 7,350 r.p.m.

6. Take-offs during the hours between 10 p.m. and 7 a.m. will be made on Runways 25 or 22 only.

In reality, what these regulations meant to the Comet could best be understood by considering the aircraft's take-off and climb performance at maximum all-up weight of 158,000 lbs in relation to each of the runways available for jet airliner operations. The map shows the layout of the runways and the proximity of dense urban areas.

For Runways 22 and 25 - with zero or light winds, or when the wind was in the south-west quarter, the Comet would use runway 25. The map showed the line of this runway to be over the sea and there are thus no noise problems. Alternatively runway 22, which wass in line with the Rockway community could be used and it was then a simple matter for the pilot to make a gentle turn of 30° to the right to clear the area.

Each of these runways was 8,000 feet long - more than enough for a maximum-weight take-off under any conditions likely to be encountered.

For runways 13R and 31L - if the cross-wind component on runways 25 and 22 exceeded 20 knots, then runways 13R or 31L were used, the choice being dependent on the direction of cross-wind.

Left: Captain Roy Millichap and the crew of G-APDC shortly before departure from London Airport on the morning of 4 October 1958

Below: First regular transatlantic jet travellers: the departure from London Airport of the first-ever jet airliner service across the Atlantic Ocean. Official sanction from the Port of New York Authority had been announced the previous evening. Bookings, eastbound and westbound, some having been made with BOAC years beforehand, were confirmed overnight. This picture shows the passengers boarding G-APDC for the flight to New York.

Three views from the De Havilland archives showing the take-off of G-APDC from Heathrow Airport on the first ever scheduled service pure jet crossing of the Atlantic on October 4 1958.

The press were out in force that day, photographing and filming every move, including the spectacular climb out.

If runway 13R was used then the line of flight was towards the Inwood and Cedarhurst communities. A steady 15° banked turn to the right, through 120°, however, enabled the aircraft to avoid the area completely. In any event the nearest houses were some 3.5 miles from the start of take-off and a straight-ahead climb on a hot day (80°F. -into wind component 20 knots) would by then have enabled the Comet to attain 1,800 feet, using the procedure laid down by the Port of New York Authority which called for a reduction to climbing power before over-flying built-up areas. This altitude is half as high

again as the Authority's minimum of 1,200 feet and had been laid down to allow the Boeing 707 to operate out of the airport and was a clear example of the difference in take-off performance!

If runway 31L was used - when a right-hand circuit was in force - the aircraft had to pass over the Lindenwood community - approximtely 2.5 from the start of take-off. With a 20-knot headwind and maximum all-up weight of 158,000 lb. the Comet would, in theory, be at 1,100 feet at this position on a hot day (80°F.); on a standard day (60°F.) it would have reached 1,300 feet. However, practical operating experience at Idlewild showed that the combination of an 80°F. air temperature and a strong down- or cross-wind component on runway 25 were unlikely eventualities.

Runway 07 had to be used if the cross-wind component over runways 13R or 31L exceeded 20 knots and its direction was downwind on runway 25. Once again there was a community - Rosedale - at a distance of approximately 2.5 miles. The Comet would thus be at the altitude indicated in the previous paragraph for runway 31L. It was, however, entirely practicable to make a steady 15° banked turn to the right through 180° and this made it possible to avoid over-flying the built-up area.

The conclusion was that one remote contingency alone - a strong downwind component on runways 22 or 25, between the hours of 22.00 and 07.00 -

"Those were the days…"

" The lady says she's so comfortable she doesn't want to leave the ship."

The c ompany magazine the *De Havilland Gazette* regularly ran cartoons that featured the Comet. These reproduced here gives a flavour of what appeared.

" Easy enough to pick out our passengers from the flagged-victims of the old horse-drawn wooden-wheeled airliners . . ."

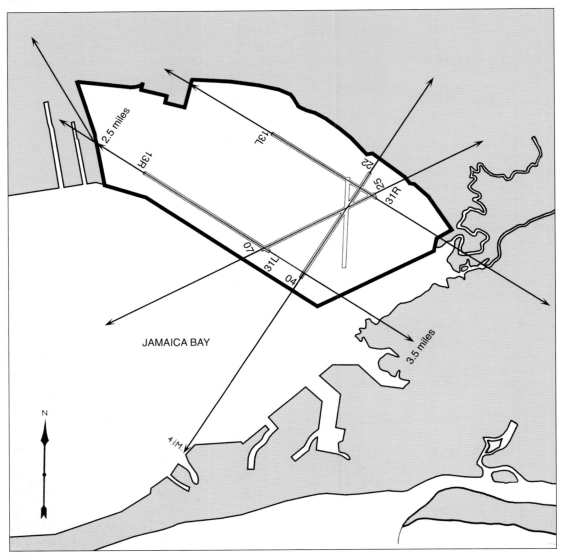

Idlewild International Airport, New York. This sketch-map shows the proximity of the built-up areas which surrounded airport on three sides. The Comet had no difficulty in meeting the Port of New York's stringent noise regulations.

would not affect the Comet. The Port of New York Authority ruled that jetliners must use runways 22 or 25 between these hours which could affect operators. BOAC, however, scheduled their New York-London Comet 4 flights outside this period. Cancellations or delays on this account were, therefore, most unlikely.

The Comet's good power-to-weight ratio and low wing loading provided a runway and climb performance unequalled among jet airliners and better than many contemporary piston-engined airliners. These qualities enabled it easily to meet the Port of New York Authority`s restrictions without loss of range or payload, a fact which was proved in practice by daily Comet 4 operations

Basil Smallpeice again: *'After the initial excitement we had to get down to work preparing for the service to leave New York in the morning. The DC-7C and the Britannia 312 still had to operate overnight eastbound because of their long flight times. Only the jets made it possible to schedule daytime flights from west to east. If we were to leave early from Idlewild (as Kennedy Airport was then called) and if the flight took no more than six and a half hours, we could reach London shortly before dark.*

Operationally, there was no problem. The aircraft

in New York was fully serviceable, as was its sister aircraft in London, and both crews were on standby. So, on Saturday, 4 October, 1958, BOAC made aviation history by operating the first transatlantic jet service ever - and, to cap it, both ways on the same day. Capt Tom Stoney, our Comet flight manager, in command eastbound, took the aircraft up to 1,850 ft while still inside the perimeter fence of the airport, at which point he throttled back to reduce the noise level within limits acceptable to the authorities.

Out over the Atlantic we passed the other aircraft, out of sight, with Pops d'Erlanger on board and Capt Roy Millichap in command. Our eastbound flight to London took only 6 hours 12 minutes, thanks to a tailwind of 92 mph and the priority given us by Air Traffic Control over the UK. The aircraft glided in to a smooth touch-down at London Airport. A warm welcome was given us on the tarmac, and it gave me a particular glow of pleasure to find Miles Thomas among those who had come to greet us.

Not until nearly three weeks later were Pan American able to introduce their own transatlantic jet service with their newly delivered Boeing 707. Our team had scored another BOAC first.

BOAC's important 'first' was very nearly spoiled by an Engineering strike by BOAC's staff at London Airport and subsequent Comet services were held up

until 14 November when the aircraft took over the daily Monarch services between London and New York from the Britannia 312s. In 1959 the three organisations concerned with getting the Comet back in international air service, De Havilland, Rolls-Royce and BOAC, were given the Hulton award for the most outstanding contribution to British prestige.

Cut to the bone.

To say that American pride was hurt with the arrival of the transatlantic Comets was an understatement. Legend has it that the first passengers were booed as they stepped of the aircraft in New York by some. None were more incensed at being beaten than the Boeing Aircraft Company. Even 50 years later Boeing's publicity machine were still coming out with mealy-mouthed words that twist the truth and conceal the facts.

'...the advances in passenger experience that the 787 will introduce are reminiscent of the advances first experienced 50 years ago when Pan American World Airways blazed a trail across the Atlantic Ocean with its brand-new Boeing 707.

On Aug. 15, 1958, Pan Am took delivery of the United States' first commercial jet airliner, a Boeing 707-120, and began plans for Oct. 26, 1958, when Pan Am and the 707 would make history by inaugurating the first 707 service and the first daily

One of BOAC's Comet 4s undergoing servicing in the maintenance facility at London Airport before re-entering passenger service. *(DH Hatfield)*

transatlantic jet service from New York to Paris'.

The deception - almost to the point of revising history - continues to this day when Boeing placed the 367-80, the famous 'Dash 80', forerunner to the 707, in the Smithsonian Institution's Steven F. Udvar-Hazy Center near Washington Dulles International Airport, claiming it to be the prototype of the passenger airliner, even going to the lengths of painting 'Boeing 707' on the tail!

In reality the Dash 80 was and is at least two steps removed from the earliest 707, the -120 model which itself came from the KC-135 Stratotanker for the US Air Force. The list of differences is almost endless, but probably the biggest was that of fuselage diameter - the Dash 80 was 132 inches; the KC-135 was increased by 12 inches to 144 inches and the 707 was widened even further by four inches to 148 inches!

Boeing targetted Pan American World Airlines, which had traditionally 'bought Boeing' and which the U.S. government considered its 'chosen instrument' to represent the American commercial air fleet abroad. Undoubtedly a pioneer in embracing jet aviation, Juan Trippe, the airline's legendary chief executive officer, had early on expressed a keen interest in operating a passenger jet service capable of flying nonstop across the North Atlantic. Having seen the bright promise of the British Comet fade,

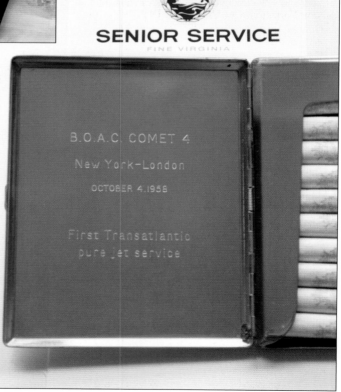

BOAC produced sales leaflets, brochures and other items to mark the first transatlantic pure jet service.

Possibly the nicest, and the most understated was this gold-plated, dark blue leatherette covered cigarette case, complete with silver 'Speedbird' emblem.

The cigarette case was engraved inside

BOAC Comet 4

New York - London
October 4 1958

First Transatlantic
pure jet service'

This of course was flown by G-APDB, which BOAC sold in 1965 to Malayan Airways System and was eventually purchased by Dan-Air who placed it on long-term loan to the East Anglian Aviation Society at Duxford, where it resides to this day.

Trippe played off two of the biggest domestic airplane builders, Boeing and Douglas. Both companies vied to appeal to Pan American's needs and offered the Boeing 707 and DC-8 respectively.

In October 1955, Trippe signed contracts with both companies to buy 45 of these jets (20 707s and 25 DC-8s). Exactly two years later, Boeing rolled out the first operational 707, a Boeing 707-120, and on 26 October 1958, amid much fanfare, Pan American inaugurated its New York-London route, ushering in a new era in the history of passenger aviation. On the very first flight, which made a stopover in Newfoundland, there were 111 passengers, at the time the largest number ever to board a single regularly scheduled flight. Coach fares were $272, about the same as one would expect to pay for a piston-engine flight across the Atlantic.

At first BOAC tried hard to compete. With its rapidly expanding use of the Boeing 707, especially on the transatlantic route, Pan American began a period of almost unchallenged success in the international airline industry. The airline, for example, was the first to recognize the importance to passengers of non-stop flights on long trips; it negotiated with Boeing for a version of the 707 that could fly for a longer time without refuelling, known as the 707-320. This allowed the airline to introduce true intercontinental service with non-stop London-to-New York flights on 26 August 1959. This was a perfect case of a dominant air carrier playing the lead role in defining the characteristics of a new class of jets that the industry would produce. The 707-320 was eventually adopted by as many as eleven other airlines within a year.

Comet 4 commercial operations across the Atlantic were notably trouble-free and BOAC justifiably thought that, as a result of Comet 4 experience, and because of their previous Comet experience amounting to almost 30,000 hours, that the Comet had quickly passed through the early stage during which on all aircraft minor operating difficulties were encountered and defects in the various systems could be expected to cause delays in service.

Practical experience confirmed that there were no unusual crew problems associated with Comet 4 operations, pilots having no difficulty with conversion. From the navigator's point of view work might in theory be at a rather higher intensity because of the compression in time of flight; in practice, however, trans-Atlantic Comet navigation proved easy. Good Loran coverage was available for most of the flight and radio contact with either side of the Atlantic or the two weather ships, Charlie or Juliet, was maintainable through all but fifteen minutes or so of the flight; the Comet provided a smooth platform for Astro if required.

Passenger reaction was unanimously favourable; the four-abreast standard-class seating was deservedly popular and there was plenty of room for

Displayed in the Smithsonian Institution near Washington's Dulles Airport, the 367-80 carries the registration N70700 and the legend 'Boeing 707' on the tail, which of course, it never was! *(author)*

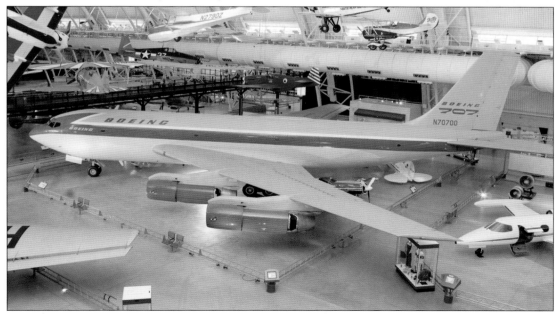

BOAC's 'Monarch' service was world renowned; now with the Comet 4, speed matched service!

the cabin staff to provide the usual incomparable BOAC Monarch service.

From the public address system, over which the Captain briefed his passengers on the new and exhilarating experience of jet travel, to the serving of a luxury meal in conditions as steady and as smooth as (and somewhat quieter than) a West End restaurant, BOAC certainly 'took good care of you'.

'As the publicity material said '...*the size*

and arrangement of the passenger accommodation enable the operator to provide a personal element in the cabin service which travellers particularly appreciate.

The Comet has proved by practical demonstration to leading airline people the world over that it goes anywhere using to-day's runways without extension or restriction. Now the passenger will decide'.

Chapter Twelve

COMET 4 IN SERVICE

The DH 106 Comet was clearly one of the most revolutionary aircraft of all time and was the pride of the British aviation industry. Although its phenomenal early successes were halted abruptly with the disastrous accidents in the early 1950s, the accident enquiry and investigations that followed enabled the aviation world to fully understand for the first time the problems of metal fatigue in pressurised aircraft. This information was made available to all and was used in the subsequent development of other first generation jet aircraft. The safety of passengers today owes a debt of gratitude to the tragedies and lives lost so many years ago.

Without doubt, no civil jet aircraft has had such a colourful history as that of the Comet, one that literally plunged from triumph to tragedy, then rose phoenix-like from the ashes to fill a historic place in the annals of aviation progress. The Comet can claim to be the very first jet airliner, the first jet airliner to cross the Atlantic, the first to start commercial passenger services, the first to fly around the world, the first to fly across the Pacific, the first to commence commercial jet services over

the Atlantic as well as many speed and technical firsts.

The Comet 4 may have inaugurated the first transatlantic jet passenger services, beating its rival Pan American with their Boeing 707s by almost a month, but the Comet 4 was not ideally suited to the Atlantic, and a year later it was replaced by the Boeing 707. The Comet 4 was however, well suited to the African and Asian routes and quickly became the flagship on BOAC routes to these destinations. It served with BOAC until the mid-1960s when it was deemed too slow and small.

Other international airlines were quick to appreciate the Comet`s impressive power and hot weather performance and so they purchased various versions for use in the Middle East and South America by East African Airways and Aerolineas Argentinas.

Capital Airlines of the US placed a substantial order for the Comet 4A, a high speed lower altitude version, but this order was cancelled when the airline was taken over by United Airlines and the Comet 4A was never completed.

British Eurpoean Airways (BEA), the UK

BOAC soon replaced the Comet on transatlantic routes with the Boeing 707, such as G-APFE seen here.

European airline, placed orders for an adaptation of the 4A called the Comet 4B which utilised the longer fuselage of the proposed intercontinental Comet 4C with the shorter wings of the Comet 4A. This version was also acquired by the Greek national airline Olympic Airways who operated it in conjunction with the BEA Comet fleet.

Here was an example of the pressures BOAC was repeatedly having to face from domestic politics. In May 1959 De Havillands were endeavouring to sell up to a further eighteen aircraft beyond the thirty-three already sold and for these eighteen were trying to negotiate a price of £1.05m per aircraft. Under the terms of BOAC's contract, de Havilland's would in that event be liable to pay the Corporation £110,000 per aircraft for each of BOAC's nineteen, a total payment of £2.09m. The Managing Director of De Havilland said that if BOAC insisted on its rights de Havilland would have serious financial problems and would have to close down the production line. BOAC's Board maintained that in view of the heavy expense BOAC had borne in the Comet programme from the start, they must insist on their contractual rights.

It was not long before the Minister despatched a letter to the Chairman dated 18 June 1959 in respect of Comets De Havillands were expecting to sell to Compania Mexicana de Aviacion (CMA), the Mexican airline, at £1.065m each. The Minister asked BOAC to waive its rights on this particular sale in the national interest and stated that if BOAC was prepared to agree, he the Minister, '...*should be happy to consider whether I might not make some public reference to the matter at some convenient time*'.

However, De Havilland claimed that the Comet mark to be sold to CMA was substantially different from BOAC's model and therefore they were not liable for any payment. BOAC differed but in view of the Minister's letter and the appeal to 'national interest', the Board agreed to the Minister's request without prejudice to the Corporation's rights in any future sales. But de Havilland again sought release from the 'Most Favoured Customer clause' when they wrote to BOAC in February 1960, but this time the request was general in respect of all their sales of Comet 4B and 4C. In view of the legal uncertainty as to whether the contract provision would apply to these types BOAC accepted the inevitable and

Comet 4 finishing. Here are aircraft for Aerolineas Argentinas, BEA, Mexicana and Middle East Airlines (MEA)

agreed. It was an odd twist of consequence that BEA was able to purchase its 4Bs at a lower price than it might otherwise have done!

The ultimate and most successful version of the Comet was the 4C, the high capacity long-range version that was purchased by Mexicana, United Arab Airlines, MEA, the Saudi Arabian Royal Flight, Kuwait Airways, Sudan Airways, the RAF and the MoD. De Havilland had projected that the break-even point for the Comet 4 was 67 aircraft, and actually broke even at 57, enabling them to pay back a £4 million loan from the UK Government, and generate a £1.5 million profit for the British taxpayer.

Comet 4 Operators in alphabetical order.
Aerolineas Argentinas
By the mid-fifties Aerolineas Argentinas was investigating the options for jet airliners to service its premier routes to Europe and North America. After review, the airline confirmed its choice of the Comet based on a combination of size, power and jet experience. Accordingly, on 19 March 1958, Aerolineas Argentinas signed a contract for the supply of six Comet 4 worth in excess of £9

million. This initial order for six aircraft was fulfilled between 1959 and July 1960, ending with LV-PPA, the initial three being the 7th, 8th, 9th and 10th airframes diverted from the BOAC order.

After a brief period of route-proving, the airline's inaugural service was flown by LV-PLM on 16 April 1959 between Buenos Aires and Santiago in Chile. The airline expanded its services on 19 May 1959 when a Comet 4 flew from Buenos Aires to Europe and then on 7 June between Buenos Aires and New York.

The airline suffered several major accidents and as a result purchased an additional Comet 4C in 1962 to supplement the remaining three Comet 4s. Aerolineas Argentinas continued to use the remaining four Comets on international services until they were gradually phased out between 1966 and 1968 to be were placed on domestic routes, eventually being withdrawn from service and sold to Dan-Air in 1971.

Air Ceylon
The airline leased a number of Comet 4s from BOAC during the early 1960s for services to London and Singapore from Colombo so as to be

Above: 'Gear Up!' LV-PLP climbs away. *(DH Hatfield)*

Right: LV-AHS taxies out for the start of another service. *(author's collection)*

G-APDA in BOAC colours and Air Ceylon markings *(DH Hatfield)*

able to compete with jet services from other airlines. The aircraft retained the standard BOAC colours and UK registrations but replaced the airline titling.

Air India
A weekly Madras - Singapore - Madras service with a Comet 4 leased from BOAC commenced on 5 April 1962. These flights were flown under Air India flight numbers, but the aircraft retained full BOAC titling, colours and registration. However, Air India titles were applied around the passenger entrance door. A series of Jakata and Kuwait flights were also made. This lease ceased on 7 July 1963.

Air Malta
Dan-Air wet-leased a single Comet 4 using an Air Malta crew on 26 May 1976 for a service between the island and Manchester.

AREA Ecuador
In 1966 AREA accounced a proposed purchase of a pair of BOAC Comets. The first G-APDI was delivered to Quito on 13 March 1966. Equipped by Mexicana and registered HC-ALT, the Comet entered into limited service from Quito to Miami. Later in 1967 two other ex-BOAC Comets - G-APDJ and 'DT -were to have served with the airline. G-APDT was to have been diverted from the Mexicana

purchase on delivery, but the AREA order was never finalised and the Comet remained with Mexicana. G-APDJ remained with BOAC until it was sold to Dan-Air in April 1967.

HC-ALT continued in service for several years until it was flown into Miami International Airport in 1968, only to become the subject of legal action. The aircraft remained at Miami, eventually becoming derelict, the BOAC colours that had been painted over with the AREA Ecuador scheme gradually becoming apparent as the AREA paintwork flaked off. The aircraft being finally scrapped in February 1978.

British European Airways
BEA ordered six 100-seater short-medium range Comet 4Bs for £7 million in 1957, and signed the agreement on 28 March 1959 with the first two aircraft - G-APMB and G-APMC - handed over at London Airport on 16 November 1959, ten weeks ahead of contract. The Comet was BEA's first jetliner and, within two weeks of delivery, proving flights on European routes had begun, to Nice on 3 December, followed by Copenhagen, Moscow, Warsaw, Stockholm and Zurich. Revenue-earning flights, did not commence until April 1960 owing to a dispute with the pilots over pay and working hours.

Before the Comet entered service, 94 BEA and Olympic pilots and engineers received training on

The former BOAC G-APDI, now registered as HC-ALT 'out to grass' in cockroach corner at Miami International sometime in the early 1970s. *(Simon Peters Collection)*

Left: G-APMA of BEA in flight.

Below: A typical scene at London Airport, with a BEA Comet taxiing past the Queens Building and a pair of Viscounts. (*both DH Hatfield*)

the 4B at the BEA Comet training base at Stansted. During the winter of 1959/60, 174 cabin crews were also trained for Comet services.

Rather surprisingly, the first scheduled flight with the Comet 4B did not originate from London but from Tel Aviv on 1 April 1960, with departure at 08.00 local for Athens, Rome and London using G-APMB flown by Captain A. N. Werner. Three further inaugural flights followed later that same day from London-Airport, the return Tel Aviv flight using G-APMD, London-Moscow using G-APMF, flown by Captain W. Baillie and London-Nice making use of flagship G-APMA. It was two months before further destinations were added to the Comet network, London-Copenhagen on 3 June 1960 using G-APMD, a weekly non-stop London-Malta service on 5 June - also making use of G-APMD, London-Oslo-Copenhagen on 1 July with G-APMA and London-Frankfurt on 1 August 1960 with G-APMC, by which time daily utilisation had risen to 7.5 hours. A seventh aircraft had been ordered on 12 August 1959 and three more on 1 July 1960. Four more were ordered on 20 November 1960.

By mid-1961, BEA's fleet of Comet 4Bs had risen to 15 aircraft, and further destinations had been added to the Comet schedules, in particular in co-operation with Olympic Airways and its newly-delivered Comet 4Bs, to Athens, Istanbul, Nicosia, Beirut and Cairo.

Operations were marred, however, by the fatal crash of G-ARJM on take-off near Ankara on 21 December 1961, which at once brought back memories of the Comet 1 disasters of the 1950s.

Confidence in the aircraft quickly recovered and by the mid-summer peak of 1963 many other European cities saw regular BEA Comet 4B schedules. Athens, Copenhagen, Milan, Nice, Nicosia, Rome, and Stockholm and Venice were all served at least once daily, as were Amsterdam, Brussels, Dusseldorf, Frankfurt, Geneva and Zurich. Naples was served six times a week, Basle, Beirut, Lisbon, Tel Aviv and five times Ankara Helsinki, Istanbul, and Malta four times, Bergen three times, Oslo, Moscow and Valencia twice, plus Cairo, Gibraltar, and Stavanger once a week. The eastern Mediterranean destinations were all served jointly with Olympic and/or Cyprus Airways, the latter using BEA Comets under a Cyprus Airways flight number.

BEA's Comet fleet gave good service throughout the sixties, the type's safety record spoilt only by the destruction of G-ARCO near the Turkish coast by a bomb on 12 October 1967.

BEA's last scheduled services with the Comets were flown in June 1969, the type being replaced by Tridents, although two aircraft - G-APMA and G-APME - remained as back-ups even after the transfer of most of the fleet to the company's new charter subsidiary BEA Airtours in the spring of 1970. Four ex-Olympic Airways Comets were purchased in 1969-70, prior to their onwards sale.

Three Airtours aircraft were leased to BEA as required to cover for the late delivery of Trident 3s. G-APMA was the only aircraft not eventually sold, and was broken up in 1972.

BEA Airtours

BEA Airtours Ltd was established to operate inclusive tour charter flights as a wholly-owned, non-IATA subsidiary of the national airline in March 1969. Seven of the parent company's Comet 4Bs were allocated to the new airline when the type was withdrawn from scheduled BEA service in June 1969. BEA Airtours was based at Gatwick Airport with a staff of 200, with former Flight Operations Chief Captain W. Baillie appointed as Managing Director. The Comet 4Bs were re-configured in a 109-seat all-tourist layout, with eight aircraft transferred between 1 March and 1 April 1970. BEA Airtours' first service was from Gatwick to Palma on 6 March 1970 with G-ARJL. Two further Comet 4Bs were transferred from the parent company in May and August 1970 respectively and, by mid-summer, the Comets were operating a large network of IT flights from Gatwick to destinations throughout the Mediterranean, especially to Spain (Barcelona, Alicante), Palma-Majorca, Italy, Greece, Turkey and Cyprus. During the winter season, many ski-related charters were undertaken to such destinations as Munich in Germany, Salzburg in Austria, and Geneva and Zurich in Switzerland. Year-round charters were also operated to Basle-Mulhouse. During their first year of operation, the Comets flew 15,067 hours. Most flights were operated from Gatwick, although a limited programme was also flown from Manchester.

By November 1970, BEA Airtours were already looking for replacements for its Comets and applied for permission to buy a fleet of seven ex-American Airlines Boeing 707-123Bs. Political pressure forced the airline to buy from either BEA or BOAC and replacements for the Comets started arriving from 30 December 1971 in the shape of ex-BOAC Boeing 707-436s. Two Comet 4Bs were sold in 1972, followed by three further aircraft in January/February 1973, all of which went to Dan-Air. With the delivery of the remaining Boeing 707s, the last five Comet 4Bs were withdrawn at the end of the 1973 summer season, the final flight being a Paris to Gatwick charter on 31 October 1973 with the same aircraft - G-ARJL - that had inaugurated services just three and a half years earlier. All five remaining Comets had been sold to Dan-Air by 9 November 1973, including G-ARJL, which made its last flight that day. The same month the airline was renamed British Airtours on the merger of BEA and BOAC into British Airways. When BEA finally ceased Comet flying, their aircraft had carried over seven million passengers and flown 110 million miles between 1959 and 1973.

British Overseas Airways Corporation

The BOAC purchase of 19 Comet 4s was announced in the House of Commons on 29 March 1955 when Viscount Thurso Sir Archibald Sinclair asked for details which were provided by The Earl of Selkirk Mr George Douglas-Hamilton and the contract was signed in April 1957.

As already mentioned, the first two Comets to be delivered were G-APDB and G-APDC in September 1958 and the final aircraft - G-APDJ - completed the order on 11 January 1960. In the first six months after the first delivery, 40% of hours were used for training and non-revenue flying, by October 1960 this had dropped to 0.7%.

BEA Airtours became the charter arm of BEA, commencing services in March 1970. The Comets served for three years until they were withdrawn, most going across the airfield at Gatwick to Dan-Air. Here G-ARJL is captured by the camera getting airborne from Gatwick.

BOAC's Comet 4 flagship G-APDA is seen low over Hatfield, with Hatfield House in the lower right corner
(DH Hatfield)

On average BOAC employed 117 Comet crews to operate its nineteen Comets.

The Comets were not ideally suited to the Atlantic route due to their limited size and range, and on 16 October 1960, flight number 512 flew BOAC's last service on this premier route. BOAC Comets had made 2,304 crossings, carried 94,000 passengers and had averaged three crossings per day. BOAC had flown the Atlantic to New York, Toronto and Boston increasing their Atlantic traffic by 40%.

Comets were then utilised on routes more suited to their performance and size, flying to South Africa, South America, the Far East, Australia and the Caribbean. Comet services were extended to Montreal on 19 December 1958, Tokyo on 1 April 1959, Hong Kong 1 June, Singapore on 10 August, Sydney and Melbourne on 1 November, and Johannesburg on 2 December 1959. In 1960 services were started to Buenos Aires and Santiago on 25 January and Montego Bay on 2 February. During 1960 the BOAC fleet of 18 aircraft were

G-APDT, seen here surrounded by ground equipment in the Heathrow engine detuner bay, was being used by the apprentices as a training aid.
(authors collection)

flying 400,000 miles a week and with the full complement of 19 in October 1960 the airline had carried 327,000 passengers.

In 1963 BOAC began to put Comets up for sale, with a single aircraft for £656,000 and an option of a second to any interested organisation. By November 1965, Comets were being withdrawn from service and were being offered for £250,000. The company stated that the Comets '...with 81 seats, were not big enough and were also 100 mph slower than the 707'.

The last BOAC Comet service was flown on 23 November 1965 from Auckland to London under the command of Captain Cliff Alabaster, the Captain of the first Comet 1 service to Johannesburg. In October 1965 BOAC had already sold six of their 18 remaining aircraft and were actively selling the remainder. In January 1968, they had five Comets remaining and by December 1969, BOAC had sold all but G-APDT, which had just been returned from lease to Mexicana and was withdrawn from use on its return to London.

Central African Airways
CAAs 'The Rhodesian' service was operated during the early 1960s under flight numbers CE892 and CE893 using BOAC Comets between London and Johannesburg. The services departed on Tuesday and returned Thursday, changing to a Thursday returning Saturday during the winter.

Channel Airways
In 1970, Channel Airways, an inclusive tour operator based at Stansted, purchased a single ex-BEA and four ex-Olympic Comet 4Bs for just under £2 million. The Comets were fitted out in a 106-seat configuration for the airline's holiday charter work.

The ex-Olympic Comets had been in storage at Cambridge after their withdrawal from service in late 1969 and were subsequently flown to Stansted between 26 January and 25 June 1970, the first arrival being G-APYC. All retained the basic colours of their previous owners.

During the 1970 holiday season, flights were made from Birmingham, Bristol, East Midlands, Glasgow, Manchester, Newcastle and Stansted. On 21 September 1971 G-ARDI was flown into retirement at Southend, reducing the fleet to four. In June 1971 Channel purchased XA-NAP (G-APDR) the ex-BOAC and Mexicana Comet, for its desperately needed Rolls-Royce Avon engines and it was flown from Mexico to Stansted to be reduced to spares.

One year later XA-NAP was donated to the fire school and became the primary fire airframe during the 1970s. Channel Airways Ltd went into receivership on 1 February 1972 and the remaining Comet 4Bs were sold to Dan-Air in April and were flown to Lasham to be refitted and painted prior to entering service.

Cyprus Airways
In May 1961 Cyprus Airways - then 22% owned by BEA - signed an agreement with BEA to commence Comet services to a number of destinations in the region considered important in promoting Cyprus as a tourist centre. Cyprus Airways used BEA flight crews and Cyprus Airways cabin staff on routes from Nicosia to Athens, Istanbul, Beirut and the Persian Gulf region.

Unfortunately the airline suffered two major Comet incidents, the first being on 21 December 1961 when the 4B G-ARJM operating a Cyprus Airways sector, stalled shortly after take-off at Ankara, Turkey. The three BEA flight crew, four Cyprus Airways cabin staff and 20 passengers all lost their lives but seven passengers were thrown

Channel Airways' G-APMB, still in its basic BEA colours, rests between flights. *(authors collection)*

clear and survived. Later in-depth investigations revealed that the accident had been caused by a tiny screw becoming loose in one of the instruments, making the pitch pointer read incorrectly. After take-off the Comet climbed too steeply and at 450ft it stalled, falling in a level pitch to the ground and bursting into flames on impact.

The second incident occurred on 12 October 1967 when G-ARCO, operating a joint service as BE/CY284, was blown up by a terrorist bomb killing all 59 passengers and seven crew, the aircraft crashing into the Mediterranean near Rhodes. The official accident report concluded that G-ARCO had been the subject of an explosion caused by a bomb placed under either Seat 4A or 5A in the economy section of the aircraft that when exploded, caused the aircraft to become uncontrollable and to descend rapidly from 29,000 ft and break up at about 15,000 feet.

Dan-Air Services

UK-based airline Dan-Air became the largest Comet operator, ultimately owning well over half of all the Comet 4s built. Established in 1953, the airline purchased its first Comet, G-APDK, from BOAC in 1966, followed several days later by G-APDO. Additional Comet 4s were added from Malaysia-Singapore Airlines, BOAC, East African and Aerolineas Argentinas and a former BOAC machine from Kuwait Airways.

In 1969 the airline purchased its first Comet 4C and then in 1972 the airline acquired the first of

Right: Captain Kurt Lang's stunning picture of a pair of Dan-Air Comet noses in the latter colour scheme one frosty morning at Gatwick. (Capt Kurt Lang)

Below: From an earlier time, Gatwick in the early 1970s with Dan-Air Comets G-APDD and G-APDP cloest to the camera. (authors collection)

many Comet 4Bs. The airline used the Comet to fly to most of the major European cities and sunny Mediterranean holiday destinations.

In 1975 Dan-Air purchased five former RAF Comets which were in excellent condition with low flying hours. In 1976 they made their final Comet purchase, taking the EgyptAir fleet of four aircraft. These aircraft had low residual wing life, and rectification would have been uneconomical, so one was stripped for spares at Cairo and the other three were flown to Lasham for spares recovery and scrapping.

Between 1966 and 1976 Dan-Air purchased 49 of the 77 Comet 4s built, although a number were utilised only for spares and never flew commerically.

As the Comet became increasingly more expensive to operate Dan-Air gradually started replacing Comets with other newer types such as Boeing 727s. 1980 became the last Comet season with four ex-RAF machines maintaining passenger services, until most finally retired in late October.

The world's last commercial Comet service DA8874, was operated by G-BDIW with a special

G-BDIT - the former RAF C.4 XR395 climbs out after maintenance at Dan-Air's Lasham facility. The aircraft is in the final Dan-Air scheme worn by the Comets. *(Kurt Lang)*

Ian Allan enthusiasts' charter on 8 November from Gatwick. The one hour ten minute flight was made around the south of England conducting low passes at London Heathrow, RAF Brize Norton and then finally its home for many years, RAF Lyneham, before returning to Gatwick. A number of airframes were earmarked for preservation, some of which fell through.

East African Airways

The governments of Uganda, Tanganyika and Kenya jointly owned East African Airways. Facing an increasing competitive threat from the new BOAC Comet jet services, the airline placed an order for two Comet 4s in August 1958 for delivery in July and September 1960. EAA ordered a third Comet 4 VP-KRL - in 1960 (the final Comet 4 built) for delivery in April 1962.

Services were started on 17 September 1960 when VP-KPJ flew a reverse service from London to Nairobi. The network was expanded on routes to Frankfurt, Paris, Rome, Athens and Cairo. In 1965 the Comets were re-registered to reflect the newly independent countries, with prefixes 5H for

Tanzania, 5X for Uganda and 5Y for Kenya.

By the mid-1960s the Comets were withdrawn from EAA's premier routes and were replaced by a number of Vickers VC-10s. The Comets were placed on routes to Pakistan and India until November 1967 when they were used on medium and short-haul routes. A re-skinning programme occurred in October 1967 to prolong airframe life. EAA added to its route capacity between November 1965 and March 1967 by leasing G-APDL from BOAC, re-registering it as 5Y-ADD. In 1968 several of the aircraft were utilised by the wholly-owned subsidiary Seychelles Kilimanjaro Air Transport for work on charter services.

In November 1969 corrosion was discovered in 5X-AAO and 5H-AAF so they were withdrawn from service before being sold to Dan-Air and flown to the UK for spares use. EAA then leased three Comets from Dan-Air, returning them during 1970 and 1971. The leased 5Y-AMT operated the last EAA Comet service on 19 February 1971, after which all the Comets were then flown back to Dan-Air's maintenance base at Lasham for disposal.

VP-KPK is re-stocked by BOAC Cabin Services at London Airport. *(BAe Hatfield)*

G-APDA appeared for a short time during 1961 in a hybrid BOAC/Ghana Airways colours and named *Osagyefo*. *(BAe Hatfield)*

Ghana Airways

Originally a part of the West Africa Airways Corporation network involving Sierra Leone, Gambia, Nigeria and Ghana, when the latter gained independence in 1957, co-operation with BOAC followed.

There had been some interest from Ghana Airways in the purchase of Comet 4s, but this did not come to fruition, although de Havilland did produce mock-ups and literature to support this interest.

In March 1961 Ghana Airways did lease G-APDA from BOAC to transport Ghana's first President, President Nkrumah to New York for a conference. The Comet had the BOAC markings replaced by those of Ghana Airways and was named 'Osagyefo', translated as 'The Redeemer'. In 1962 Ghana terminated the agreement with BOAC, and the following year Ghana Airways state owned.

Guest Aerovias Mexico SA

In December 1960 Mexicana signed an operating agreement with Guest to provide for the lease of two Comet 4Cs.

Guest crew training started in January 1961 in conjunction with Mexicana Comet crews. In April 1961 route-proving began between Mexico City and Paris with a return stopover in Lisbon.

In mid-1961 Guest Aerovias Mexico SA started their jet services from Mexico City to key cities in South America and Lisbon, Paris and Madrid. The Guest Comets continued in service for several years and were seen occasionally at London Airport in Mexicana livery but with the addition of the titles 'Guest'.

Kuwait Airways

Kuwait Airways placed an order for two Comet 4Cs in August 1962 for delivery in 1963 and 1964 prior to delivery of two Trident 1Es in 1966. They accepted Comet 4C 9K-ACA on 18 January 1963 and 9K-ACE on 2 February 1964, and then added the ex-BOAC Comet 4 G-APDG as 9K-ACI in 1965 along with the lease for one year of the BOAC Comets G-APDN and G-APDS to supplement its services.

Kuwait Airways utilised the Comets on routes to London, Frankfurt, Paris, Cairo, Beirut, Doha, Karachi and Bombay before retiring them from service in 1968. The aircraft were reactivated during late 1968 and leased to Middle East Airlines to replace those lost during the 28 December 1968 Israeli raid on Beirut. The Comets served only until March 1969 when they were withdrawn from service and stored at Beirut pending sale by Kuwait Airways. This happened

Guest Aerovias Mexico SA made use of a pair of Mexicana Comets. XA-NAT is seen here with Guest titles on the fusealge roof, and the Guest logo on the pinion tanks. *(BAe Hatfield)*

Kuwait Airways' 9K-ACE seen in flight. *(BAe Hatfield)*

a year later when Dan-Air acquired the fleet and they were subsequently flown back to the UK.

Malayan/Malaysian Airlines/MSA

Malayan Airlines became a jet operator in 1962 when it leased a BOAC Comet to operate their Silver Kris Jet Service. Following the formation of Malaysia in 1963, the company changed its name to Malaysian Airways in December 1963. Malaysian Airways continued jet services by leasing two BOAC Comets until they ultimately purchased five Comets from BOAC in September 1965.

In 1966 the company name was changed again to Malaysia-Singapore Airlines (MSA) and three aircraft were re-registered with the Singapore registrations 9V-BAS, BAT and BAU. MSA used their Comet fleet to serve Kuala Lumpur, Kuching, Colombo, Madras, Bangkok, Hong Kong, Taipei, Manila, Jesselton, Perth and Sydney. Additional routes were also introduced including the Singapore to Manila service which was inaugurated on 2 July 1966.

In 1967 two Comets were discovered to have had suffered from corrosion around the front spar bolts and both aircraft were withdrawn from service immediately. MSA leased two Comets from BOAC - G-APDR as 9V-BBH, and G-APDM, which became 9V-BBJ to maintain services while the other two Comets were repaired.

The airline retired its Comet fleet in late 1969 and they were sold to Dan-Air in October and November.

Mexicana Airlines

On 30 October 1959, Mexicana signed a $14 million contract for three Comet 4Cs for delivery in 1960. To assist with meeting the Mexicana order two Comet 4Bs - G-APMD, G-APME - destined for BEA were allocated to become the first and second Comet 4Cs and the BEA Comets were re-allocated further down the production line. Mexicana also purchased a Comet 4C simulator from Redifon and this was shipped to Mexico City.

Mexicana's first Golden Aztec service was started on 4 July 1960, Captain Roberto Pini commanding XA-NAS on the flight from Mexico

MSA Comet 9M-AOD in the strikingly elegant colour scheme. *(BAe Hatfield)*

MSA Comet 9M-BAU in the same colour scheme thatb appears to have faded somewhat! *(BAe Hatfield)*

Mexicana's XA-NAS banks away from the camera revealing an underside free from dangling engine pods and the bulges of the undercarriage doors.

The aircraft bears 'CMA' under one wing, which stands for 'Compañía Mexicana de Aviación, S.A. de C.V.' - the airlines full title.

Both these pictures are the product of De Havilland's flight test department and their staff photographers.
(BAe Hatfield)

City to Los Angeles. With the other two Comets being delivered by the end of 1960, Mexicana placed the Comets on its premier routes to Chicago, Los Angeles, New York, San Francisco and San Antonio.

Mexicana had an option on two more Comet 4Cs but the airline was facing fierce competition from both domestic and foreign carriers and the option was not taken up, the aircraft going to Sudan Airways instead.

On 15 December 1964, Mexicana entered into a long-term lease with BOAC for one Comet 4 G-APDT/XA-NAB and purchased another - G-APDR as XA-NAP to supplement their jet services including commencing services direct from Dallas to Mexico City.

XA-NAB was returned to BOAC as G-APDT in 1969 and a year later XA-NAP was sold to Channel Airways for its engines and spares and flown to the UK. The three remaining Comet 4Cs and the simulator were sold to the US aviation dealer Westernair.

Middle East Airlines

MEA, which was established on 31 May 1945, placed a £5.5 million order for Comet 4Cs in January 1959, receiving the first of four in 1960 with the final delivery in March 1961 after a two-year study which concluded that the Comet had '...*technical and economic suitability*' for MEA routes. The airline also held an option on a fifth Comet 4C - G-AROV - but this was not taken up and it was subsiquently sold to Aerolineas Argentinas.

The Comet fleet was used on westbound routes to the UK and central Europe and also eastbound to Pakistan and India. Routes served included London, Geneva, Vienna, Frankfurt, Rome, Athens, Baghdad, Teheran, Kuwait, Dhahran, Bahrain, Karachi, Istanbul, Jeddah, Bombay and Aden.

MEA also leased several Comets including BOAC examples G-APDG and G-APDK in the early 1960s and then G-APDM in 1967 as OD-AEV. They also leased three Comets Kuwait

Cedar tree jet! MEAs
OD-ADR is captured by
a Hatfield photographer
for a publicity picture.
(BAe Hatfield)

Airways in 1968-1969 as 9K-ACA, ACE and ACI, these being withdrawn from service in March 1969 shortly before the delivery of two Boeing 707s.

On the night of 28 December 1968 Israeli commandos attacked Beirut Airport and destroyed thirteen aircraft including three MEA Comets - OD-ADQ, OD-ADR and OD-ADS. OD-ADT survived and continued in service until October 1973 when it was sold to Dan-Air and flown to Lasham for spares.

Misrair/United Arab Airlines/EgyptAir

Over two years. United Arab Airlines evaluated options for a jet airliner fleet and in 1959 decided on the Comet 4C due to its '...reliability, performance and applicability to the UAA routes' and the £4 million contract for three Comet 4Cs was signed on 30 December 1959. The first Comet, SU-ALC, was delivered in June 1960 and the last, SU-ANI, in 1964. Services with the initial

two aircraft were started on 16 July 1960 with return trips from Cairo to London. From late July two return services were introduced between Cairo and Jeddah and two on the Cairo-Khartoum route.

On 15 January 1961 UAA placed a further order for two more Comets. Once the full fleet had been established the airline expanded Comet routes to include London, Rome, Frankfurt, Geneva, Zurich and Kuwait. Routes expanded further in the sixties, servicing Far East, European and extra Middle East destinations.

Three more Comets were ordered in 1962 and in February 1964 the airline ordered their final Comet, SU-ANI to replace SU-ALD which had crashed in the sea on approach to Bombay. Although the airline had ordered a total of nine Comets, the number in use never reached this level due to several accidents.

In 1969 UAA introduced the Boeing 707 and in October 1971 with a change of name to

Comet SU-ALD, part of the United Arab Airline conglomorate, with Misrair titles. *(BAe Hatfield)*

Comet SU-ANI, with full United Arab Airline titles. *(BAe Hatfield)*

EgyptAir the airline gradually phased the Comets onto the domestic routes which they served until they were withdrawn from service.

Finally in 1976 EgyptAir withdrew their Comets at Cairo and they were subsequently purchased by Dan-Air who flew three aircraft to Lasham for spares and reduced the last (SU-ALL) to spares, leaving its remainsin situ on the airfield to be scrapped later.

Nigeria Airways
In the mid-1960s Nigeria Airways chartered a BOAC Comet for use on the London to Lagos route The aircraft were operated by BOAC crew and had no changes to the airline livery.

Olympic Airways
The legendary Greek shipowner Aristotle Onassis, who started Olympic Airways in 1957, had determined from the first to take the airline into the jet age. For this he sought a consortium agreement with a foreign major airline - preferably one with jet experience - in order to gain maximum

financial and operational advantage. After a reorganization of the airline, a pooling of services with British European Airways (BEA) was signed in Monaco on 20 July 1959. Onassis signed on behalf of Olympic, and BEA chairman Lord Douglas of Kirtleside for BEA.

The Greek government duly endorsed the agreement, sharing the general optimism that it would generate new traffic. More first-class seats were planned on both routes. There was no sale of stock on either side, and thus each airline's identity was maintained. The Comet's manufacturer, De Havilland, was also pleased as Olympic promptly ordered two 4Bs in addition to the seven which BEA had on order.

By the terms of the agreement, BEA provided the Comet flight crews until such time as Greek crews could be trained on the new aircraft. The Comet would prove to have high passenger appeal and the consortium agreement gave Olympic Airways an economical way of entering the jet club. Olympic and British European Airways agreed to create the first codeshare flights; later the

G-APYC - later to be registered SX-DAK and named *Queen Frederica* - is seen on a pre-delivery test flight. *(BAe Hatfield)*

Just at the time that Olympic Airways introduced the Comet they changed from the logo above to the famous 'five Olympic rings' although the logo remained as a sign by the main passenger door.

Olympic Airways operated their Comet 4Bs mainly around Europe, but occasionally ranged further afield. Flagship was SX-DAK, which appeared on much of the airline's promotional material.

companies expanded their cooperation. When Hellenic crews had to spend a night in London, British crews would fly the Olympic Comets to BEA destinations, and the same with Greek crews and BEA Comets.

Olympic's first two Comet 4Bs were delivered on schedule in early 1960. The first, registered SX-DAK (ex G-APYC) and named *Queen Frederica*, was delivered on 26 April 1960. Flying to Athens four days after its handover, it set a record time on the route of 3 hours 14 minutes.

The second Comet, SX-DAL (ex G-APYD), named *Queen Olga*, was handed over on 14 May 1960. The two Comets formally began to operate the Athens-London route, in conjunction with BEA, four days later. Itineraries to Rome, Paris, Zurich, Frankfurt, Brussels, Amsterdam, Istanbul, Tel Aviv, Beirut, Cairo and Nicosia (this last in conjunction with BEA affiliate Cyprus Airways) followed.

Olympic Airways' Comet 4Bs, identical to those flown by BEA, were configured for 22 first class and 64 economy class passengers. Unlike the British airline, however, Olympic employed a flight engineer as part of the cockpit crew.

All Comet crews, including about fifty ground maintenance staff, were at the De Havilland factory in Hatfield. Experienced BEA crews also served as trained instructors.

When the British airline acquired a flight simulator, Olympic's crews were able to make good use of it as well.

By mid-1960 growing traffic made the acquisition of a third Comet necessary. On 14 July of that year the *Queen Sophia* was leased from BEA, retaining its British registration of G-APZM. The lease remained in effect, until 13 April 1966, when the aircraft was re-registered as SX-DAN.

In mid-March 1961 Olympic decided to operate a fourth Comet 4B. On 25 March G-ARDI was leased to the Greek airline. Like its predecessor, the Princess Sophia kept its British registration until 1966, when it was re-registered SX-DAO.

At the end of the 1960s the leases began to expire, SX-DAO in November 1969 and SX-DAN in March 1970. Both aircraft were returned to BEA and subsequently sold to Channel Airways. At about this time, after a decade of service, Olympic Airways phased out its Comets. The original two purchases, SX-DAK and SX-DAL, were sold back to BEA towards the end of 1969. They, too, were later sold to Channel Airways. All four ended their flying days in the service of Dan Air.

Queensland and Northern Terrirories Aerial Services Ltd (QANTAS)

Qantas leased BOAC Comet 4s in the early 1960s mainly to supplement Boeing 707s on the eastern end of its premium routes to Europe. Largely used for the Sydney to Singapore sections of the joint BOAC/Qantas Kangaroo service between London and Sydney, the Comets retained their BOAC crew and basic livery, with the BOAC markings replaced by those of Qantas. The use of BOAC Comets had been phased out by the early sixties when the airline's own Boeing 707s were used exclusively.

Redmond Air

Redmond Air, a US 'flying travel club' that operated in a similar manner to a European charter airline based in Redmond, Washington State, purchased the ex-Mexicana Comet 4Cs, refurbished by Westernair, in the late seventies. The airline had intended to use the Comets to provide charter flights from Washington State to Las Vegas, but these plans came to nothing and only one Comet - N888WA - was delivered to Everett. The other two remained at Mexico City and Albuquerque respectively.

Royal Aircraft Establishment

The Royal Aircraft Establishment's long association with the Comet started in 1949 with the prototype and ended with the retirement of Boscombe Down's Comet 4C *'Canopus'* in 1997. Although the RAE was not directly involved in the design and production of the Comet, it provided much assistance with aeronautical data collection and advice.

Although the RAE had requested a Comet for high altitude trials, none of the BOAC machines proved to be suitable and it was not until 1959 that the RAE had a dedicated trials aircraft Comet 2E XN453.

After modification, G-AMXD was re-registered XN453 and was used for radio and avionics work at Farnborough until it was replaced by the ex-BOAC Comet 4 XV814, formerly G-APDF. The other Comet 2E - XV144 formerly G-AMXK, was delivered to the Blind Landing Experimental Unit (BLEU) at Bedford and remained in service until 1974 when it was flown to Farnborough and scrapped. Also allocated to the BLEU was Comet 3 G-ANLO which served as XP915 until it was retired for various ground tasks in April 1972.

In 1963 the RAE purchased XS235, the first of four Comet 4s that would provide experimental airframes for almost thirty years. Three ex BOAC Comets were acquired, two directly from the airline and the other, G-APDP from Dan-Air. Unfortunately this last aircraft was found to have severe corrosion and was grounded in 1975. The remaining Comet 4s provided excellent service, however, conducting various trials and in the case of XW626, becoming a part Nimrod AEW.3 prototype.

After a tour to Australia in late 1993 XV814, the longest flying Comet, was retired to Boscombe Down to provide spares for the last flying Comet XS235 which was itself retired in 1997. XV814

G-APDC on lease to Qantas. *(BAe Hatfield)*

Above: The Redmond Air Comet 4C N888WA spent many years abandoned at Paine Field, Everett, Washington State.

Left: It was eventually re-painted by Boeing Aircraft in BOAC colours - which it never originally wore and was finally placed under restoration by the Museum of Flight, where it is seen here (author)

was scrapped at Boscombe Down in August 1997, although the nose was preserved. The de Havilland Trust purchased XS235, with the help of private donations from the public, for preservation at Hatfield. Various difficulties resulted in the aircraft being re-acquired by British Aerospace and then by David Walton at Bruntingthorpe, to where the aircraft was flown in October 1997.

The RAE also utilised the last two Comet airframes (c/n 06476 and 06477), which had become the prototype Nimrods XV147 and XV148 respectively. XV147 was used by the RAE for Nimrod systems evaluations while XV148 operated from RAE Bedford on Nimrod radar work. XV147 retired to Farnborough for spares use and was finally sold to British Aerospace. XV148 was retired in 1982 to BAE Systems at Woodford for structural testing and was scrapped in April 1999.

Royal Air Force

At the 1962 Farnborough Air Show the RAF announced the purchase of five Comet 4C to be designated C.4s for use in transport and VIP duties. The first Comet C.4 to be delivered to 216 Squadron at RAF Lyneham was XR395, followed closely by the remaining aircraft later in 1962 and into 1963.

By 1965 the Comet 2s and 4s were being used on the SLIP service - the 2s were used around the Mediterranean (Cyprus, Malta and Gibraltar) and the C.4's were used on the Far East service to RAF Changi in Singapore. The route was first to El Adem, then on to Khormaksar in Aden. Here the crew would 'slip' and the aircraft would continue to Gan and Singapore with another crew. The turnaround was 90 minutes in Aden and three hours in Singapore. The return flight with fresh crew took the same route back to Lyneham. Later this route became Akrotiri, Bahrain/Muharraq then Gan and Changi. The flights left at 10:00 local time on a Monday and a Thursday, and the aircraft was back in the UK within three days whereas the crews took 14 days to get back.

In addition to the Far East flights the RAF used Comets on flights to Europe for troop moves, Casevac operations, 'States Trainers' to the USA and around-the-world trips with VIPs etc. There was a set of priorities for the use of the Comet C.4; first was VIP Ops, second was Casevac, third was Troop Moves and fourth was Scheduled Ops i.e. the Slip.

There was also an Maintenance Unit (MU) at RAF Lyneham located in C2 Hangar, although during the mid-sixties the main servicing hangar was the J4 Hangar. Then when the MU closed the whole of Comet Servicing operations went over to the C2 Hangar where there was a large servicing dock for the aircraft.

Each aircraft was given a full air test once a year. The Comet would carry two Flight Engineers, one to

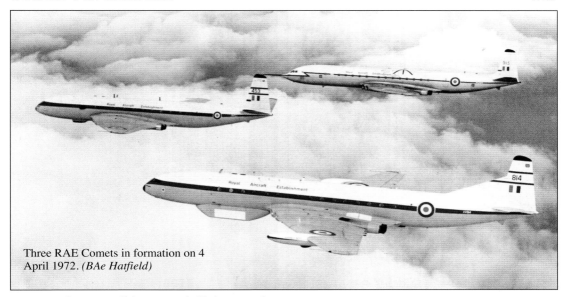

Three RAE Comets in formation on 4
April 1972. *(BAe Hatfield)*

operate and one to call in turn each flight test to be
carried out. Among these tests, the crew took the
aircraft to the full stall and tested the fuel jettison
systems.

Eventually the Comet offices were moved to
Comet Training Flight at the old Guardroom at the
North of the main site near to the Electronics

Centre, After the VC-10s took over the Slip in
around 1971 the Comets' were mainly tasked with
VIP Ops.

216 Squadron reduced to only six crews after
the Comet 2s were withdrawn and the Squadron
continued under Wg Cdrs Basil d'Oliveira and Phil
Walker amongst others.

An object lesson in how to take a beautiful, graceful design and turn it into possibly the ugliest thing ever to fly -
XW626, the former BOAC G-APDS - nicknamed by some as the 'ComRod' - after modification at Woodford for
Nimrod AEW.3 test work. It is seen here on final approach to RAE Farnborough. *(BAe Hatfield)*

C.4 XR399 of 216 Squadron. The early colour scheme was for a highly polished underside, but this was later replaced with light grey paint when polishing was found to damage the skin. *(BAe Hatfield)*

Somewhat surprisingly, the Comet appeared in one the Ian Fleming's James Bond novels *'Thunderball'* from 1961 in which *'... five Mark IV Transport Comets, should make their run in at ten thousand feet at an airspeed of 300 mph...'*. They never survived the transition to the big screen and this 'appearance' has largely been forgotten!

The Comet C.4s remained in service until 1975, when they were withdrawn and flown to RAF Leconfield for disposal. Dan-Air purchased all five Comets and flew them to Lasham for conversion to airline use.

Saudi Arabian Royal Flight

The Saudi Arabian Government placed an order with de Havilland for a single unique Comet 4C. The aircraft was to be a special VIP version for use by King Saud and operated by a Saudi Arabian Airlines crew. Although the Comet was officially delivered on 15 June 1962. it primarily remained based in the UK for training purposes. The American crew received training from de Havilland pilots flying to the Middle East and European destinations. During the night of 19 March 1963 during a positioning flight from

The ill-fated Comet 4C SA-R-7 of the Saudi Arabian Royal Flight seen at Hatfield. the aircraft was painted green, white and gold. *(BAe Hatfield)*

The same aircraft, from a badly damaged, but unique negative showing crew training at Stansted.*(author's collection)*

Geneva to Nice. the Comet struck a mountain crest in the Italian Alps destroying the aircraft and killing all the crew on board. No members of King`s family or staff were on board.

Sudan Airways

Sudan Airways purchased two Comets in 1962, which had originally been destined for Mexicana. ST-AAW was diverted from pre-delivery flights to join the Sudanese independence celebrations in Khartoum, but returned to Hatfield shortly afterwards. The second aircraft, ST-AAX, the final Comet built at Hatfield, was delivered on 21 st December 1962. ST-AAX was at times also used as a VIP transport for the Sudanese Govemment. ST-AAW was delivered to Khartoum in early January 1963.

The Comets operated primarily on routes in the Gulf, Middle East and Europe until November 1972 when they were retired from service.

Upon retirement ST-AAW was flown to Tees-side in the UK while ST-AAX remained in Khartoum.

Both Comets were sold to Dan-Air in June 1975, although due to the limited remaining spar life of ST-AAW, it never entered service and was scrapped, while ST-AAX was re-registered G-BDIF and remained in service until November 1979, becoming the last fully civilian Comet to remain in service.

Transportes Aereos Portugueses - TAP

BEA and TAP of Portugal entered into a charter agreement on 9 June 1959 to operate a joint service from London Heathrow, which lasted until 1962. The two airlines used several Comet 4Bs to operate a three times a week service to Lisbon. The

Comets retained their BEA colours receiving the addition of small TAP logos along the cheat line placed over the BEA red squares.

Westernair

Westernair, an aviation dealer from New Mexico, acquired the former Mexicana Comet 4Cs in 1973 and proceeded to repaint and refurbish the aircraft ready for resale. The aircraft received new registrations and individual colour schemes, XA-NAR becoming N888WA, XA-NAS to N999WA and XA-NAT to N777WA.

Westernair hoped to sell the aircraft as a complete airline along with ground vehicles, a large source of spares and a Redifon Comet 4C simulator, Two of the Comets, N888WA and N999WA, were sold subsequently to independent organisations and were flown to the US, neither aircraft ultimately entering passenger services again. After passing through other owners, N888WA now resides in the Seattle Museum and the other aircraft - N999WA - was scrapped at Chicago in the early nineties. The third, N777WA, which had been damaged on its last Mexicana flight, was grounded at Mexico City for many years. The aircraft was moved some years later to a children's playground within the Irapuato Zoo in northern Mexico.

'Not Taken Up'...

The introduction of the Comet 4 provided de Havilland with a new opportunity to recapture opportunities lost due to the Comet accidents, but, although the Comet 4 order book developed well, the aircraft was never to realise its true potential.

The primary markets for Comet 4 came from the UK, Middle East and Africa. Several airlines

ST-AAW of Sudan Airways *(BAe Hatfield)*

De Havilland employed a team of photographers and artists to create 'artists impressions' of proposed colour schemes and new aircraft designs. This is the late 1950's drawing of the Comet 4A for Capital Airlines.
(BAe Hatfield)

placed orders for the Comet 4 series, but many were subsequently cancelled, including two aircraft for Mexicana and a single Comet 4C for MEA.

The Comet 4 almost entered the US market in substantial numbers following the 26 July 1956 Capital Airlines' order for four Comet 4s and ten Comet 4As. The Capital Airlines order was based around the specially designed Comet 4A, a short range, lower altitude version.

The order was valued at around £19 million with aircraft scheduled for delivery between 1958 and 1959.

Capital Airlines, based on the US east coast, stated: '...*The decision to purchase the Comet has been made after a most comprehensive and detailed study of all flight equipment either in production or projected, both in the United States and England. The economical and operating characteristics of the Comet 4A are ideally suited to the Capital system. The Comets will go into service on our major and most competitive routes.'*

The airline, which had already successfully operated Vickers Viscounts, was in financial difficulties and was absorbed by United Air Lines in 1961; the Comet order was cancelled and the Comet 4A was never built.

CAUSA (Compania Aeronautica Uruguaya SA) were to have purchased a BOAC Comet in 1967, but the sale fell through.

Chapter 13

THE WORLD'S LARGEST COMET OPERATOR

The UK independent airline Dan-Air came into being in 1953 and survived until being taken over by British Airways in 1993. For a number of years it was the world's largest operator of the Comet; this came about when BOAC decided to put their Comet 4 fleet on the market after retirement in the autumn of 1965.

Operation of the Comet by Dan-Air was first evaluated by Commercial Director Frank Horridge, but negotiations were handled by Alan Snudden of Dan-Air and Mr 'A Rabbits', the Manager of BOAC Aircraft Sales. This series of documents provides a rare insight into the intricacies of aircraft purchase.

A written proposal was sent to Alan Snudden on 10 January 1966, offering two aircraft, engines and spares for £1,074,000. The first aircraft - with 1500 hours to run to the next major service known as a Check 4 and with Front Spar Mod completed - was offered at £425,000. The second machine, which was time expired needing a major service and Front Spar Mods was offered at £400,000. The proposal went on to state that '...*I understand from our conversation that it is your intention at the moment to pay cash for the first aircraft and a substantial part of the cost of the second. We would agree that the balance due, together with the cost of spares and engines could be payable over a period of four years at 7% interest'*.

Further meetings took place and discussions occurred at Board level, and it was not until a month later - on 10 February - that Alan Snudden wrote a formal offer, confirming that '...*we wish to confirm that it is our intention to go ahead with the lease purchase arrangements for Comet aircraft GAPDK and GAPDO'*.

The basic price was

£380,000 per aircraft 'as is' for delivery at London Airport. The letter set out payment terms: £5,000 per aircraft as a deposit with the purchasers having the option of up until five days after budget day 1966 to declare if they would take the second aircraft or not. £12,500 per aircraft was payable on signing contract, £182,500 payable on completion of the Check 4, this being expected as 1 September 1966 for the first aircraft and 1 March 1967 for the second. The balance would be over four years at six-monthly intervals, plus the interest at 7% per annum on the outstanding amount at the time of each payment.

As part of the deal BOAC were to arrange, at their expense, class-room training for two crews per aircraft, including Flight Engineer, commencing in October that year. BOAC were also to provide, if required, class-room courses, starting 1 January, 1967 at a price to be agreed. They were also to provide an aircraft and crew for basic flying training at a cost of £250 per hour. Finally on crew training, BOAC were to assist in obtaining the services of a Check Captain for route flying if required.

When it came to engineering assistance, Dan-Air drove a hard bargain. BOAC agreed to undertake to arrange engineering training with De Havillands at Dan-Air's expense; BOAC would provide an X Licence Instrument - General - Navigation Engineer for a period of at least three months per aircraft during Check 4 period.

BOAC would also provide two complete sets of aircraft manuals, including auxiliaries and radio, and where applicable component overhaul specification sheets. They would also provide a complete range of Operation and

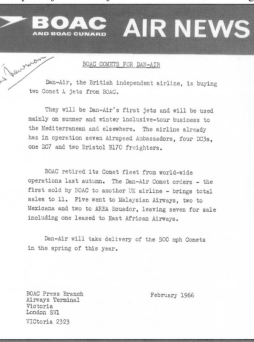

BOAC COMETS FOR DAN-AIR

Dan-Air, the British independent airline, is buying two Comet 4 jets from BOAC.

They will be Dan-Air's first jets and will be used mainly on summer and winter inclusive-tour business to the Mediterranean and elsewhere. The airline already has in operation seven Airspeed Ambassadors, four DC3s, one DC7 and two Bristol B170 freighters.

BOAC retired its Comet fleet from world-wide operations last autumn. The Dan-Air Comet orders - the first sold by BOAC to another UK airline - brings total sales to 11. Five went to Malaysian Airways, two to Mexicana and two to AREA Ecuador, leaving seven for sale including one leased to East African Airways.

Dan-Air will take delivery of the 500 mph Comets in the spring of this year.

BOAC Press Branch
Airways Terminal   February 1966
Victoria
London SW1
VICtoria 2323

Cabin Staff Manuals, Route Manuals, along with those for Flight Engineering and Training.

BOAC would also provide Spar Modification Kits for each aircraft, free of charge, and an allowance for the cost of labour would be made. They would also undertake to give Dan-Air the first refusal of associated ground equipment if available.

With the lease-purchase arrangements in place, it fell to Captain Arthur Larkman to oversee the introduction of the Comet into use with Dan-Air:

'G-APDO, a Comet 4, was acquired from BOAC in October 1966 and a second aircraft, G-APDK, a month later. Lasham carried out a number of modifications, which included increasing the number of seats to 99. Technical, performance and simulator training for our crews was carried out by BOAC at Cranebank, their training headquarters at Heathrow. Two of their retired training Captains, initially Clive Houlder and later Tom Walters, were contracted to carry out the training of our first crews converting onto the aircraft. A period of intensive activity ensued to obtain Ministry approval for the addition of the aircraft to our Air Operating Certificate. Before an airline operates a new type of aircraft it must demonstrate that it has thoroughly prepared for every aspect relating to its use, from trained maintenance engineers with the requisite servicing schedules and the necessary equipment and spares, to all administration, traffic handling, management structure, flight crew training and proficiency checks, the provision of Manuals and so on. Prior to operating for hire and reward a number of route proving flights are carried out under the supervision of Ministry Inspectors. Among my responsibilities was the planning of flight crew training and procedures for the periodic checks of competency and the various examinations that pilots must pass. All of this was completed satisfactorily by that December.

One of my problems was to ensure that the production of fully trained crews kept pace with the

requirement for the programmed flights which increased in number as the season progressed. The limiting factor was the required number of line flights under the supervision of a Line Check Captain which the trainee pilots and flight engineers had to complete before they were cleared to operate. We did not have sufficient flights booked during this phase of the training to produce the number of pilots required to crew the rapidly increasing number of flights. I solved the problem in various ways, such as selecting flights which had empty sectors; for example those when the aircraft was positioning empty, as happens when the first flights of a series take the passengers to their resort but there are not yet any returning passengers. I arranged that on these empty sectors the aircraft would make touch and go landings at airfields en-route, so that what was programmed as one sector could be split to accomplish two or more sectors.

I spent many hours wrestling with this problem but eventually was able to make up the shortfall by arranging with Captain Davidson, the Operations Director of East African Airways, for some of our pilots to fly with them on their routes, under the supervision of their Line Check Captains. The CAA Inspectorate approved the plan and we were able to train sufficient crews in time to avoid sub-chartering other carriers to perform our flights.

The base and upper airwork training for crews converting onto piston engined aircraft posed a different problem to that on jets. This was because of the cost of fuel. The tax on petrol uplifted and used in the UK was very high. If this petrol was used away from the UK the tax was refunded provided a 'Drawback' form was completed. In the early days of Dan-Air our operations management was not fully aware of this and usually failed to take advantage of the cost savings available. Crews were not asked to return from overseas with maximum fuel in the tanks if the aircraft's next flight was internal; for example, positioning to Lasham or when the next flight programmed was a service within the UK;

Bob Atkins, one of the Dan-Air Stewardesses, Arthur Larkman and Jock Mills pose for pictures after inspecting the first Dan-Air Comet, purchased from BOAC, at Heathrow. *(Dan-Air Staff Assn)*

or the aircraft was planned for crew training. I had always taken a keen interest in economical methods of aircraft operation and eventually persuaded management to set up a system to take advantage of this tax concession.

When we bought the Comets it was necessary to give extensive conversion training to our crews who, almost without exception, had flown only piston engined aircraft. This meant that the training involved a great number of flying hours and hundreds of circuits, so I investigated the most economical way of achieving this. Gatwick was out of the question because of the increased traffic and high charges, so I explored other alternatives. Clive Houlder had planned to do the circuit training at Shannon, which he had always used in BOAC. He was rather put out therefore when I vetoed the plan on the grounds that fuel prices were higher and there was no discount on the landing fees. The most suitable airfields were Newcastle and Teesside as both had all the necessary facilities and were not very busy, thus enabling us to achieve more circuits per hour. Teeside had been recently extended and a new terminal built and it was now in fierce competition with Newcastle to gain more traffic to justify the expenditure. I had gone to talk to both Airport Managers, detailing the very large training activity that I had planned. By letting them compete against each other for our training I obtained very good offers which included no charge for touch-and-goes and only one sixth of the normal landing fee for each full stop landing. These were real bargain rates, but in addition, because both airports were their own fuel contractors, I achieved a

Right: Bob Atkins and Arthur Larkman at the controls of a Dan-Air Comet.

Below: G-APDM in the first Dan-Air colour scheme with the 'compass and flag' on a white tail, the aircraft registration sitting in the middle of two red lines.

reduction in the fuel price which, I discovered, was actually lower than the Company's contracted commercial rate. Neither airport made much money from this deal but the advantage to them was that each landing, including each 'touch and go', was counted in the all important total of aircraft movements at the airports.

Newcastle was the preferred venue as we had established our own traffic office there, complete with a Station Manager and his staff. Another advantage was a hotel on the airfield, thus avoiding transport costs. Although most of the training was carried out there, we used Teeside fairly often when Newcastle's visibility was poor or it had a busy period, and also when the wind direction was wrong for the Newcastle

Left: The Comet Simulator. At the controls is First Officer Pete Goddings and First Officer David Shorrock. Supervising their training is Fleet Manager Capt John Cotter and Engineer Officer Joe Clarke. *[J. Cotter]*

Gordon Anderson with Comet Simulator computer. *[J.Cotter]*

Instrument Landing System. During the long periods of time spent at Newcastle I became very friendly with Jim Denyer, the Airport Manager, who was unfailingly helpful to the Company. These arrangements continued for the rest of Dan-Air's existence, although I often had to explain the advantages, both for economy and training efficiency, to successive Fleet Training Managers.

My own conversion training onto the Comet was carried out on the second course and was completed in January 1967 after route checks to Gibraltar and Nairobi with fellow trainees Tom Phethean, Frank Hatchard, Gordon Pumphrey and Flight Engineers Bill Snow, Neville Stacey and Frank Albert. Others now flying on the Comet were Bob Atkins, Dennis Barty, Brian Martin, Monty Montgomery, Colin Duthie and Brian Ridge, with Flight Engineers C.I. 'Charlie Item' Smith, the training engineer, Cliff Lewton, George Keene, Brian Leversha, Alec Ewen and Tim Ware. The latter had been with 216 Squadron on Comets and subsequently with Sudan Airways and later succeeded C I Smith as Dan-Air's Chief Flight Engineer. We once again had to recruit Flight Navigators and the first of these was Ricky Richards, who had flown for many years with BOAC and was now our Chief Navigator. Denis Revell, another ex-Nav from BOAC, had also joined. He became our Operations Planning Manager when he retired from flying.

The training Captain for part of my course was John Dalrymple, who had been a fellow member of Malayan Airways. He and I had flown the first

commercial flight out of Paya Lebar, the new airport which had been built to replace Kallang in Singapore. The first flight I made in command of the Comet was to Bombay, followed by charters to various European and North African destinations. By the beginning of March, when I had flown about 100 hours on the Comet, the Civil Aviation Authority had approved me to fly and train on the DC-7, in addition to conducting training on the Comet. I also continued to carry out training on the Ambassador and the DC-3. The authorisation to train on both the Comet and the DC-7 was very unusual, as the commercial operation of both piston and jet engined aircraft at the same time was normally prohibited. In June 1967 I was checked out as an Authorised Examiner on the Comet by the CAA and commenced Alan Barker's conversion in the simulator and on the aircraft and carried out the bi-annual Competency Checks on some of the Comet crews. We normally avoided carrying out these tests in the busy summer season as far as possible, but these were unavoidable because of the timing of the conversion training in the previous winter.

The Comet proved popular with both the passengers and our charterers, who kept the aircraft busy. Several of the ITs which had been flown by the Ambassador were now transferred to the Comet and the 99 seats were filled without difficulty. Longer flights to North Africa and the Canary Islands were included in the programme and these could be flown without re-fuelling stops. This increased demand led the Company to buy another Comet 4 from BOAC, and G-APDJ arrived in May 1968 in time to perform a full programme in the following summer.

The fleet now consisted of three DC-3s, as XK had been taken out of service in the winter, one DC-7, three Comets and six Ambassadors. The last two B-170s had been sold in 1966 to Lamb Air in Canada and unfortunately one of them, after landing on a frozen lake, had broken through the ice and sunk. The Ambassadors were flying less ITs now but had taken over more of the schedules. Flights from Liverpool increased and Manchester was very active with scheduled flights to Munich, Ostend, Perpignan, Genoa, Biarritz, Basle, Dinard and Tarbes. Schedules out of Gatwick to Jersey, Newcastle/Kristiansand, and Ostend were now flown on the Ambassador, as well as services from Newcastle to Stavanger and from Prestwick to Ronaldsway.

Captain Bill Peacock, the CAA Flight Inspector assigned to us, was responsible for ensuring that our operation conformed to the requirements laid down in our AOC (Air Operators Certificate).

When we introduced the Comets I had outlined all aspects of the training required for the flight deck and cabin crews. Much of the content

was taken from BOAC's Operations Manuals, although I had altered several procedures which did not suit our type of operation. I had also added detailed procedures for the conversion training for pilots and flight engineers adjusted for their varying qualifications and experience.

Bill asked me to produce a Company Training Manual incorporating this material and detailing all the training procedure and mandatory requirements for all the types of aircraft which we were operating. I launched into this task thinking that it could be completed without too much trouble. The first and most important step, I decided, was to inspect the other airlines' Training Manuals and benefit from their work. I was surprised to find that Company Training Manuals did not exist as such, but that Manufacturers Manuals were generally used in combination with Company Instructions.

I spent night after night writing out every aspect of our training procedures. Included were the criteria for selection of the candidate, the educational qualifications and the minimum flying experience required for each type of aircraft we operated, or for promotion from the right to the left hand seat. Detailed syllabi for each phase of the training, with the appropriate progress reports plus guidance to the Trainers and Examiners, were included along with the details of all the legislative requirements and much more. Bill had pulled a 'fast one' on me which resulted in Dan-Air possessing the first manual specifically devoted to company Training and Examining procedures. The CAA Inspectorate was delighted, as they now had a precedent with which to pressure the other airlines; they, of course were able to refer to the Dan-Air Manual.

At my instigation some changes to BOAC's

At one stage Dan-Air set aside G-APDE as a training aircraft, a role which it undertook during 1971/2. Note the modification of a servicing platform over the bonnet of the Morris Minor pick-up truck! (DASA)

procedures were made in our operation of the Comet, As well as being of very robust construction the aircraft was, in fact, overpowered. So much so that suggestions were often made that more economical operation would be achieved if one of the inner engines was shut down during the cruise. One of the consequences of this power was a spectacular rate of climb after take-off. When complaints about aircraft noise became more vociferous, airlines were instructed to reduce noise levels in the vicinity of airports. As the greatest amount of noise is produced on take-off and the initial climb at low levels, procedures were introduced to climb as rapidly as possible while reducing power as soon as practicable. These manoeuvres were designed, essentially, to produce the minimum decibel readings when flying over the noise monitoring units and are known as 'Noise Abatement Procedures'. The procedure laid down for the Comet by BOAC demanded a very early reduction in power at the same time as climbing as rapidly as possible. This meant flying the aircraft at a low speed, not much above the safety margin. I found this uncomfortable and soon realised that, if the aircraft was climbed without this very early reduction of power, by the time it had passed the airfield boundary it would gain sufficient height to enable normal climb power and speed to be used without breaching the noise limits. In the interest of a safer operation I changed the technique as well as some other procedures which BOAC had used.

There had been many accidents and close shaves on the Comet. A recurring problem had been instances of descent below the safety height. I recounted earlier the story of the BOAC aircraft landing in the Game Park seven miles short of the runway at Nairobi because it was below the required altitude, and the incident when the same aircraft clipped the top of a hill at Madrid when approaching to land. Other instances included two BEA aircraft hitting trees on hilltops at Rome when letting down for landing approaches. In Dan-Air we had a mandatory drill which required the Captain, First Officer and Flight Engineer to each confirm the height required for each stage of climb and descent and for each to warn when the designated altitude was being approached. Another problem which had been repeated several times had been the inadequate crew monitoring of the approach to land. For example, on an approach to land at Calcutta the BOAC Comet descended below the correct approach path and hit the tree tops on the final approach. He climbed away and made another approach but the same thing happened. On the third approach the pilot was determined not to undershoot and this time touched down too far along the runway to be able to stop and over-ran the end of the runway.

Our procedure was for all three crew members to monitor the approach and to call out the height when crossing the marker beacons and, also, the appropriate speeds for the approach phase. Many other modifications to improve the operation were made. When we were regularly flying to the Canaries I was asked by a Corporation Manager to explain our techniques for achieving non-stop regularity with a full load, as they were having difficulty in doing this. In fact I had made modifications to BOAC's operating techniques because of my continuing concern with economical operation and fuel usage. Soon after we had commenced flying the Comet I gave Keith Stokes the task of recording the fuel used for each flight on each route, and this provided a comparison of each Captain's performance and the cost of the fuel used could thus be ascertained. This was a result of my ongoing concern, which I had expressed to Mr. Davies, when I had first joined the Company, about the fuel usage by the Yorks on the Singapore flights. I reproduce below a part of the

G-APDJ seen at Gatwick in the early 'white tail' colour scheme.

Six 'Dan-Air Girls' in their dark blue and white uniforms walk away from Comet G-APDO. The uniform was typical of late 1960s Air Hostesses.

memo recording my ideas which I wrote to Alan Snudden in 1967, and copied to the Operations Manager, Chief Pilot, Chief Navigation Officer and the Chief Flight Engineer, which indicates some of my ideas on operating costs.

"At present, economical operation is judged by average fuel consumptions. These are usually misleading; for example:-

1. The slower the cruising speed, the lower the fuel consumption, but the longer the flight time.
2. The longer the taxi time, the lower the average fuel consumption for the flight if measured, as at present, from chock to chock.

A more realistic measure of the Captain's operation would be to average the outbound and inbound flights, preferably over several flights on the same route. Account should be taken of factors outside his control such as:- weight, flight level, en-route winds, taxying delays, unfavourable runway direction in use, delayed clearances from Air Traffic Control for climb or descent, enforced holding patterns and delayed approach, and inability to obtain optimum cruising level and preferred routes. Further adjustment should be made for temperature variation. All calculations must be made using fuel weight and not volume as happens at present.

Kilos per Ground Mile would be a better indicator, but could be misleading as a low KPGM could be achieved at the expense of an increase in time. I suggest that a more accurate assessment would be on a COST basis. We now have sufficient data to determine the average actual cost of the round trip in terms of fuel usage and engine and airframe time. Fixed overhead and finance costs which at present are incorporated in the hourly cost should be excluded as they exist regardless of whether the aircraft flies or not. Thus we would be able to compare actual flight cost against the commercial quote, which would be helpful to the Commercial Department in the future. Additionally we can identify individual Captain's variations from the average with a view to correcting any non –

standard operation.

As the Company does not wish to reveal its contracted fuel prices, I propose that the following method is used.

1. An average fuel usage when taxying is established, and this amount is deducted from the total fuel used on each flight.
2. Average in-flight fuel consumption for the round trip on each route is determined and the price of the fuel used on that route is accurately calculated, instead of our present system of averaging European prices.
3. When these figures are determined, any variations from the standard on individual flights for each route, can be shown as a percentage deviation from the average fuel consumption and from the average flight time, thus concealing confidential information but still giving a true picture of the operation."

Alan Snudden, the General Manager, decided to adopt this system and Keith Stokes was able to easily extract the necessary information for each flight from the figures entered in the technical log by the Flight Engineer. The results were distributed to the various departments and were used by us, eventually, to improve an area of performance which I had found the most difficult to influence. This had been the limited success of my attempts to make Engineering's management more aware of the effect on economic performance of imperfections on the aircraft exterior, such as ill-fitting panels, leaking door seals, drag inducing projections etcetera. The difficulty had arisen, as usual, from DAE's reluctance to incur what they considered unnecessary costs, and for management in general to appreciate that cost effectiveness was more important than the effect on one division's budget.

I was pleased that, after years of trying, some progress had been made, but there was still a long way to go. I had not yet been able to formalise a system for ensuring that the Captain's decision on the amount of the fuel uplift took adequate account of the price differentials at the airfields to which we flew. Some time later, when Alan became sufficiently convinced of its importance, he and I devised a scheme which gave the crew sufficient information with which to judge whether maximum or minimum fuel should be uplifted. Keith, who I was using to extract the figures for each flight was, incidentally, the father of John Stokes who became one of our elite group of Operations Supervisors.

Two more firsts in the Company's progress were achieved when C I Smith, the Chief Flight Engineer, was appointed to the newly created position of Company Safety Officer, and the second was that I produced our first detailed Terms of Reference for the position. Once again I had engendered more work for myself as I then had to create them for all the other appointments. To replace 'Charlie Item', Tim Ware, who was a very experienced flight engineer and had flown Comets when he was with Sudan Airways, was promoted to Chief Flight Engineer. Another who joined was Pat Fry, who had flown with us on the Ambassador before moving to Sudan to fly Comets. In November I carried out Instrument Rating renewals and Competency checks on several of the DC-7 crews and then flew with John Cotter on the DC-7 to Singapore. As well as flying the DC-7, I also flew services and carried out training on the DC-3, Ambassador and Comet. These tasks continued into the winter and I conducted, in addition, the periodic tests on most of our crews in the BOAC simulator. In between these activities I once again set to and planned the training task for the winter and spring to meet the following year's establishment requirements.

The method I had developed to arrive at these proposed establishments was to estimate the number of crews required week by week to operate the programme on each fleet as the flights increased progressively in number throughout the spring and into the summer. This was not as straight forward as it sounds as the programme was never firmly fixed for the coming year and changed constantly according to the Charterers' estimations of the number of bookings. I made my own assumptions on the utilisation of each fleet therefore, and based the overall Training Plan on these. Starting from the end point of my projection, where the flights were notionally fully crewed at the time the peak summer activity was reached, I worked backwards through each stage of the training. From this I was able to produce flow charts showing the progress of each trainee, at each stage of the training, in the weeks and months before the peak. Thus I ensured that the flights could be crewed as the aircraft programme's activity increased.

Off to the sun!

Some of the activities of the time in which the airline became involved may seem slightly strange now, but at the time air travel was still very much a novelty for many of the general public. This interest could not be better demonstrated than when Clarksons, Gold Case Travel and the Newcastle Evening Gazette newspaper organised a 'Holiday Spectacular' for one mid-January evening at Tees-Side Airport. The organisers had expected about two thousand people to turn up, but when the night arrived, over fifteen thousand

A scene typical of the Comet days at Lasham, with all the panels open as one of the Dan-Air aircraft undergoes deep maintenance.

With flaps fully extended, Comet 4B G-APMG comes in to land at Gatwick during the summer of 1975. The aircraft wears the second, or 'red tail' colour scheme with a red, white and blue cheat line. *(Kurt Lang)*

potential passengers queued, often in driving rain showers, to take a look inside a Dan-Air Comet 4 that was parked on the airport apron!

Peter and Nola Wilde took one of the early Dan-Air Comets on a five night Clarkson 'City Break'.

'We went to escape the English winter at the end of March, after the birth of our second child. When we arrived over Venice the pilot apologised to us for orbiting the city, but he was awaiting clearance to land as a 'light aeroplane's whereabouts was uncertain'. We were sitting on the 'wingdown' side of the cabin and the view below us was breathtaking! The pilot apologised again, but we shall be eternally grateful for that unknown Italian pilot for giving us such an extended view of what is without doubt the most beautiful city in the world. I've always felt well disposed to Dan-Air ever those lovely five days, and we could hardly blame them for the snowstorm which greeted us at Gatwick on our return!'

The publicity that use of the Comet could achieve was considerable. In May 1967 Dan-Air Comet G-APDK landed at Glasgow to the cheers of 30,000 football fans welcoming home the Glasgow Celtic football team that had just won the European Cup. The team had flown out to Lisbon earlier that week in the same machine, and following the result Intercontinental Caterers were contacted with orders to quickly bake a celebratory cake to be consumed with glasses of Champagne on the flight home!

In order to make better utilization of the Comet fleet, Dan-Air started flying Inclusive Tours from West Berlin to the Mediterranean on behalf of the West German tour operator Neckerman und Reisen. The first flight occurred on 31 March 1968 when a Dan-Air Comet lifted off from Tegel Airport bound for Malaga. Almost 300 flights were made that summer, making the basing of one aircraft permanently in the city a necessity.

The operation of this aircraft from the city involved positioning a Comet from Gatwick to Berlin early on Monday morning, and returning to Gatwick late on the following Friday. Initially this was an entirely British operation, with staff operating on short stays away from Gatwick. Gradually the Company began to recruit local cabin and ground staff until almost the entire operation (apart from the flight-deck crews) was run by Berliners.

1968 also saw a number of Comet crews heading for the sun - but not for leisure! Captain Larkman explains: *'Over the years Dan-Air had operated many aircraft for other airlines, but possibly none was more remarkable than when in July 1968 we were approached by Kuwait Airways to fly their entire Comet fleet whilst they sent all of their own flight deck crews over to the USA to train on the Boeing 707 (a number of which they were obtaining to replace their own Comets).*

A lot of preparation went into this, and we were in close contact with them for about a year before, so eventually we were contracted to operate all their services from October 1968 and detached a number of flight-deck crews out to Kuwait. Our pilots flew out to the UK, through the Middle East to India and so on - for a number of months until their own crews returned with the 707s, It was quite a thing (and possibly unique) for one airline to say to another 'We have the trust in you to take-over our entire operation'. That was a feather in everyone's cap'.

The company was also purchasing six Comet 4s, three from East African Airways and another three aircraft from Kuwait Airways.

In February 1971 Dan-Air began a series of Comet flights to Toronto and New York following the granting in October 1970 if traffic rights to the United States and Canada.

The loss of Delta November

Two of the Comets were replacements for two of our fleet which had been lost. The first loss happened on 3 July 1970, when Comet G-APDN was flying a charter from Manchester to Barcelona under command of Captain George Neal, with a crew of seven and 105 passengers on board. The flight departed Manchester at 1608 hrs. At 17.53 hrs the pilot established contact with Barcelona Air traffic Control Centre on 124.7 MHz and after reporting that he had passed the Spanish frontier requested clearance to descend further; and was cleared to descend from 22,000 feet to 9,000 feet. The Captain followed these instructions as he was confident that the aircraft's progress was being monitored by radar.

According to the later accident report, at 17.57 hrs Delta November reported passing the Barcelona FIR boundary and that it was leaving FL160, giving an ETA of 18.01 hrs for Point Berga. At 17.59 hrs the pilot received instructions to contact Barcelona Approach on 119.1 MHZ; a few seconds after changing to that frequency G-APDN was instructed to turn left on to heading 140°. The pilot acknowledged the turn and reported that he was leaving FL130, and immediately afterwards gave an ETA for Sabadell of 18.07 hrs.

At 18.00 hrs Barcelona Approach requested confirmation of this estimate and the pilot corrected it to 18.05 hrs. On receiving this information, Air Traffic Control cancelled the turn on to 140° and told the pilot to proceed to Sabadell. At 18.01 hrs, Delta November reported leaving FL100 for FL90. Barcelona Approach enquired whether it had DME on board and the pilot replied that it did not. G-APDN was then cleared to descend to FL60.

At 18.02 hrs, Barcelona Approach instructed the pilot to turn left on to 140°. The pilot acknowledged this instruction and informed ATC that he was leaving FL85 for FL60. Immediately after this transmission, Barcelona Approach requested confirmation that G-APDN was passing Sabadell, and the pilot replied 'in about 30 seconds'; 15 seconds later the pilot said 'Barcelona, G-APDN passing Sabadell'. Barcelona Approach acknowledged the message and added 'radar contact, continue descent to 2,800 feet, altimeter 1017, transition level five zero'.

At 18.03 hrs DN requested information on the duty runway, Barcelona Approach replying that Runway 25 was in use, which the pilot acknowledged.

At 18.05 hrs, Air Traffic Control requested aircraft altitude and Delta November reported passing 4,000 feet. At 18.07 hrs Barcelona Approach called the aircraft for confirmation that it was still on course; G-APDN did not reply to this transmission, nor to other calls that were subsequently made.

The Comet had crashed between 18.05 and 18.06 hrs, in daylight on a hillside site at Sierra del Montseny, some 65 kilometres to the northeast of Barcelona Airport which was covered by cloud, due to the phenomenon known as 'barrage' effect.

The accident site was on the beech-covered

'Like jewels in a wine-dark sea...' the Greek island of Corfu, with Mouse Island in the middle distance. The building in the foreground is the Viacherna Monastry, which is connected to the main island by a causway. Oh, and the 'dot' over Mouse Island is a Dan-Air Comet on final approach to Corfu Airport, the end of the runway being literally just out of shot on the right! *(author)*

Former Prime Minister Alexander 'Alec' Frederick Douglas-Home, KT, PC was invited by Edward Heath to join the cabinet. Thus, as Foreign Secretary he made many tours with his wife on behalf of Her Majesties Government.

One such tour, using Dan-Air Comet G-AYWX, which had its interior converted for its VIP role, starting on 31 January 1972 took the Foreign Secretary and his party to Istanbul - Dubai - Delhi - Hong Kong - Delhi - Rawalpindi - Ankara - Heathrow.

Former Beatle Paul McCartney, his wife Linda and daughter Stella board a chartered Dan-Air Comet for a flight to Nice. Also on board were other pop stars including the Rolling Stones' Mick Jagger, who was about to marry Bianca de Macias on 12 May 1971 at a Roman Catholic ceremony in Saint-Tropez

CELEBRITIES ABOARD COMETS!

One of the check-in desks at Luton Airport and a Comet interior were used for filming scenes for a spin-off movie from the TV comedy series 'Steptoe and Son'. Here actors Harry H Corbett and Wilfred Bramble are seen with Air Stewardesses Caroline Brown and Kay Dudley-Smith. *(Dan-Air Staff Assn)*

northeast slopes of the Les Angudes peak, at an altitude of about 3,800 feet, in the municipal district of Arbucias . The heading of the aircraft before impact was approximately 145°, and its flight path was descending between 5° and 10° as indicated by the path cut through the trees by the aircraft. Later, two goniometers (direction finders) were found which indicated a heading of 142°. On detailed examination of the crash it was ascertained that the longitudinal axis of the aircraft at the moment of impact was at an angle of approximately 45° up from the horizontal, that is roughly equal to the angle of the mountain slope, it being noted that the main side marks were produced by the auxiliary fuel tanks and not by the fuselage. The fuel tanks exploded and caught fire on impact with the ground.

Arthur Larkman remembers the whole tragic event vividly: '*Bob Atkins and I flew to Barcelona that night and when we arrived at the crash site we thought that there was inadequate security. With the help of the British Consul in Barcelona, who assisted us greatly, we were able to persuade the Guardia Civil to increase the 24 hour guard around the site to deter looters and souvenir hunters. The point of impact was on the side of a very steep mountain slope, and apparently the pilot had seen the mountain at the last minute because it appeared that the aircraft was in a nose-up attitude when it hit. Although the initial impact gouged a large section of the hillside away, the forward part of the fuselage and the cockpit had cut a wide swathe through the trees for two to three hundred yards up the mountain.*

Due to the uneven terrain, a bulldozer and excavator shovels had to be used to widen paths and open up a new one to facilitate evacuation of the victims. Since the Spanish health authorities reported that 'it was technically impossible for the remains of the bodies to be embalmed and preserved, due to the extreme mutilation and scattering of the remains as a result of injuries of exceptional violence caused by an explosive shock-wave, and that death was presumably instantaneous in every case', the court ordered the bodies to be removed and taken to the municipal cemetery at Arbucias where they were buried.

Bob and I examined the wreckage to gain an initial picture of what had happened and gathered up as much as we could locate of the documents, navigation logs, log books etc., many of which were blood stained Most of the bodies had been removed by this time, but there were still many body parts scattered about, some even hanging on tree branches. Bob carried on at the site and had to continue to endure the grisly and malodorous experience, while I drove to the Air Traffic Control Centre in Barcelona. I was fortunate enough to persuade the ATC Officials to give me a copy of the voice tape of DN's communications with ATC up to the time of the crash.

With this valuable information, together with the navigation log which we had rescued, I returned to London and was able to plot the course of the events which led up to the crash and this sequence seemed to exonerate the crew. First thing the next morning I gave the originals to the CAA's Air Accident Board investigators and copies to the Board of Trade. I then explained the sequence of events to our company Board members immediately afterwards. When all the bodies had been recovered they were examined by the Spanish Authorities, the Spanish and British Accident Investigators and their pathologists. Permission for the interment of the bodies was then given. The relatives of many of the crash victims did not request their return to the UK. As a result the British Consul, in conjunction with Kenyons, our Company's appointed funeral directors, arranged a mass burial service at the Cemetery in Arbucies near Barcelona, which Bob and I attended. A memorial service for all the victims was subsequently held in Manchester Cathedral, which the Chairman and Peggy his wife, Frank Tapling and I attended as representatives of the Company. After the service we went to the cemetery where the bodies which had been returned to the U.K. were interred, after another funeral service, in a communal grave.

G-BBUV gets airborne for another flight to the sun from Gatwick. *(Kurt Lang)*

Dan-Air had long had a happy association with sport in general, the Comets being used on many sporting charters, as with G-BBUV seen in approach to Gatwick. *(Kurt Lang)*

Right: clearly a publicity photo - two girls - supposedly employed by Liverpool and Everton football clubs, attempt to keep rival supporters apart before they flew out to watch their teams play in the 1971 European football competitions. *(DASA)*

Further investigation revealed that one spoiler was extended and the other was retracted, but it was impossible to establish whether the latter had been closed by the impact although this appears most likely in view of the manner of operation of these brakes. The main landing gear was retracted. No flaps were extended. Safety belts were in use. The life jackets were not removed from their normal position. The turbine and compressor blades showed evidence of heavy abrasion as a result of their having been functioning normally. The accident took place at 1805.30 hrs, this figure being obtained from data in the flight recorder.

The summary of the Inquiry revealed that the combination of erroneous information regarding reporting points, together with the existence of a radar echo over Sabadell NDB (coinciding with the report from the aircraft of passing that reporting point), led both the aircraft and Barcelona Approach to believe, erroneously, that the aircraft was already over Sabadell; this was an involuntary error on both sides - both ATC and aircraft - which was physically impossible to correct when Air Traffic Control realised it had occurred.'

This accident came just two days after Dan-Air announced that it had signed a four year deal with Global worth £25 million which covered the operation of all Global's flights from Birmingham from April 1971 onwards. The same year, the Birmingham based consortium Midland Air Tour Operators introduced a series of two-week holidays from Birmingham's Elmdon Airport to the Greek islands of Rhodes and Corfu using Dan-Air Comets. Prices ranged from what today seems an incredible £73 for a two week stay in the Messongi Beach hotel on Corfu during the low season to £108 for the equivalent holiday at the Coreyra Beach. So that everything would proceed smoothly, four days before the first departure the airline flew out a party of 100 travel agents for an 'educational visit', a quite common occurrence during the late 1960s and early 1970s when any new destination was about to be served. One presumes that in the case of Greece, it was to explain the intricacies (and hazards) of drinking the local Ouzo to the agents so that they could pass it on to their customers!

The 1970 Inclusive Tour season saw a fleet of twelve Comet 4s in service, operating mainly from Gatwick and Manchester. From Gatwick the airline operated to Alicante, Athens, Djerba, Dubrovnik, Faro, Gerona, Ibiza, Ismir, Malaga, Palma, Rhodes, Rimini, Sardinia, Tenerife, Tunis and Vama. The Comets flying from Glasgow served Alicante, Gerona, Ibiza, Palma and Rimini. From Manchester they flew holiday-makers to Alicante, Gerona, Ibiza, Palma, Rimini and Venice. Edinburgh also was the start of a weekly Comet service to Palma.

More and more Comets...

Two more Comet 4Cs were purchased in March 1971 and were placed on some of the longer-distance European charters in a 119- seat configuration. Charters operated to Las Palmas, Tenerife and the Greek islands, which were just becoming popular with British holiday-makers.

A number of BEA Comet 4Bs had been transferred during the early 1970s to their newly formed associate company BEA Airtours for non-scheduled Inclusive Tour work. Airtours gave the Comet only two years of economic life and thus had already started looking for a suitable replacement. The Comets were progressively replaced during 1973 by a number of Boeing 707s, allowing Dan-Air to obtain them. The last BEA Airtour Comet flight occurred on 31 October 1973 and the remainder of the 4B fleet soon found its way to Lasham for storage and re-painting for use by Dan-Air as required.

Arthur Larkman again: *'A second Comet, G-APDL, was taken out of service in October 1971. 'Delta Lima' was engaged on a training detail at Newcastle during which the Training Captain was conducting a recurrent six-monthly Competency Check on a First Officer. This included the simulation of various failures so that the Pilot undergoing the Check could demonstrate his ability to deal with these emergency situations. On the final circuit of the airfield the Training Captain simulated a complete failure of the aircraft's flap system. The F/O then carried out the appropriate drills, completed a circuit and made a 'Flapless' approach and landing. All went well although the landing roll was unusually short despite the increased landing speed required because the flaps were retracted. The Captain immediately realised that the short landing run was the result of the wheels not having been lowered. On a normal approach a Warning Horn would have sounded when power was reduced if the wheels were retracted. However, if the flaps were not lowered the system assumed that a landing was not being made and the Warning system was not armed. The damage to the aircraft was confined to the skin of the lower fuselage and was not serious.*

The quickest way to remove the aircraft from the runway was to raise it up so that the wheels could be lowered, and then it could be towed away. Our engineers employed large inflatable airbags to lift the aircraft to the height necessary for the undercarriage to be extended. Unfortunately the bags they used were of differing sizes and when the bags were fully inflated the aircraft was not kept in a level attitude and it slid off the bags. Much damage had now been inflicted on the structure and our engineering management assessed the cost of repairs as being so great that it would not be economical to restore it. The aircraft was scrapped.

This aircraft, 'Delta Lima', had borne a charmed

A rainy day at Gatwick, with Mike Bravo closest to the camera. Also visible are another pair of Comets, a company 707 and 1-11.

life when it was in service with BOAC. In an earlier chapter I recounted the story of its brush with a hilltop when it was making an approach to land at Madrid. Later, while it was still in service with BOAC, yet another extraordinary incident befell it. The aircraft was on a night approach to Nairobi when, to the great surprise of the crew, it touched down in the game park west of the runway although it was still seven miles from the threshold. The pilot immediately opened up the throttles and climbed to regain the correct approach path, he then landed on the runway without further incident. The manner in which the service of this aircraft was ended was extremely ironic. It had valiantly avoided potential disasters to its occupants throughout its chequered history only to be destroyed by 'Finger Trouble'.

Dan-Air also had a number of Comets operating on the Hadj, which included flying pilgrims out of Kabul and Kandahar in Afghanistan to Mecca.

Although the Comet found favour with many thousands of passengers, there were times when Dan-Air's high-density seating configuration of the main cabin caused problems. Peter Neighbour recalls possibly the most uncomfortable flight he ever had... "In the mid-1970s I was employed by Occidental Oil and regularly commuted between Gatwick and Tripoli. The Company always used British Caledonian Airways, for it was possible to leave Houston, Texas one evening, arrive at Gatwick at 09.00 the next morning, catch the 1000 flight to Tripoli and be there in the early afternoon.

Unfortunately, there was all the cargo door problems with the DC10 and every one was grounded. B.Cal maintained their trans-Atlantic services using 707s but were compelled to charter-in replacement aircraft to use on the Tripoli run. The aircraft used were Dan-Air Comet IVs which had been used on holiday flight.

Whilst they were adequate for this, they were totally unsuitable for the carriage of large Texans from Gatwick to Tripoli, especially after a long trans-Atlantic flight! Several guys were physically incapable of getting into the seats and I vividly remember some of the (unrepeatable) comments prior to the removal of the armrests. I genuinely felt sorry the crew, who strove valiantly to make everyone happy, but in some cases, I am sorry to say, they were unable to succeed. Luckily the DC10s were soon back in service, otherwise I had visions of mass lynchings at Occidental's Travel Department!

Bruce Fardell remembers one episode when the Comet's performance was required to the fullest extent... "One day I got a call that I had to be at Gatwick within two hours to take a Comet with a full medevac team aboard out to Abidjan on a mercy Flight. Some Costain construction workers had been injured there in a car crash. First I had to find out where I was going and then work out the route. Abidjan was a tiny little airport near Lake Chad, so the route was out to Malta and down across the Sahara. The charts told us that they had a runway, but on arrival we discovered that it was not in commission, so we had to do a visual flypast to work out what was going on. Eventually we got down and rigged up a lorry to get the stretcher cases aboard.

The strip was tight, even for a lightly loaded Comet, so first we measured its length with the mileometer on a borrowed Land Rover, then paced it on foot before working it out on the charts as to how much fuel we could uplift. The figures told us we could not make it back direct to Malta, so we would have to call into Kano; by the way, all of this went on in temperatures of around 35 degrees Celsius!

We had to 'hurry up' the Africans to get a move on before those on board started to 'cook' in the heat! The girls meanwhile were searching through their flight-bags for anything they could use to make them as cool and comfortable as possible!"

One of the former RAF Comets undergoes servicing at Lasham. *(Kurt Lang)*.

Twilight of the Comet

By the mid-1970s the Comet was starting to reach the end of its useful life. Nevertheless, it says much for the skills and expertise of the Lasham engineers, for they obtained a contract from the Ministry of Defence to partially modify one of the fleet, G-APDP, into a test-bed aircraft for the Nimrod Airborne Early Warning (ADE) machine. This aircraft, now serialled XX944, was delivered to the Royal Aircraft Establishment at Bedford in June 1973.

For a number of years the airline's engineers had experienced problems in the location and acquisition of spares to keep their Comets flying, so Dan-Air scoured the world for any examples they could obtain as spares or replacement aircraft for their fleet. In 1975 the airline acquired a number of low-hour Comet C.Mk.4s from the Ministry of Defence that were in excellent condition.

These aircraft were brought up to civil standards by the engineers at Lasham and quickly placed into service along with three ex-Egyptair machines, allowing some of the earlier aircraft to be retired. The problems of finding ways of keeping the Comet fleet airborne still existed, so further examples were obtained from East African Airways, Aerolineas Argentinas, Middle East Airways and others. Most of these aircraft were flown into Lasham, where they languished for a while, donating items every now and then to keep the others flying. Eventually, almost all were broken up.

With the fuel crisis it could be expected that the Comet would be retired in favour of more economic aircraft, but with the book value written down to practically zero and adequate spares backing available, the type still retained its appeal. It says much for the passenger appeal of the Comet to the public - and the part the aircraft played in the story of the airline - that one source quotes that during the

Dan-Air's Comets were replaced mainly by the Boeing 727. These two Kurt Lang shots show both aircraft types.

1979 IT season, a massive 30% of all British holiday-makers carried overseas used Dan-Air Comets!

Out to grass...

Not all the examples of the world's first jet airliner were scheduled to end their days on the scrap-heap, as a number of Dan-Air Comets managed to escape the breaker's torch intact. A landmark event occurred on 12 February 1974 with the delivery of Comet 4 G-APDB from Lasham to Duxford airfield, the home of the famous aviation museum. Delta Bravo was the second aircraft off the Comet 4 production line and, when it entered service with BOAC, was the first of the Comet aircraft to fly the Atlantic. By the time it had completed its service with Dan-Air, it had flown 36,268 hours with 15,733 landings. Tom Walters, who had flown DB in its earlier years with BOAC and was now the Chief Training Captain on the Dan-Air Comet fleet, took the aircraft off from Lasham for Duxford, and flew via Hatfield, the airfield where the aircraft was built. Here he made two low passes down the runway in a final salute before flying on to Duxford. The aircraft was then handed over to the safe keeping of the East Anglian Aviation Society. Dan-Air retained the title to the aircraft but the society had undertaken to maintain it in good condition and to keep it in Dan-Air's livery. A *coup d'elat* saw the East Anglian Aviation Society replaced by the Duxford Aviation Society in the late 1970s. Delta Bravo is still there to this day, and they have put it back into BOAC colours, despite the original agreement.

Dan-Air's lady pilots.

Arthur Larkman: '*A large number of First Officers were recruited in 1972, to crew our fleets, including John Mayes and Graham Peck. Another who joined in the autumn as a 748 Second Officer was Marilyn Booth. She had previously been an Air Hostess with* us and, with the Company's help, gained a scholarship to train as a pilot at the Oxford Aviation College.

The three who were currently flying with us included Yvonne Pope who has had a remarkable career, combining triumph and tragedy. She began her pilot training while flying as a stewardess with BOAC and married her instructor. Tragically, the day before their second son was born her husband died. Although she was now a single mother with two young children, her determination to follow a career in aviation was undiminished. She qualified as an instructor at a Flying Club, and soon began training with the Ministry of Aviation to become the first female Air Traffic Controller. She continued to build up her piloting hours and gained her Commercial Licences and, with difficulty, managed to persuade Mortons Air Services to employ her as a First Officer on their Dove and DC-3 aircraft. She left them to join Dan-Air and flew on the DC-3 initially, converted to the Ambassador and then to the Comet within a year. Throughout her unique career her achievements have been recognised by many honours and awards.

Yvonne herself picks up the story: *I joined the Comet fleet in November 1969. There were so many innovative systems in the design of the Comet that the technical course lasted four weeks. It was held at the Russ Hill Hotel near Gatwick and conducted by experienced engineers. Unfortunately, one of our instructors went down with a virulent 'flu just before Christmas and I caught it and was prostrate throughout the festivities.*

Next came the simulator training. Fortunately the cockpit layout was not completely new to me. On hearing that I might be posted to the Comet, I had requested two more supernumerary flights and, during a visit to RAF Lyneham with the British Ninety Nines, had managed to persuade the pilots to allow me to return to do an hour on their Comet simulator. I was very grateful; hands on was very much better

The end of the last flight for G-APDB - arrival at Duxford for preservation. *(author)*

Literally put out to grass - G-BDIV awaits its fate at Lasham. *(Kurt Lang)*.

than just watching.

During subsequent training sessions we practiced coping with various failures and emergencies. Then, at the beginning of February 1970, came the really exciting part – the actual flying of the aircraft. Familiarization started en route from Gatwick to Teeside, previously the RAF Middleton St George. I was the last in line of the trainees and to my amazement was talked down on the approach and allowed to do the landing!

Even though it was early February, the weather on the whole was kind to us. I was able to fly eight days out of ten, practising handling the aircraft in normal and emergency situations, including landing with and without flaps and with simulated engine failures. The instructors were very good and I found the training exhilarating. Whilst awaiting my turn I would stand outside the terminal building watching this wonderful aeroplane thinking 'do I really fly her?'! She climbed like a 'home-sick angel' and I didn't want her to stop. She flew like a dream and was amazingly flexible in descent.

There was so much power available from the four Rolls Royce Avon engines embedded in the wings that one could only tell if one had failed from the instruments. There were no physical symptoms and she would fly happily on three. Indeed there was an idea put forward to do so whilst at cruising altitude to save on fuel. The ministry did not approve! Her big flaps were a special design feature which enabled this clean, streamlined aircraft to slow down very easily from a fast approach speed to the landing one, the last selection giving the braking effect of huge 'barn doors'.

It was great having a Flight Engineer as part of the crew. He looked after all the different systems, including transfer of fuel from one tank to another in the huge wings and any de-icing if required. One of the engineers, big Jock Mills, had kindly tried to teach me something about the various systems on a supernumerary flight, but his Scottish accent was so strong that I wasn't able to catch all of it!

During training all the pilots were checked to the standard required of a Captain, so that if he became

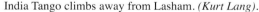
India Tango climbs away from Lasham. *(Kurt Lang)*.

ill the second pilot could take over. Having finished at Teeside , we started three months supervised route flying to prove that we could cope with all that was required before sharing the actual hands-on flying.

My first route flight was on the 14th February to Las Palmas and took 4 hours 23 minutes. The normal procedure was for the pilot not flying the aeroplane to do the R.T. With the faster speed of the Comet the setting up of the radio aids and position reporting came somewhat rapidly. It wasn't until we were on the long sector from Lisbon to the Canary Islands that I really appreciated that we were serenely flying over the Atlantic at 35,000 ft! However, I also learned how intermittent the long distance H.F. (high frequency) radio contact could be. It required patience and persistence.

During route training I flew to several different and interesting destinations, including Venice, Berlin, Tenerife, Malaga, Faro, Alicante, Tunis and Pula on the tip of the Yugoslav Peninsular. It was really great when we didn't have to restrict our climb after take-off and could soar upwards. Unfortunately, due to noise restrictions at busy airports, aircraft usually had to reduce power and be restricted in height whilst following sometimes complex departure routes, avoiding built up areas and inbound traffic. I always felt it was degrading to curb our superb aircraft's ascent and resented it every time!

On one occasion as we relaxed in the cockpit at Gatwick after a route flight, a senior training Captain came on board to take over and stood talking to us. Unknown to us, he quietly pressed a test button for a fire alarm. Half out of the cockpit we fell back into our seats, not really knowing whether to believe, but thinking we should do something about it. He just said it could have been for real. We weren't sure whether to forgive him!

Towards the end of my route training I had a nightmare in which the Captain collapsed and I hadn't done a landing since completing my initial training at Teeside. Fortunately my next flight was with Keith Moody,

another training captain who understood and let me 'save his life'. I soon learned that there was a great camaraderie in Dan-Air.

Another strong memory was when three Dan-Air Comets participated in the Dutch bulb flights, transporting people who wanted to see the beauty of the massed bulbs in full bloom. We all night-stopped in an over-full hotel in Rotterdam. I would not have believed it possible that all three crews could somehow fit into a small single bedroom to enjoy an evening drink together. A crew comprised two pilots, an engineer and four hostesses. One crew sat on the floor side by side, backs to the wall, another crew did the same on the opposite side, with the third crew on the bed and any chair available! Needless to say we only caught a glimpse of the bulbs on our way back to the airport for an onward flight to Berlin, which was an experience in itself.

The aircraft was only safe within one of the corridors fanning out on the western side of the city. They crossed Russian occupied German territory. Maintaining an exact heading and height were vital.

Once fully checked out as a First Officer, I flew farther afield to many places I had not seen before (mostly airports!). These included Corfu, Athens, Rhodes, Nicosia in Cyprus, Istanbul and Izmir in Turkey and Dubai in the Arab Emirates. I will never forget the beautiful view from miles high of the islands of Crete and Rhodes set in the blue of the Mediterranean Sea.

Dan-Air was chartered to fly Berliners to many favourite holiday destinations in Spain, Italy, Yugoslavia and North Africa. My first week entailed

First Officer Yvonne Pope on the flight deck of a Dan-Air Comet.

flying to Palma, Rimini and Dubrovnik. During time off between flights, we explored some of the city of Berlin. I was impressed by the wide tree-lined avenues and the ease with which one could get out of the centre into the green wooded countryside – 'Grunewald' – and take a trip on the river. It was, however, sad and depressing to see the 'Wall' being built, dividing East and West Germany, the actual boundary being in the centre of the river. The grey police boats patrolling the drab eastern side of the river were in great contrast to the pleasure steamers and working barges plying the western half with its little sandy beaches filled with cheerful families.

Shortly afterwards I was rostered to do an RAF charter with Captain Atkins, our Chief Pilot. I had not flown with him before so was somewhat in awe. After take-off, the undercarriage wouldn't come up. We went to Mayfield, Gatwick's holding beacon, to sort the problem out. To lighten things, I asked if he was glad he had left his office that morning. I don't think he appreciated it! However, all went well thereafter and we landed at Akrotiri in Cyprus five hours and eleven minutes later.

As there were no passengers for the return flight I was allowed to fly the aircraft. Coming up towards Athens, Air Traffic suddenly advised me that our Company wished us to divert to 'Gili'. Captain 'Atkins was in the cabin at the time. Having only heard of the opera singer by that name, I had to ask for the four letter code. It turned out to be Izmir. One of our Comets had gone 'sick' (developed a fault) so that it couldn't return to the U.K. with passengers on board. Knowing that we were returning empty, the Captain had requested our diversion. On arrival, we had no trouble in being given permission to land, but when the passengers had been transferred and we requested start-up clearance, it was denied. We were told the authorities concerned had not yet given us permission to land! Our poor passengers had to wait yet another hour. As our duty day would exceed

fifteen hours, Captain Atkins had to ask the crew if they were prepared to continue. We all naturally said 'yes'. We had taken off at 08.10 and finally landed back at Gatwick at 23.25. We definitely enjoyed a drink on arrival! It had been a worthwhile day.

As the Comets were used mainly on Inclusive Tour Charters, the summer was a very busy one. As well as flying out of Gatwick, we flew from Glasgow and Edinburgh, Manchester, Liverpool and Berlin, being based away from home for up to five days at a time.

Our Comets were fairly busy that winter. Just before Christmas we flew to Venice for the day. Arriving early, we changed into civilian clothes in the hotel and then started exploring by taking a boat to St Mark's Square where we seemed to be the only people wandering across it. The air was crisp and clear and we couldn't believe that we had the famous square almost to ourselves.

On one occasion I was called out to position an aircraft to Shannon for the onward crew to take it across the Atlantic. Only a few of us were checked out on that route. You could be fined by American Air Traffic if you misunderstood their clearance procedure! On another occasion I was called out to go to three different destinations in the space of fifteen minutes, ending up with a flight to Dubai. I didn't have any summer clothing to hand so had to make do and buy a swimsuit and kaftan in a market near the hotel during our two-day wait for the returning aircraft. I soon learned why the kaftan is so comfortable in the heat!

We also had a day charter to Paris. Landing at Beauvais, the passengers, followed by ourselves, were transported by coaches to the centre of the city. We set off in search of the famous River Seine. I

The end of an era!

Representatives of the media gather around Comet G-BDIW prior to departure on the last commercial flight.
(via Tom Singfield)

Captain John Kelly, with Captain Simon Searle as Co-pilot and Gordon Moores, the flight engineer, try to look interested as the press invade the flight deck before the start of the last-ever commercial Comet flight.

eventually had to ask a gendarme directing traffic in the middle of a busy thoroughfare, 'Ou est la Seine?' 'La bas' he condescendingly replied to the mad English tourist – and there it was, just below the next block! We found a bar/café for lunch and explored on our way back to the coach pick-up area. Our transport was delayed so the passengers arrived at Beauvais ahead of us. There was no time to change into uniform so I had to fly the Comet back in my smart black and white dress and court shoes!

I also flew to places I had not yet been – Zaragoza, Rome, Naples, Ibiza, Bucharest, Constanta, Frankfurt, Zurich, Barcelona, Gerona, Helsinki and Stockholm. I even flew to Mahon in Menorca once! At one time, whilst I was holding off over the runway before touching down at Barcelona, a sudden sharp rain shower occurred and it felt as if the Comet had landed itself because my vision was impaired. It was also really beautiful to see the Bay of Naples on a clear day, and funny to at last see the snow covered runway at Stockholm delineated by soft little fir trees.

I felt really privileged when I was able to escape a gloomy day on the ground by climbing through the grey clouds up into the bright sunlight above and look down on the shimmering carpet of white cloud tops far below.

At the end of 1971 I learned that I was not going to escape to that bright sunlight quite so easily. I was offered a captaincy on the Avro 748. I had flown one thousand and thirty two hours on the Comet and was grateful for every minute.

Above: The extra-special flight crew for DA8874 try to pose for the cameras as passengers hurry to board behind them.

Left: the sparkling performance of the Comet could not be better demonstrated that during the climb-out from Gatwick on the last commercial flight. When viewed against the horizon the wing is at approximately 30 degrees! (both John Hunt)

A fond farewell to a legend of the air . . .

Daily Mail, Saturday, November 8, 1980   PAGE 9

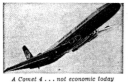

A Comet 4 . . . not economic today

By ANGUS MacPHERSON
Air Correspondent

THE once-proud Comet is set for its final approach.

Twenty-eight years after the first one roared up out of Heathrow the famous jet airliner is being retired.

The last one to carry passengers leaves Gatwick tomorrow on a £34-a-head flight of nostalgia before a future as a museum piece.

Comet 4 India Whiskey of the independent airline Dan-Air will take more than 100 aviation enthusiasts to Bournemouth and back.

'They are all sorts of people, and all ages from schoolboys upwards,' said John Hunt, of the Ian Allen publishing and travel group, which is organising the farewell. 'But they all want a final ride in this historic plane.'

India Whiskey, built at Hatfield, Hertfordshire, in 1962, is the last of four Comets in flying condition owned by Dan-Air.

'A lot of people will be sorry to see them go,' said the airline.

'They are very comfortable — they've been good old workhorses, but their engines are just too thirsty and noisy to be economic today.'

Comets will go on flying in its Nimrod version with the RAF, but not with commercial passengers.

There was a time when the Comet, the world's first jet airliner, was more than just a workhorse.

It was a technological marvel which carried all Britain's pride

as it set out to herald a new age of passenger jet flying and capture the world's aviation markets for Britain.

It was said that it broke the heart of old Sir Geoffrey de Havilland, who had already lost his test pilot son Geoffrey trying to break the sound barrier, and who had staked all on this effort to open a new age of flying.

The Comet was later reborn as the Comet 4, and entirely rebuilt. It was bought by a dozen airlines, including BOAC and BEA.

Above: the build up to the last Comet commercial flight, as reported by the *Daily Mail*.

Right: All passengers on DA8874 received a commemorative certificate marking that they were indeed on the last commercial flight. The document was signed by all the crew.

The last flight

Arthur Larkman: '*We were forced to end our Comet flights as operating costs were now prohibitive. Some 'last flights' on the Comet were advertised and were quickly filled. The final commercial flight was on a 4C, 'India Whisky', on 9 November 1980, which was chartered by a group of enthusiasts. The aircraft was commanded by Captain John Kelly, with Captain Simon Searle as Co-pilot and Gordon Moores the flight engineer. Val Barnett, the Fleet Stewardess and my daughter Sue, who was a Comet Number One, were in charge of the cabin crew.*

Flight number DA8874 had been chartered by John Hunt of Ian Allan Travel Ltd. Before moving John had been reservations manager with Dan-Air and was determined that the Comet was to go out in a blaze of glory.

119 passengers boarded with others waiting up to seven hours for the possibility of a standby seat! The aircraft made low flypasts of the airfields at Heathrow, Brize Norton, Lyneham, and Bournemouth before landing back at Gatwick.

Thus the era of Dan-Air's Comets passed, but a commercial concern could not become sentimental. The Comet design had come to a premature twilight of its years as a fuel thirsty and expensive-to-operate jet, so it was time again to consider the future. With the demise, someone within the Company calculated that during the fleet's life, the legendary Comet had flown a total of some 238,000 hours in Dan-Air service, which equated to a distance of 95,400,000 miles!

DAN AIR

Farewell Flight of the

'COMET 4C' *prior to retirement.*

This is to certify that _____

was a passenger aboard the

farewell flight from

London - Gatwick on Sunday,

November 9th 1980.

Chapter 14

NIMROD - THE MIGHTY HUNTER

The search for an aircraft to replace the fleet of Avro Shackletons in what was then RAF Coastal Command began with objectives set out in Air Staff Requirement 381 during 1958, which laid out six tasks, of which the most important was the ASW role — to detect, fix and destroy submarines either on the surface or submerged, and whether conventional or nuclear. The others included search and rescue, wide-area surveillance, detecting and shadowing enemy surface units and forces, with the ability to make limited air-to-surface strikes against individual vessels, and trooping in case of emergency.

The required performance called for an aircraft having a large fuselage capacity, a long range/endurance, a high maximum speed in order to be able to reach search areas far off-shore in the minimum time and good handling and 'ride' characteristics at low speed and altitude during the search. As with any other aircraft design exercises, meeting these requirements called for an assessment of possible trade-offs and decisions on the precise points at which to pitch compromises, and Hawker Siddeley set about a series of design feasibility studies. As the Manchester Division (originally Avro) had been responsible for the Shackleton, the design activity for ASR381 was naturally centred there.

The designs studied between 1960 and 1965 centred on turboprop power as this was thought to offer substantially better fuel consumption - and therefore endurance - than the pure jet, so some of the earliest studies concentrated upon large four-engined turboprop types, such as the Avro 784. At the other extreme, Hawker Siddeley studied the feasibility of a variable geometry design with turbojet engines. The chief advantage of the latter type lay in its ability to cruise at high speed in transit to and from the search area with wings swept back and then to loiter with wings forward, but the cost and length of development of such a type made it a fairly obvious non-starter from the outset.

Other designs were also considered - including the use of mixed power plants - for example, the

The Nimrod production line at Woodford. Hawker Siddeley Aviation never made a single overseas sale.

Avro 775 with two wing-mounted turboprops and a turbojet in the tail and in a derivative of the Breguet Atlantic with two RB 153-61 turbojets in pods under the wings to supplement the two Tyne turboprops during the cruise; and pure-jet types were also studied, such as the Avro 776 with three rear engines.

In addition modifications of various existing aircraft were considered, including the Trident, Comet, Vanguard and VC10. Examples of these civil types were demonstrated to Coastal Command and flown on typical high and low altitude missions from St Mawgan. By 1964, it was becoming clear that the timescale for replacement of the Shackleton and the funds available combined to make acquisition of a new aircraft impracticable, and of the adapted civil aircraft available, the Comet began to emerge as the favourite.

At the time it was considered that the use of turbojets for maritime aircraft was not a good idea as their relatively high fuel consumption made it difficult to achieve the required range and endurance in an aircraft equal in size and cost to one with turboprop engines. However, the advent of a new generation of turbofan engines with improved fuel consumption made it possible to reconsider this type of engine, and further advantage could be derived from operating procedures to minimise fuel flow, such as shutting down one or more engines during the patrol, when high speed was not required.

The deciding factor became the ability of the aircraft to survive the failure of one of the engines still running. Calculations showed that a version of the Comet re-engined with the then new Spey turbofans in place of the original Avon 500s would normally start its patrol at a weight at which a positive rate of climb could be maintained on two engines, and in the course of a long patrol this would go down to the point where climb away on one engine would be possible.

Thus, it was possible to suggest an operational procedure in which the aircraft made a high speed dash to the search area on all engines, and then stopped one engine and retained a second at flight idle power for immediate response in the event of failure of one of the other two engines. Then, when the critical weight for single-engined climb was reached, the 'flight idle' engine could also be stopped, both engines being re-started for the high speed cruise back to base.

The Comet was particularly suited to this kind of operational procedure, since the engine location was close inboard in the wing roots and few problems arose in the case of asymmetric power. The relatively low wing loading of the Comet represented a good compromise between the needs of high-speed cruise and low-speed search, and it had the added, somewhat fortuitous, advantage of providing a comfortable ride and good controllability at low speeds and altitudes. Its size was adequate for the mission requirements of crew, equipment and weapon load and the aircraft fitted into available RAF airfields without any problem. The Spey engine could be installed in place of the Avons with only the minimum of engineering changes.

De Havillands, of course had been bought by Hawker Siddeley in 1960, but kept it as a separate company until 1963. In that year it became the De Havilland Division of Hawker Siddeley Aviation and all types in production or development changed their designations from 'DH' to 'HS'.

With the Manchester design office designation HS.801, the maritime Comet took shape during 1964. The version of the Spey adopted was a military equivalent of the civil Spey 25 used in the BAC One-Eleven and HS Trident, the principal modifications being concerned with anti-corrosion treatment for operation in a salt-laden atmosphere, the elimination of some magnesium components for the same reason, and a change in the accessory gearbox to drive the larger alternators needed for the extensive avionic fit in the aircraft. The increased mass flow of the Spey over that of the Avon resulted in larger air intakes and exhausts being required

The basic structure of the Comet was retained for the maritime version, and the problem of how the weapons could be accommodated in an airliner was elegantly solved by adding an un-pressurised ventral pannier for almost the whole length of the fuselage, fairing forward and upward round the nose to provide a housing for the ASV 21 radar scanner. The basis for the HS 801 design was the Comet 4C, this being the final version of the commercial jetliner, but the fuselage length reverted to that of the earlier Comet 4, which was 6 feet shorter. Most of the fuselage windows were eliminated, and the size of the pilots' windscreens was increased, with the addition also of an eyebrow window each side.

Magnetic Anomaly Detection (MAD) equipment was provided in a conventional 'sting' fairing at the rear of the aircraft, and Electronic Countermeasure - also called Electronic Support Measures - was located in a fairing on top of the fin. The extra side area of the weapons bay pannier had an adverse effect on directional control, so a small dorsal fin was designed for the maritime Comet - that was increased to have a larger area after prototype flight testing. The starboard wing pinion tank — a feature of the original Comet—provided a convenient housing for a 70-

When the Nimrod was designed, the flight deck was completely redesigned, including fitting more up-to-date seats. *(Warrant Officer Paddy Porter BEM)*

million candlepower Strong Electric searchlight, controlled directionally by joy-stick at the co-pilot station, and two wing strong points were introduced to allow for the carriage of air-to-surface missiles on pylons. With the gross weight increased from the Comet 4C's 162,000 lb to a maximum of 177,500 lb, a stronger undercarriage was called for, and a Rover APU was provided for engine-starting. The entire cabin was, of course, laid out for the maritime role.

By 1964 the maritime Comet became the solution to ASR381, and in June 1965 was selected to replace the Shackleton with Instruction To Proceed (ITP) issued to Hawker Siddeley. The requirement was for 38 aircraft, plus two prototypes which were to be converted from Comet airframes. This was a convenient arrangement, not only because an extremely tight schedule was established by the RAF to achieve an Initial Operational Capability (IOC) only 48 months from ITP, but also because two Comet 4C airframes remained unsold from the Chester production line, where the jigs were still intact, although commercial orders had dried up with the delivery of the 75th Comet 4. While these jigs were being refurbished and the final assembly line for the HS801 was being set up at Woodford, Cheshire, modification of these two Comets proceeded at Chester.

What's in a name?

According to the Bible's Book of Genesis and Books of Chronicles, Nimrod was a legendary king of Babylonia, the son of Cush and great-grandson of Noah and the king of Shinar. He is depicted in the Tanakh as a man of power in the earth, and a mighty hunter. He is described as the son of Cush, grandson of Ham, and great-grandson of Noah; and as *'a mighty one on the earth'* and *'...a mighty hunter before God'*.

One prototype was brought up to the

Inside a Nimrod, with the tactical and routine navigators stations visible, along with other operators stations. *(Warrant Officer Paddy Porter BEM)*

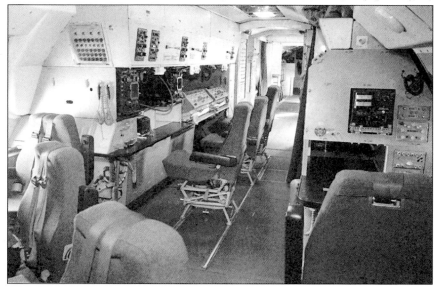

The tactical navigator's station, dominated by the large circular radar screen from which he was able to control the scenario surrounding the aircraft. *(Warrant Officer Paddy Porter BEM)*

prototype followed, this also being externally up to HS 801 standard but retaining Avon engines and being assigned the task of flight development of the nav/tac system. So that the electrical power quality was the same as on the Nimrod, a special

aerodynamic status of the HS 801, including installation of the Spey engines, the external changes to the airframe and representative electrical generating, fuel and hydraulic systems and XV148, the modified aircraft, made its first flight on 23 May 1967. The pilot was John Cunningham, who had been responsible for all Comet flight development and the flight took the aircraft from Chester to Woodford, with Jimmy Harrison assuming responsibility for the flight test programme. Two months later, on 31 July 1967, XV147, the second

installation was designed to adapt the generators to the Avons which permitted these units to be slung under the nacelles in external pods.

As already noted, flight testing led to an increase in the size of the dorsal fin, and the location of the pitot and static vent positions was changed to reduce the initially rather large position error, but as would be expected with a developed airframe, no other significant changes were called for. Evaluating the nav/tac system represented the major part of the programme, which also involved the first four

The Nimrod Weapons Pannier. At the rear are the canisters for the Lindhome rescue equipment. This was five cylinder-shaped containers joined together by lengths of floating rope. The centre container would house a nine-man inflatable dinghy with the other containers housing survival equipment such as emergency rations and clothing. The Gear would be dropped in a long line up-wind of the survivors. The Dinghy would inflate on impact and then drift towards the survivors. Survivors could then use the dinghy, haul in the containers of equipment and await rescue. *(BAe Hatfield)*

XV254 gets airborne for another sortie.
(Warrant Officer Paddy Porter BEM)

production aircraft, one of which flew in June 1968 and the other three in the first half of 1969, the production contract having meanwhile been confirmed at the end of 1967. Knowing that the success of the Nimrod would rest largely upon the performance of its various systems. Hawker Siddeley chose to assume complete responsibility for systems management, expanding its avionics and systems development capability in order to do so. Consequently, the contract - worth nearly £100m - was at the time the biggest fixed-price deal ever concluded with a single company in the British aerospace industry.

The prototype and second and third production aircraft spent some time at the A&AEE in 1968/69, leading to CA release in the autumn of 1969, by which time three more production aircraft had flown, and IOC was achieved in mid 1970. The Maritime

Operational Training Unit at St Mawgan began to receive Nimrods on 2 October 1969, and a start was made on training crews for the first operational squadrons. With 10 Nimrods delivered to the RAF by July 1970, formation of the first squadron - 201 - began at RAF Kinloss, to be followed by 204 at St Mawgan, where the training unit in due course became 236 OCU. Completion of the batch of 38 Nimrod MR Mk Is in August 1972 allowed the RAF to build up its planned force of five squadrons, including 120 and 206 at Kinloss and 203 at Luqa, Malta, with a detachment from one of these units normally based at Singapore.

The naughty Nimrods

While Nimrod production was getting underway, it was realised that the Nimrod airframe would also make an ideal replacement for the ageing Comet 4Cs

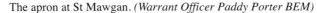

The apron at St Mawgan. *(Warrant Officer Paddy Porter BEM)*

XV242 seen low over Newquay in Cornwall. Built as as MR1, it was later converted to a MRA.4.
(Warrant Officer Paddy Porter BEM)

still used by the RAF for Electronic Intelligence (ELINT) duties. The Comet offered ample internal space for electronic equipment and good cruise performance. Three additional airframes were ordered under the designation Nimrod R.Mk 1, with the first being delivered to 51 Squadron at RAF Wyton as virtually an empty shell in July 1971. Over the next three years a complex array of sophisticated electronic eavesdropping equipment was installed in the three aircraft, resulting in a large number of antennae appearing on the fuselage. The aircraft initially only differed externally in having the MAD probe in the tail deleted and dielectric radomes in the nose of each external wing tank and in the tailcone.

Although the airframe of the R1 was essentially the same as the Nimrod MR1 ASW variant, internally the aircraft were completely different, apart from the flight deck area which was used by five crew - two pilots, two navigators and a flight engineer - but additional space was available for two supplementary crew to provide relief on long sorties. Accurate navigation is essential and the aircraft were fitted out with AD360 ADF, AD260 VOR/ILS, AN/ARN-172 TACAN, AN/ARA-50 UFH DF, LORAN, and a Kollsman periscope sextant. The ASV-21D radar

from the ASW variant was retained with a 32in diameter dish, but provision was made for an antenna up to 5ft. Up to 23 SIGINT specialists were accommodated at thirteen side-facing equipment consoles in the fuselage; consoles 1-5 were located on the port side with consoles 6-13 on the starboard. Each was designed to accommodate two 4ft modules with provision for a single seat placed centrally but able to slide on transverse rails. Consoles 1-4 and 9-12 had provision for a pair of side-by-side seats. These double consoles were later augmented by three forward facing single-man consoles.

The first Nimrod R1, XW664, was delivered to Wyton on 7 July 1971 and took over 2 years to fit out and test. The first training sortie (Captained by Flt Lt Gordon Lambert) was flown on 21 Oct 73. The first operational sortie was flown on 3 May 1974 and the type was formally commissioned into RAF service on 10 May. Two more Nimrod R1s entered service soon after, XW665 in August and XW666 in January 1975, allowing the retirement of the last Comets and Canberras. For pilot training 51 Sqn also received standard Nimrod MR.1 XZ283 on 8 April 1976; this airframe stayed with the squadron until June 1978, when it was returned to BAe for conversion to AEW3

Nimrod R.1 XW664 gets airborne from RAF Wyton on another sortie to who knows where!
(Warrant Officer Paddy Porter BEM)

standard. Another Nimrod MR1 XV252 then briefly acted as the trainer until the squadron reverted to the three operational aircraft.

In 1980 the aircraft were upgraded by replacing the ASV21 ASW radar with an ECKO 290 weather radar displaying in the cockpit this allowed the radar navigator crew position to be removed. The workload of the single navigator was improved by removing one of the LORAN sets and replacing it with a Delco AN/ASN-119 Carousel IVA INS. As a result of this upgrade one of the LORAN external aerials was removed and a variety of other external antennae appeared, believed to be used for direction finding. NWingtip pods, similar in appearance to the Yellow Gate Electronic Support Measures (ESM) fitted to the Nimrod MR2 also appeared on XW664 and then the other two aircraft.

The requirement for in-flight refuelling became apparent as a result of Operation *Corporate*, the plan to recapture the Falkland Islands following the Argentinean invasion in 1982, however, none but XW664 had received IFR probes by the Argentine surrender on 14 June. Where the aircraft operated from during the conflict is still open to speculation, but some sources believe the aircraft operated from

a base in Chile alongside a detachment of RAF Canberra PR9s. Along with the refuelling probe each aircraft also gained a large ventral fin, overwing vortex generators and rectangular tailplane finlets. Underwing pylons were fitted at the same time and these carried a modified BOZ pod believed to contain a towed radar decoys. It is believed the aircraft was also fitted with a Marconi Master satellite communications system.

In 1995 51 Sqn finally left RAF Wyton after 32 years in residence and moved to RAF Waddington in Lincolnshire. Only since the end of the Cold War has the role of the aircraft been officially acknowledged; they were once described as 'radar calibration aircraft'.

This close-up of the rear end of R.1 XV249 shows the modified tail boom which housed ELINT equipment and the inflight refuelling 'finlets' put on to improve stability. The aircraft was also fitted with assorted aerials all over the airframe. *(Warrant Officer Paddy Porter BEM)*

Nimrod R1 XW666 was jokingly referred to by some personnel on 51 Squadron as 'The Beast' or 'Damian', because of the satanic connotations of the number 666. Unfortunately, on 16 May 1995, during an air-test following a lengthy stay at the Nimrod Major Servicing Unit at Kinloss, a starter motor disintegrated and the debris punctured the wing and fuel tanks. A fire broke out which was so severe that there was every likelihood the main spar holding the wing onto the fuselage would burn through and fail. The pilot of the aircraft, Flt Lt Art Stacey, had no choice but to carry out an immediate ditching in the Moray Firth from which all the crew survived. The aircraft was later recovered and scrapped. A Nimrod MR2, XV249, was identified as a suitable replacement and after a major overhaul at Kinloss the aircraft was ferried to BAe Woodford and stripped of all ASW equipment. After the installation of some antenna fairings, the aircraft was ferried to RAF Waddington on 19 December 1996.

When XW666 was lost, the three Nimrod R1s were in the middle of a major modification programme known as Starwindow. The project had been launched to equip the R1s with a new Open Systems architecture digital SIGINT suite, probably based on those carried by the RC-135 Rivet Joint aircraft operated by the USAF. The Starwindow system incorporated two high-speed search receivers, a wide band digital direction finding system and 22 pooled digital intercept receivers. New workstations were fitted for the 'specialists' in the rear of the aircraft. The Starwindow installation on XV249 began on 27 December 1996 and the aircraft eventually flew as a fully equipped R1 on 11 April 1997. In addition to the Starwindow package the R1s were also fitted with a new 'Special Signals' intercept facility with a digital recording and playback suite, an enhanced pulse-signal processing capability and multi channel digital data demodulator.

On 21 September 2005 it was announced that the RAF had completed flight trials and acceptance testing of a new airborne reconnaissance system named Extract that was designed specifically for the three Nimrod R1 SIGINT aircraft. Developed by Raytheon Intelligence and Information Systems, Extract examined routine radio and radar emissions whilst providing electronic combat support to military commanders and provided enhanced automated capabilities. In addition to the Extract system on the Nimrod R1s, the company also supplied ground-based analysis systems and a rear crew trainer, as well as providing continued contractor logistic support for Extract.

In addition to the new Extract system, Northrop Grumman were selected to execute a £2 million first stage assessment phase for Project Helix, a programme to provide a new mission suite, associated ground stations and training facilities to enhance the overall reconnaissance mission capabilities of the Nimrod R1. Also in competition for the final £200 million project were L-3 Communications' Integrated Systems and Lockheed Martin's Integrated Systems and Solutions, both of whom had also been awarded Phase 1 assessment contracts. In 2007 L-3 Communications Integrated Systems (L-3 IS) won a £11.5M contract to carry out the risk reduction studies for Helix Assessment Phase Stage 3.

Following the retirement of the Nimrod MR2 fleet in 2010, the final two Nimrods, in service with

XV249, with the RAF Waddington crest and '1995-2011' on the tail in low visibility markings and the 51 Squadron 'droopy goose' emblem behind the flight deck windows and the words 'Nimrod R1 1974-2011'. The assorted collections of lumps, bumps and aerials are particularly noticable. *(authors collection)*

51 Squadron, bowed out to a 700-strong audience of serving and retired RAF personnel at a ceremony held at RAF Waddington.

Leading the thanks and tributes to 51 Squadron and the R1 supporting elements, the Chief of the Air Staff, Air Chief Marshal Sir Stephen Dalton, said: *'Today is a day of celebration. There is no question this aircraft has given us the ability to do things that would be very much more difficult, and could have cost us more, if we hadn't had it.*

The ceremony saw parades by two flights of Nimrod R Force elements, including personnel from 51 Squadron, 54(R) Squadron, 56(R) Squadron, Electronic Reconnaissance Operations Support Squadron and the Electronic Warfare and Avionics Detachment. They were accompanied by the Band of the Royal Air Force Regiment.

Flying for the last time, Nimrod R1 XV249, piloted by Flight Lieutenant Mike Chatterton, made two spectacular flypasts directly over the parade, the second concluding with a roaring climb before disappearing into the clouds.

Reflecting on flying the Nimrod for the last time he said: *'It's a great honour to fly the Nimrod R1 today. When you're flying you're too busy to take stock of how significant a day this is. Only after I had landed did it really hit home.*

The Nimrod R1 flew over Afghanistan in support of Operation *Herrick* for ten years, making it one of 51 Squadron's longest operational commitments. Due for retirement at the end March 2011, the Nimrod R1 was given a three-month reprieve to enable participation in Operation *Ellamy*, supporting the NATO mission over Libya.

The replacement for the Nimrod R1 will be the Rivet Joint aircraft, due into service with the RAF in 2014. For now, RAF crews from 51 Squadron are already co-manning US Rivet Joint aircraft in missions over Libya and Afghanistan, continuing their support to operations.

Watching the Nimrod's final flight, RAF Waddington Station Commander, Group Captain Chris Jones, said: *'There's a touch of sadness, but a sense of great pride. The Nimrod has delivered a fantastic service to the RAF and at RAF Waddington since 1995. And it's a fitting way to say farewell'.*

Nimrod MR2

Starting in 1975, 35 aircraft were upgraded to MR2 standard, being re-delivered from August 1979. The upgrade included extensive modernisation of the aircraft's electronic suite. Changes included the replacement of the obsolete ASV Mk 21 radar used by the Shackleton and Nimrod MR1 with the new EMI Searchwater radar, a new acoustic processor capable of handling more modern sonobuoys and additional ESM pods on the wingtips.

Provision for in-flight refuelling was introduced during the Falklands War (as the MR2P), as well as hardpoints to allow the Nimrod to carry the AIM-9 Sidewinder missile to counter enemy Argentine Air Force maritime surveillance aircraft. In preparation for operations in the Gulf War theatre, several MR2s were fitted with new communications and ECM equipment to deal with anticipated threats; at the time these modified aircraft were given the designation MR2P(GM), thus demoting 'Gulf Mod'.

The MR2 carried out three main roles – Anti-Submarine Warfare, Anti-Surface Unit Warfare and Search and Rescue . Its extended range enabled the crew to monitor maritime areas far to the north of Iceland and up to 4,000 km out into the Western Atlantic. With Air-to-Air Refuelling, range and endurance was greatly extended. The crew consisted of two pilots and one flight engineer, one tactical navigator and a routine navigator, one Air Electronics Officer, the sonobuoy sensor team of two Weapon System Operators and four Weapon System

MR.2 XV248 of the Kinloss Wing taxies past the camera. *(Warrant Officer Paddy Porter BEM)*

XV255 in it's element, down low over the ocean. *(Warrant Officer Paddy Porter BEM)*

Operators to manage passive and active electronic warfare systems.

On 2 September 2006 XV230 was on a routine mission over Helmand Province in Southern Afghanistan in support of NATO and Afghani ground forces when it suffered a catastrophic mid-air fire, leading to the total loss of the aircraft and the death of all those on board.

When rumbles started to surface about the safety of the Nimrod, the Secretary of State ordered an independent review into the broader issues under Charles Haddon-Cave QC.

A Board of Inquiry (BOI) was convened and presented its Report to the Convening Authority on 20 April 2007. An Addendum to the Report was issued on 25 July 2007. The Board's findings were made public on 4 December 2007.

The Inquiry concluded that the loss was caused by the escape of fuel during Air-to-Air Refuelling, occasioned by an overflow from the blow-off valve to No. 1 tank, causing fuel to track back along the fuselage, or alternatively, a leak of fuel from the fuel system (fuel coupling or pipe), leading to an accumulation of fuel within the No. 7 Tank Dry Bay. Although of a lower probability, the fuel leak could have been caused by a hot air leak damaging fuel system seals, the ignition of that fuel following contact with an exposed element of the aircraft's Cross-Feed/Supplementary Cooling Pack (SCP) duct.

The BOI found that fuel was most likely to have accumulated in the Refrasil insulation muff around the SCP elbow at the bottom of the starboard No. 7 Tank Dry Bay.

The BOI also found that a 'Safety Case' prepared in respect of the Nimrod MR1 and MR2 aircraft between 2002 and 2005, the Nimrod Safety Case, contained a number of significant errors.

The independent review discovered that there were a number of previous incidents and warning signs potentially relevant to XV230; in particular, the rupture of the SCP duct in Nimrod XV227 in

The nose refuelling probe of XV254 makes it look like the aircraft is about to participate in a jousting tournament! *(Warrant Officer Paddy Porter BEM)*

November 2004 should have been a 'wake up call' – thus the loss of XV230 was avoidable

The Nimrod Safety Case was drawn up between 2001 and 2005 by BAE Systems (Phases 1 and 2) and the MoD Nimrod Integrated Project Team (Third Phase), with QinetiQ acting as independent advisor. This represented the best opportunity to capture the serious design flaws in the Nimrod which had lain dormant for years. If it had been drawn up with proper skill, care and attention, the catastrophic fire risks to the Nimrod MR2 fleet presented by the Cross-Feed/SCP duct and the Air-to-Air Refuelling modification would have been identified and dealt with. Unfortunately, the Nimrod Safety Case was a lamentable job from start to finish. It was riddled with errors. It missed the key dangers. Its production is a story of incompetence, complacency, and cynicism. The best opportunity to prevent the accident to XV230 was, tragically, lost.

The independent review found that the Safety Case process was fatally undermined by a general malaise: a widespread assumption by those involved that the Nimrod was 'safe anyway' (because it had successfully flown for 30 years) and the task of drawing up the Safety Case became essentially a paperwork and 'tickbox' exercise.

The MR2 was based at RAF Kinloss in Scotland and flown by 201, 120, 206, and 42(R) Squadrons.and were withdrawn on 31 March 2010, a year earlier than planned, for financial reasons. The last official flight of a Nimrod MR2 took place on 26 May 2010, with XV229 flying from RAF Kinloss to Kent International Airport to be used as an evacuation training airframe at the nearby MOD Defence Fire Training and Development Centre.

AEW3

The Nimrod AEW3 was a planned airborne early warning (AEW) aircraft intended as to provide airborne radar cover for the air defence of the United Kingdom by the RAF. It was designed to use the existing Nimrod airframe, in use with the RAF as a maritime patrol aircraft, combined with a brand new radar system and avionics package developed by Marconi Avionics.

In 1977 an RAF Comet 4 was modified for flight testing with the nose radome and conducted a series of trials, the results of which proved promising enough for an order for three prototype Nimrods to be built using redundant MR1 airframes. The first of these was rolled out in March 1980 and flew for the first time in July, and was intended to test the flight characteristics, with the second airframe planned to carry out trials on the Mission Systems Avionics (MSA) package. The MSA was based around a GEC 4080M computer, which was required to process data from the two radar scanners, the ESM system, IFF and inertial navigation systems. The integration of all of these systems into a single package proved too difficult for the underpowered computer. Additionally, when operating at full power the radar scanners and on-board electronic systems generated a significant amount of heat. A system was developed to channel this via the fuel system, from where it could then dissipate, but which only worked when the fuel tanks were at least half full.

Despite the problems, the AEW3 continued, and eight production aircraft were ordered (all from existing airframes), the first of them flying in March 1982. Even while the technical problems were being worked on, the aircraft was delivered to the RAF,

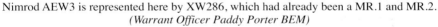

Nimrod AEW3 is represented here by XW286, which had already been a MR.1 and MR.2.
(Warrant Officer Paddy Porter BEM)

Two views of AEW3 XZ285. Both radomes were planned to be the same shape and size, but the front 'dome was changed for ground clearance aerodynamic and reasons. The AEW3s were withdrawn from use, stored at Abingdon and eventually scrapped.

with 8 Squadron, the RAF's AEW squadron which at that time operated the Shackleton, receiving its first in 1984 to begin crew training. By the time of the Falklands War, the Nimrod AEW had been originally scheduled to be in service; however the technical problems proved insurmountable to be deployed in the conflict. To provide some degree of cover, several Nimrod MR.2 were quickly modified to undertake the airborne surveillance role for the task force.

The MoD then undertook a complete review of the AEW programme. The result was the start of a bid process to supply AEW aircraft for the RAF that began in 1986. The primary bidders were GEC Marconi with the Nimrod, and Boeing with its Sentry. In December 1986, the Sentry was finally chosen and the Nimrod AEW programme was cancelled.

By all accounts the Nimrod programme had cost in the region of £1 billion up to its cancellation, contrasting with manufacturer claims in 1977 that the total cost of the project would be between £200-300 million. The unused airframes were eventually stored and used as a source of spares for the Nimrod R1 and MR2 fleets, while the elderly Shackleton aircraft that had been commissioned in 1971 as a 'stop-gap'measure for AEW cover until the planned entry of the Nimrod were forced to soldier on until 1991

and the entry into RAF service of the Sentry. The scandal over the collapse of the Nimrod AEW project was a major factor in Prime Minister Margaret Thatcher's stance to open up the UK defence market to competition.The Nimrod AEW project was hugely complex and expensive for the British government, as a result of the difficulties of producing brand new radar and computer systems and integrating them successfully into the Nimrod airframe.

MRA.4

In 1992, the RAF started a Replacement Maritime Patrol Aircraft (RMPA) procurement programme to replace the Nimrod MR2 aircraft. To meet the requirement British Aerospace proposed rebuilding each Nimrod MR2 with new engines and electronics which it called Nimrod 2000. The RAF considered bids from Lockheed with its P-3 Orion, Loral Corporation with rebuilt ex-US Navy Orions, and Dassault with the Atlantique 3. In December 1996 the contract was awarded to British Aerospace for the Nimrod 2000, under the designation Nimrod MRA4. British Aerospace became BAE Systems in 1999 and continued development on the Nimrod MRA4.

The MRA4 was to be essentially a new aircraft. Significant changes included the installation of current-generation Rolls-Royce BR710 turbofan engines, a larger and more efficient wing, and a fully refurbished fuselage. Much larger air intakes were required on the MRA4 because the airflow requirements of the BR710 engine were significantly higher than that of the Spey 250s powering the original Nimrods. The MRA4 also borrowed heavily from Airbus technology; the glass cockpit was derived from the Airbus A340.

According to BAE Systems, the Nimrod MRA4 systems was to enable the crews to gather, process and display up to 20 times more technical and strategic data than the MR2. The Searchwater 2000 radar was stated to have been capable over land as well as water; with the ability to have swept an area the size of the UK every 10 seconds. The Aircraft Synthetic Training Aids (ASTA) provided by Thales Training & Simulation was an electronic training suite to allow the training of crew members to transfer from active MRA4 aircraft to ground-based training systems; this change was made to increase the availability of the aircraft for operational missions and allow for more intensive training exercises.

The scheduled date of entry into service for the MRA4 was April 2003, but development proved far more protracted than anticipated. An independent company, Flight Refuelling Ltd., was contracted to undertake the conversions to MRA4 standard, but BAE discovered that the Nimrod airframes supplied by the RAF were not built to a common standard and this considerably complicated the refurbishment process. The task of converting the existing airframes was transferred in-house to BAE Systems Woodford. The Woodford team then found that the new wing was flawed, which resulted in the project being put on hold while another wing design was developed.

The contract was renegotiated for the second time in 2002, when the aircraft requirement was reduced from 21 to 18. BAE Systems then issued a shock profit warning in December 2002 due to cost overruns of the Nimrod MRA4 and the Astute class submarine projects. On 19 February 2003 BAE took a charge of £500 million against the MRA4 contract. The company had previously taken a £300 million 'loss charge' in 2000, *which was expected to cover '...all the costs of completion of the current contract'.*

Announcing plans for the future of the British military on 21 July 2004, the Defence Secretary Geoff Hoon detailed plans to reduce the upgrade programme to cover only 16 MRA4 aircraft, and suggested that an fleet of 12 might suffice. PA02, the second development MRA4, achieved its first flight in December 2004 and was used to test elements of the mission system and the air vehicle. BAE Systems received a contract worth £1.1 billion for 12 MRA4s on 18 July 2006; three were to be development aircraft and nine more converted to production standard. The Nimrod MRA4 successfully released the Sting Ray torpedo for the first time on 30 July 2007.

Further disputes over 'affordability' meant that the number of MRA4s to be delivered was further reduced to nine by Spring 2008. The first production aircraft took its maiden flight on 10 September 2009. At the time of the flight, each MRA4 was to cost at least £400 million. The Ministry of Defence announced in December 2009 that the introduction of the MRA4 would be delayed until 2012 as part of defence spending cuts. The first MRA4 was delivered in March 2010 to the RAF for acceptance testing and initial operational capability was expected to be reached in October 2012. The MRA4 was to operate from its main base at RAF Kinloss, Scotland; all nine aircraft were due to be delivered by 2012.

In the 2010 Strategic Defence and Security

At Kinloss the fuselage of XV242 is loaded aboard an Antonov 124 of HeavyLift Ltd for transportation to Hurn.
(Warrant Officer Paddy Porter BEM)

MRA.4 ZJ518 in flight over the Welsh Coast.

Review of the Armed Forces, the UK government announced the cancellation of the MRA4 on 19 October 2010 and consequently that RAF Kinloss, the intended base for the Nimrod fleet, would be closed. Although late and over-budget the decision to cancel the MRA4 was controversial as the remaining airframes had all been near completion.

The aircraft would have been used in civilian search and rescue, as the Nimrod MR2 had often been used. In this respect the Strategic Defence and Security Review stated that the UK '...will depend on other maritime assets to contribute to the tasks previously planned for [the Nimrod MRA4]'.

Following the cancellation, Defence Secretary Liam Fox used the Nimrod MRA4 procurement as an example of the worst of MoD procurement performance: '...*The idea that we ever allow ourselves into a position where something that was originally Nimrod 2000 - where we ordered was reduced to nine, spent £3.8bn and we still weren't close to getting the capability - is not to happen again.*'

In January 2011 it was reported by the *Financial Times* that when the decision was taken to scrap the aircraft, '[The MRA4] *was still riddled with flaws.... Safety tests conducted* [in 2010] *found there were still 'several hundred design non-compliances' with the aircraft. It was unclear, for example, whether its bomb bay doors functioned properly, whether its landing gear worked and, most worryingly, whether its fuel pipe was safe.*' According to *Air Forces Monthly*, '...*significant aerodynamic issues and associated flying control concerns in certain regimes of flight meant that it was grounded at the time of cancellation and may not have been signed over as safe by the Military Aviation Authority.*" The magazine also stated that the reason for the cancellation was that the RAF and Navy placed a higher priority on fast jets and frigates than on maritime patrol.

On 24 November 2010, 382 sub-contract workers previously working on the MRA4 were laid off at BAE Systems Warton and Woodford. After the airframes were stripped of electronic equipment, the remaining fuselages were scrapped at BAE Systems Woodford, beginning on 26 January 2011. Although the process was conducted behind screens intended to hide the process from the media, the BBC flew a helicopter over Woodford and broadcast footage of the scrapping in process. Six former defence chiefs publicly criticised the decision to scrap the Nimrods the following day.

Press reports in February 2011 claimed the Royal Navy's Fleet Air Arm had established a committee to consider the acquisition of maritime patrol aircraft to replace the scrapped Nimrod MRA4 in the anti-submarine role. The budget was expected to be up to £1 billion, contrasting with the MRA4 program's cost of £3.6 billion. Further reports in mid-2011 suggested that a purchase of up to five Boeing P-8 Poseidons was under consideration. According to *Jane's*, a decision regarding a replacement maritime patrol aircraft is expected in the 2015 defence review.

So was the last roll of the dice for the Comet design - ending not with a bang but a whimper. However, the Comet lives on in the form of many airport/airfield road signs!

Bibliography

Air Crash. The clues in the wreckage. Fred Jones, Robert Hale Ltd, London. 1985. ISBN 0-86379-094-1

Air Disaster - Volume 1. Macarthur Job, Aerospace Publications, Australia 1994. ISBN 1-875671-11-0

Airplane Stability and Control: A History of the Technologies That Made Aviation Possible. Malcolm J. Abzug and Eugene Larrabee. Cambridge, UK: Cambridge University Press, 2002. ISBN 0-521-80992-4.

Antennas and Propagation, Part 1. London: Institution of Electrical Engineers, 1978. ISBN 0-85296-196-0.

Assorted BEA publicity brochures.

Assorted BOAC publicity brochures.

Assorted Dan-Air publicity brochures

Assorted Olympic Airways publicity brochures.

Behaviour of Skin Fatigue Cracks at the Corners of Windows in a Comet I Fuselage. R. J. Atkinson, W. J. Winkworth and G. M. Norris; Ministry of Aviation via Her Majesty's Stationery Office, 1962.

Beyond the Black Box: The Forensics of Airplane Crashes. George D. Bibel; JHU Press, Baltimore, Maryland 2008. ISBN 0-

Black Box: Why Air Safety is no Accident, Nicholas Faith; The Book Every Air Traveller Should Read. London: Boxtree, 1996. ISBN 0-7522-2118-3.

Boeing Aircraft since 1916. Peter M Bowers. Putnam, London 1968. SBN 370-00016-1

British Airways publications:
Comet 4 Flying Manual (BOAC),
Comet 4B Flying Manual (BEA)

British Civil Aircraft 1919–1972: Volume II. A J Jackson. London: Putnam (Conway Maritime Press), 1988. ISBN 0-85177-813-5.*Classic Civil Aircraft 3: De Havilland Comet.* Phillip J Birtles. Ian Allen Ltd Shepperton, UK 1990. ISBN 0-7110-1947-9

Bush Pilot with a Briefcase: The Incredible Story of Aviation Pioneer Grant McConachie. Ronald A Keith. Vancouver: Douglas & McIntyre Ltd., 1997, First edition 1992. ISBN 978-1-55054-586-9

Challenging Horizons: Qantas 1939–1954. John Gunn. St Lucia, Queensland: University of Queensland Press, 1987. ISBN 0-7022-2017-5.

Civil Aircraft of the World. F G Swanborough. London: C. Scribner's Sons, 1980. ISBN 0-684-12895-0.

Comet Highway. Henry Hensser MBE. John Murray Ltd, London 1953.

Comet 4C Operations Manual, Technical Volume
Comet 4C Systems and Design,
Goblin Engine,
Ghost Engine,

Comet Resurgent: A decade of D.H. Jet Transport Design'. Flight, 28 March 1958, pp. 420–425.

Comet: The World's First Jet Airliner. R.E.G. Davies and Philip J. Birtles. McLean, Paladwr Press, Virginia: 1999. ISBN 1-888962-14-3.

Dan-Air Services staff newspapers

"Database: D.H. 016 Comet." Barry Jones. Aeroplane, Volume 38, No. 4, Issue no. 444, April 2010.

De Havilland Aircraft Since 1909. A J Jackson, Putnams, London 1962. ISBN 0-370-30022-X

De Havilland Comet: the world's first jet airliner. Phillip Birtles, & REG Davies. Paladwr Press, 1999. ISBN 1-888962-14

De Havilland Comet. Kev Darling; Crowood Press, Ramsbury, Marlborough, Wiltshire, UK: 2005. ISBN 1-86126-733-9

De Havilland Gazette Edition 49 - February 1949
De Havilland Gazette Edition 50 - April 1949
De Havilland Gazette Edition 51 - June 1949
De Havilland Gazette Edition 52 - August 1949
De Havilland Gazette Edition 53 - October 1949
De Havilland Gazette Edition 54 - December 1949
De Havilland Gazette Edition 55 - February 1949
De Havilland Gazette Edition 56 - April 1950
De Havilland Gazette Edition 57 - June 1950
De Havilland Gazette Edition 58 - August 1950
De Havilland Gazette Edition 59 - October 1950
De Havilland Gazette Edition 60 - December 1950
De Havilland Gazette Edition 61 - February 1951
De Havilland Gazette Edition 62 - April 1951
De Havilland Gazette Edition 63 - June 1951
De Havilland Gazette Edition 64 - August 1951
Comet SupplIment to Edition 64 - August 1951
De Havilland Gazette Edition 65 - October 1951
De Havilland Gazette Edition 66 - December 1951
De Havilland Gazette Edition 67 - February 1952
De Havilland Gazette Edition 68 - April 1952
De Havilland Gazette Edition 69 - June 1952
De Havilland Gazette Edition 70 - August 1952
De Havilland Gazette Edition 71 - October 1952
De Havilland Gazette Edition 72 - December 1952
De Havilland Gazette Edition 73 - February 1953
De Havilland Gazette Edition 74 - April 1953
De Havilland Gazette Edition 75 - June 1953
De Havilland Gazette Coronation Issue - June 1953
De Havilland Gazette Edition 76 - August 1953
De Havilland Gazette Edition 77 - October 1953
De Havilland Gazette Edition 78 - December 1953
De Havilland Gazette Edition 79 - February 1954
De Havilland Gazette Edition 80 - April 1954
De Havilland Gazette Edition 81 - June 1954
De Havilland Gazette Edition 82 - August 1954
De Havilland Gazette Edition 83 - October 1954
De Havilland Gazette Edition 84 - December 1954
De Havilland Gazette Edition 85 - February 1955
De Havilland Gazette Edition 86 - April 1955
De Havilland Gazette Edition 87 - June 1955
De Havilland Gazette Edition 88 - August 1955
De Havilland Gazette Edition 89 - October 1955
De Havilland Gazette Edition 90 - December 1955
De Havilland Gazette Edition 91 - February 1956
De Havilland Gazette Edition 92 - April 1956
De Havilland Gazette Edition 93 - June 1956
De Havilland Gazette Edition 94 - August 1956
De Havilland Gazette Edition 95 - October 1956
De Havilland Gazette Edition 96 - December 1956
De Havilland Gazette Edition 97 - February 1957
De Havilland Gazette Edition 98 - April 1957
De Havilland Gazette Edition 99 - June 1957
De Havilland Gazette Edition 100 - August 1957
De Havilland Gazette Edition 101 - October 1957
De Havilland Gazette Edition 102 - December 195
De Havilland Gazette Edition 103 - February 1958
De Havilland Gazette Edition 104 - April 1958
De Havilland Gazette Edition 105 - June 1958
De Havilland Gazette Edition 106 - August 1958

De Havilland Gazette Edition 107 - October 1958
De Havilland Gazette Edition 108 - December 1958
De Havilland Gazette Edition 109 - February 1959
De Havilland Gazette Edition 110 - April 1959
De Havilland Gazette Edition 111 - June 1959
De Havilland Gazette Edition 112 - August 1959
De Havilland Gazette Edition 113 - October 1959
De Havilland Gazette Edition 114 - December 1959
De Havilland Gazette Edition 115 - February 1960
De Havilland Gazette Edition 116 - April 1960
De Havilland Gazette Edition 117 - June 1960
De Havilland Gazette Edition 118 - August 1960
De Havilland Gazette Edition 119 - October 1960
De Havilland Gazette Edition 120 - December 1960
De Havilland Gazette Edition 121 - February 1961
De Havilland Gazette Edition 122 - April 1961
De Havilland Gazette Edition 123 - June 1961
De Havilland Gazette Edition 124 - August 1961
De Havilland Group original publications:
    Comet Passenger Liner, Series 1,
    Comet Passenger Liner, Series 2,
    Comet 1 & 1A Pilot's Notes,
    Comet C2 Pilots Notes,
    Comet 4 Flying Manual,
    Comet 4 Crew's Manual,
    Comet 4 Operating Data
    (fuel consumption/climb tables),
    Comet 4C Flying Manual,
Falklands - The Air War. Guild Publishing, London. 1987.
Famous Airliners - The Comet. Derek Harvey ARAeS. Cassels,
    London 1959.
Of Comets and Queens. Sir Basil Smallpeice: Airlife,
    Shrewsbury UK. 1980. ISBN 0-906393-10-8
RAF publications:
    Comet 4 Pilot's Notes,
    Comet C.4C Pilot's Notes,
    Comet C.4C Operating Data,
    Comet C.4C Flight Reference Cards.
Report of the Court of Inquiry into the Accidents to Comet G-
    ALYP on 10 January 1954 and Comet G-ALYY on 8
    April 1954. Baron L Cohen of Walmer, W S Farren, W
    J Duncan and Alan H Wheeler. HMSO 1955.

Report on Comet Accident Investigation. RAE Accident Report
    270. Ministry of Supply London 1954.
Soviet Transport Aircraft since 1945. John Stroud. London:
    Putnam, 1968. ISBN ISBN 0-370-00126-5.
Strange Encounters: Mysteries of the Air. David Beaty;
    Atheneum, London, 1984. ISBN 978-0-689-11447-2.
The Avro Canada C102 Jetliner. Jim Floyd Erin, Ontario:
    Boston Mills Press, 1986. ISBN 0-919783-66-X
The Brabazon Committee and British Airliners 1945-1960.
    Mike Phipp Tempus Publishy, Stroud, Glos. 2007
    ISBN 978-0-7524-4374-4
The Comet Riddle. Timothy Hewat and W A Waterton.
    Frederick Muller Ltd London. 1955
The de Havilland Comet Srs. 1–4. Aircraft in Profile, Volume
    5. Phillip J Birtles. Profile Publications, London 1967.
The DH. 106 Comet: An Illustrated History. Martin Painter.
    Tonbridge, Kent, UK: Air Britain (Historians) Ltd.,
    2002. ISBN 0-85130-330-7.
The First Jet Airliner: The Story of the de Havilland Comet.
    Timothy Walker. Newcastle upon Tyne, UK: Scoval
    Publishing Ltd., 2000. ISBN 1-902236-05-X.
The History of BOAC - 1934-1976 - unpublished thesis
The Nimrod Review: an Independent Review into the Broader
    Issues Surrounding the Loss of the RAF Nimrod MR2
    Aircraft XV230 in Afghanistan in 2006. Charles Haddon-
    Cave. London: The Stationery Office, 2009.
The Spirit of Dan Air. Graham M Simons GMS Enterprises,
    Peterborough 1993. ISBN 1-870384-20-2
"*Triumph, Tragedy and Triumph Again… The Comet Story.*"
    Bill Withun. Air Classics Airliner Special No. 2, Summer
    1976
Turbine-engined Airliners of the World. F G Swanborough.
    London: Temple Press Books, 1962.
Who's Who in Aviation 1955. Temple Press, London.
Who's Who in Aviation 1963. Temple Press London.
Wings Across the World: an illustrated history of British Airways
    Harald Penrose. Cassells, London 1980. ISBN 0-304-
    30697-5
"*World Beater: Homage to the DH. 106 Comet.*" François
    Prins. Air Enthusiast, Issue 78, November/December
    1998

IINDEX